C# and the .NET Framework

The C++ Perspective

Robert Powell and Richard Weeks

SAMS

201 West 103rd St., Indianapolis, Indiana, 46290 USA

C# and the .NET Framework

Copyright © 2002 by Sams Publishing

International Standard Book Number: 0-672-32153-x

Library of Congress Catalog Card Number: 2001093492

Printed in the United States of America

First Printing: September 2001

04   03   02   01   4 3 2 1

Trademarks

Warning and Disclaimer

PUBLISHER
Jeff Koch

ACQUISITIONS EDITOR
Neil Rowe

DEVELOPMENT EDITOR
Kevin Howard

MANAGING EDITOR
Matt Purcell

PROJECT EDITOR
George E. Nedeff

COPY EDITOR
Pat Kinyon

INDEXER
Johnna Dinse

PROOFREADER
Plan-It Publishing

TECHNICAL EDITOR
Mattias Sjögren

MEDIA DEVELOPER
Dan Scherf

INTERIOR DESIGNER
Aren Howell

COVER DESIGNER
Anne Jones

PAGE LAYOUT
Ayanna Lacey

Contents at a Glance

Table of Contents

PART II   The C# Language

2.1   C# Basics   105

2.2   Advanced C#   169

About the Authors

Bob Powell is an Englishman abroad. He currently lives in North Carolina with his wife Chrissy and their children Laurence, Mike, Robyn, Jeremy, Abigail, and Charlie. Currently, Bob is VP of Development at NetEdge Software Incorporated, a consulting company that provides .NET and C++ software design services. Bob's e-mail address is bob@netedgesoftware.com.

Richard Weeks is the CTO and Chief Architect for Crystal Sharp Consulting specializing in .NET applications development. Richard has been writing software for the better part of 10 years, specializing in C++, MFC, COM, ATL, and now C#. His major areas of interest include custom control development, compiler theory, distributed applications development, and design patterns. During the past 10 years, he managed to make time to earn his B.S. degree in Computer Science from Western Carolina University; it proudly hangs next to his G.E.D. When not working, he enjoys video games, go-cart racing, and good beer. Richard Weeks can be reached at rweeks@nc.rr.com.

Dedication

My portion of this book is dedicated to Chrissy, my wonderful wife,
who has put up with me sitting at the computer till the early hours of the morning
bashing keys, to my children whom I love dearly, and to my Dad whom I miss very much
because he's on the other side of the pond in England and I don't travel enough.

—Bob Powell

To my family, things really do always work out for the best.

—Richard Weeks

Acknowledgments

Primarily I would like to thank the whole crew at Sams Publishing for their patience in guiding me through the task of becoming an author. I would also like to thank Eric Andrae, Chris Anderson and Mattias Sjögren of Microsoft for their help while writing this book.

—Bob Powell

I would like to thank the entire Sams team who worked with Bob and myself on this project. Without the support of Neil, George and others, this project would certainly not have succeeded. I would also like to thank Chris Anderson for getting my questions answered and pointing me in the right direction when all seemed lost.

—Richard Weeks

Tell Us What You Think!

As the reader of this book, *you* are our most important critic and commentator. We value your opinion and want to know what we're doing right, what we could do better, what areas you'd like to see us publish in, and any other words of wisdom you're willing to pass our way.

As a Publisher for Sams Publishing, I welcome your comments. You can fax, e-mail, or write me directly to let me know what you did or didn't like about this book—as well as what we can do to make our books stronger.

Please note that I cannot help you with technical problems related to the topic of this book, and that due to the high volume of mail I receive, I might not be able to reply to every message.

When you write, please be sure to include this book's title and author as well as your name and phone or fax number. I will carefully review your comments and share them with the author and editors who worked on the book.

Fax: 317-581-4770

E-mail: feedback@samspublishing.com

Mail: Jeff Koch
          Publisher
          Sams Publishing
          201 West 103rd Street
          Indianapolis, IN 46290 USA

Introduction

Another platform change is upon us. Just as with the transition from DOS to Windows, we must now move into the realm of .NET. The .NET platform strives to finally provide a common playing field for all languages to seamlessly interoperate with a common type system and base class library. Along with this new platform, Microsoft has created a language specifically designed to take advantage of the .NET platform, C#, which serves as the basis for this book and the examples herein.

Unlike Visual Basic, Microsoft has submitted both C# and the CLS to the ECMA standards organization to ensure adoption of the platform and the C# programming language. With open standards as the cornerstone for the .NET platform, it is sure to gather momentum and an adoption rate that exceeds proprietary systems and languages. With the introduction of C#, Microsoft has proven once and for all that the Internet and interoperability are key components for today's software requirements.

The goal of this book is, first and foremost, the exploration of the .NET platform and its underpinnings. Next, the coverage of the C# language is an essential part of .NET; considering that a vast majority of the base class library was developed entirely in C#. For the die-hard enthusiast, examples are provided for Intermediate Language and managed C++.

This book is divided into five parts to give to provide an in-depth look at the major topics in .NET. These topics include:

- .NET Platform
- Intermediate language
- C#
- Windows Forms Development
- ASP.NET
- COM Interoperability
- .NET Threading

As with any new platform, exhaustive coverage of any one topic could easily span a large volume on its own. Our goal in writing this book is to provide in-depth information about the major areas of .NET, to provide you with the knowledge required to develop for the .NET platform and to jump start your productivity. The requirements for software today far exceed what anyone could have envisioned in the early years of computer programming. The need for Internet-aware, peer-to-peer, XML-consuming/producing applications requires that programmers have a breadth of knowledge at their fingertips. The focus from the beginning of this book is to provide you with that breadth of knowledge from the foundations of .NET all the way to Windows Forms and Web Forms application development. Welcome to .NET.

The .NET Framework

PART
I

IN THIS PART

A Quick Introduction to .NET

IN THIS CHAPTER

It is possible that Microsoft has made some of the boldest moves in the computer industry. The enormous success of DOS was based on a gutsy move by Bill Gates and Steve Ballmer when they told IBM that they had an operating system to sell. Microsoft did it again with the creation of the most widely used operating system in the world by plagiarizing the Apple Macintosh's look and feel.

Now, in possibly the boldest move yet, Microsoft has done it again by totally reinventing the way we will use and program our computers. If you're a programmer of C++, or if you've come to rely on the Windows operating system or Microsoft Foundation Classes (MFC) for your livelihood, then you will without doubt be deeply affected by the implications of .NET.

In the recent past the Internet has become the medium in which we do our business, visit our friends, run our bank accounts, play, chat, and keep in touch with loved ones. This has all been made possible, practical, and affordable by the software written to perform Internet Protocol (IP) communications for the World Wide Web. As the Web has grown in capability and complexity, so has the software required to perform all the millions of IP data transfers to and from our computers. Using e-mail, browsing Web pages, interacting with databases, and running distributed applications have become more complex, and the programming skills and techniques required to create and maintain the software have grown more sophisticated as well. A programmer will often be faced with COM, COM+, DCOM, ASP, SOAP, XML, and XSL on a daily basis, with an ever-growing array of complex SDKs and manuals to contend with.

Microsoft, like many of us in the industry, has been building up operating systems, toolkits, and applications incrementally, depending on the requirements of the current technological focus, adding to existing work with an SDK here and a standard there. The outcome is that operating systems and libraries are not portable, are top heavy, and are full of add-ins, extensions, and compromises. The .NET framework radically changes that. It is not an increment, and it is not a consolidation of work. It's a huge, bold, go-for-it rip that redefines just about everything you know about programming for personal computers of all shapes and sizes, including the languages themselves.

Dispelling the Myth of the .NET Virtual Machine

One of the most important facts about the .NET framework (and probably the most misquoted) is that it does not employ virtual machine technology like Java. The software running on .NET is wholly compiled and runs at the machine level just like the compiled code from a C program. The popular misconception comes from the fact that .NET uses an intermediate language that has been often described as "P-Code." In reality, .NET employs a technique of multistage compilation: an initial compile to a portable intermediate format and, at runtime, a just-in-time (JIT) compile to the final executable form.

A Quick Introduction to .NET

CHAPTER 1.1

7

1.1

A QUICK
INTRODUCTION TO
.NET

This system, while relatively complex, gives an enormous advantage to the programming community. It means that all languages have a common level that they share in their intermediate form. Therefore, a mixture of modules, written in C#, Visual Basic, Eiffel, FORTRAN, COBOL, or any language that will be supported in the future, can be used to create a single application. The reason for this lies in the fact that a module, once compiled to intermediate language (IL), is packaged along with a full description of itself. Its interfaces, properties, methods, and classes are available as metadata to other modules or to integrated rapid application development environments like Visual Studio .NET.

When the .NET runtime is used to execute a program that has been converted to IL, it uses a JITer to compile the IL to full, native machine code that runs on the microprocessor of the machine. The JITers are very fast and efficient, even to the point of not compiling unused portions of the intermediate code. Obviously, this compilation process takes time, so when load times are important or portability is not needed, the system provides a pre-JIT compiler that converts the IL-based code to a permanent, native format.

The diagram in Figure 1.1.1 shows the strata of the .NET framework as seen by the programmer. The portions in gray are the additions that have been made by .NET.

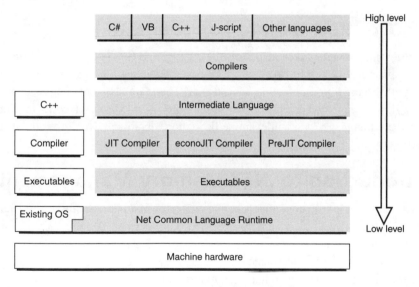

FIGURE 1.1.1

A compilers-eye view of .NET.

The .NET framework provides four native languages: C#, Visual Basic, C++ with managed extensions, and JScript. Several other languages are in the pipeline from other companies. For example, Fujitsu has a version of COBOL.

There are basic sets of compilers that take .NET-supported languages and produce the interme-diate language modules. Below that are the IL-to-machine-code JITers. There is a standard JITer that is used primarily by systems with plenty of memory and power. This compiles a standard form of IL to an optimized form on the host machine. Then there's the econoJIT com-piler that is very fast but does little optimization and relies on a subset of pre-optimized IL. Finally, there is preJIT that creates a native code executable that can be distributed in its ready-compiled form. This method is used only when there is no chance of the program being dis-tributed to another hardware platform.

Finally, sitting partially upon the hardware and partly upon the existing operating system of the machine is the .NET Common Language Runtime (CLR). This functional block provides all the services that components use to interact with the computer or the native OS of the machine. It's interesting to note that the machine hosting the CLR is not identified as a PC, and the oper-ating system does not have to be DOS or Windows. Microsoft has a definite strategy for deploying the .NET framework on many platforms, from the smallest appliances, handhelds, phones, and PDAs right through to Unix and Linux systems. Although it is not immediately available on anything other than an I386 Windows 2000 system, this portability will eventually afford developers a write-once, run-anywhere programming environment.

Microsoft Intermediate Language (IL)

The interesting thing about Microsoft Intermediate Language (IL) is that it is not hidden in the depths of the machine. IL is a full-fledged, stack-based language a bit like assembly code that can be written by hand if you're feeling adventurous. There are also tools that enable you to disassemble IL and view the contents of the system objects and your own code. In Chapter 1.3, "IL Intermediate Language," we will examine IL in more detail and even use it to write some programs directly.

An Introduction to .NET Memory Management

A .NET fact that has a lot of people interested, worried, or just plain dumbstruck is that .NET runtime memory management is a garbage-collected (GC) system. Old programmers in partic-ular have nightmares about the days of Lisp, when waiting for the garbage collector was a painful experience because he only came on Tuesdays. C++ programmers have had memory management drummed in to them so hard that to relinquish control of those allocations and deletions is anathema to them.

The .NET memory management system approaches the allocation of memory resources differ-ently. A block of memory allocated in the garbage collected or managed heap maintains a record of all the objects that refer to it. Only when those references have been released is the object destroyed. This relieves the burden of memory management from the programmer. You no longer have to remember to delete memory; you just stop using it. A class no longer has to keep track of reference counts. It knows when to delete itself. To reduce heap fragmentation, the GC also moves objects to consolidate the used and free spaces in the managed memory store.

This prevents memory leaks and improves performance of heavily stressed server systems. The managed heap also ensures that unsafe accesses, like buffer overflows and crashes, cannot modify the data associated with other programs running on the same system. This makes the whole operating system more reliable and secure. Garbage collected systems have an unfair reputation for being slow and inefficient, but Microsoft has gone to considerable lengths to ensure that garbage collection in .NET really works. It's very fast and does not impose a significant load on the CPU. Generally, on a Windows 2000–based machine, the GC will require only around 1/1000 of the total processor time.

Finally, for programmers who require the use of pointers to blocks of memory, there is provision in the system for what is called "unmanaged" or unsafe memory and code. This is so that you can use your old structures or legacy C++–based applications side-by-side with.NET features.

The .NET Framework Type System

C++ programmers in particular will be surprised by the changes in the basic storage types used by the .NET framework. An integer is no longer just a couple of bytes in a memory block somewhere. Of course, the data is stored in memory, but you can now treat that integer like an object, accessing methods that it exposes.

There are two distinctly different families of types. Value types, including chars, ints, and doubles to name a few, are accompanied by reference types such as arrays, interfaces, classes, and a native string type.

Because the .NET framework itself defines the types, languages such as C#, Visual Basic, and others can use them in the same way. This means that the integer used by VB is the same as the integer used by C#, and painful conversions between "real" types and types such as variants are unnecessary.

The .NET Framework System Objects

The working parts of the .NET framework are contained within a set of DLLs that holds the system object model. The system namespace holds class hierarchies for collections, security, file I/O, graphics, Win32 API access, XML serialization, and many other important functions. All of the .NET system is available from C#, VB, or any of the supported languages.

C#—A New Programming Language

C# is possibly the biggest source of the controversy that has dogged the .NET framework since its unveiling to the public in early 2000. Previously named Cool and shrouded in mystery, disinformation, and speculation, C# is actually a very good, totally object-oriented, simple language.

It is obvious that the designers of C# went to a lot of effort to create a language that was palatable to C++ programmers. It is easy to adapt to and has many of the same language constructs as C++. A few things are very conspicuous by their absence, however.

Multiple inheritance does not figure in the C# scheme. A C# class may declare that it implements one or more interfaces, but multiple inheritance of base classes is not possible. To some programmers, especially ATL lovers, this might be a shortcoming.

The C# system does not allow for any sort of templates, either. There are ways around that problem, though, which we will show you later in this book. Most of the C# controversy has been from the reactions of people who have dismissed it as a blatant effort to rip off Java. We believe that C# and Java are horses for different courses and can coexist happily. C# and the whole .NET framework are better suited to a mixture of client-side and server-side work, whereas Java has definite shortcomings for the client.

It was mentioned that C# is "totally object-oriented." C++ came from C. It was at first a tricky add-on to C, then a true attempt at object orientation. At best, C++ is a compromise that still retains some of the characteristics of a non–object-oriented language. It has standalone functions and global variables. C# on the other hand, does not have a non–object-oriented bone in its body. All the variable types, even simple value types, can be treated as objects. All functionality must be contained within a class. Global variables are not allowed. (Don't despair, though. You can have classes with static functions or variables. These can be used in lieu of true global variables if you must have them.)

Just to give you a snippet of real code, here is the famous, infamous, beloved, hated, hello world example, written in C#.

```
using System;
class helloworld
{
    public static int Main()
    {
    Console.WriteLine("Hello World");
    return 0;
    }
}
```

See, you understood that just fine!

How Objects Describe Themselves

Metadata is the key to language interoperation in the .NET framework. In every DLL or executable assembly, there is a complete description of the classes, methods, parameter lists, and class data members it contains. The metadata stored in the assembly enables the object to be used in developer tools such as Visual Studio.NET. This means that your C# objects can be used on a Visual Basic form with ease. Furthermore, the metadata is available at runtime. Other objects can access it to find out about the services your class provides and invoke methods that it exposes. This enables you to use metadata as a simpler replacement for IDispatch.

Component Object Model (COM) Interoperability

The .NET framework takes all the stress and strain out of the Component Object Model (COM). To systems accessing your .NET-based objects remotely, the objects look just like COM objects. Similarly, COM objects can be manipulated by .NET classes and objects without having to worry about marshaling. The CLR does it all for you behind the scenes.

Windows Forms, Web Controls, and GDI+

If you were developing programs for Windows clients or servers at any time in the last 10 years, it's very likely that you were using Microsoft Foundation Classes. MFC is a great system for producing consistent and fairly complex user interfaces that are easy to create using wizards. The disadvantage of MFC comes from the fact that management of operational items such as collections, graphics, file management, serialization, and so on was built into the MFC framework classes themselves. Probably about 85% of what you deal with in MFC involves an object-oriented class "wrapper" on some low-level construct. .NET breaks that mold. The system namespace—with all the operational bits and pieces like native data types, collections, XML serialization, and so on—is a grab bag of ready-made, inherently object-oriented components. The framework for creating applications is consequently simpler.

On the client, Windows Forms is the vehicle for the windowing application. It is unlike MFC inasmuch as a Windows Forms application is mostly all code. Dialog boxes and form views that under MFC were laid out in resources are now created by code that sets properties in classes based on `System.Windows.Forms.Form`. Windows Forms applications are constructed from a class hierarchy and use the capabilities of the CLR to create a powerful but compact Windows application.

Web Controls employ a different type of user interface paradigm. They work on the principle of the disconnected GUI. Java programmers have had the servlet, an application that runs on the server, effectively on behalf of the client, for some time. The servlet performs computations, assists in user interactions, and works the business logic of a Web application while the user is at the other end of a Web connection using a "thin client" browser. The complexity of a Web application might be such that the HTML displayed on that thin client will change from moment to moment, such as when a user clicks a button that results in a UI change. The page will be refreshed behind the scenes, and a new HTML page that reflects the differences will be sent to the client browser. Generally, the HTML stream is constructed on-the-fly as the page is sent, so the GUI seen by the user is rich and dynamic.

Microsoft has answered this with its own version of servlets: server-side Web Controls. These components provide the subportions of a distributed application in the same way that MFC extension controls enhance a desktop application. The application and the controls that help to produce its look and feel run on the server, and the user interface is projected back to the client machine as an ASP-like stream of dynamically created HTML.

GDI+, like its predecessor GDI (the graphics device interface) is a much refined, immediate mode, graphics API that includes such niceties as 2D rotation and scaling plus alpha blending and transparency. It is also very fast and takes advantage of advances made to raster graphic processing that DirectX provides to older systems.

Tools

The basic .NET SDK comes with tools that make the developer's life easier. There are tools for building and viewing IL: the Intermediate Language Assembler (ILASM) and the Intermediate Language Disassembler (ILDASM). Also included are the C Sharp Compiler (CSC) and a debugger. Visual Studio.NET is the development environment of choice and is obviously a big part of the whole .NET developer experience, but it's not included with the basic SDK. You can do useful development without VS.NET using Notepad or some other simple text editor if you can't afford VS.NET or if you just want to try out the concepts. We have written a C# syntax highlighting editor that can be downloaded from the Stingray Web site at `http://www.stingray.com/csharpeditor.asp`.

Assemblies, the .NET Packaging System

The assembly is the .NET component packaging medium. An assembly contains the intermediate code generated by the different sources for a particular component—the metadata for the components and all the extra files and information needed to run the component. Each assembly has a manifest that enumerates the files in the assembly and defines on what other assemblies the component depends. The manifest also holds information about what is exposed to users of the assembly.

Programming with Attributes

.NET makes practical use of an attributed programming system that allows objects or methods to be extended in a particular way. C# has no provision for templates or macros. These are well known to C++ programmers as a way to aggregate functionality or provide cookie cutter behaviors. Attributes, like macros or templates, insert code into your software that applies certain rules to replaceable elements. For example, it is possible to turn a seemingly mundane C# class with three or four lines of code into a full-blown Internet Web service by using the attribute [WebMethod] in the source code. Using this technique, it is possible to create something akin to a full IIS server extension DLL in just a few moments, and have the service running live on the Internet in a minute or two. It's even possible to design your own attributes.

Security

Any programming system that works on today's Internet must be secure and safe. The .NET runtime employs a system that verifies and enforces the component's permissions to access the system on which it runs. These security settings can be adjusted very precisely and allow you to adjust the permission granted to an application, from complete sandbox paranoia to any level of access you feel you can stand.

Ready, Set, GO!

This book is broken into sections that deal with all the major ideas of .NET. It is intended to provide a running start for programmers who need to cut through the shock and get productive from week 1. It would be silly of us to try to give an in-depth byte-for-byte analysis of .NET because that is already very well provided by the Microsoft documentation. However, we will try to bring to your attention all the salient points of .NET operations and give you the insights it took a year or more to soak up from wading through what is after all an enormous endeavor on the part of the Microsoft crew.

The Common Language Runtime

IN THIS CHAPTER

Overview

The Common Language Runtime (CLR) serves many roles within the .NET system. It is an important part of the execution system, but it also plays an active part in the development and deployment of software that runs on the framework. It provides multilanguage support by managing the compilers that are used to convert source to intermediate language (IL) and from IL to native code, and it enforces program safety and security.

Let's take a look at these roles in a little more detail.

Simplification of Development

The CLR's development role is important in reducing the load that we carry in our day-to-day tasks. Using .NET, you don't need to worry about the nitty-gritty details of GUIDS, IUnknown, IDispatch, or type libraries. All this "plumbing" is taken care of by the CLR on your behalf.

Code is much more reliable because memory management is also the CLR's responsibility. The objects instantiated under the CLR do not need explicit reference counting; data that you allocate is automatically reclaimed by the Garbage Collector when your code ceases to use it. Metadata also allows dynamic binding of executables. This means that those out-of-date DLL linkage problems go away completely. Reliability is also enhanced through type safety. No detail of a structure size or the organization of members within an object is unknown, so there is never any need to worry about alignment or packing issues. Furthermore, you never need to worry about bounds-checking for arrays or buffers.

Tool Support

The CLR works hand-in-hand with tools like Visual Studio, compilers, debuggers, and profilers to make the developer's job much simpler. You don't even need Visual Studio.NET for a great development experience. A debugger provided with the SDK is almost as good as the one integrated into VS.NET. Other tools, such as the Intermediate Language Disassembler (ILDASM), take advantage of services provided by the CLR.

Multiple Language Support

The basis for multiple language support is the Common Type System and metadata. The basic data types used by the CLR are common to all languages. There are therefore no conversion issues with the basic integer, floating-point, and string types. All languages deal with all data types in the same way. There is also a mechanism for defining and managing new types.

All top-level languages compile to IL. Once the compilation is made and the metadata is generated for the object, it is easily accessible from other languages. This means that objects written in one language can be inherited in a second language. It is possible to write a class in VB and inherit from it in C#.

So far, about 15 languages are supported by the .NET framework, including C++, Visual Basic, C#, Perl, Python, JScript, Pascal, COBOL, and Smalltalk.

Deployment Made Easier

With the .NET framework, there is never any need to register components in the system. You can simply copy a component to a directory, and the CLR will make sure that it is compiled and run correctly. In the case of code written for ASP.NET, you just need to copy the basic C#, JScript, or VB source code, and the correct source to IL compiler will be invoked.

There are effectively two places into which components can be deployed. The first is the directory in which the application lives. This allows different versions of the application to coexist on the same machine. The other place is the Global Assembly Cache. This is a central store for assemblies that are accessible to all .NET applications.

Wherever the components are stored, the update procedure is very simple. You just copy the assembly into the correct directory, even if the object is running (you can't do that with a Windows DLL), and the system makes it work.

Software Isolation

Applications are isolated from one another by the CLR so that they cannot affect each other. Resources may be shared, but the share must be made explicitly. This means that a .NET system can have a sandbox approach to system security if needed. When more relaxed security or access to any particular system resource is desirable, permissions for access to files or other resources on the system are tunable on an application-by-application basis.

Type Safety and Verification

The CLR enforces security and reliability through type safety, verification and trust. Type safe code is built to conform to contracts laid out by the CLR. It only uses recognized types, only uses memory allocated to it by the memory manager and cannot access non-public data or methods of other applications or processes. A type safe program cannot get into a crash situation where it runs off into outer space and writes all over some other processes memory blocks. Verification of type-safety takes place when the code is loaded and run by the CLR. The CLR, during the process of JITing each method, looks at the metadata description of the method and verifies that it is typesafe. There are circumstances when this verification is impossible, for example, when the CLR needs to use unmanaged code from a managed object. This is often the case when a .NET class calls a Win32 DLL. In these cases code must be trusted by the CLR.

Security

The issue of security is very high on the radar for systems that can run active content or execute user scripts. As a client you don't want to allow errant programs to run wild on your machine, destroying valuable data. As a service provider you don't want to allow attacks or simple mistakes by users to bring down your whole system.

The CLR manages system security through user and code identity coupled with permission checks. The identity of the code, for example the publisher and the origin of the code, can be known and permission for the use of resources granted accordingly. This type of security is called Evidence Based Security and is a major feature of .NET. The .NET framework also provides support for role-based security using Windows NT accounts and groups.

The CLR in Relation to .NET

The block diagram shown in Figure 1.2.1 shows the CLR in relation to the general .NET framework.

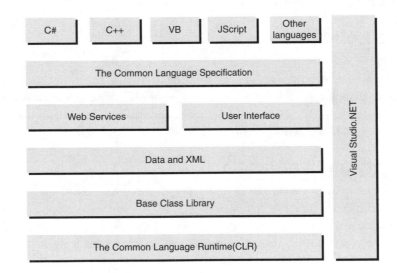

FIGURE **1.2.1**
The CLR and the .NET framework.

The CLR in Detail

As a subcomponent of the .NET framework, the CLR itself is built up from individual parts. Figure 1.2.2 shows those pieces in relation to one another.

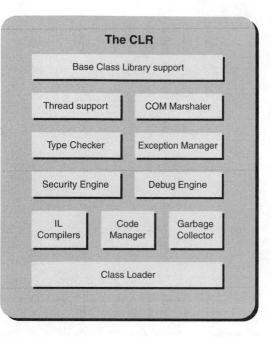

FIGURE 1.2.2

Detail of the CLR subsections.

As you can see from Figure 1.2.2, the primary function of the CLR is as a class loader. It loads classes that you create or that are supplied as part of the base class library, prepares them for use, and then either executes them or assists in their design-time use.

Classes are loaded from assemblies, the .NET equivalent of the DLL or EXE. The assembly may sometimes contain native code but is most likely to contain classes that have been compiled to IL and the metadata associated with them. At design time, the CLR interfaces with tools such as Visual Studio.NET to provide the Rapid Application Development (RAD) experience that VB programmers have used for so long, but for all modules in all languages. At runtime the class loader executes the classes.

The CLR at Runtime

When the class loader opens an assembly at execution time, it has a number of important steps to take before the classes can actually be run. Figure 1.2.3 illustrates the execution model for the CLR.

The class loader uses the Code Manager to assign memory for the objects and data. The layout of the classes in memory is computed, and each of the methods that are stored as intermediate language is given a stub that is used to invoke the compiler the first time it is run.

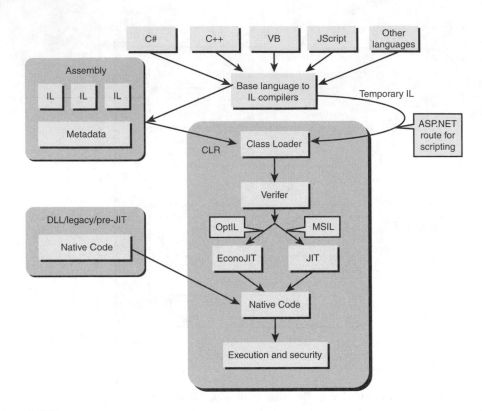

FIGURE 1.2.3

The CLR execution model.

NOTE

You will notice that in the model in Figure 1.2.3 there are two distinct types of intermediate language, MSIL and OptIL, that are compiled by their own JIT compilers. OptIL is a highly optimized subset of MSIL that is designed specifically for use by host systems that don't have the luxury of lots of memory or computational speed. Because of the extra work that the high-level language compiler puts into the optimization, OptIL is more suited to PDAs, intelligent phones, and the like. EconoJIT is the compact, portable compiler that turns OptIL into machine code.

Whenever a function first references a class stored in a different assembly or a data type that hasn't been used before, the class loader is invoked again to bring in the required objects.

The process is probably best understood by looking at a flowchart. The Common Language Runtime's virtual execution system (VES) and the major control paths are shown in Figure 1.2.4.

The Common Language Runtime

CHAPTER 1.2

21

1.2

THE COMMON
LANGUAGE
RUNTIME

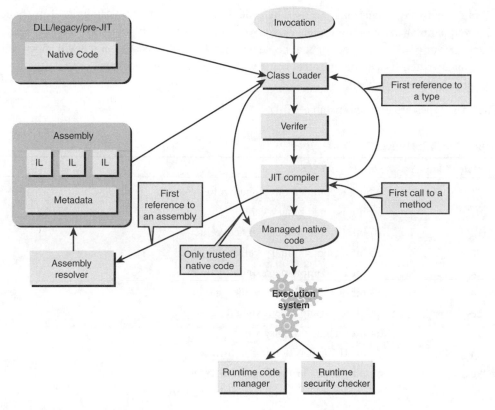

FIGURE 1.2.4

The virtual execution system.

Install Time Code Generation

A part of the VES not shown in Figure 1.2.4 is the install time code generation that sometimes takes place when assemblies are first put onto a host system. This will create native code in the assembly that reduces the startup time of a particular object. Generally, verification of this code is done at install time, but if a runtime version or security checks are needed, the code will be recompiled by the standard JITer in the usual manner.

Data Types Supported by the CLR

As was mentioned earlier, the .NET framework has a set of native data types that are used by all languages. These include integral types like 8-, 16-, 32-, and 64-bit integers and chars. The list also contains floating-point types and pointers to both managed and unmanaged memory.

All of the native data types may be used by code written in IL, and you can write IL by hand. IL is very similar to assembly language, so if you've ever rolled up your sleeves and played with a Z80 or 6502, you'll feel right at home with IL. Later in this section we will show you some handwritten IL and the tools that come with the .NET framework that can be used to assemble and disassemble it.

The basic types are detailed in Table 1.2.1.

TABLE 1.2.1 Native CLR Data Types

Type Name	Description
I1	8-bit 2's complement signed value
U1	8-bit unsigned binary value
I2	16-bit 2's complement signed value
U2	16-bit unsigned binary value
I4	32-bit 2's complement signed value
U4	32-bit unsigned binary value
I8	64-bit 2's complement signed value
U8	64-bit unsigned binary value
R4	32-bit IEEE 754 floating-point value
R8	64-bit IEEE 754 floating-point value
I	Natural size 2's complement signed value
U	Natural size unsigned binary value, also unmanaged pointer
R4Resul	Natural size for result of a 32-bit floating point computation
R8Result	Natural size for result of a 64-bit floating point computation
RPrecise	Maximum-precision floating point value
O	natural size object reference to managed memory
&	Natural size managed pointer (may point into managed memory)

Table 1.2.1 mentions "natural" sizes for data types. This refers to sizes that are dictated by the hardware. For example, a machine with a 16-bit bus probably has a 16-bit natural integer, and a machine with a 32-bit bus will have a correspondingly large integer. This can be a problem when programs are supposed to talk to software at the other end of an Internet connection. Without explicit instructions, it is difficult to know how big an integer is at either end, and type size mismatches and structure misalignments can occur. To address this and other similar problems, the CLR uses only a select few data types when actually evaluating and running software. The native type that doesn't fit the few chosen sizes is carefully packed and unpacked to

and from the more portable types. This happens behind the scenes, and you don't have to worry about it.

Managed Data and Code

The CLR contains the Code Manager and the Garbage Collector (GC). These functional blocks are responsible for the memory management of all .NET native objects, including all the managed data types. The Code Manager allocates storage space; the Garbage Collector deletes it and compacts the heap to reduce fragmentation.

Because the GC is responsible for compacting the heap, data or objects used in the .NET managed space are often moved from place to place during their lifetimes. This is why, under normal circumstances, objects are always accessed by reference. In the C++ world, a reference is not very different from a pointer. The mechanism used to find the object referred to is the same—a pointer to a memory block somewhere. C++ references are the compiler's way of saying that it guarantees that you are pointing to a particular type. Under C++ it's possible to store a reference to an object, delete the object, and then use the stored, out-of-date reference to access the place where the object used to be. This is often the cause of disastrous failure in a C++ program.

Under the .NET system, however, this problem is eliminated. Whenever a reference to an object is made, the object knows it's being referred to, and the GC will never delete it unless it's free of encumbrance. Furthermore, when the GC tidies up the heap and moves the object in memory, all of the references to that object are automatically updated so that components that use the object get the right one when they access it next.

Through the Code Manager, the CLR is responsible for the actual memory layout of objects and structures that it hosts. Usually this layout process is automatic, but when you need to do so you can specify the order, packing, and specific layout of memory in the metadata. This is made possible by the fact that the metadata is available to the programmer through a set of well-defined interfaces.

Unmanaged Code and Data Access

It might not be apparent how .NET type safety, security, and verification enable you to protect your investment in the C++ code that you have lavished care and attention on for so long. Microsoft was in exactly the same boat and, as a consequence, the .NET framework has excellent capabilities for reusing your legacy code.

There are three basic mechanisms for managed/unmanaged interoperation under .NET. COM Interop enables your COM objects to be used by the .NET framework as if they were .NET objects. The Platform Invoke (or P/Invoke) method lets managed objects call static entry points in DLLs the same as `LoadLibrary` and `GetProcAddress`. Finally, IJW (It Just Works) in its most basic form enables you to recompile your code and . . . it just works. A more complex form enables you to enhance your code using managed extensions to C++. This lets you create full GC memory-managed objects that your old C++ source code uses.

COM Interop Via the CLR

You can see in Figure 1.2.2 that the CLR contains a COM marshaler. This functional block is responsible for the COM/.NET Interop. There are two scenarios that require COM Interop with the .NET framework. The first is when you want to access your old COM objects from new C# or VB code you've written. The second is when you want to implement a well-known interface and have your COM objects access it.

For both of these scenarios, the CLR plays a very dynamic role by creating a specialized wrapper at runtime and then marshaling data in and out of the COM object as needed. The diagram in Figure 1.2.5 shows a COM object being accessed by a .NET client object.

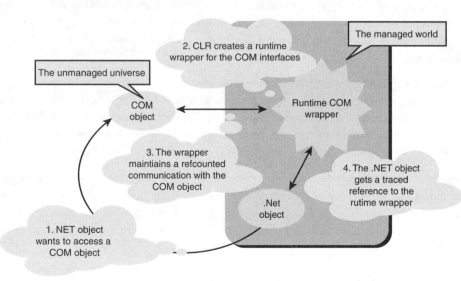

FIGURE 1.2.5

Managed code to COM Interop.

To use COM objects with your .NET programs, you need to import the type library definition. VS.NET will do this for you automatically when you add a reference to the COM object in the IDE, in the same way that VB programmers have done for many years. You can also use the type library import utility (TLBImp) explicitly. TLBImp will refactor the COM method signatures into .NET method signatures for you. For example, the COM method signature

```
HRESULT MyMethod(BSTR b, int n, [out, retval]int *retval);
```

is transformed to

```
int MyMethod(String b, int n);
```

As a result, when you call the method you don't have to worry about interpreting HRESULTs, you can simply assign the integer return value to a variable in your code. In fact, the whole .NET-to-COM Interop picture is very easy to use. You don't have to worry about data conversions. As you can see from the example, the COM data types such as BSTR map to sensible equivalent .NET types. You don't have to manage the reference counting and there are no GUIDS. If you do get a failure HRESULT, the runtime wrapper generates an exception that you can catch.

When you want to call a .NET object from existing COM objects, the process that the CLR uses to facilitate the connection is similar to that shown in Figure 1.2.5. Figure 1.2.6 illustrates the COM-to-.NET connection.

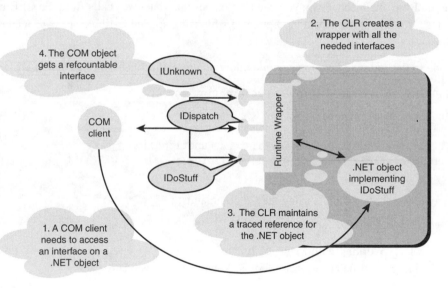

FIGURE 1.2.6

Accessing a .NET object from COM.

COM objects can access only public methods of your .NET objects, but they can be used from the COM world.

First, create a typelib from your object using the .NET tool TlbExp. Next, register the assembly created by TlbExp with the tool RegAsm. This is the only time you'll need to register anything under .NET; COM running in the unmanaged portion of your host computer needs to activate the object in the standard way. Finally, from COM you can use `CoCreateInstance` and `QueryInterface`, use `AddRef` and `Release` as normal, and use the `HRESULT`s that the wrapper provides.

Later, in Part 5.3, we have a chapter dedicated to COM Interop where we will go into more detail and show you examples.

Platform Invoke (P/Invoke) from the CLR

One of the most common requirements for interoperation will be the use of a DLL that already exists on the local system. For example, you might need to continue to use tools that you've invested in and that are available only as DLLs.

The .NET framework provides the P/Invoke mechanism for this purpose. The internal mechanism is very similar to COM Interop, but because the DLLs that you use are always going to be local (on the same machine), the system is simpler to use.

To use the P/Invoke mechanism, you need a wrapper that delegates calls from the CLR to the actual DLL function. You create these wrappers by using special attributes in your method definitions.

The code in the following example would allow you to call a function in a custom DLL.

MyDll.Dll contains a function int MyFunction(int x):

```
public class MyDllWrapper
{
    [DllImport("MyDll.Dll",EntryPoint="MyFunction")]
    public static extern int MyFunction(int x);
}
```

You may now access the DLL using the C# commands:

```
int r=MyDllWrapper.MyFunction(12);
```

In Chapter 1.4, "Working with Managed Extensions to C++," we will examine the P/Invoke mechanism in greater detail when we look at Managed Extensions to C++.

IJW ("It Just Works")

The simplest way to migrate your C++ applications to the .NET framework is to gather all the source code for your EXE or DLL. Recompile them all with the /CLR compiler switch and run them. Microsoft says "It Just Works." This is probably true if you've been programming in a reasonably modern way. If your code still contains good old K&R-style declarations, then it won't.

There are a few limitations to this process. You cannot recompile all your class libraries and then inherit from them in the managed world. You cannot easily pass managed code pointers to your functions and classes.

Both the IJW and P/Invoke methods prolong the life of your code and give you an opportunity to migrate to the .NET framework.

Managed Extensions to C++

When simply reusing your old code isn't enough, and you need a more integrated approach from a C++ programmer's perspective, managed extensions to C++ are an ideal solution or migration path.

The .NET framework adds some significant concepts to memory management and the use of data. These features are all available from the C# and VB languages but not natively to C++. The additions to the programmer's arsenal are discussed in the following sections.

Garbage Collected (GC) Classes

Garbage Collected (GC) classes are objects for which all memory management is performed by the CLR. Once you stop using a GC class, it is marked automatically for deletion and reclaimed by the GC heap. A GC class may also have a delete method that can be called explicitly.

You can create GC classes by using the new __gc class modifier on your classes:

```
__gc class MyClass
{
    public:
        int m_x;
        int m_y;
        SetXY(int x, int y)
        {
            m_x=x;
            m_y=y;
        }
}
```

MyClass is now a Garbage Collected class.

CAUTION

If you use _asm or setjmp in your C++ methods, the compiler will issue warnings; attempting to run the code may result in failure if the method uses any managed types or managed code. Your GC classes may employ only single inheritance. They may not have a copy constructor and may not override operator & or operator new.

Value Classes

The new __value keyword enables you to create complex value types in your C++ code. For example, you may want to create a 3D_point structure with x,y,z coordinates to be used as a value type. These types are created on the heap but may be boxed or wrapped in a sort of object skin, using the __box keyword to use them as managed objects. (There is an extensive discussion of boxing and unboxing in Part II of this book, "The C# Language.") When they are boxed, these value types can be used by .NET managed code, held in .NET collection classes, serialized simply with XML, and so on.

Classes and structs created with the __value keyword inherit from the .NET framework class System.ValueType and may override any of the methods that are needed from that object. Putting any other virtual methods on your value class is not allowed. For example, you can override System.ValueType.ToString to render a string that describes the object. For example, int32.ToString() returns the number as a string. Like itoa(...). You may also wish to override System.ValueType.GetHashCode for use in a map collection.

These value classes act like C++ classes when used from C++ but can be used by the managed runtime, too. They cannot be allocated directly from the managed heap, but they can be used by managed objects when boxed.

There are some other rules that apply to value classes. You may derive the value class from one or more managed interfaces, but you cannot define a copy constructor for it. A value class cannot have the __abstract keyword as a modifier. Value classes are always sealed, which means that they cannot be derived from. You can't declare a pointer to a value class.

As with the __gc keyword, you should not use _asm or setjmp if the class uses any managed code, accepts managed types as parameters, or returns a managed type. It might compile, but it will probably fail to work correctly.

Properties

.NET C# classes can have properties with get and set accessors. The __property keyword allows you to create GC classes that support properties. A property looks like a data member in your class but is really a piece of code. The example below shows how a property would be created and used.

```
#using "mscorlib.dll"

__gc class My3DPoint
{
    // members are private by default
    int m_x;
    int m_y;
    int m_z;
```

The Common Language Runtime

Chapter 1.2

29

1.2

THE COMMON
LANGUAGE
RUNTIME

```
public:
    __property int get_x(){return m_x;};
    __property void set_x(int value){m_x=value;}
    __property int get_y(){return m_y;};
    __property void set_y(int value){m_y=value;}
    __property int get_z(){return m_z;};
    __property void set_z(int value){m_z=value;}

    // other 3D operations go here...
};

void main(void)
{
    My3DPoint *pP=new My3DPoint();
    pP->x=10; // calls set_x(10);
    int X = pP->x; // calls get_x();
}
```

Pinning Values

The Garbage Collected heap will regularly move objects from place to place during the course of its operation. Whenever you need to pass a pointer to a managed object or to an unmanaged C++ function, you can pin the object in place using the __pin keyword. The pinning operation forbids the GC from moving the object until it's unpinned.

Exceptions

All exceptions within the .NET framework are handled by the CLR. This provides a very consistent and powerful mechanism for trapping and handling errors wherever they may occur.

Exceptions in the CLR use exception objects, usually derived from the .NET framework class System.Exception and one of four types of exception handlers. These handlers are

- A finally handler is executed whenever a block exits. This handler is called during the normal shutdown of an object as well as when a fault occurs.

- A fault handler runs when a true exception occurs.

- A type-filtered handler services exceptions from a specific class or its derived classes. For example; catch(MyExceptionType e)

- A user-filtered handler can figure out whether the exception should be ignored, handled by the associated handler, or passed on to the next exception handler available.

Every method in every class in the .NET framework libraries or in your code has an exception handler table associated with it. The entries in the array describe a protected block of code and the exception handler associated with it. There may be either no handler at all, a catch handler, a finally handler, or a fault handler for each table entry. When an exception occurs, the

CLR looks for an entry in the table of the method that threw the exception for a handler. If one is found, control is passed to the handler as usual; if not, the CLR proceeds through a stack walk to the calling method and so on, back up the chain of callers until a handler is found. If one is not found, the CLR aborts the application and produces a stack dump.

As we progress through this book, examples will give more detailed information on how to create your own exception classes and handlers.

Debugging Support

The .NET framework has debugging built into it at a very low level. Unlike the debug schemes that C++ programmers are used to, which are often intrusive, the CLR, which runs all the code anyway, manages debugging and sends events to the connected debugger whenever needed.

The .NET SDK has its own debuggers, in addition to the one that's integrated with Visual Studio.NET. All debuggers operate through the public APIs provided by the framework.

Summary

The Common Language Runtime is the heart of the .NET system. It loads and manages code, interacts with the development tools and debuggers for you, enforces the safety and security of your system, and allows your software to integrate with legacy systems like COM and user DLL's. As a component of .NET it is unlikely that you will think about it much at all.

Read on now as we travel into the world of Intermediate Language and examine how it's possible to write code, by hand, in the true native language of .NET.

IL Intermediate Language

IN THIS CHAPTER

In the current day and age of software development, developers use high-level languages such as C++, Visual Basic, or Java to implement applications and components. I personally don't know any working binary developers and few assembly language programmers.

So why is IL, Intermediate Language, so important to .NET? To answer this question requires a brief tour of compiler theory 101. The basic task of a compiler is to transform readable source code into native executable code for a given platform. The compilation process includes several phases, which include but are not limited to lexical scanning, parsing, abstract syntax tree creation, intermediate code creation, code emission, assembler, and linking. Figure 1.3.1 shows a basic diagram of this process.

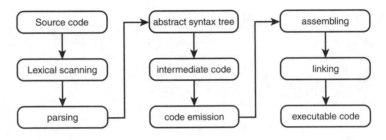

FIGURE 1.3.1

The basic compilation process.

The intermediate code creation poses an interesting question: What if it's possible to translate a given set of languages into some standard intermediate code? This is where IL fits into the scheme of things. The ability to translate high-level language constructs into a standardized format, such as IL, allows for a single underlying compiler or just-in-time (JIT) compiler. This is the approach taken by .NET.

With the introduction of Visual Studio .NET, Microsoft is providing Managed C++, C#, Visual Basic, and ASP.NET, each of which produce IL from their respective source code. There are also several third-party language vendors providing .NET versions of their respective languages. Figure 1.3.2 shows the basic .NET compilation process.

It is important to note that IL is not interpreted. Rather, the .NET platform makes use of various types of just-in-time compilers to produce native code from the IL code. Native code runs directly on the hardware and does not require a virtual machine, as is the case with Java and early versions of Visual Basic. By compiling IL to native code, the runtime performance is increased compared to interpreted languages that run on top of a virtual machine. We will be covering the various types of just-in-time compilers later on. (From here on out I will refer to the just-in-time compiler(s) as the *jitter*).

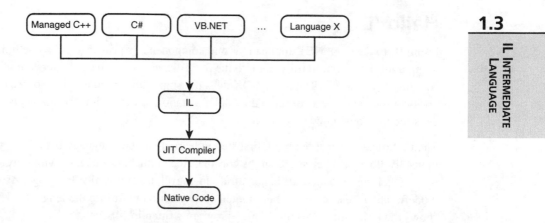

FIGURE 1.3.2
.NET compilation.

IL is a full, stack-based language that you can use to implement .NET components. Although it is definitely not suggested for the sake of productivity, you can use IL to do things that you can't do with C#. For example, in IL, you can create global functions and call them from within IL.

Language Inter-Op

Like the quest for the Holy Grail, the ability to seamlessly inter-op between languages has been on the forefront. On the various Windows platforms, the standard for cross language development has been the Component Object Model (COM). An entire industry was born whose sole purpose was developing COM components and ActiveX controls. Because COM is a binary standard, any language capable of consuming COM components is able to use them regardless with which language the COM component was created.

Although COM allowed for reusable components, it was far from perfect. Certain languages, such as scripting languages, could only make use of the default interface provided by the COM object. Also, it was not possible to inherit from a COM component to extend its basic function-ality. To extend a binary object, developers were forced to wrap the COM component, not a very OO approach.

With the advent of .NET and IL, such barriers no longer exist. Because every language tar-geted at the .NET platform understands IL and the metadata of a .NET component, a new level of interoperability is born. The metadata allows inspection of a .NET component to discover the classes, methods, fields, and interfaces that it contains. The topic of metadata will be cov-ered later in this section.

Hello IL

Using IL to develop .NET applications and components is probably not something you'll be doing a lot. However, to truly dig into the .NET framework, a basic understanding of the IL structure is important. The .NET SDK does not ship with the underlying source code. This does not mean you can't dig into the implementation of the various components. However, it does require some knowledge of IL.

The traditional, almost required, first step in learning a new language is to display the infamous "Hello World" message on the console. Accomplishing this task with only IL is not as painful as it might sound. IL is not a truly low-level, assembly-like language. As with most modern languages, there is a fair amount of abstraction built into the language. Listing 1.3.1 shows the now famous "Hello World" program written in MSIL.

LISTING 1.3.1   Hello World

```
 1: //File               :Hello.cil
 2: //Author          :Richard L. Weeks
 3: //
 4: //
 5:
 6: //define some basic assembly information
 7: .assembly hello 8: {
 9:     .ver  1:0:0:0
10: }
11:
12:
13: //create an entry point for the exe
14: .method public static void main( ) il managed
15: {
16:
17:     .entrypoint
18:     .maxstack   1
19:
20:
21:     //load string to display
22:     ldstr "Hello World IL style\n"
23:
24:     //display to console
25:     call void [mscorlib]System.Console::WriteLine( class System.String )
26:
27:     ret
28: }
29:
```

To compile Listing 1.3.1, issue the following command line:

```
ilasm hello.cil
```

The IL assembler will produce a .NET `hello.exe`.

This IL code displays the message "Hello World IL style" by using the static `Write` method of the `System.Console` object. The `Console` class is part of the .NET framework and, as its use implies, its purpose is to write to the standard output.

Notice that there is no need to create a class. IL is not an object-oriented language, but it does provide the constructs necessary to describe objects and use them. IL was designed to accommodate a variety of language constructs and programming paradigms. Such diversity and openness in its design will allow for many different languages to be targeted at the .NET runtime.

There are a number of directives that have special meanings within IL. These directives are shown in Table 1.3.1.

TABLE 1.3.1 IL Directives used in "Hello World"

Directive	Meaning
`.assembly`	Name of the resulting assembly to produce
`.entrypoint`	Start of execution for an `.exe` assembly
`.maxstack`	Number of stack slots to reserve for the current method or function

Notice that the `.entrypoint` directive defines the start of execution for any `.exe` assembly. Although our function has the name `main`, it could have any name we want. Unlike C, C++, and other high-level languages, IL does not define a function to serve as the beginning of execution. Rather, IL makes use of the `.entrypoint` directive to serve this purpose.

Another directive of interest is the `.assembly` directive. IL uses this directive to name the output of the assembly. The `.assembly` directive also contains the version number of the assembly.

Functions

The Hello World IL example encompasses only one method. If only all software development requirements were that simple! Because IL is a stack based language, function parameters are pushed onto the stack and the function is called. The called function is responsible for removing any parameters from the stack and for pushing any return value back onto the stack for the caller of the function.

The process of pushing and popping values to and from the call stack can be visualized as shown in Figure 1.3.3.

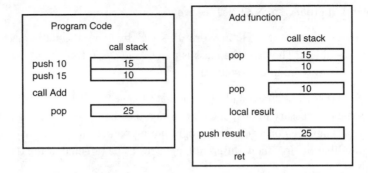

FIGURE 1.3.3

The call stack.

Although Figure 1.3.3. depicts a very simplified view of the actual process, enough information is provide to gain an understanding of the overall steps involved. Translating Figure 1.3.3 into IL produces the source in Listing 1.3.2.

LISTING 1.3.2 IL Function Calls

```
 1: //File      :function.cil
 2:
 3: .assembly function_call 4: {
 5:      .ver 1:0:0:0
 6: }
 7:
 8:
 9: //Add method
10: .method public static int32 'add'( int32 a, int32 b ) il managed
11: {
12:
13:      .maxstack    2
14:      .locals      (int32 V_0, int32 V_1)
15:
16:      //pop the parameters from the call stack
17:      ldarg.0
18:      ldarg.1
19:
20:      add
21:
22:      //push the result back on the call stack
```

LISTING 1.3.2 Continued

```
23:    stloc.0
24:    ldloc.0
25:
26:    ret
27: }
28:
29: .method public static void main( ) il managed
30: {
31:    .entrypoint
32:    .maxstack 2
33:    .locals ( int32 V_0 )
34:
35:    //push two parameters onto the call stack
36:    ldc.i4.s 10
37:    ldc.i4.s 5
38:
39:    call int32 'add'(int32,int32)
40:
41:    stloc.0              //pop the result in the local variable V_0
42:
43:    //Display the result
44:    ldstr "10 + 5 = {0}"
45:    ldloc  V_0
46:    box        [mscorlib]System.Int32
47:    call void [mscorlib]System.Console::WriteLine(class System.String,
➥ class System.Object )
48:
49:    ret
50: }
51:
```

The function.cil code in Listing 1.3.2 introduces a new directive: .locals. This directive is used to reserve space for local variables used within the current function. The add method defined on line 10 declares space for two local variables. The parameters that were passed to the add method are loaded into the reserved space using the ldarg statement. After the add instruction has been issued, the next step is to store the result and then to push the result back onto the call stack.

The main method only allocates space for a single local variable. This local variable will be used to hold the result returned from the user-defined add method. The process of pushing the values 10 and 5 onto the stack, calling the add method, and popping the result correspond to the depiction in Figure 1.3.3.

You've no doubt noticed the box instruction on line 46. Boxing is something new to .NET. *Boxing* allows for value-types, such as primitives, to be treated as objects.

Classes

As previously stated, IL is not an OO language in itself. For IL to support multiple source languages and constructs, IL supports the notion of creating classes and creating instances of classes. Looking at the IL for declaring and creating classes will give you a better understanding of the Common Language Specification (CLS). Listing 1.3.3 shows the IL code for creating and using a class.

LISTING 1.3.3   Creating a Class in IL

```
 1: .assembly class_test as "class_test"
 2: {
 3:   .ver 1:0:0:0
 4: }
 5:
 6:
 7: .module class_test.exe
 8:
 9:
10: //Create a class Dog with two public fields
11:
12: .class public auto ansi Dog extends [mscorlib]System.Object {
13:
14:   //public data fields
15:   .field public class System.String m_Name
16:   .field public int32 m_Age
17:
18:
19:   //Create a method to display the fields
20:   .method public hidebysig instance void Print() il managed
21:   {
22:     .maxstack  8
23:     ldstr      "Name : {0}\nAge  :{1}"
24:     ldarg.0
25:     ldfld      class System.String Dog::m_Name
26:     ldarg.0
27:     ldfld      int32 Dog::m_Age
28:     box        [mscorlib]System.Int32
29:     call       void [mscorlib]System.Console::WriteLine(
➥class System.String,
30:                                          class System.Object,
31:                                          class System.Object)
```

LISTING 1.3.3   Continued

```
32:       ret
33:     }
34:
35:     //The Constructor
36:     .method public hidebysig specialname rtspecialname instance void .ctor()
 ↪ il managed
37:     {
38:       .maxstack  8
39:       ldarg.0
40:       call       instance void [mscorlib]System.Object::.ctor()
41:       ret
42:     }
43:
44: }
45:
46: .method public static void Main() il managed
47: {
48:       .entrypoint
49:
50:       .maxstack  2
51:
52:       .locals (class Dog V_0)
53:
54:       newobj     instance void Dog::.ctor()
55:       stloc.0
56:       ldloc.0
57:       ldstr      "Daisy"
58:       stfld      class System.String Dog::m_Name
59:       ldloc.0
60:       ldc.i4.3
61:       stfld      int32 Dog::m_Age
62:       ldloc.0
63:       call       instance void Dog::Print()
64:       ret
65: }
66:
```

Creating a class in IL is a fairly straightforward process. The Dog class declared in Listing 1.3.3 derives from the System.Object class, which is the base class of all .NET classes. In .NET, data members are known as fields and as such are marked with the .field keyword.

To define a class method, all that is required is to define the method within the scope of the class to which the method belongs. The Print method is declared on line 20 of Listing 1.3.3. Notice the instance method modifier that is applied to the Print method. For the Print method to be invoked, an instance of the Dog class is required.

The same is true for the constructor of the Dog class. IL provides two modifiers that must be applied to instance constructors. The rtspecialname modifier is used by the runtime, whereas the specialname is provided for various .NET tools, such as Visual Studio .NET.

ILDASM

The .NET ships with several tools, ranging from compilers to form designers. However, the most important tool is ILDASM, Intermediate Language Disassembler. ILDASM allows for peeking into various .NET assemblies. Regardless of the language used to implement the assembly, ILDASM is capable of displaying the resulting IL.

The main window of ILDASM creates a treeview detailing the contents of a .NET assembly. The treeview is grouped by namespace with each namespace containing one or more nested namespaces, structs, classes, interfaces, or enumerations (see Figure 1.3.4).

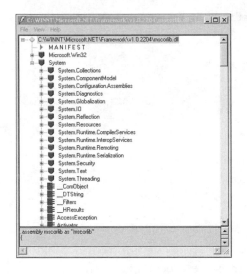

FIGURE 1.3.4
ILDASM with mscorlib.dll *loaded.*

Locate the .NET assembly mscorlib.dll and use ILDASM to view the contents. Depending on the install of the .NET SDK, the .NET assemblies should be located in

<rootdrive>:\<windows directory>\Microsoft.Net\Framework\vN.N.NNN.

Make the appropriate substitutions. Figure 1.3.5 shows the various symbols and their meanings for ILDASM.

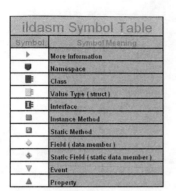

FIGURE 1.3.5
ILDASM symbol table.

At the heart of the .NET framework is the `mscorlib.dll` assembly. This assembly contains most of the standard classes and interfaces that comprise .NET. Certainly there are other assemblies for database access, networking, security and such, but at the root of it all is `mscorlib.dll`.

Using the symbol table in Figure 1.3.5, you can visually determine entity types found within `mscorlib.dll`. Locate `System.Object` and double-click the node to expand it (see Figure 1.3.6).

FIGURE 1.3.6
`System.Object` *in ILDASM.*

The `System.Object` class is the base class of all .NET classes. The `System.Object` base class provides shared functionality used throughout .NET. Locate the `ToString` method and double-click it to view the underlying IL code that comprises it (see Figure 1.3.7).

FIGURE 1.3.7
IL code for `System.Object.ToString()`.

MFC developers were accustomed to having the Visual C++ source code to the MFC framework readily available for their inspection. This is not the case with the .NET framework. Currently, the only way to get a peek under the covers is to use a tool such as ILDASM to view the IL implementation. Although IL is not as easy to read as, say, C# or VB.NET, it will allow for an understanding of the internal workings of the .NET classes none the less.

ILDASM provides the ability to produce a text file with the complete IL source for a given .NET assembly. Launching ILDASM from the command line and using the `/OUT=<filename>` parameter, ILDASM will direct the disassembly output to the specified file rather than displaying the ILDASM GUI.

Metadata

Every component in .NET contains metadata. Metadata describes the runtime `types`, `classes`, `interfaces`, `structs`, and all entities within a .NET component. Metadata also provides implementation and layout information that the .NET runtime makes use of to JIT compile IL code.

Metadata is available to all tools through two different sets of APIs. There exists a set of low-level, unmanaged APIs and a set of managed APIs that can be used to gather information about a .NET component. There also exists a set of APIs for emitting Metadata. This emit API is used by compilers during compilation of a given source language into IL for the .NET runtime. A full description of the Metadata APIs and infrastructure would require another book in itself, but this text will present a small sample of how to use the Reflection API to inspect a .NET component.

Reflection API

Reflection represents an extremely powerful mechanism for working with .NET components. Through the use of reflection, .NET components can be dynamically loaded and their contents discovered at runtime. Metadata is the heart of this functionality and, as such, Metadata can be thought of as a TypeLib on steroids.

The .NET CLR provides for strong runtime type information and provides a System.Type class. After a .NET component is loaded, it is then possible to obtain the type or types contained within the given assembly. To demonstrate the power of Metadata and the Reflection API, create a text file named **employee.cs** and copy Listing 1.3.4 into it. To compile the listing, issue the following command:

```
csc /t:library employee.cs
```

This will build the employee.dll assembly.

LISTING 1.3.4 The Employee Class

```
 1: //File         :employee.cs
 2: //Author       :Richard L. Weeks
 3: //Purpose      :Create a .NET component and use the reflection
 4: //             API to view the component
 5:
 6: using System;
 7:
 8: namespace stingray {
 9:
10:
11:     //Create a basic class
12:     public class Employee {
13:
14:         //private data members
15:         private string   m_FirstName;
16:         private string   m_LastName;
17:         private string   m_Title;        //Job Title
18:
19:         //Public Properties
20:         public string FirstName {
21:             get { return m_FirstName; }
22:             set { m_FirstName = value; }
23:         }
```

LISTING 1.3.4   Continued

```
24:
25:            public string LastName {
26:                    get { return m_LastName; }
27:                    set { m_LastName = value; }
28:            }
29:
30:            public string Title {
31:                    get { return m_Title; }
32:                    set { m_Title = value; }
33:            }
34:
35:            //Public Methods
36:            public void ShowData( ) {
37:                object[] args = { m_LastName, m_FirstName, m_Title };
38:
39:                Console.WriteLine("********************\n");
40:                Console.WriteLine("Employee : {0}, {1}\nTitle      :{2}\n",
➥ args);
41:                Console.WriteLine("********************\n");
42:            }
43:
44:            //Private methods
45:            private void Update( ) {
46:                //TODO: Update Employee information
47:            }
48:        }
49: }
50:
```

The `Employee` class resides in the `stingray` namespace and contains three private data members, corresponding public properties, and two methods. Using the Reflection API, it is possible to dynamically load the `employee.dll` at runtime. After the assembly has been loaded, all types contained within the assembly can be queried and their Metadata accessed. Listing 1.3.5 makes use of the `Reflection` API to peek into a .NET component.

LISTING 1.3.5   Metaview Source Listing

```
1: //File         :metaview.cs
2: //Author        :Richard L. Weeks
3: //Purpose       :Use the Managed Reflection API
4: //                to inspect a .NET component
5:
6:
```

LISTING 1.3.5   Continued

```
 7: using System;
 8: using System.Reflection;
 9:
10:
11:
12: public class ClsView {
13:
14:
15:     public static void Main( String[] args ) {
16:
17:        try {
18:
19:             //Load the assembly
20:             Assembly asm = Assembly.LoadFrom( args[0] );
21:
22:             //Get the Types contained within the Assembly
23:             System.Type[] Types = asm.GetTypes( );
24:
25:             //Display basic information about each type
26:             foreach( Type T in Types ) {
27:                 Console.WriteLine("Type {0}", T.FullName);
28:                 DisplayFields( T );
29:                 DisplayProperties( T );
30:                 DisplayMethods( T );
31:                 Console.WriteLine("");
32:             }
33:
34:        } catch( Exception ex ) {
35:             Console.WriteLine( ex );
36:        }
37:
38:     }
39:
40:
41:     public static void DisplayFields( Type T ) {
42:         Console.WriteLine("*****[ DisplayFields ]*****");
43:         FieldInfo[] Fields = T.GetFields(
➥System.Reflection.BindingFlags.Instance |
44:
➥System.Reflection.BindingFlags.Public |
45:
➥System.Reflection.BindingFlags.NonPublic );
46:
47:         foreach( FieldInfo F in Fields )
48:             Console.WriteLine( "FieldName = {0}", F.Name );
```

LISTING 1.3.5   Continued

```
49:      }
50:
51:      public static void DisplayProperties( Type T ) {
52:          Console.WriteLine("*****[ Display Properties ]*****");
53:        System.Reflection.PropertyInfo[] Properties = T.GetProperties(
➥ System.Reflection.BindingFlags.Instance |
➥System.Reflection.BindingFlags.Public |
➥System.Reflection.BindingFlags.NonPublic );
54:
55:          foreach( PropertyInfo pi in Properties )
56:              Console.WriteLine( pi.Name );
57:      }
58:
59:      public static void DisplayMethods( Type T ) {
60:          Console.WriteLine("*****[ Display Methods ]*****");
61:          System.Reflection.MethodInfo[] Methods = T.GetMethods(
➥ System.Reflection.BindingFlags.Instance |
➥System.Reflection.BindingFlags.Public |
➥System.Reflection.BindingFlags.NonPublic );
62:
63:          foreach( MethodInfo mi in Methods )
64:              Console.WriteLine( mi.Name );
65:      }
66: }
```

Listing 1.3.5 makes use of the most basic Reflection APIs to detail information about each field, property, and method with the loaded employee assembly. Although the C# language has not been covered yet, most of the code should speak for itself. I encourage you to implement a robust version of Metaview, complete with a Windows Forms GUI. Such a project will no doubt increase your knowledge of .NET and the rich set of features it provides.

Summary

We've covered a lot of ground in this chapter. Topics included IL, ILDASM, metadata, and Reflection. The .NET framework certainly gives a hint as to the future of software development. No longer is language a barrier; the .NET platform provides languages targeted to the superior interoperability that, until now, has not been easy to use or extend.

Gone are the days of using IDL and DEF files to describe the interfaces exposed by objects. Rather, all objects, interfaces, and members are fully described with metadata. Those developers who are familiar with Java will appreciate the decision to include Reflection in .NET because it provides a powerful paradigm to extend the life of applications and use new components dynamically.

Working with Managed
Extensions to C++

IN THIS CHAPTER

In the previous chapter we looked briefly at managed extensions to C++ as a way to use your C++ skills, either in the managed environment of .NET or as a vehicle for reusing your existing code. If you're the typical C++ programmer looking at migration to .NET, the questions foremost in your mind will be "Can I protect my investment in all that C++ code?" and "Can I use C++ and C# together easily?" Thankfully, due to the efforts of the Microsoft engineers, both of these questions have positive answers. Let's take a short sidetrip into managed extensions to C++ and get a feel for where your old code can fit into the new world of .NET.

The managed extensions add a few keywords to the C++ language. Obviously this is not going to amuse language lawyers the world over, but remember that in reality, managed C++ is not an attempt to corrupt ANSI specifications but a compromise that allows many of the benefits of the managed runtime without the pain of having to learn a whole new language. As an aside, the Visual Studio.NET C++ compiler is actually more ANSI compliant than its predecessors when used in native C++ mode. When used to compile ordinary C++ code, the compiler generates x86 object code for linking in the normal manner. When used to compile managed C++, the `/CLR` command-line argument is used, and the compiler creates IL instead.

The C++ Extension Keywords

`__abstract`   indicates that a class is an abstract base class and requires implementation of some or all of its declared methods.

`__box`   makes a managed object from a value type like a structure or variable. The boxed object is reallocated on the Garbage Collected heap and then subject to GC lifetime management.

`__delegate`   is the .NET answer to the callback. It is a declaration for a function signature that provides information about function return types and parameters. The delegate declaration allows both static members and instance members of a class to be called. It is used to map an event handler to a specific stimulus. There are two distinct types of delegate: `Single Cast` and `Multicast`. These allow either a simple event handler or a list of handlers for a single stimulus to be called.

`__gc`   makes your classes or structures manageable by the Garbage Collected runtime.

`__identifier`   allows you to use keywords from C++ as identifiers, such as `class` or `for`. The documentation from Microsoft says that its use is "strongly discouraged as a matter of style."

`__nogc`   declares that instances of structures or classes should not be managed by the GC runtime.

`__pin`   is used to prohibit the Garbage Collector's compacting mechanism from moving the managed class or value type. Once an instance of an object is pinned, it might be referred to

Working with Managed Extensions to C++

CHAPTER **1.4**

49

1.4

WORKING WITH
MANAGED
EXTENSIONS TO C++

reliably using a pointer. An unpinned object is likely to be moved "out from under your feet" by the actions of the Garbage Collector, which moves objects around as it cleans up the heap. This can have disastrous results.

__property   Classes under the C# language can be given properties. These look like data members to external objects and are set or read by accessor functions called get_ and set_. In reality, the property could perform some calculation or access some other function, using data supplied to the set accessor or before returning data via the get accessor.

__sealed   has two uses. It can be used as a class modifier to signify that the class may not be derived from. It also might be used as a modifier on a final implementation of a virtual method to prevent it from being overridden again.

__try_cast   allows you to try to cast a class to a particular type but will throw an exception at runtime if the cast fails. The syntax for __try_cast is

```
__try_cast<type_id>(expression)
```

If the cast is unsuccessful, System::InvalidCastException is thrown. __try_cast should be used during the construction and test phases of program creation and then replaced by static_cast or dynamic_cast as required.

__typeof returns the System::Type of a declared object. Similar to [object]->GetType(), which requires an instance of an object, the __typeof keyword can return the type of an abstract declaration; for example

```
MyObjct o=new MyObject;
Type *pt = o->GetType(); // requires an instance of a MyObject
Type *pt2 = __typeof(MyObject); // does not require an instance of MyObject
```

__value   Structures and simple classes might be turned into managed value types by the application of this modifier. A value type can be allocated on the GC heap and can be reclaimed by the GC runtime when it is no longer needed. Remember that value types are best kept simple because there is some overhead when they are used.

Using the C++ Compiler for Managed C++

The compiler has a new /CLR command-line switch that signifies that code should be compiled for the Common Language Runtime.

Using the /LD command-line switch will create a DLL instead of an EXE.

When using the compiler in this mode, the linker will be invoked automatically to produce an executable file that requires the .NET CLR to make it work. This implies that you cannot create executables and run them on systems that do not support the .NET runtime. You can disable the link step by using the /c command-line switch. In this case, an .obj file is created in the normal way.

You can use the /link compiler command-line option to pass the remainder of the command line directly to the linker. The /link directive is the last one the compiler notices. All other directives are passed to the linker command line.

Garbage Collected Classes

Classes under C++ are usually allocated on the stack or the heap as required. Classes allocated with the new keyword must also be deleted in an orderly fashion to prevent memory leaks. Garbage Collected classes are allocated on the GC heap, are subject to lifetime management and movement by the GC, and will be deleted from the system only after the final reference to them has been released.

The declaration for a Garbage Collected class under managed C++ is as follows:

```
__gc class SomeClass
{
};
```

Under .NET, all classes that have no explicit base class are implicitly derived from System::Object. The managed C++ classes declared with __gc are also added to in this manner by the compiler. This base class has methods that you can override to improve interaction between your GC class and the system. See the System::Object methods in the .NET SDK documentation for more details.

The #using Directive

#using can be considered equivalent to the import statement and is used to refer to the .NET libraries. For example, to use some of the .NET framework classes in your C++ code, you first employ the following:

```
#using <mscorlib.dll>
```

This directive should be followed by the declaration for exactly which namespaces you need.

Listing 1.4.1 shows the creation of a simple application containing a GC class.

LISTING 1.4.1   managed.cpp: A First Look at Garbage Collected C++

```
#using <mscorlib.dll> // import the library
using namespace System;

__gc class MCPPDemo
{
public:
    void SayHello()
```

LISTING 1.4.1 Continued

```
    {
        Console::WriteLine("Hello Managed C++");
    }
};

void main()
{
    MCPPDemo *pD=new MCPPDemo;
    pD->SayHello();
}
```

There are a few things in this code that need explanation. First of all, there is a distinct difference between #using and using namespace. The #using directive refers to a DLL that will be imported. The using namespace maintains its classic meaning. Next, the main function creates a pointer and assigns a new class to it, uses it, and then exits without deleting. This, surprisingly, is correct because the __gc keyword applied to the class defines it as being managed by the .NET runtime. The Garbage Collector concerns itself with the lifetime of such objects and will delete it for you when you stop using it. The result is no memory leaks.

Because __gc classes are specifically created on the managed heap, you cannot just create an instance on the stack as follows:

```
MCCPDemo d;
```

If you try this you will get an error. You must always create GC classes with the new operator and use the -> fleche when you invoke its methods or use its data. This is an odd paradox of managed C++ because C# and other managed languages use dot notation exclusively when referring to class members.

If you want to run the program in Listing 1.4.1, type it in with Notepad, save it to the file managed.cpp, and then use the following command line to compile it:

```
CL /CLR managed.cpp
```

It will create managed.exe, which you can run from the command line. Notice the distinct lack of an explicit link step. The linker is invoked automatically.

The String

The .NET framework has extensive support for strings. The System namespace has a System.String class that can be used to store text.

The managed extensions to C++ also allow you to use the System.String object through the String extension.

You can define a string under managed C++ as follows:

```
String *pS=S"Hello World";
```

These strings are created on the Garbage Collected heap and are subject to lifetime management.

Notice the S prefix to the string literal. All instances of identical strings prefixed by S are essentially the same string. A string literal can also be prefixed with L. This signifies that it is a wide character string:

```
String *s=L"This is a wide string";
```

Each string is immutable. Once you've made it you can't change it. However, there are functions in the String object that allow you to create new, altered strings from the original. There is also a StringBuilder class that helps in the process.

Listing 1.4.2 shows an example.

LISTING 1.4.2   strings.cpp: Using Managed Strings in C++

```
#using <mscorlib.dll>
using namespace System;

void StringCompare(String *a, String *b)
{
    Console::WriteLine("a=\"{0}\" b=\"{1}\" same string? {2}\n",
                       a,b,a==b ? S"true":S"false");
}

void main()
{
            String* a=S"Hello";
            String* b=S"Hello";
            StringCompare(a,b);
            a=a->Concat(a,S" World");
            StringCompare(a,b);
            a=a->Remove(5,6);
            StringCompare(a,b);}
```

In addition to the String being available as a native type, there are some classes specifically designed to manipulate strings. The StringBuilder class is available from the System::Text namespace, and a stream writer for strings called StringWriter is available in the System::IO namespace.

The StringBuilder class provides a set of string manipulation features such as appending characters to a string or snipping a substring from the middle of a string. The StringWriter

Working with Managed Extensions to C++

CHAPTER 1.4

53

1.4

WORKING WITH
MANAGED
EXTENSIONS TO C++

provides a stream-style interface to strings and enables you to use the .NET style string formatting features instead of having to rely on `sprintf` all the time. There is also a complementary `StringReader` class that can be used to stream in a string as if from a file.

Examples of `StringBuilder` and `StringWriter` are in some of the listings in the rest of this chapter, particularly Listing 1.4.10.

Mixing Managed and Unmanaged Code

Mixing managed and unmanaged code is quite simple, but it must follow some specific guidelines.

To create (or maintain) a block of unmanaged code in your programs, you need to bracket the code with the `#pragma_unmanaged` and `#pragma managed` directives as needed. For example, Listing 1.4.3 shows a function in unmanaged code.

LISTING 1.4.3 Using `#pragma unmanaged`

```
#pragma unmanaged

void timestwo(int* pToMultiply)
{
    *pToMultiply*=2;
}

#pragma managed
```

As you can see, the `timestwo` function multiplies the integer pointed to by the `pToMultiply` pointer and is specifically implemented as unmanaged code because of the use of the `#pragma unmanaged` directive.

Pinning Managed Code

The code in Listing 1.4.3 would have a problem if you wanted to pass a pointer to an integer owned by a managed type. You will remember that managed objects can be moved around in memory by the Garbage Collector's compacting system, so pointers passed to unmanaged code must be guaranteed not to move. This is accomplished by pinning the object in place with the `__pin` keyword.

Listing 1.4.4 illustrates how a managed code object can be pinned to allow a pointer to be used.

LISTING 1.4.4 `pinned.cpp`: Fixing Pointers by Pinning

```cpp
#using <mscorlib.dll>
using namespace System;

#include "stdio.h"

__gc struct ManagedStruct
{
    int p;
    int q;
};

#pragma unmanaged

void timestwo(int* pToMultiply)
{
    *pToMultiply *= 2;
}

#pragma managed


void main()
{
    ManagedStruct* pStruct=new ManagedStruct;
    pStruct->p=1;
    pStruct->q=2;

    int __pin* pinnedp=&pStruct->p;
    int __pin* pinnedq=&pStruct->q;

    timestwo(pinnedp);
    timestwo(pinnedq);

    printf("p=%d, q=%d\n",pStruct->p, pStruct->q);

}
```

Managed Interfaces

The __interface keyword can be used to create COM-style interfaces with a minimum of fuss and no IDL. This keyword is not specifically listed in the first part of this chapter because it applies to other technologies, too.

Working with Managed Extensions to C++

Chapter 1.4

55

1.4

WORKING WITH
MANAGED
EXTENSIONS TO C++

However, when used in conjunction with the __gc managed C++ extension, it creates a managed interface. A simple interface is shown in Listing 1.4.5.

LISTING 1.4.5   managedif.cpp: A Simple Managed Interface

```cpp
#using <mscorlib.dll>
using namespace System;

__gc __interface IDoSomething
{
    String * SayHello();
};


__gc class CDoSomething : public IDoSomething
{
    String * SayHello()
    {
        return new String("Hello");
    }
};

void main()
{
    CDoSomething* pD=new CDoSomething();

    IDoSomething *pI=static_cast<IDoSomething*>(pD);

    String* s=pI->SayHello();
    Console::WriteLine(s);
}
```

A big advantage to the combination of the managed object and the interface is that the compiler has support for ambiguous method names. If you have two interfaces with methods of the same name, you can identify which implementation goes with which interface. Listing 1.4.6 shows how to resolve ambiguous interfaces.

LISTING 1.4.6   Ambiguous.cpp: Resolving Ambiguous Interfaces

```cpp
#using <mscorlib.dll>

using namespace System;
```

LISTING 1.4.6 Continued

```
__gc __interface IFirst
{
    void TheMethod();
};

__gc __interface ISecond
{
    void TheMethod();
};

__gc class AClass : public IFirst, public ISecond
{
    void IFirst::TheMethod()
    {
        Console::WriteLine("Invoked IFirst::TheMethod");
    }

    void ISecond::TheMethod()
    {
        Console::WriteLine("Invoked ISecond::TheMethod");
    }
};


void main()
{
    AClass* c=new AClass();

    IFirst *pF=static_cast<IFirst*>(c);

    ISecond *pS=static_cast<ISecond*>(c);

    pF->TheMethod();

    pS->TheMethod();
}
```

The class AClass distinguishes between the two interface definitions by specifying which of the TheMethod entries is being implemented.

Creating Value Types

The .NET framework recognizes two distinct families of types: value types and reference types.

Value types are relatively simple, small structures that can be created and used directly on the stack. Reference types are essentially objects in their own right, are created on the managed heap, and are subject to Garbage Collected lifetime management.

A value type might be a simple storage type such as an `int` or a `float`. It could also be a small structure or class such as `time_t` or `CPoint`. A reference type is a class, an interface, an array, and so forth.

Value types created and used on the stack are not subject to GC management because they are effectively deleted by the movement of the stack pointer when they go out of scope. This implies that they are simple to create and take minimal time to manage. It might be necessary to create a structure on the stack and pass it to some other function. For this reason, the managed runtime uses the technique of boxing the simple structure in a wrapper object that holds a copy of the original data but is reassigned on the managed heap.

To prepare your own simple structures for use as value types, you can use the `__value` keyword:

```
__value struct Birthday
{
    int day;
    int month;
    int year;
};
```

Note also that the `__value` keyword does not imply the `__gc` keyword, so if you want to be able to assign your value type on the managed heap as well, you must use both modifiers where appropriate:

```
__value __gc struct Birthday
{
    int day;
    int month;
    int year;
};
```

NOTE

The order of modifiers is important. If you use `__gc __value`, you'll get an error.

Listing 1.4.7 shows a technique that would make any C++ programmer cringe with pain. It creates simple values on the local stack and passes a pointer to them for inclusion in a collection. Under unmanaged C++, this would cause a disastrous error when the collection tried to reference items that had already gone out of scope. Under managed C++, the Garbage Collector takes over lifetime management of the values referred to and won't allow them to be deleted until everything has let go of them.

LISTING 1.4.7   refdemo.cpp: Value Types Under GC Control

```cpp
#using <mscorlib.dll>
using namespace System;
using namespace System::Collections;

__value struct simple
{
    int i;
    float f;
};

__gc class refdemo
{
    ArrayList* l;

public:

    refdemo(){l=new ArrayList;}

    void Add(Object* o)
    {
        l->Add(o);
    }

    void create(int n,Object **pO)
    {
        simple s;
        s.i=n;
        s.f=n*3.1415926;
        *pO =__box(s);
    }

    void init()
    {
        for(int x=0;x<10;x++)
        {
            Object *pO;
```

LISTING 1.4.7 Continued

```cpp
            create(x,&pO);
            Add(pO);
        }
    }

    void show()
    {
        for(int x=0; x<l->get_Count(); x++)
        {
            try
            {
                simple* pS=__try_cast<simple*>(l->get_Item(x));
                Console::WriteLine("{0} * PI = {1}",__box(pS->i), __box(pS->f));
            }
            catch(System::InvalidCastException *)
            {
                Console::WriteLine("Bad __try_cast...");
            }
        }
    }
};

void main()
{
    refdemo *pD=new refdemo;
    pD->init(); // create the list of values
    pD->show(); // iterate the list and display the contents.
}
```

Creating a value type with the __value keyword changes your simple structure into a class derived from System::ValueType. This means that the value type itself can override some of the methods in the base class to allow it to participate more fully in operations with managed code. One of the more common uses of a value class is to extract a string from it. This mechanism allows you to send a boxed integer or float to the Console::WriteLine parameter replacement function and get your types to print themselves out. In this way you don't have to worry about the correct printf format code for an integer, float, or string. The object knows how to return a string describing itself.

Creating and Using Delegates

Delegates are the .NET equivalent of callbacks and function pointers. They are used primarily to route events to handlers as they arrive.

A delegate declaration describes a function signature with a specific pattern of parameters and a specific return type. Once this pattern is established, it might be used to invoke any function with the same signature. A difference between delegates and callbacks implemented by C++ classes is that, although callbacks in C++ must always be static members of the class, delegates can be used to invoke instance members, too.

A delegate is declared like this:

```
__delegate <return type> MyMCDelegate(<parameter list>);
```

> **NOTE**
>
> Delegates can have many parameters. The delegate matching pattern relies on the return type and the parameter list. Therefore
>
> ```
>     __delegate char MyDelegate(int x, int y, double d)
> ```
> can be used on both of the following method declarations:
> ```
>     char AFunction(int a, int b, double dData)
>     static char Foo(int moo, int hoo, double doo)
> ```

Listing 1.4.8 shows the delegate in action. It illustrates a simple delegate, a delegate that takes input parameters, delegates that return values, and those that return data throughout parameters.

LISTING 1.4.8   delegate.cpp: Using Delegates

```cpp
#using <mscorlib.dll>
using namespace System;

#include <stdio.h>


// first declare the delegate signatures we will use.

__delegate void SimpleDelegate(void);

__delegate void DelegateWithParameter(int);

__delegate int DelegateWithReturn(int);

__delegate void DelegateWithOutParam(int,int *);


__gc class AClass
```

Working with Managed Extensions to C++

CHAPTER 1.4

61

1.4

WORKING WITH
MANAGED
EXTENSIONS TO C++

LISTING 1.4.8 Continued

```
{
public:
    static void StaticHandler(int n)
    {
        printf("I am a static handler and Simple parameter is %d\n",n);
    }

    void InstanceHandler(int n)
    {
        printf("I am an instance handler and Simple parameter is %d\n",n);
    }

    void HandlerA()
    {
        printf("I am handler (a)\n");
    }

    void HandlerB()
    {
        printf("I am handler (b)\n");
    }

    void HandlerC()
    {
        printf("I am handler (c)\n");
    }

    void HandlerD()
    {
        printf("I am handler (d)\n");
    }

    int WithReturn(int x)
    {
        printf("Returning %d*5\n",x);
        return x*5;
    }

    void WithOutParam(int x, int *retval)
    {
        printf("Returning %d*14 through the out parameter\n",x);
        *retval = x*14;
    }

};
```

LISTING 1.4.8   Continued

```
void main()
{
    // instantiate the handler class..
    AClass* pC=new AClass();

    // Create the delgates
    DelegateWithParameter* sh=
            new DelegateWithParameter(NULL,&AClass::StaticHandler);
    DelegateWithParameter* ih=
            new DelegateWithParameter(pC,&AClass::InstanceHandler);

    DelegateWithReturn* wr=new DelegateWithReturn(pC,&AClass::WithReturn);

    DelegateWithOutParam* wo=new
DelegateWithOutParam(pC,&AClass::WithOutParam);

    //Invoke the static...
    sh->Invoke(10);
    //and the instance handlers.
    ih->Invoke(100);

    //Now a multicast which is the invocation
    //of all the handlers on a list

    SimpleDelegate* mc=new SimpleDelegate(pC,AClass::HandlerA);
    mc=static_cast<SimpleDelegate*>(Delegate::Combine(mc,
            new SimpleDelegate(pC,&AClass::HandlerB)));
    mc=static_cast<SimpleDelegate*>(Delegate::Combine(mc,
            new SimpleDelegate(pC,&AClass::HandlerC)));
    mc=static_cast<SimpleDelegate*>(Delegate::Combine(mc,
            new SimpleDelegate(pC,&AClass::HandlerD)));

    mc->Invoke(); // One invoke makes four calls

    //Now a delegate with an out parameter

    printf("Invoking delegate with value 5\n");
    int r = wr->Invoke(5);
    printf("WithReturn sent back %d\n",r);

    //finally a delegate with an out parameter

    printf("Invoking delegate with value 11\n");
    wo->Invoke(11,&r);
```

Working with Managed Extensions to C++

CHAPTER 1.4

63

1.4

WORKING WITH
MANAGED
EXTENSIONS TO C++

LISTING 1.4.8 Continued

```
    printf("WithOutParam sent back %d\n",r);

}
```

Calling Custom .NET DLLs from Your Managed C++ Code

Managed C++ uses .NET DLLs whenever it imports runtime elements such as MSCORLIB.DLL with the #using statement. It is also useful to be able to implement a portion of your code in managed C++ and a portion in C# or VB. This means that you will have to import and use your own custom DLLs. The process is simple and is described in this section.

First we'll create a C# DLL that we can import and invoke. Listing 1.4.9 shows a very simple DLL that has one class and one method.

LISTING 1.4.9 mydll.cs: A Simple C# DLL

```csharp
using System;

namespace mydll {

public class myclass
{
    public void MyMethod()
    {
        Console.WriteLine("MyMethod invoked!!!");
    }
}
}
```

You don't have to be a C# expert to see how this works. Note that the class is declared with the public modifier. This will allow it and its methods to be exported from the library. Enter this file with Notepad in a scratch directory, save it as mydll.cs, and compile it with the C# compiler as follows:

```
csc /t:library mydll.cs
```

The /t: command-line option tells the compiler to create a library DLL. You should see no errors or warnings.

This has nothing to do with the function of writing or using the DLL but just as a matter of interest, you might want to type in the following command line, too:

```
Ildasm mydll.dll
```

This will bring up the Intermediate Language Disassembler (ILDASM), which will enable you to examine the DLL that you've just created. Figure 1.4.1 shows this.

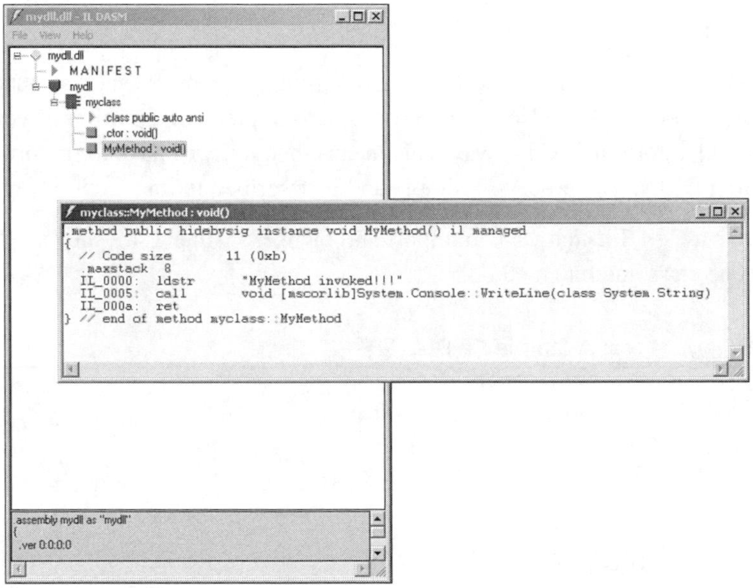

FIGURE 1.4.1
ILDASM, showing the contents of the test DLL.

You could also use ILDASM to examine some of the other executable files we have created in this chapter.

Listing 1.4.10 shows a simple C++ class that uses the MyMethod call in the mydll namespace.

LISTING 1.4.10 useCSdll.cpp: A C++ Program That Uses a Custom C# DLL

```
#using <mscorlib.dll>
#using <mydll.dll>

using namespace System;
using namespace mydll;
```

LISTING 1.4.10   Continued

```
void main(void)
{
    myclass *pM=new myclass();

    pM->MyMethod();
}
```

Enter this file using Notepad and save it as useCSdll.cpp. Notice that the #using statement and the using namespace directive both reference the C# DLL we created in Listing 1.4.9.

Compile the file with the following command:

```
cl /CLR useCSdll.cpp
```

Run it by typing **usecsdll** at the command prompt.

You will see that the C# DLL you created is loaded and invoked automatically.

Using Managed and Unmanaged C++ DLLs in Your .NET Programs

Dynamic library linkage and use is simple using managed extensions for C++ under .NET. C++ DLLs compiled to IL, like their native .NET language counterparts, are tagged with metadata that provides the calling program information about the classes and methods stored in the DLL. This means that you can use them just like ordinary .NET objects written in C# or VB.

Other DLLs that you might use, such as the system DLLs or those you create, require a little more work but are still straightforward thanks to the Interop services provided by the Common Language Runtime.

Listing 1.4.11 shows a managed C++ component that will be compiled as a DLL.

LISTING 1.4.11   cppdll.cpp: A Simple Managed C++ DLL

```
#using <mscorlib.dll>

using namespace System;
using namespace System::Text;
using namespace System::IO;

// This is a managed C++ DLL that uses .Net framework classes
// compile with...
// cl /CLR /LD cppdll.cpp
```

LISTING 1.4.11   Continued

```
namespace cppdll {

//Demonstrates calling a class method....
public __gc class AClass
{
public:
    void FirstMethod(int n)
    {
        String* pS=S"Hi from Firstmethod  ";

        StringBuilder* pB=new StringBuilder(pS);

        StringWriter* pW=new StringWriter(pB);

        for(int x=n;x>=0;x--)
        {
            pW->Write(__box(x));
            if(x)
                pW->Write(S", ");
            else
                pW->Write(S"...");
        }
        pS=pW->ToString();
        Console::WriteLine(pS);
    }
};

}
```

Type in this code and save it as `cppdll.cpp`. Then compile it with this command line:

```
cl /CLR /LD cppdll.cpp
```

This DLL will be called as if it were a simple .NET managed object.

Listing 1.4.12 shows a standard unmanaged C++ DLL that performs a function equivalent to the C# DLL we created in Listing 1.4.9. As you can see, it has a standard `DllMain` function and a `DllFunction` that can be called to do some processing and print a message.

LISTING 1.4.12   straightdll.cpp: A Simple x86 DLL

```
// This is a straight C++ DLL that will be called using the p-invoke
// system interop services from .NET

#include <windows.h>
```

Working with Managed Extensions to C++

CHAPTER 1.4

67

1.4

WORKING WITH
MANAGED
EXTENSIONS TO C++

LISTING 1.4.12 Continued

```c
#include <stdio.h>
#include <string.h>

static char *buffer;

char* __stdcall DllFunction(int n)
{
    sprintf(buffer,"Hi From DllFunction! ");
    for(int x=n;x>=0;x--)
    {
        char temp[100];
        sprintf(temp,"%d%s",x,(x==0 ? "..." : ", "));
        strcat(buffer,temp);
    }
    return &buffer[0];
}

BOOL __stdcall DllMain(HINSTANCE hInst, DWORD dwReason, LPVOID resvd)
{
    switch(dwReason)
    {
        case DLL_PROCESS_ATTACH:
            buffer = (char *)malloc(1000);
            memset(buffer,0,1000);
            printf("Straightdll loaded\n");
            return TRUE;
        case DLL_PROCESS_DETACH:
            free(buffer);
            printf("Straightdll unloaded\n");
            return TRUE;
        default:
            return FALSE;
    }
}
```

The following is the old-style DEF file that is used to export the functions from the DLL.

```
EXPORTS
    DllFunction @1
    DllMain @2
```

Type to a file and save `straightdll.def`, then build the DLL with the following command line:

```
cl /LD straightdll.cpp /link /DEF:straightdll.def
```

These DLLs can both be used by C# or VB programs that you write. This ability to call old-style DLLs with new-style code or languages maintains your investment in legacy code, applications, and tools as you make the transition to .NET. For this demonstration, we will write a very simple C# program that shows how to use the managed C++ class and the unmanaged DLL. Listing 1.4.13 shows the code for the host executable cppdllusr.exe.

LISTING 1.4.13   cppdllusr.cs: A Simple C# Program Showing DLL Use

```
 1: using System;
 2: using System.Text;
 3: using System.IO;
 4: using System.Runtime.InteropServices;
 5:
 6: using cppdll;
 7:
 8: class dlltester
 9: {
10:
11:     [DllImport("straightdll.dll")]
12:     [return:MarshalAs(UnmanagedType.LPStr)]
13:     public static extern String DllFunction(int n);
14:
15:     static void Main()
16:     {
17:
18:         // First the method in the C++ dll "cppdll.dll" is invoked...
19:         AClass pC=new AClass();
20:         pC.FirstMethod(10);
21:
22:         //Now to invoke the wrapper function for the unmanaged DLL
23:         Console.WriteLine(DllFunction(10));
24:
25:     }
26: }
```

Using the managed C++ DLL is straightforward, but the unmanaged one is more complex. Let's examine the part that makes interaction with unmanaged code possible.

The code on lines 11, 12, and 13 in Listing 1.4.13 shows how to create a wrapper for a function in an unmanaged DLL. This uses attributes to create a proxy for the unmanaged code and to marshal the parameters and return types to and from the unmanaged part of the system.

The attribute [DllImport(...)] specifies that the following function signature is one exported by the named DLL, in this case straightdll.dll, which we created in Listing 1.4.11. This function returns a char * to a buffer that it allocates. The managed runtime, however, will

Working with Managed Extensions to C++

CHAPTER 1.4

69

1.4

WORKING WITH
MANAGED
EXTENSIONS TO C++

require the returned data to be packaged in a more .NET-friendly object, so instead of using char * as the return type for our function, we use String and tell the system that it needs to marshal the data when it returns from the function. This is accomplished with the [return:MarshalAs(...)] attribute. Its position before the function declaration signifies that it is the return type that is to be marshaled. The same attribute could be used on a parameter to transfer data from a string to a char *. The argument to the MarshalAs attribute is one of a list of recognized types from the System::Runtime::InteropServices namespace.

The invocation of the DllFunction is on line 23. It's a simple argument to the Console.WriteLine method. This accepts only System.Object-based items, so you can see that the marshaling of the returned char * to a String object has taken place.

Type Listing 1.4.13 into a file called cppdllusr.cpp and compile it using the following command line:

```
csc /r:cppdll.dll cppdllusr.cs
```

The program will compile, and you can run cppdllusr from the command line.

Using Properties in Your C++ Classes

Properties are pseudo-data members of your classes. They are accessed just like public data members but in reality they are functions within the class.

Adding properties to Garbage Collected C++ classes is accomplished by the use of the __property keyword. Listing 1.4.14 shows a simple GC class with properties.

LISTING 1.4.14   props.cpp: Simple Properties in a GC Class

```
#using <mscorlib.dll>

using namespace System;
using namespace System::IO;


__gc class PropClass
{
    int m_x;
    int m_y;
    int m_z;

public:
    PropClass() : m_y(19762), m_z(3860)
    {
    }
```

LISTING 1.4.14   Continued

```cpp
    // read / write properties for a data member

    __property int get_x(){return m_x;}
    __property void set_x(int v){m_x=v;}

    // read only properties for a data member

    __property int get_y(){return m_y;}

    // write only properties for a data member

    __property void set_z(int v){m_z=v;}

    // properties that don't act on data at-all

    __property int get_bogus()
    {
        Console::WriteLine("Read the bogus property!");
        return 10;
    }
    __property void set_bogus(int v)
    {
        Console::WriteLine("Wrote {0} to the bogus property!",__box(v));
    }

    String* ToString()
    {
        StringWriter *w=new StringWriter();
        w->Write("PropClass; m_x = {0}, m_y = {1}, m_z = {2}",__box(m_x), __
➥box(m_y), __box(m_z));
        return w->ToString();
    }

};

void main()
{
    PropClass *pP=new PropClass();
    Console::WriteLine("At Creation...{0}",pP);
    pP->x=50;
    Console::WriteLine("Wrote to x...{0}",pP);
    pP->z=100;
    Console::WriteLine("Wrote to z...{0}",pP);
    pP->bogus = 150;
```

Working with Managed Extensions to C++

CHAPTER 1.4

71

1.4

WORKING WITH
MANAGED
EXTENSIONS TO C++

LISTING 1.4.14 Continued

```
    Console::WriteLine(pP);
    int x=pP->x;
    Console::WriteLine("Read x, Return ={0}, {1}",__box(x),pP);
    int y=pP->y;
    Console::WriteLine("Read y. Return ={0}, {1}",__box(y),pP);
    int z=pP->bogus;
    Console::WriteLine("Returned value = {0},  {1}",__box(z),pP);
}
```

The props.cpp program shows properties that directly access data members within a class and properties that perform some computation that is not necessarily related to class attributes at all.

The program also shows the technique of creating read-only or write-only properties. To create a read-only property, simply include only the get_ accessor. Write-only properties have only set_ accessors.

Finally, the program shows the interesting technique of overriding the ToString() method. Remember that classes declared with __gc are derived implicitly from System::Object. This class defines the ToString method, which is used to output a text representation of the class to text streams.

Ensuring the Alignment and Packing of Your C++ Structures

Because the Garbage Collector does so much of the assignment and layout of the code for you, it's sometimes difficult to know how a particular structure is laid out in memory. This can be of crucial importance if you are bringing in byte-ordered structures from previous C++ applications or DLLs and using them in the context of .NET. The Platform Invoke services has attributes that you can use to specify exactly how your structures are laid out so that you can read them into managed code and still be sure that the order and alignment of memory-based variables are well known.

The StructLayout attribute can be used to lay out a structure sequentially, to place member variables at an exact offset within a structure or to declare a union. Sequential layout is the simplest form, and you can additionally specify the packing of structure members.

The most common scenario that you will come across is one where you already have a predefined C++ structure in an application and you need to use that same structure from the managed world, possibly from a managed C++ program or with some code written in C#. This is what interop is all about. Take a look at the simple C++ structure in Listing 1.4.15:

LISTING 1.4.15   `simplestruct.h`: A Simple C++ Structure

```
#pragma pack(8)

typedef struct{
    char name[17],
    int age,
    double salary,
    short ssn[3],
}simple;
```

The declaration shown in Listing 1.4.15 defines a structure with a particular packing. To see how this structure actually looks in memory, we'll fill it with some well-known values and then write to the variables in the structure. Listing 1.4.16 shows this process and dumps the contents of the structure to the screen.

LISTING 1.4.16   `simpletest.cpp`: A Program to Test the Simple Structure

```
 1: #include <stdio.h>
 2: #include <memory.h>
 3: #include "simple.h"
 4:
 5: void dump(unsigned char *pC,int count)
 6: {
 7:     printf("Dumping %d bytes\n",count);
 8:     int n=0;
 9:     while(n<count)
10:     {
11:         int i;
12:         int toDump=count-n>=16 ? 16 : count-n;
13:         for(i=0;i<toDump;i++)
14:             printf("%02x ",pC[n+i]);
15:         while(i++<16)
16:             printf("   ");
17:         printf("  ");
18:         for(i=0;i<toDump;i++)
19:             printf("%c",pC[n+i]>0x1f ? pC[n+i] : '.');
20:         printf("\n");
21:         n+=toDump;
22:     }
23: }
24:
25:
26: void main(void)
```

Working with Managed Extensions to C++

CHAPTER 1.4

73

1.4

WORKING WITH
MANAGED
EXTENSIONS TO C++

LISTING 1.4.16 Continued

```
27: {
28:     simple s;
29:
30:     memset(&s,0xff,sizeof(simple));
31:     memcpy(&s.name[0],"abcdefghijklmnopq",17);
32:     s.age=0x11111111;
33:     s.salary=100.0;
34:     s.ssn[0]=0x2222;
35:     s.ssn[1]=0x3333;
36:     s.ssn[2]=0x4444;
37:
38:     dump((unsigned char *)&s,sizeof(simple));
39: }
```

Compile this code with the following command line:

```
cl simpletest.cpp
```

Now run it from the command line.

```
Dumping 40 bytes
61 62 63 64 65 66 67 68 69 6a 6b 6c 6d 6e 6f 70    abcdefghijklmnop
71 ff ff ff 11 11 11 11 00 00 00 00 00 00 59 40    q    ..........Y@
22 22 33 33 44 44 ff ff                            ""33DD
```

The code in Listing 1.4.16 shows that the structure `simple` is filled with data. First, on line 30, it gets filled with hexadecimal `ff` to contrast the real data with the blanks left over from the structure packing. Line 31 shows the `age` member being filled with 17 letters, and lines 32 through 36 show all the numeric variables being assigned. The code in lines 5 through 23 simply dump the structure to the screen.

The output shows clearly, wherever the `ff` code is seen, that there are gaps in the structure. Another clue is that 17+4+8+2+2+2 does not equal 40, the declared size of the structure by `sizeof`.

NOTE

To pass this structure to your legacy code from managed C++ or C# might be a problem because memory management is different and the CLR does not allow you to create managed structures with fixed size arrays. The data will require both layout and marshaling between the managed and unmanaged world.

Listing 1.4.17 illustrates how a structure can be created with exact placement of the members and how the transportation of array data can be accomplished.

LISTING 1.4.17   managedsimple.txt: The Managed Version of the Simple Structure

```
[StructLayout(LayoutKind::Explicit,Size=40)]
public __gc struct managedsimple {
    [FieldOffset(0)]
    [MarshalAs(UnmanagedType::ByValTStr,SizeConst=17)]
    System::String *name;
    [FieldOffset(20)]
    int age;
    [FieldOffset(24)]
    double salary;
    [FieldOffset(32)]
    [MarshalAs(UnmanagedType::ByValArray,SizeConst=3)]
    short ssn __gc[];
};
```

NOTE

Remember that whenever you use these attributes in your software, you should declare that you are using namespace `System::Runtime::InteropServices`.

Here you see that not only has the physical layout of the structure been carefully controlled by the use of the `StructLayout` and `FieldOffset` attributes but also the `char` and `short` fixed length C arrays have been replaced by the garbage collector friendly `System::String` and `System::Array` types.

So that the program knows how these managed arrays should be transported to the old code, the `MarshalAs` attribute, which we saw before in conjunction with return types, has been employed to specify that the arrays need to be marshaled as a 17 character string array and an array of three `short` integers.

Listing 1.4.18 is a modification of the code in Listing 1.4.16. Here, we define an unmanaged C++ DLL that performs the same dump task for us. This DLL will be driven by a managed C++ program, which could equally be a VB.NET or C# module. The results will be shown on the screen again. First is the unmanaged DLL.

Working with Managed Extensions to C++

CHAPTER 1.4

75

1.4

WORKING WITH
MANAGED
EXTENSIONS TO C++

LISTING 1.4.18   structuredll.cpp: The Unmanaged DLL

```
 1: #include <windows.h>
 2: #include <stdio.h>
 3: #include "simple.h"
 4:
 5: void dump(unsigned char *pC,int count)
 6: {
 7:     printf("Dumping %d bytes\n",count);
 8:     int n=0;
 9:     while(n<count)
10:     {
11:         int i;
12:         int toDump=count-n>=16 ? 16 : count-n;
13:         for(i=0;i<toDump;i++)
14:             printf("%02x ",pC[n+i]);
15:         while(i++<16)
16:             printf("   ");
17:         printf("  ");
18:         for(i=0;i<toDump;i++)
19:             printf("%c",pC[n+i]>0x1f ? pC[n+i] : '.');
20:         printf("\n");
21:         n+=toDump;
22:     }
23: }
24:
25: void __stdcall ShowSimple(simple *s)
26: {
27:     printf("Unmanaged DLL\n");
28:     dump((unsigned char *)s,sizeof(simple));
29:     printf("Name=%17s\n",&s->name[0]);
30:     printf("Age=%d\n",s->age);
31:     printf("Salary=%f\n",s->salary);
32:     printf("SSN=%d-%d-%d\n\n",s->ssn[0],s->ssn[1],s->ssn[2]);
33:     printf("Changing the salary...\n");
34:     s->salary=999999.0;
35:     printf("Changing the name...\n");
36:     strcpy(s->name,"Mavis      ");
37:     printf("Changing the ssn...\n");
38:     s->ssn[0]=99;
39:     s->ssn[1]=999;
40:     s->ssn[2]=9999;
41: }
```

Listing **1.4.18** Continued

```
42:
43: BOOL __stdcall DllMain(HINSTANCE hInstance,DWORD dwReason,LPVOID)
44: {
45:     switch(dwReason)
46:     {
47:     case DLL_PROCESS_ATTACH:
48:     case DLL_PROCESS_DETACH:
49:         return TRUE;
50:     default:
51:         return FALSE;
52:     }
53: }
```

The DEF file exports the method you will invoke. Save it as structuredll.def.

```
EXPORTS
    DllMain @1
    ShowSimple @2
```

Compile this DLL with the following command line:

```
Cl /LD structuredll.cpp /link /DEF:structuredll.def
```

Listing 1.4.19 shows the managed C++ application that uses the DLL created in Listing 1.4.18 through the platform invoke system, passing the specially-defined and marshaled-managed structure.

Listing **1.4.19** simpledump.cpp: The Managed C++ Test Application

```
 1: // This is the managed C++ test
 2: // program for the simpledump dll
 3:
 4: #using <mscorlib.dll>
 5:
 6: using namespace System;
 7: using namespace System::Runtime::InteropServices;
 8:
 9: // Here we declare the managed structure that we will use
10: [StructLayout(LayoutKind::Explicit,Size=40)]
11: public __gc struct managedsimple {
12:     [FieldOffset(0)]
13:     [MarshalAs(UnmanagedType::ByValTStr,SizeConst=17)]
14:     System::String *name;
15:     [FieldOffset(20)]
16:     int age;
17:     [FieldOffset(24)]
```

Working with Managed Extensions to C++

CHAPTER 1.4

77

1.4

WORKING WITH
MANAGED
EXTENSIONS TO C++

LISTING 1.4.19 Continued

```
18:     double salary;
19:     [FieldOffset(32)]
20:     [MarshalAs(UnmanagedType::ByValArray,SizeConst=3)]
21:     short ssn __gc[];
22: };
23:
24:
25: //This class imports the DLL function we need
26: __gc class StDll {
27: public:
28:     [DllImport("structuredll.dll")]
29:     static void
ShowSimple([In,Out,MarshalAs(UnmanagedType::LPStruct,
30:     SizeConst=40)]managedsimple *);
31:
32:     // if you import other functions from the DLL
33:     // they can be added here.
34: };
35:
36: void main(void)
37: {
38:     managedsimple *m=new managedsimple;
39:
40:     m->age=24;
41:     m->salary=180000.0;
42:     m->name=new System::String("Beavis");
43:     m->ssn=new short __gc[3];
44:     m->ssn[0]=10;
45:     m->ssn[1]=100;
46:     m->ssn[2]=1000;
47:
48:     managedsimple __pin* pS=m;
49:
50:     StDll::ShowSimple(pS);
51:
52:     pS=0;
53:
54:     Console::WriteLine("Back in managed code");
55:     Console::WriteLine(m->salary);
56:     Console::WriteLine(m->name);
57:     Console::WriteLine("{0}-{1}-{2}",__box(m->ssn[0]),__box
(m->ssn[1]),
58:     box(m->ssn[2]));
59: }
```

Compile this file with the following command line:

```
cl /clr simpledump.cpp
```

Now run it from the command line. You should see the following output.

```
Unmanaged DLL
Dumping 40 bytes
42 65 61 76 69 73 00 00 00 00 00 00 00 00 00 00    Beavis..........
00 00 00 00 18 00 00 00 00 00 00 00 00 80 66 40    .............Çf@
0a 00 64 00 e8 03 48 00                            ..d._.H.
Name=          Beavis
Age=24
Salary=180.000000
SSN=10-100-1000

Changing the salary...
Changing the name...
Changing the ssn...
Back in managed code
999999
Mavis
99-999-9999
```

Starting with the main function on line 36, we create the new managed structure on line 38 and populate it in lines 40 to 46. Line 50 calls the DLL function, and we jump to Listing 1.4.18 line 25.

This method does a hex dump of the contents of the structure, showing how our managed structure with both the string and the array of short integers marshaled out to the unmanaged world of the DLL. In lines 29 to 40 of the structured listing, the data in the unmanaged structure is modified by good old unmanaged C++. When this process is finished, the .NET marshaling takes over again and brings the unmanaged structure back into the managed world where lines 54 to 58 of Listing 1.5.19 confirm the changes by printing out the new data to the console.

As you can see from the code in this section, interoperability between the managed and unmanaged world is well catered and will keep your existing intellectual property current well into the .NET years.

Summary

C++ programmers working with .NET are very well looked after. Your existing code can be brought into the .NET fold, and you don't have to throw out everything and start over. It would be possible to write an entire book on the subject of migration alone, and we're sure that someone will do so, but this chapter sets you on the right path and gets you up and running.

Introducing Visual Studio.NET

IN THIS CHAPTER

The Integrated Development Environment (IDE)

If you're already familiar with Visual Studio 5.x or 6.x, the look and feel of Visual Studio.NET won't be too unfamiliar to you. However, there are some differences that should be pointed out to get you on the right path to productive development with this new tool.

Visual Studio.NET is a more advanced, bigger brother to the older VS family. In the past, development of, for example, C++ and Visual Basic has taken place using different applications. Now, however, you are offered a choice of C++, C#, JavaScript, Visual Basic, and a plethora of other languages that all run side-by-side on the framework. It's also becoming common to create an application that requires many languages or many distributed components. Consequently, the development environment is more sophisticated and able to handle all parts of your application in a unified manner.

As with most of the topics we cover in this book, Visual Studio probably merits five hundred pages on its own, but, in this chapter, we'll give you enough of an overview to get you familiar with the software.

Figure 1.5.1 shows the initial view of Visual Studio.NET. The major components of Visual Studio are annotated A through E.

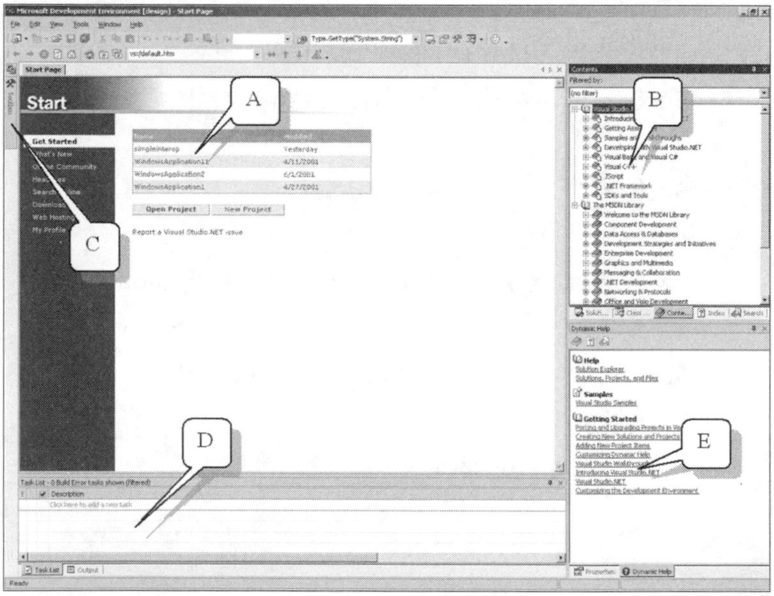

Figure 1.5.1
Visual Studio.NET.

Introducing Visual Studio.NET

CHAPTER 1.5

81

1.5

INTRODUCING
VISUAL
STUDIO.NET

Section A: The Main Editing Area

The first thing you'll see in this area is the Start Page. Like many of the VS.NET windows, it is an HTML browser window that shows your last few projects, links to the customer support site, and gives other useful information about the VS.NET package. This area is also where the editing of all your source files takes place. Above this window is a tabbed bar that allows you to easily select any of the currently open files for editing (see Figure 1.5.2).

FIGURE 1.5.2
Selecting open files.

Here you can see that the Form1.CS is open for editing in Design Mode, just like a form in Visual Basic, and as a C# source file. To the far right of this bar are controls that allow you to scroll the tabs left or right and to close the current window.

Section B: Solutions, Classes, Items, and Help

In this portion of the IDE window, you will see another tabbed control with multiple panes. This is a recurring theme in VS.NET because the IDE is so busy that there's nowhere else to put all the information. Figure 1.5.3 shows the tabs generally contained in this panel.

FIGURE 1.5.3
The right pane tabs.

By default, this pane contains the Solution Explorer, the Class View, Help Contents, Help Index, and Help Search windows. Some other tabs appear in this pane also; we'll explain those as we go.

Solutions and the Solution Explorer

The Solution is the fundamental package of work in VS.NET. A Solution can hold projects of many different types. For example, you might want to create a complete client/server application with many individual sub-projects ranging from MFC-based client code to ASP.NET server code. The Solution is the top-level placeholder for all sub-projects associated with that application. A Solution can be built all at once and dependencies between sub-projects can be defined so that the projects contained in it are built in a particular order.

Selecting the Solution Explorer tab brings up a pane with a tree of items. The tree contains projects, folders, files, resources, and other miscellaneous data that defines your current scope of work.

A Solution has properties that affect all the projects within it. As with most of the other items in Visual Studio.NET, right-clicking a Solution and selecting Properties will allow you to adjust the characteristics of your solution.

Figure 1.5.4 shows the solution pane and a solution properties dialog.

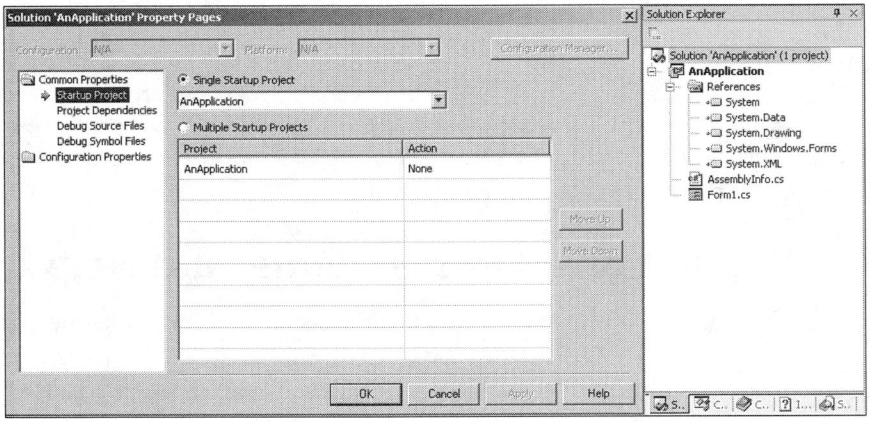

FIGURE 1.5.4
The Solution and its properties.

The Solution Explorer panel, far right, contains a single project called AnApplication. The solution Properties dialog, left, allows you to pick which sub-project is the startup project, how each project depends on another, where the IDE will search for source files when debugging, and where the debug symbol files are stored. These settings are common to all projects within a solution.

Projects

Just as Solutions contain projects, projects contain items. These items can be folders for organizing your source, header and resource files, references to other projects, Web services and system files, and all the source files that go to make up the project within the solution. In Figure 1.5.4, you can see that the open project has two files, Form1.cs and AssemblyInfo.cs, and a set of references. These references are analogous to the #include directive in a C++ file; they allow access to the metadata in the namespaces shown. These references are to actual files

Introducing Visual Studio.NET

CHAPTER 1.5

83

1.5

INTRODUCING
VISUAL
STUDIO.NET

and data that exist on your machine. They could also refer to the Web Service Description Language (WSDL) description of a Web service, for example. This type of reference is called a *Web reference*.

Each project within a solution has properties. Figure 1.5.5 shows the properties of the AnApplication project.

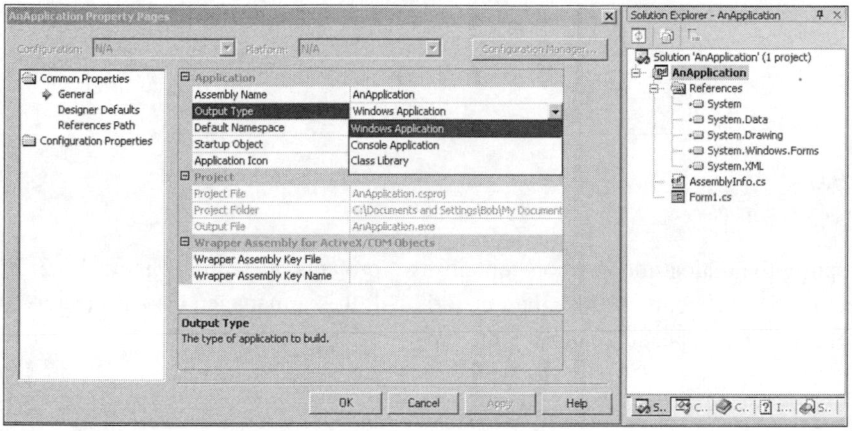

FIGURE 1.5.5
The project Property dialog.

In the dialog shown in Figure 1.5.5, the property that defines what type of project will be built is being used. As you can see, these properties are very easy to use and are far more concise than the old settings for VS 6.0.

Project properties include build options such as optimizations, start options, including command line entries, and debugging options.

Right-clicking the project will show a context menu that allows you to build the project individually, add items and folders to the project, or add references.

Multiple Projects in a Single Solution

Adding a project to a solution is simple. Right-click the solution and select Add. You will be presented with the choice of creating an object, using one you already have locally on your machine, or going to get one from the Web. Adding new project brings up a dialog to select the project type.

Figure 1.5.6 shows the New Project Wizard in action. In this case, we'll add a managed C++ project to the solution.

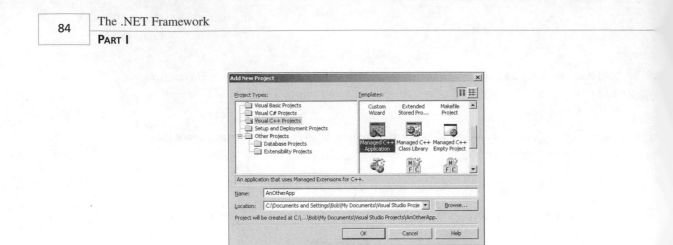

FIGURE 1.5.6

Adding a project to a solution.

After accepting the dialog, the solution contains two projects, as seen in Figure 1.5.7. The second project is of a different structure than the original. It is a managed C++ project, so it contains folders for source, header, and resource files.

FIGURE 1.5.7

A solution with multiple projects.

In both of these projects, there is a file called AssemblyInfo. This file will be in all projects that use the framework. It is analogous to the VS_VERSION_INFO resource used in Visual C++. An Assembly is the basic packaging unit of the framework. It can contain one or more executable modules and resources. It also contains an assembly "manifest." This is the metadata associated with the assembly. You can add information, such as code version numbers, trademarks, descriptions, and other data, to the manifest by filling out the contents of the AssemblyInfo file. Later, in Section 5 of this book, "Component Usage," we will explain assemblies and how to manage them.

Project Dependencies

Now that there are two projects in the solution, we can show how dependencies are managed. Right-clicking a project and selecting Project Dependencies from the context menu will allow you to decide which projects must be built before the selected one. The dialog shown in Figure 1.5.8 shows that AnOtherApp depends on AnApplication and that the projects will be built in the order shown. The image shows both panes of the dialog. Remember that settings are available through the Solution properties as well.

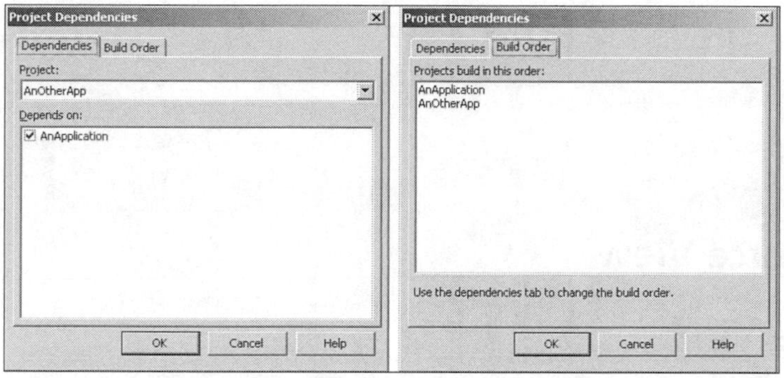

FIGURE 1.5.8
Setting project dependencies.

The Class View

If you're familiar with Visual C++ 6.0, you'll feel right at home in the Class View tab. This is a multi-project class viewer that allows you to navigate your projects by class, member, and function. Clicking an entry takes you to that place in the editor. Right-clicking a class will bring up a context menu that has entries for adding methods, properties, fields, and indexers. Classes also have their bases and interfaces available for browsing. Figure 1.5.9 shows the contents of the Class View pane for our solution.

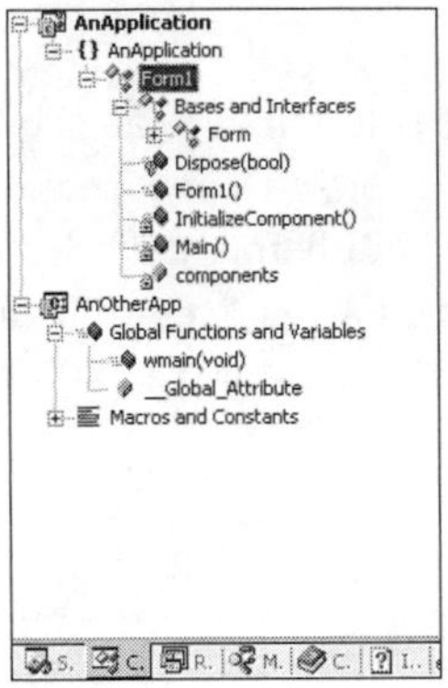

FIGURE 1.5.9
The Class View pane.

The Resource View

The tab control that contains the Solution Explorer and the Class View can also host the Resource View. When you're creating a Windows Forms application, you won't see this tab, but you can explicitly request it by selecting View, Resource View from the main menu or by pressing the shortcut Crtl+Shift+E. This pane allows you to edit the old style resource files that you know from C++ and MFC development. Note that Visual Studio.NET will allow you to create and edit MFC and ATL applications alongside your .NET framework projects.

The Macro Explorer

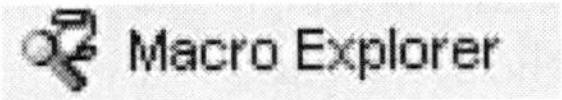

It is possible to make extensive use of macros in your day-to-day development tasks. Visual Studio 7.0 has a comprehensive object model that allows scripting of just about every function you can imagine. The Macro Explorer is where you'll find all the macros associated with your own version of VS.NET.

Manual Help

There is a distinction between the help found in the remaining three tabs of this pane and the Dynamic Help system that we will show you in a moment. The Help system works pretty much as you would expect and includes a Contents, Index, and Search tab. Figure 1.5.10 shows the help system.

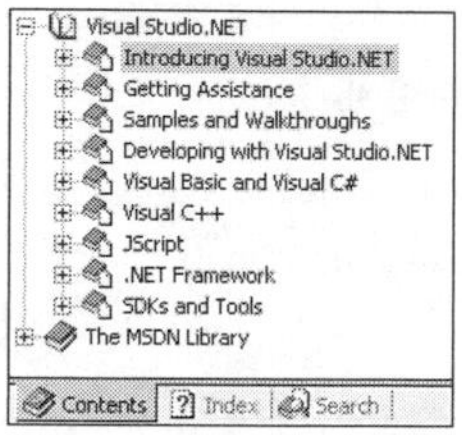

FIGURE 1.5.10
The help tabs.

The Index tab allows you to type in a simple phrase and the index searches to the nearest match straight away. The Search tab allows you to perform a more complex inquiry. Document entries can be searched for using search expressions. For example, "Thread AND blocking" will search for all documents containing the words thread and blocking. There is also a check box to allow searching for similar words, so in this case, threading and blocked might be found too. You can also use the word "NEAR" in the place of "AND". This ensures that the words found are within a group of eight words. You can also control the nearness of words so that they are within three words of one another, for example. Many searches will return 500 entries. To refine this, you can search again within the previous search results. Ordering the entries as they are found is also useful. For example, a search that provides 500 entries might not seem particularly useful and will have results that are from all over the help database. Ordering this search by "Location" will allow you to get an idea of what section the title was found in, so if you search for "text NEAR box," you'll get 500 entries. Only about 30 of these are in the .NET Framework Class Library, so ordering by location narrows the field substantially.

Section C: The Toolbox and Server Explorer

Floating the mouse over this toolbar will cause it to concertina out so that you can access the individual components. The animated toolbox is a screen real-estate saving device. If you're lucky enough to have a 36-inch monitor, you won't need any of the space saving innovations. Therefore, you can pin all the controls immovably in place with the pushpin icon that you'll see in the top-right corner of the pane. Also, if you have that big monitor and you love to write really long lines of code, you can cause the other panes on the right side, the Solution Explorer and so on, to concertina away by unpinning their pushpins.

The Toolbox

The Toolbox is another toolbar that contains multiple sections, the primary one being the component toolbox. Editing Windows Forms layouts, adding items to dialogs, and placing other resources all rely on the toolbox as the drag-source for the palette of available items.

The contents of the Toolbox are very dynamic and will change according to the task you are performing. When editing a Windows Form, you'll see the Forms list; when editing a UML diagram, you'll see UML components.

Figure 1.5.11 shows the Toolbox in its expanded and pinned state. The interface is similar to that of Microsoft Outlook's Outlook Bar but more compact.

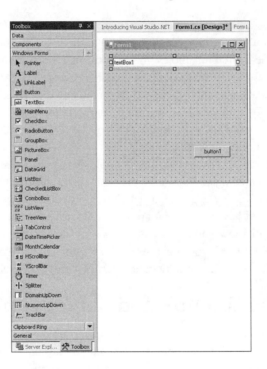

FIGURE 1.5.11

The Toolbox.

Here, you can see that a Windows Form is being edited. Components are dragged from the Toolbox and placed on the form. They can be moved, sized, and manipulated, as you would expect.

Introducing Visual Studio.NET

CHAPTER 1.5

89

1.5

INTRODUCING
VISUAL
STUDIO.NET

The Server Explorer

The companion to the Toolbox in this toolbar is the Server Explorer. This is a brand new feature for VS.NET and enables some advanced features that are a real time saver when programming against database servers, message queues, system services, and system event logs.

The Server Explorer displays a set of tree nodes for all the servers to which it is connected. You can select various categories of nodes and drag them onto your Windows Form where VS.NET creates a set of adapters for you that allow your program to access the chosen node.

Figure 1.5.12 shows the Server Explorer with the performance counter nodes expanded.

FIGURE 1.5.12

The Server Explorer window.

Using the Server Explorer, you can drag one of the performance counters onto a Windows Form. For example dragging the _Global_ performance counter from the # of CCWs node onto a form will create a Performance Counter component that you can use to find out how many times marshaling between managed and unmanaged code took place.

Similarly, dragging the Access database from the Data Connections node onto a form creates an oleDBConnection to the database. Expanding the database node in the Server Explorer allows you to drag the tables, stored procedures, and views to the form, creating the correct adapters for them as well.

You can add a server to the explorer window by using the Tools, Connect to Server menu selection from the main toolbar. After you've connected to the server, you can access its performance counters and system logs, if you have permission.

Section D: Tasks, Output, Search Results, and Watches

In this section, you will again find a tabbed window with several panes. This section of the screen deals with tasks, output from the build process, debug trace information, results of searches from the help Index and Search panes, and the results of symbol searches within your applications. Figure 1.5.13 shows a view of area E from the illustration in Figure 1.5.1.

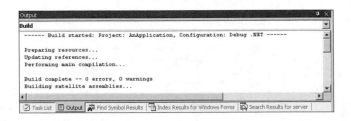

FIGURE 1.5.13

The task, output, and search results panel.

Tasks

Programmers working with Visual C++ over its last few incarnations will be used to the // TODO comments that appear in the wizard-generated code. These comments usually told you what portions of the auto-generated implementation still needed to be filled in. You only needed to find the TODO markers with a quick file search and you could see how complete the code was.

Visual Studio.NET now automates the task tracking process for you. Whenever you enter the // TODO comment in your code, the IDE will place a task in the task list for you. Double-clicking that task will take you to the comment in the code. In addition to the built-in tags TODO, HACK, and UNDONE, you can put in your own custom tags that will also show up in the task list.

Figure 1.5.14 shows the task list in relation to a TODO task that has been placed in the code.

To add your own task list tag, select Tools, Options from the main menu, and then select Environment, Task List from the tree of setup options in the left pane of the dialog. By default, these tasks might be hidden in the task window. To see all your tasks, right-click the task pane, select Show Tasks, and select All.

Output Details

Selecting the Output tab might show you several panes of information. Build messages, including warnings and errors, will be displayed here. Messages from debugging traces are also available here, as well as certain messages from other programs such as those invoked through the command line and by the IDE.

Introducing Visual Studio.NET

CHAPTER 1.5

91

1.5

INTRODUCING
VISUAL
STUDIO.NET

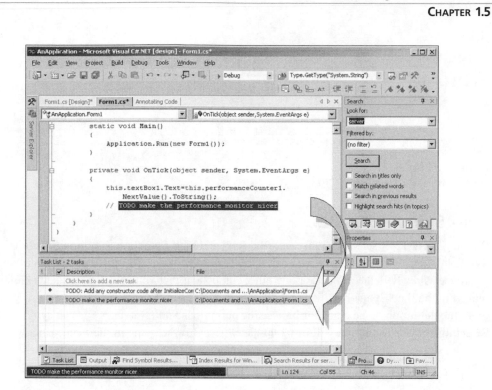

FIGURE 1.5.14
The task list.

You can place your own messages here, particularly when debugging, by using the
System.Diagnostics.Trace object. For example, when handling a timer event in a C# program, the code shown in Listing 1.5.1 illustrates this technique.

LISTING 1.5.1 Using the Trace Object to Output to the Debug Pane

```
private void OnTick(object sender, System.EventArgs e)
{
   System.Diagnostics.Trace.Write("The timer ran!!\n","Timer");
}
```

This snippet of code produces the result seen in Figure 1.5.15.

As you can see, the message "The timer ran!!" was displayed for category "Timer" several
times as the program ran.

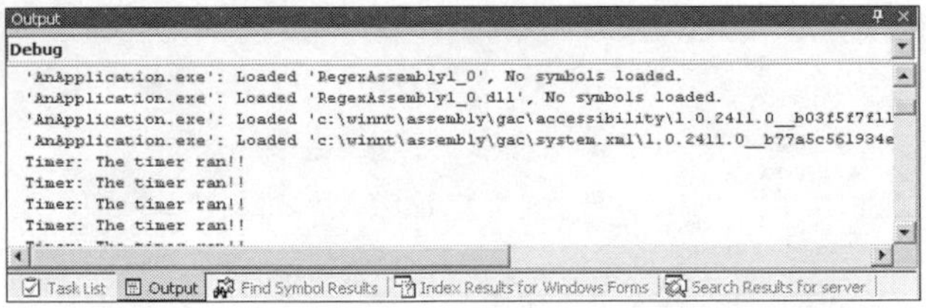

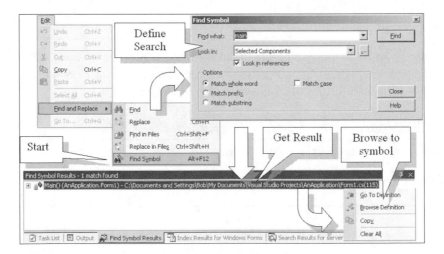

FIGURE 1.5.15

Trace activity in the output pane.

Find Symbol Results

Pressing Alt+F12 or selecting Edit, Find and Replace, Find Symbol will bring up the Find Symbol dialog. With this dialog, you can search for a symbol in your own application files, references already in the project, or any other component that you select. The results are displayed in the Find Symbol results pane. Right-clicking an entry in that pane will allow you to go to the definition in the editor or browse the definitions and references for that symbol. Selecting Browse Definition will bring up the Object Browser pane in the main window where you can see the whole object hierarchy tree for the selected object and others in its assembly.

Figure 1.5.16 shows the steps required to do a symbol search in VS.NET.

FIGURE 1.5.16

Using the Find Symbol dialog.

The object browser interface is a little different than the Browser Info in VS 6.0. The browser information in the previous version had to be built explicitly. The Object Browser in VS.NET is available all the time, even before you do your first build, and is far more useful for your general day-to-day development tasks. The browser consists of three panes—the Object pane (left), the Members pane (right), and the Description pane (bottom). In addition, a toolbar above it allows you to select other options. Using the Object Browser, you can explore namespaces, classes, types, interfaces, enums, and structures. You can optionally sort objects in the Browser Pane by using the Object Browser toolbar to sort members alphabetically, by type, by object access, or grouped by object type. The image in Figure 1.5.17 shows the results of a search for InitializeComponent and the resultant state of the Object Browser.

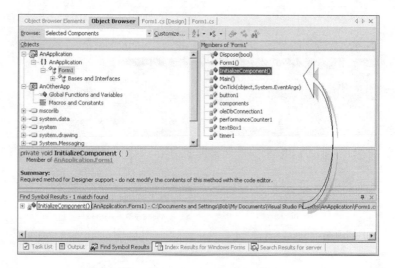

FIGURE 1.5.17
The Object Browser.

Index and Search Results

Both of these panes display the results of help contents searches, either by a simple index request or through a more complex search. Clicking a search result takes you to the help entry.

Debug Windows

Some other panes appear in this section. They are the Breakpoint pane and the immediate command window. We will explain these panes in the "Debugging Programs" section later in this chapter.

Section E: Properties, Dynamic Help, and Favorites

Now let's examine what is arguably the most well-used corner of the IDE real estate.

The Property Browser

Almost every aspect of .NET is configured, controlled, and examined through the property system. Objects within .NET have the ability to display their parameters through special attributes that are tied to their properties. If you're familiar with Visual Basic, the property grid will make you feel right at home. If you're a veteran C++ programmer, the property system might take a little getting used to. Figure 1.5.18 shows the Properties pane being used to edit a Windows Form control.

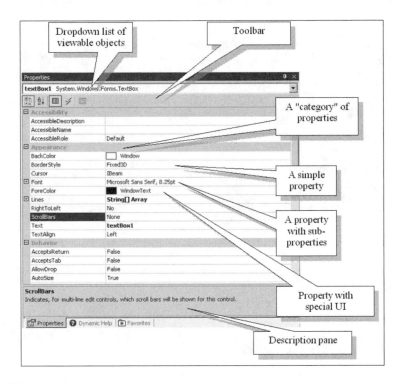

FIGURE 1.5.18

The Property Browser.

The Property Browser pane displays a grid of name-value items that can optionally be grouped into categories. Some items might have their own sub-properties. These can be displayed by expanding them using the + icon on the left side. Similarly, whole categories can be expanded and collapsed by using the + or – icons appropriately. Generally, the property grid deals exclusively with simple values, for example, a number or a string value. However, values that are represented by numbers can sometimes be more easily represented using some other form, for example, a box containing a swatch of color. The Property Browser has the ability to convert certain types of information, say a color value in numeric RGB, to a UI element, such as the

Introducing Visual Studio.NET

CHAPTER 1.5

95

1.5

INTRODUCING
VISUAL
STUDIO.NET

color swatch seen in Figure 1.5.18. Furthermore, a simple `enum` value might be stored internally as its numeric value, but the Property Browser can show the actual mnemonic values. Figure 1.5.18 shows a property called `Cursor` and the value currently selected is `Ibeam`.

The Property Browser doesn't just display information in a user-friendly or mnemonic fashion. It also allows you to edit it in a more useful way. The color swatches shown in Figure 1.5.18 can be altered using a specialized color picker that pops up when you try to change the value. Figure 1.5.19 shows the Property Browser editing one of the color values.

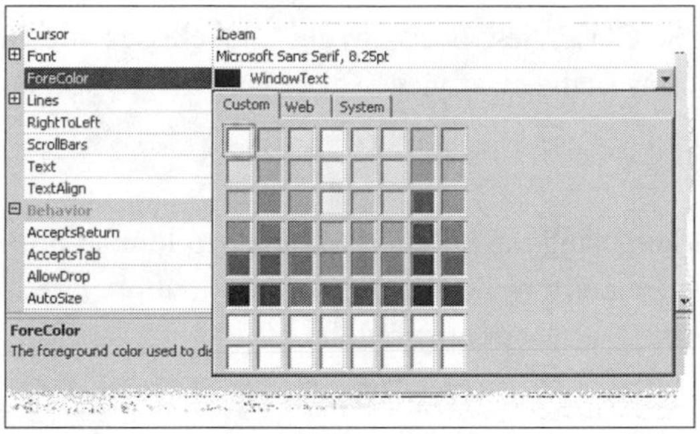

FIGURE 1.5.19

Editing a color value with the Property Browser.

There are several specialized UI editors for properties of framework objects. The `Anchor` and `Dock` properties of a Windows Form control have editors with intuitive, graphical interfaces.

The Property Browser toolbar, just above the main Property Browser, is used to display different types of information or order the data in a different way. Depending on the context of the properties you are viewing, you will see some of the following buttons.

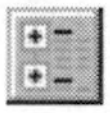

Categorized—Selects a property browser view that shows items grouped into categories, such as Appearance or Behavior.

Alphabetic—Sorts all properties into alphabetic order, ignoring the category.

Events—Lists all the event properties of a component and allows you to create an event handler for them. Events are used in the framework in place of message maps. To create or edit a handler for a particular event, click the event name in the list. The IDE will allow you to type in a name for your handler or select an existing handler from a drop-down list. After a handler has been created or selected, you can double-click it to go to the code. If you want to create a handler with a pre-selected name, simply double-click an event with no handler and the IDE will create one with a name indicative of the object and function to which the handler is assigned.

Messages—This button will appear on the toolbar when the Class View pane is displaying a Windows C++ application. You can view, edit, and add message handlers to your C++ classes through the Property Browser. The method of adding message handlers to your C++ classes is similar to that of the Event Editor mentioned earlier.

Overrides—When the Class View is displaying C++ classes you can edit, add, and view overrides for a selected class in the class view by clicking this button on the Property Browser toolbar.

Property pages—When using the Solution Explorer to look at project or solution configurations, the toolbar of the Property browser will show this button. Use it to display a dialog with the available properties for that configuration.

Properties—If you have used the Property Browser to view events or other information, you can switch back to the normal property view with this button.

Dynamic Help

The new dynamic help system in Visual Studio.net makes a big difference to the busy programmer. It's not often now that you need to search the help database as you're programming, because Dynamic Help keeps an updated list of information relevant to what you are typing all the time. It even keeps information about the windows you're using in the IDE. For example, if you select the Dynamic Help tab in section E and then select the Class View, a help item on using the Class View pane will be made available.

Experience has shown, however, that Dynamic Help requires a lot of processing power, because it is searching and collating data almost with every keystroke. There is an option to turn Dynamic Help off, and you might want to consider this if your machine seems sluggish when using VS.NET.

The Favorites Window

Your Internet Favorites list is also available from this section of the IDE. Selecting a favorite link will display it in the browser interface in the main editing pane.

Debugging Programs

Even the greatest programmers make mistakes, so a good debugger is of paramount importance. Debugging with Visual Studio is very easy, and you have a wide range of options for stopping programs and examining code. The simplest is to debug code as you are building it. The debugger can also trap an unhandled error condition and attach itself to the offending process, or you can explicitly attach the debugger to a process. Let's examine the simple case first.

To debug the program, it must be built in Debug mode. Select this using the project Configuration Manager selectable from the main Debug . . . menu. Figure 1.5.21 shows the Configuration Manager and illustrates the use of the drop-down menus for selecting the build configuration currently in use.

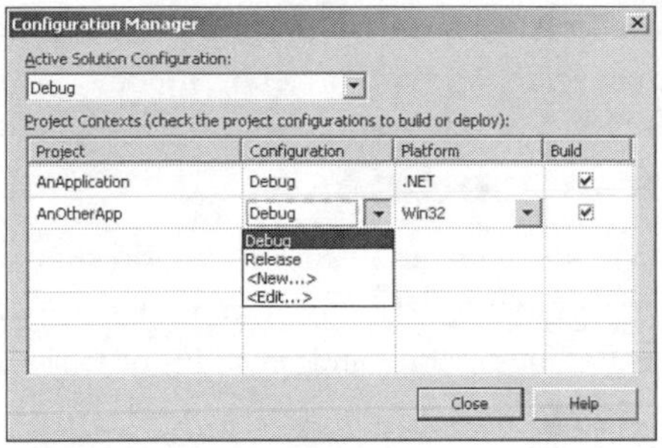

FIGURE 1.5.21
The project Configuration Manager dialog.

After the debug configuration is selected, you are ready to decide where you want the program to stop. This is accomplished by setting a breakpoint. You can do this by selecting the line of code where you want to stop and pressing F9. A red mark will appear in the margin of the code editor to show that the breakpoint is active. You can also set a breakpoint by clicking the mouse in the gray left margin of the editing window, or by pressing Ctrl+B.

Earlier in this chapter, we mentioned the Breakpoints pane that is found near the task window. To activate this pane, select Debug, Windows, Breakpoints or press Ctrl+Alt+B.

Breakpoint Glyphs

A hollow red circle is an inactive breakpoint. It can be activated or deactivated with the breakpoints pane. Select Debug, Windows, Breakpoints or press Ctrl+Alt+B.

> A breakpoint with a question mark in it might not be hit, because the process it is associated with might never run. For example, this happens if you set a breakpoint in application a and then run application b from the same solution. As soon as the process that contains the potential breakpoint is loaded, the breakpoint becomes active.
>
> A breakpoint with an exclamation point cannot be set because of an error, possibly the breakpoint location is invalid or the breakpoint might be subject to a condition that can never be satisfied.
>
> A breakpoint with a dot in it is set in an ASP page, and the break is mapped to the corresponding HTML page generated by the ASP.

After a breakpoint has been successfully set, the program can be run with the expectation of hitting the break. Press F5 to execute the code in debug mode.

Advanced Breakpoint Settings

Sometimes you need more than just a place to stop, so the breakpoints in VS.NET can also be set to trigger after so many passes through the breakpoint or when some condition is met. To create a new breakpoint, select a line of code and press F9 or Ctrl+B. F9 will automatically fill in the function and line of code where you want to stop. Ctrl+B will require you to fill this information in manually. When you use Ctrl+B, you will see the New Breakpoint dialog, as shown in Figure 1.5.23.

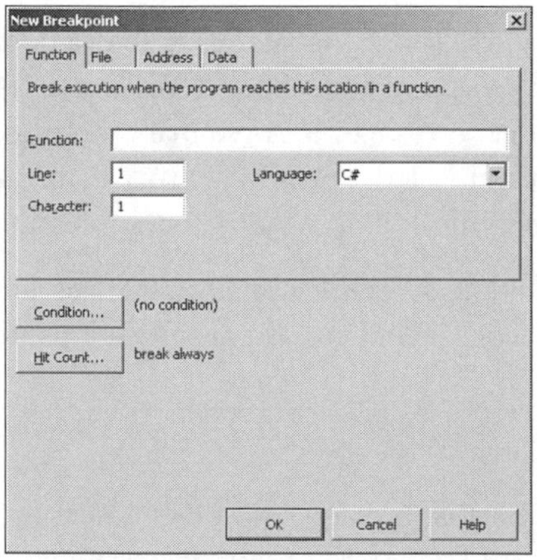

FIGURE **1.5.22**
The New Breakpoint dialog.

There are two buttons on this dialog, Condition and Hit Count. To edit a breakpoint that has already been set, find the breakpoint in the Breakpoints pane and right-click it. This action lets you select Properties from a context menu that brings up a Breakpoint edit box that has similar options.

Conditional Breakpoints

Choosing this option allows you to decide when you want the program to halt, depending on one condition or another. For example, you might want to have the program stop when a variable reaches a specific value if it has changed since the last time through the breakpoint.

Hit Counts

This option allows the breakpoint to execute as normal until it has been hit a certain number of times. You can set it to Break Always, Break When Hit-Count is Equal to a Specific Value, Break When the Hit-Count is a Multiple of Some Number, or Break When the Hit-Count is Greater Than or Equal To a Value.

Combining these options is possible so you can say you want the program to break on the fifth pass through the breakpoint, on the condition that a variable is greater than or equal to fourteen.

What to Do When the Code Is Paused

Some old familiar options are available to the programmer when code is paused. You can examine variables, step through lines of code one at time, and even send direct commands to objects in the application via the command window.

Figure 1.5.24 shows a timer service handler stopped at a breakpoint. It also shows the local variables that can be edited or examined and the call stack for the application at that point.

A feature that will be familiar to Visual Basic programmers, but probably not to C++ programmers, is the command window. This pane, located in the bottom-right tab bar when debugging, allows you to write commands directly to objects that are halted in the debugger. In the case of the previous timer code, for example, it is possible to type in `this.timer1.Enabled = false<enter>` and the timer will be disabled. If F5 was pressed to run the program from the breakpoint again, the breakpoint in the timer would no longer be hit. Using the command window, you can easily change the contents or configuration of objects in the code to try out scenarios that help you fix your bugs.

Attaching the Debugger to a Process

This is a useful feature if you're debugging a collection of applications from the same solution or perhaps debugging a DLL. You can run the application, start the debugger, and chose to break into the application by stopping it. You will be asked what kind of application you want to debug. Common choices are a CLR-based app, a Microsoft T-SQL, a native code program, possibly C++, and a script. Attaching to another process can also be done on a remote machine if you have permission to access it.

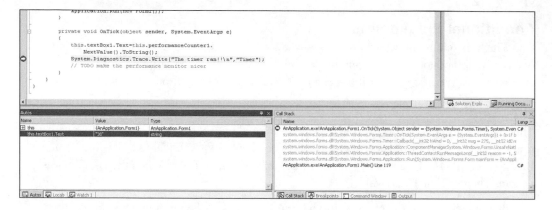

Figure 1.5.23
Code stopped at a breakpoint.

JIT Debugging

Just in time (JIT) debugging occurs when a piece of code throws an unhandled exception and is not attached to a debugger. You have several options for debugging when this happens. You will be presented with a dialog that allows you to choose which debugger you want to use. Note that even if you don't have Visual Studio installed, you will have debugging options. If you do have Visual Studio installed, though, it's best to choose this as your debugger because the features VS.NET has are more advanced than the other choices. Figure 1.5.24 shows the JIT debug dialog after an unhandled exception.

Here, you see that the options are to use the debugger that's already running (this is the one being used to edit the AnApplication used in this chapter), to use the CLR debugger (a stand-alone debugger), or a new instance of Visual Studio.NET. Choosing a debugger and clicking Yes will run the selected debugger, which will break at the point the error was trapped. If the program that caused the exception was built with a debug configuration, you should be able to see the code and step through it to find the error. If the offending application was built with a release configuration, JIT might not be very useful because you will probably be presented with X86 assembly code to debug.

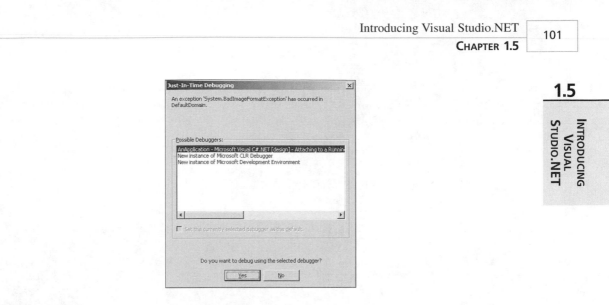

FIGURE 1.5.24
The Just-In-Time Debugging dialog.

Summary

This quick introduction to Visual Studio.NET will enable you to navigate the IDE and use all the major features. This chapter concludes the introduction to .NET. Part 2 of this book, "The C# Language," deals with the intermediate language and with C#. Read on to discover the mechanism that will make .NET the ubiquitous programming system of the future.

The C# Language

IN THIS PART

C# Basics

IN THIS CHAPTER

C# represents a modern object-oriented language that was designed to allow for the expressiveness of C++ with RAD style development found in 4GLs, such as Microsoft Visual Basic. The design of C# was driven by Anders Hejlsberg, the principle language architect at Microsoft. The design and evolution of C# was influenced by such languages as C++, SmallTalk, Java, and other OO languages.

This section will explore the C# language, semantics, and the grammar that comprise the language. It is this careful design that will allow you as a developer to concentrate on the task of building applications that drive your business requirements. The book will also reduce the initial learning curve associated with a new language and framework.

It is important to cover some basic topics before diving into the language itself. First and foremost is that everything in C# is an object. Unlike procedural languages, the C# language does not allow for global data or global functions. All data and methods must be contained within either a `struct` or a class. This is a key concept in any OO language. All data and the methods that operate on that data should be packaged as a functional unit. These functional units are reusable objects that are self-contained and self-describing.

Although it is not the goal of this text to cover OO design patterns and software engineering, it is important to understand the key concepts of OO design and implementation. C# will allow both advanced and new developers to implement solid code with minimal effort.

The C# Type System

In the .NET framework, there is a common type system that is used to allow all languages targeted at the .NET environment to interoperate with each other. C# makes use of this underlying type system. Earlier it was stated that everything in C# is an object. Well this is almost true. Primitive data types are not objects and the reason for this is performance. Because objects are allocated on the heap and managed by the GC, this would introduce a significant amount of overhead to deal with basic types such as `int` and `char`. For this reason, C# implements primitive types as `struct`s, which are considered value types. In C#, a value type is allocated on the stack as opposed to being allocated on the heap and managed by the GC. Because value types are allocated on the stack, their lifetime is limited to the scope in which they were declared.

Table 2.1.1 presents a listing of the available types within C#.

With the exception of the `string` type, all types represented within Table 2.1.1 are implemented as a `struct`. The `string` type is special in the fact that its implementation is actually a sealed class. A *sealed class* is a class that cannot be inherited from and thus terminates the inheritance chain.

TABLE 2.1.1 C# Types

Type	Description
object	Base class of all objects in C#
string	Unicode sequence of characters
sbyte	8-bit signed integral
short	16-bit signed integral
int	32-bit signed integral
long	64-bit signed integral
byte	8-bit unsigned integral
ushort	16-bit unsigned integral
uint	32-bit unsigned integral
ulong	64-bit unsigned integral
float	Single-precision floating point
double	Double-precision floating point
bool	Boolean—true or false
char	A Unicode character
decimal	28 significant digit decimal type

Value Types in Action

When a primitive type is declared, C# requires that the variable is initialized before any attempt is made to use that variable. In C++, the value of an un-initialized variable is undefined; the same rule applies in C#. The difference is that in C++, the variable can be used with unknown results.

Declaring a variable in C# has the following syntax:

```
type variable-name [= initialization]
```

Where *type* represents the variable type, and the variable name can consist of any combination of alphanumeric characters and the underscore. However, a variable name must begin with either an underscore or an alpha char and cannot begin with a numeric value.

The following are examples of variable declarations:

```
int _999;       //valid
int a_dog;      //valid
int 123_go;     //invalid
```

> **NOTE**
>
> C# allows for the `//` and `/*…*/` comment markers. The `//` denotes that all text to the right on the current line is a comment. The `/*…*/` marker is used for multi-line comments.

C# also enforces strict type checking and assignment. This means no fudging! In C++, it was possible to declare an unsigned integer and then assign the value of −1 to the variable. The C# compiler will quickly catch the assignment and produce a compiler error pointing out the invalid assignment.

```
unsigned int cpp_fudge = -1;        //valid C++
uint csharp_fudge = -1;        //error in C#
```

The error produced by the C# compiler will declare that the constant value of −1 cannot be converted to an unsigned integer. Talk about strict!

The `struct`

In languages such as C/C++, it was not possible to create a primitive type. The primitive types were like little magic entities that just existed—their meaning known, their implementation a mystery. C# implements primitive types as simple `struct`s. This means that it is possible for developers to create types that are treated in the same manner as the C# primitive types.

When creating a `struct`, it is important to keep the implementation to a bare minimum. After all, if additional functionality is required in its implementation, it would be better to implement the entity as a full blown object. `struct`s are often used to represent small pieces of data that generally have a restricted lifetime and tend to be inexpensive to manage in terms of memory requirements.

In contrast to C++, `struct`s and classes are two totally different entities. In C++, the only difference between a `struct` and a class is the default member visibility. In C#, `struct`s and classes seem to share many similarities on the surface, but they are not related and actually have many differences.

A `struct` in C# cannot inherit from another `struct` or class, however a `struct` can implement one or more interfaces. Structs may contain data members and methods. A `struct` cannot define a parameter less constructor. All `struct`s contain an implicit constructor that is responsible for initializing all data members to their default values. However, a `struct` can define a construct that accepts parameters. A construct in C# is the same as a constructor in C++ or Java. The big difference between a `struct` and a class is, of course, that `struct`s are value-types that are allocated on the stack and not reference counted.

The following is the syntax for declaring a struct:

```
struct name {
    [access-modifier] members;
}
```

The syntax is similar to both C++ and Java with respect to the declaration and construction. Member visibility defaults to private in C#. Members of a struct can have the following access modifiers applied to them: public, private, or internal. Because a struct cannot serve as the base from which another struct can inherit, the protected modifier has no place; if used, the C# compiler will quickly point out the error.

Listing 2.1.1 shows the declaration of a struct named Fraction. Notice that the member access is achieved by use of the dot operator, this can be seen on lines 13 and 14. In C#, all member access is through the dot operator regardless of whether it is a struct or class.

LISTING 2.1.1   A Simple struct

```
 1: //File        :part02_01.cs
 2: //Author     :Richard L. Weeks
 3: //Purpose     :Declare a simple struct
 4:
 5: struct Fraction {
 6:     public int numerator;
 7:     public int denominator;
 8: }
 9:
10: public class StructTest {
11:     public static void Main( ) {
12:         Fraction f;
13:         f.numerator   = 5;
14:         f.denominator = 10;
15:     }
16: }
```

Value-types also have a built-in assignment operator that performs a copy of all data members. In C++, this functionality was achieved by implementing the assignment operator and providing the code necessary to copy the data members. Listing 2.1.2 uses C# built-in assignment operators to copy the value of one struct to another struct of the same type.

LISTING 2.1.2   struct Assignment

```
 1: //File         :part02_02.cs
 2: //Author      :Richard L. Weeks
 3: //Purpose      :Declare a simple struct
```

LISTING 2.1.2   Continued

```
 4:
 5: using System;
 6:
 7: struct Fraction {
 8:     public int numerator;
 9:     public int denominator;
10:
11:     public void Print( ) {
12:         Console.WriteLine( "{0}/{1}", numerator, denominator );
13:     }
14: }
15:
16:
17: public class StructTest {
18:     public static void Main( ) {
19:
20:         Fraction f;
21:         f.numerator   = 5;
22:         f.denominator = 10;
23:         f.Print( );
24:
25:         Fraction f2 = f;
26:         f2.Print( );
27:
28:         //modify struct instance f2
29:         f2.numerator = 1;
30:
31:         f.Print( );
32:         f2.Print( );
33:     }
34: }
```

Listing 2.1.2 extends the implementation of the Fraction struct by implementing the Print method on line 11. The Print method makes use of the Console.WriteLine method to display the current value of the Fraction.

To demonstrate the assignment operator provided by C# for structs, two instances of the Fraction are declared. Line 25 declares a variable f2 and initializes it with the previous Fraction variable f. When f2.Print() is invoked, the same 5/10 output will be displayed as the call to f.Print().

It is important to realize that a copy has occurred and not a reference assignment of f to f2. When f2 is modified on line 29, the following Print method invocations display two different values. The call to `f.Print()` will still produce the 5/10 output, whereas the call to `f2.Print()` will now output 1/10.

Reference Types

C# has many circular references when trying to describe the concepts of the language. It seems that to discuss one aspect of the language, knowledge of a different aspect of the language is necessary. To this end, a brief discussion of reference types is necessary for the remaining topics to flow together.

A class construct is an example of a reference type in C#. Classes can be considered the big brother to C# structs. Reference counting means that any reference type will exist so long as there remains some active reference to the entity. In classic COM, referencing counting was visible in the `AddRef` and `Release` methods of a COM object. When the final reference was released on the instance of the object, the object took the necessary steps to clean up.

Fortunately, C# has abstracted away all the gory details of referencing counting. The GC is responsible for cleaning up memory being used by un-referenced classes and interfaces. When an object's reference count reaches zero, the GC will invoke the `Finalize` method on the object, reclaim the memory, and return it to the general application heap. The `Finalize` method is similar to the destructor concept in C++, but there is no deterministic finalization in C#. Basically, there is no way to know when an object will expire. The topic of deterministic finalization is beyond the scope of this book.

A reference is acquired in one of two ways: when an instance of a reference type is created and when an assignment takes place. Remember that when the assignment operator was used in conjunction with value types, a copy of the value type was created. This is not the case when the assignment operator is used with reference types. Changing the `Fraction struct` to a `class` changes the behavior of the assignment operator, as shown in Listing 2.1.3.

LISTING 2.1.3 Reference Types

```
 1: //File       :part02_03.cs
 2: //Author     :Richard L. Weeks
 3: //Purpose    :Reference Types
 4:
 5: using System;
 6:
 7: //A class represents a reference type in C#
 8: class Fraction {
 9:     public int numerator;
10:     public int denominator;
11:
```

LISTING 2.1.3   Continued

```
12:     public void Print( ) {
13:         Console.WriteLine( "{0}/{1}", numerator, denominator );
14:     }
15: }
16:
17:
18: public class ReferenceTest {
19:     public static void Main( ) {
20:
21:         Fraction f = new Fraction( );
22:         f.numerator   = 5;
23:         f.denominator = 10;
24:         f.Print( );
25:
26:         Fraction f2 = f;     //f2 is a reference to f and not a copy!!!
27:         f2.Print( );
28:
29:         //modify instance f2. Note that f is also effected.
30:         f2.numerator = 1;
31:
32:         f.Print( );
33:         f2.Print( );
34:     }
35: }
```

There are only two changes made to Listing 2.1.2 to create Listing 2.1.3. The first change was declaring the Fraction to be a class instead of a struct. This small change means that instead of the Fraction being allocated on the stack, it will now be created on the heap and reference counted.

The next change to the code involves the way an instance of Fraction is created. Notice that line 21 has changed. To create an instance of a reference type, the new keyword must be used. Now, an instance of the Fraction class must be created to declare the variable f. Without using the proper declaration, the variable f would be considered an un-initialized variable.

The changes to Listing 2.1.2 impact the overall semantics of the code in Listing 2.1.3. Notice that the declaration of the variable f2 on line 26 is now considered a reference to the variable f. This means that the variable f2 is the same as variable f—f2 is not a copy. This is the fundamental difference between value types and reference types. When f2 is modified on line 30, that same modification is apparent in the variable f.

The invocation of f.Print() and f2.Print() will always produce the same output. When a change is made to f2.numerator, it is the same as changing f.numerator. In C++, is was possible to define an assignment operator and to control the behavior of that operator. This ability does not exist in C#. The assignment operator cannot be overloaded or re-implemented by the developer.

Boxing and Unboxing

The concept of boxing allows for treating a value type as a reference type. Times exist when it is necessary for a value type to be treated as an object, such as storing values in an array or some other collection.

When a value type is boxed, an object instance is created on the heap and the value of the value type is copied into the object. When this happens, the boxed object and the value type are two different entities. The object is not a reference to the original value type. Any change to the value type is not reflected in the object and vise-versa.

Boxing a value type can be done with an implicit assignment. An *implicit assignment* is an assignment that does not require a type cast, as shown in the following:

```
int i = 10;
object o = i;
```

The value type variable *i* is implicitly cast to that of type object. When the value type *i* is boxed into object o, an instance of type object is created on the heap and the type information and value of the right-side of the expression is copied into the object.

To unbox an object, an explicit conversion is required, as shown in the following:

```
int i = 10;
object o = i;
int j = (int)o;    //explicit conversion from object to int
```

The integer variable *j* now holds the value that was held by the object o. It is important to understand that the variables *i*, *o*, and *j* are all independent of each other and not merely references to the same memory space.

Programming Concepts

For those of you moving from either C++ or Java, you will have a very small learning curve for C#. The syntax and productions found in the language are very similar to those found in C++ or Java. The truth of the matter is that C# was designed to be simple to learn and powerful enough to be extremely expressive.

At the time I'm writing this, Microsoft has made available the C# language reference that includes the EBNF grammar for the language. Although I happen to enjoy reading language grammars, most of my peers think that's a little excessive. So, rather than put you to sleep with such mundane details, we will look at the language from a slightly higher level.

Namespaces

In recent years, the prevalence of namespaces has come to play a major role in software engineering and component development. Namespaces provide for isolation and packaging of related classes, interfaces, and structs into a logical unit.

The .NET framework makes use of nested namespaces stemming from the System namespace. Microsoft has also provided classes and interfaces located under the Microsoft namespace for Windows-specific functionality. When developing components for the .NET platform, you should use your company name as the outer namespace in which to contain all of your classes, interfaces, and component code.

A namespace declaration should precede any code you develop, although it is not required. The syntax for declaring a namespace is as follows:

```
namespace some-namespace-name {
        //classes, interfaces, structs, and so on
}
```

Making use of entities within a namespace can be accomplished two different ways. The easiest way to access entities within a namespace is to use the using directive. Consider the System namespace, which has been used in every example presented so far. The first line of code in the previous examples is the line

```
    using System;
```

This directive instructs the compiler to use the System namespace to locate the names of classes used in the code body.

The second option is to make use of the fully qualified name of a particular entity. For example, the Console class exists within the System namespace. Rather than making use of the using directive, it is possible to use the fully qualified name instead, as shown in the following:

```
System.Console.WriteLine("Fully Qualified Name Access");
```

Let's see namespaces in action. The sample code in Listing 2.1.4 implements two namespaces. Each namespace contains a Money class. It is important to understand that the two Money classes are not the same as far as C# is concerned. Even though the Money class is identical in declaration and implementation, C# sees two distinct classes distinguished by namespace.

LISTING 2.1.4   Namespaces

```
1: //File      :part02_04.cs
2: //Date      :12.28.2000
3: //Author    :Richard L. Weeks
4: //Purpose   :Demonstrate Namespaces
```

Listing 2.1.4 Continued

```
 5:
 6:
 7: using System;
 8:
 9:
10:
11: namespace Foo {
12:
13:     public class Money {
14:
15:         private double m_Amount;
16:
17:         public Money( ) {
18:             Init( 0.0 );
19:         }
20:
21:         public Money( double Amount ) {
22:             Init( Amount );
23:         }
24:
25:
26:         public void Print( ) {
27:             Console.WriteLine("Foo.Money.Print  {0}", m_Amount );
28:         }
29:
30:
31:         private void Init( double Amount ) {
32:             m_Amount = Amount;
33:         }
34:     }
35: }
36:
37: namespace Bar {
38:
39:     public class Money {
40:
41:         private double m_Amount;
42:
43:         public Money( ) {
44:             Init( 0.0 );
45:         }
46:
47:         public Money( double Amount ) {
48:             Init( Amount );
```

LISTING 2.1.4   Continued

```
49:            }
50:
51:
52:        public void Print( ) {
53:            Console.WriteLine("Bar.Money.Print  {0}", m_Amount );
54:        }
55:
56:
57:        private void Init( double Amount ) {
58:            m_Amount = Amount;
59:        }
60:    }
61: }
62:
63:
64: public class NamespaceTest {
65:
66:    public static void Main( ) {
67:
68:        Foo.Money fm = new Foo.Money(5.00);
69:        Bar.Money bm = new Bar.Money(5.00);
70:
71:
72:        fm.Print( );
73:        bm.Print( );
74:
75:
76:    }
77: }
```

The code in Listing 2.1.4 declares two namespaces—Foo and Bar. A Money class exists within each namespace. To make use of each Money class, the Main method creates an instance of each Money class by using the fully qualified name. One caveat to note is the using statement, there does not exist a keyword to un-use a namespace. Therefore, if you have two objects with the same name residing in different namespace, be sure to use qualified names rather than the using directive.

Statements

To control the execution flow of a given section of program code, there needs to exist some notion of one or more flow control statements. That is the meat of this particular section.

if

One of the most basic control statements is the `if` statement. Simply stated, the `if` statement evaluates a Boolean expression. The result of the Boolean expression determines whether or not a given line of code or a code segment will be executed. When the result of the Boolean expression is `true`, any code within the control body of the `if` statement is executed. When the condition expression is `false`, the code contained within the control body of the `if` statement is not executed.

The syntax for the `if` statement is as follows:

```
if( conditional-expression )
    Single statement

    or

if( conditional-expression ) {
    one or more statements
}
```

The conditional-expression can be a simple expression or a compound expression. It is important to note that the conditional-expression must evaluate to a Boolean result. In C and C++, any expression with a non-zero value is considered `true` and a zero value is considered `false`. C# employs stricter type checking and requires the conditional-expression to evaluate to either `true` or `false` (see Listing 2.1.5).

LISTING 2.1.5 The if Statement

```
 1: //File      :part02_05.cs
 2: //Date      :12.29.2000
 3: //Author    :Richard L. Weeks
 4: //Purpose   :C# if statement usage
 5:
 6:
 7: using System;
 8:
 9:
10:
11: public class Statements {
12:
13:
14:     public static void Main( ) {
15:
16:         bool bSimple_1 = true;
```

LISTING 2.1.5 Continued

```
17:          bool bSimple_2 = false;
18:
19:
20:      if( bSimple_1 )
21:          Console.WriteLine("You should see this");
22:
23:      if( bSimple_2 )
24:          Console.WriteLine("You should not see this");
25:
26:      //Complex
27:      if( bSimple_1 && !bSimple_2 )
28:          Console.WriteLine("Will you see this?");
29:
30:
31:      //Multiple Statements
32:      if( bSimple_1 ) {
33:          Console.WriteLine("Statement 1");
34:          Console.WriteLine("Statement 2");
35:      }
36:  }
37: }
```

The example in Listing 2.1.5 demonstrates the basic semantics of the `if` statement. Expression evaluation also employs short-circuit evaluation. This means that when the expression is being evaluated from left to right, as soon as the expression evaluates to `false`, the entire expression is said to be `false`. Short-circuit evaluation is employed by languages such as C and C++, but Visual Basic does not make use of short-circuit evaluation for basic Boolean logic such as `And` and `Or` In VB.NET, two operators, `AndAlso` and `OrElse`, have been added that do make use of short-circuit evaluation.

if...else

The `if...else` construct is merely an extension of the standard `if` statement. Because the `if` statement only executes the code within its body when the conditional-expression is `true`, the `else` clause allows for the execution of code when the conditional-expression is `false`. Listing 2.1.6 makes use of the `if-else` construct to determine if an integer entered by the user is odd or even.

LISTING 2.1.6 `if...else` Statement Usage

```
1: //File      :part02_06.cs
2: //Author    :Richard L. Weeks
3: //Purpose   :C# if-else statement
```

LISTING 2.1.6 Continued

```
 4:
 5: using System;
 6:
 7: public class StatementTest {
 8:
 9:     public static void Main( ) {
10:         Console.Write("Enter an number between 1 and 10: ");
11:         int i = Int32.Parse( Console.ReadLine( ) );
12:
13:         //is the number in the proper range
14:         if( (i >= 1) && (i <= 10) ) {
15:
16:             //is the number even or odd?
17:             if( (i % 2) == 0 )
18:                 Console.WriteLine("The number {0} is even", i );
19:             else
20:                 Console.WriteLine("The number {0} is odd", i );
21:
22:         } else
23:             Console.WriteLine("You must enter a number between 1 and 10");
24:
25:     }
26: }
```

Let's take a minute and step through the code in Listing 2.1.6. On line 10, the program prompts the user to enter a number between 1 and 10. The next line makes use of the ReadLine method of the Console object to read the input from the user. Because the ReadLine method returns a string, it is necessary to convert the string to an integral value. This is accomplished by using the static method Parse implemented by the Int32 value-type.

The next step is to test the value entered and determine whether the value is within the required range. If the conditional-expression evaluates to true, the next step is to determine if the number is odd or even. To test for odd or even, the program makes use of the modulus operator. The modulus operator divides the right-side value by the left-side value and returns the remainder. Because the divisor is 2, all even numbers will have a remainder of zero and all odd numbers will not.

As previously stated, C# enforces strict type checking, and the expression on line 17 must evaluate to a Boolean result. In C and C++, the line of code could have been written as

```
if( i % 2 )
```

However, the expression i % 2 produces in an integer result and not a Boolean result. For this reason, C# will reject the statement and issue an error.

Conditional Operator ?:

The conditional operator can be viewed as a compact if...else statement. Its best use is for assigning values to variables based on some conditional-expression. Both C, C++, and Visual Basic implement the conditional operator; Visual Basic uses the IIf(...) expression for this purpose. Unlike VB, C# employs short-circuit evaluation. *Short-circuit evaluation* means that only the necessary result is evaluated. In VB, both the true and false conditions are evaluated. This is inefficient and can even introduce subtle bugs.

The conditional operator has the following syntax.

```
result = conditional-expression ? true expression : false expression
```

Remember that C# requires all conditional expressions to evaluate to a Boolean expression. This is enforced due to C#'s strong type checking. Listing 2.1.7 is a revision of Listing 2.1.6 and makes use of the conditional operator for determining if the number entered is odd or even.

LISTING 2.1.7   The Conditional Operator

```
 1: //File      :part02_07.cs
 2: //Author    :Richard L. Weeks
 3: //Purpose   :conditional-operator
 4:
 5:
 6:
 7: using System;
 8:
 9:
10: public class StatementTest {
11:
12:
13:     public static void Main( ) {
14:
15:         Console.Write("Enter an number between 1 and 10: ");
16:         int i = Int32.Parse( Console.ReadLine( ) );
17:
18:
19:         //is the number in the proper range
20:         if( (i >= 1) && (i <= 10) ) {
21:
22:             //is the number even or odd?
23:             string odd_even = (i % 2) == 0 ? "even" : "odd";
24:
25:             Console.WriteLine( "The number {0} is {1}", i, odd_even );
26:
```

LISTING 2.1.7   Continued

```
27:           } else
28:              Console.WriteLine("You must enter a number between 1 and 10");
29:
30:     }
31: }
```

Line 23 in Listing 2.1.9 shows the use of the conditional operator. Here, a string variable odd_even is assigned a value based on the condition that (i % 2) == 0. When the condition is true, the variable odd_even is assigned the constant string literal "even". When the expression is false, the variable odd_even is then assigned the constant string literal "odd".

In Listing 2.1.7, the conditional operator is used to replace four lines of code found in Listing 2.1.6, lines 17 to 20 specifically.

goto

Yes, the goto statement still survives. I can hear the software engineering purists screaming. Why does a modern language include the goto statement? The goto statement is used to immediately transfer program execution to a specified label. When the switch statement is covered, a concrete use of the goto statement will be unveiled.

There are times when the judicious use of the goto statement allows for tight and efficient code. On the other hand, using the goto statement as the primary means of logic control flow tends to produce spaghetti code.

There are a few constraints regarding the use of the goto statement. A goto statement cannot be used to jump into another method or out of the current method. The goto statement can only transfer control to a label that exists within the current scope.

The syntax for the goto statement should be familiar to those of you coming from C, C++, or VB. A destination label can be any combination of alphanumeric constants, given that the first position is a character element. The label name is then terminated with a colon (:) to denote that it is, in fact, a label and not some statement, expression, or variable.

The goto syntax is as follows:

```
goto label-name;
```

Listing 2.1.8 illustrates the basic use of the goto statement.

LISTING 2.1.8   The goto Statement

```
1: //File    :part02_08.cs
2: //Author  :Richard L. Weeks
```

LISTING 2.1.8   Continued

```
 3: //Purpose :Demonstrate the use of the goto statement
 4:
 5:
 6: using System;
 7:
 8:
 9: public class GotoTest {
10:
11:     public static void Main( ) {
12:
13:
14:         Console.WriteLine("about to goto label1");
15:         goto label1;
16:
17:         Console.WriteLine("This will not print");
18:
19:     label1:
20:         Console.WriteLine("label1 goto effective");
21:     }
22: }
23:
```

The example in Listing 2.1.8 demonstrates the basic use of the goto statement. On line 19, a label named label1 has been defined. The goto statement on line 15 directs the program flow to immediately jump to the specified label. This, in effect, causes all code between lines 15 and 19 to be jumped over. Notice that the WriteLine statement on line 17 states that This will not print.

When compiling the example, the C# compiler will issue a warning stating that there exists "Unreachable Code detected." The unreachable code is found on line 17. Because the control execution jumps this segment of code, there is no reason for it to exist. Always be sure to heed compiler warnings and treat them as if they were compiler errors.

switch

There are many times when it is necessary to evaluate some condition and select among several possible choices or cases. This is the role of the switch statement. Given some expression to evaluate, the switch statement can be used to select a constant case to execute. Think of the switch statement as a multiple-choice implementation. Instead of using multiple nested if statements, the switch statement can be used.

The switch statement consists of an expression to evaluate and one or more constant values that represent the possible outcome cases.

```
switch( expression ) {
    case constant-expression:
        statement(s)
        jump-statement

    [default: statement(s); jump-statement]
}
```

The controlling expression for the switch statement can be an integral or string type expression. Each constant case expression must be of the same type as the controlling expression, and no two cases can have the same constant expression.

Unlike C and C++, C# does not allow for one case to fall through into another case. To accomplish fall-through style execution, the goto keyword can be used to transfer control to another case. Each case must make use of a jump statement including the last case or the default case. Listing 2.1.9 shows the basic use of the switch statement.

LISTING 2.1.9 The switch Statement

```
1: //File      :part02_09.cs
2: //Author    :Richard L. Weeks
3: //Purpose   :The switch statement
using System;
4:
public class SwitchTest {
5:
    public static void Main( ) {
6:
        Console.WriteLine("Please make your selection");
7:          Console.WriteLine("1 Hamburger");
8:          Console.WriteLine("2 Cheese Burger");
9:          Console.WriteLine("3 Fish");
10:
        int Selection = int.Parse( Console.ReadLine( ) );
11:
        switch( Selection ) {
            case 1:
12:                 Console.WriteLine("Hamburger");
13:             break;
14:
            case 2:
15:                 Console.WriteLine("Cheese Burger");
16:             break;
17:
            case 3:
```

LISTING 2.1.9   Continued

```
18:                 Console.WriteLine("Fish");
19:             break;
20:
        default:
21:                 Console.WriteLine("Unknown choice");
22:             break;
23:         }
24:     }
25: }
```

Listing 2.1.9 presents an example of the switch statement in action. Each case expression is represented by some constant integral value. Notice that the break jump statement separates each case.

Because C# does not allow for case fall through (that is, execution cannot continue from one case to another), the goto statement can be used to transfer control to another case or the default case. Listing 2.1.10 uses the goto statement to transfer control from one case statement to another.

LISTING 2.1.10   Using the goto Inside a Case Statement

```
1: //File      :part02_10.cs
2: //Author    :Richard L. Weeks
3: //Purpose   :The switch statement and the use of goto
4:
5: using System;
6:
7: public class SwitchTest {

8:     public static void Main( ) {

9:         Console.WriteLine("Please make your selection");
10:     Console.WriteLine("1 Hamburger");
11:     Console.WriteLine("2 Cheese Burger");
12:     Console.WriteLine("3 Fish");
int Selection = int.Parse( Console.ReadLine( ) );

13:     switch( Selection ) {
        case 1:
14:                 Console.WriteLine("Hamburger");
15:             goto case 4;

16:         case 2:
17:                 Console.WriteLine("Cheese Burger");
```

LISTING 2.1.10 Continued

```
18:             goto case 4;
19:         case 3:
20:             Console.WriteLine("Fish");
21:           break;
22:         case 4:
23:             Console.WriteLine("Transferred to case 4");
24:             Console.WriteLine("Transferring to default case");
25:             goto default;
26:         default:
27:              Console.WriteLine("Unknown choice");
28:           break;
29:     }
30:   }
31: }
```

Listing 2.1.10 is a modification of the code found in Listing 2.1.9. Cases 1, 2, and 4 make use of the `goto` statement to transfer control from the current case to another case. Again, the `goto` statement can be used to transfer control to another case label or to the default case label.

for

The `for` statement is one of the most basic iteration statements. Whenever there is a fixed number of iterations, the `for` statement fits the bill. Like C and C++, the `for` statement consists of an initialization, conditional expression, and an iteration statement. The syntax is as follows:

```
for( initialization(s); conditional-expression; iteration(s) )
    statement;
```

The initialization can be a comma-separated list of variable declarations and assignments. The conditional expression must evaluate to a Boolean expression and is used to determine when the `for` loop terminates. The iteration section is used to increment or decrement the controlling variables used by the `for` statement (see Listing 2.1.11).

LISTING 2.1.11 The for Statement

```
1: using System;
2:
3: public class ForStatement {
4:
5:     public static void Main( ) {
6:
7:         for( int i = 0; i < 10; i++ )
8:             Console.WriteLine( "i = {0}", i );
9:     }
```

Listing 2.1.11 shows the for statement in action. The integer variable *i* is used to control the number of iterations to be performed by the for statement. The output produced by Listing 2.1.11 is as follows:

```
i = 0
i = 1
i = 2
i = 3
i = 4
i = 5
i = 6
i = 7
i = 8
i = 9
```

Notice that the value of *i* ranges from 0 to 9, and not 0 to 10. This is due to the conditional expression *i* < *10;*. Notice that the expression that equates to *i* is less than 10. When the value of *i* is equal to 10, the for statement will terminate and program execution will continue with the statement following the for statement construct.

The for statement controls only the next statement or statement block. To execute multiple statements, the statements must be contained within a statement block. A *statement block* is a section of statements within the opening and closing {} brackets. Listing 2.1.12 shows a for statement controlling a statement block.

LISTING 2.1.12   Statement Block

```
 1: using System;
 2:
 3: public class ForTest {
 4:
 5:     public static void Main( ) {
 6:
 7:         for( int i = 0; i < 10; i++ ) {
 8:             Console.WriteLine("value of i to follow");
 9:             Console.WriteLine("i = {0}", i);
10:         }
11:     }
12: }
```

With the addition of a statement block, the for statement now controls the execution of statements within the block. The output from Listing 2.1.12 should look like the following:

```
1: value of i to follow
2: i = 0
```

```
 3: value of i to follow
 4: i = 1
 5: value of i to follow
 6: i = 2
 7: value of i to follow
 8: i = 3
 9: value of i to follow
10: i = 4
11: value of i to follow
12: i = 5
13: value of i to follow
14: i = 6
15: value of i to follow
16: i = 7
17: value of i to follow
18: i = 8
19: value of i to follow
20: i = 9
```

A small note about variable scooping. In each of the examples detailing the use of the `for` statement, the control variable was declared and initialized within the `for` statement itself. As such, the variable *i* is only visible within the `for` statement, and any attempt to access the variable after the `for` statement will result is a compiler error.

while

The `while` statement allows for the execution of the statement body as long as the conditional expression evaluates to `true`.

```
while( conditional-expression )
    statement
```

The `while` statement operates as follows:

1. The conditional expression is tested.
2. If the conditional expression is `true`, the statement body is executed.
3. This continues until the condition being evaluated is `false`.
4. When the condition is `false`, the statement exits and execution beings at the next line of code following the statement.

For this reason, the body of the `while` statement may not execute at all; if the condition is `false`, the body of the statement will not execute.

The `while` statement is useful when the number of iterations is unknown, unlike the `for` statement, which is generally deterministic and a known quantity of iterations is required.

Consider the implementation of Newton's method for determining square roots. The number of iterations is unknown because the method will need to run as long as the delta between the previous result and the current result is larger than some predefined epsilon value. Let's look at the pseudo code for Newton's method and then the C# implementation.

```
Epsilon := 1.0e-9
BaseGuess := N        //Can be any value
Value := M            //Some user defined value
NewGuess := ((Value / BaseGuess) + BaseGuess) / 2;
While abs_delta( NewGuess , BaseGuess ) > Epsilon
Begin
     BaseGuess := NewGuess;
     NewGuess := ((Value / BaseGuess) + BaseGuess) / 2;
End
```

Notice that there is no way to determine the number of iterations the while statement will execute. The controlling expression is not based on a counter, but rather a Boolean evaluation that can be true at any time. This undetermined number of iterations is well suited to the while statement rather than the for statement, which should be used when the number of iterations is deterministic. The previous pseudo code for Newton's method can easily be expressed in C# with the code in Listing 2.1.3.

LISTING 2.1.13   The while Statement

```
1: //File     :part02_13.cs
2: //Author   :Richard L. Weeks
3: //Purpose  :Make use of the while statement to
4: //          :implement Newton's method for finding
5: //          :the square root of a number.
6:
7: using System;
8:
9:
10:
11: public class Newton {
12:
13:     public static void Main( ) {
14:
15:
16:     const double epsilon   = 1.0e-9;
17:           double dGuess    = 11.0;
18:
19:     //Prompt the user for a positive number and obtain their input
20:     Console.Write("Enter a positive number: ");
```

LISTING 2.1.13 Continued

```
21:     double dValue = double.Parse( Console.ReadLine( ) );
22:
23:     //Calculate the Initial result value
24:         double dResult = ((dValue / dGuess) + dGuess) / 2;
25:
26:         Console.WriteLine( "Guess Value  = {0}", dGuess  );
27:         Console.WriteLine( "Result Value = {0}", dResult );
28:
29:     //Continue to approximate the sqr until the delta is less than epsilon
30:         while( Math.Abs(dResult - dGuess) > epsilon ) {
31:
32:             dGuess = dResult;
33:         dResult = ((dValue / dGuess) + dGuess) / 2;
34:
35:             Console.WriteLine( "Guess Value  = {0}", dGuess  );
36:             Console.WriteLine( "Result Value = {0}", dResult );
37:     }
38:
39:     Console.WriteLine(
➥ "\n****\nThe approx sqrt of {0} is {1}\n****", dValue, dResult );
40:     }
41: }
```

The implementation of Newton's method is merely a straightforward conversion of the pseudo code listed previously. There are a few subtle items to point out. Line 21 shows an example of the primitive type double and the Parse method. Remember that C# implements primitive types as structs and that a struct can also contain methods. This is the case with all primitive types in C#.

The next item of interest is the while statement and the controlling conditional expression on line 30. Notice the Abs method, which is a static method of the Math class. The Abs method returns the absolute value of the given integral expression.

do...while

A similar construct to the while statement is the do...while statement. Unlike the while statement, the body of the do...while statement will always execute at least one iteration. This is due to the fact that the conditional expression is tested at the end of each loop rather than at the beginning. Listing 2.1.14 is a modification of Listing 2.1.13 that replaces the use of the while statement with the do...while statement. The result produced by each listing is the same, only the semantics of what is happening has changed.

LISTING 2.1.14   The do...while Statement

```
 1: //File      :part02_14.cs
 2: //Author    :Richard L. Weeks
 3: //Purpose   :Make use of the do while statement to
 4: //          :implement Newton's method for finding
 5: //          :the square root of a number.
 6:
 7: using System;
 8:
 9: public class Newton {
10:
11:    public static void Main( ) {
12:
13:
14:      const double epsilon   = 1.0e-9;
15:            double dGuess     = 11.0;
16:            double dResult    = 0.0;
17:
18:      //Prompt the user for a positive number and obtain their input
19:      Console.Write("Enter a positive number: ");
20:      double dValue = double.Parse( Console.ReadLine( ) );
21:
22:      //Calculate the initial result
23:      dResult = ((dValue / dGuess) + dGuess) / 2;
24:
25:      //Continue to approximate the sqr until the delta is less than epsilon
26:      do {
27:              Console.WriteLine( "Guess Value  = {0}", dGuess  );
28:              Console.WriteLine( "Result Value = {0}", dResult );
29:
30:           dGuess = dResult;
31:        dResult = ((dValue / dGuess) + dGuess) / 2;
32:
33:        } while( Math.Abs(dResult - dGuess) > epsilon );
34:
35:
36:      Console.WriteLine(
➥"\n****\nThe approx sqrt of {0} is {1}\n****", dValue, dResult );
37:    }
38: }
```

foreach

The foreach statement will be familiar to those of you who have done development with
Visual Basic. Essentially, the foreach statement allows for iteration over the elements within

an array or any collection that implements the IEnumerable interface. Interfaces will be covered in detail later in this section.

Every collection provides some method for iterating through the contents of the container. In the C++ STL world, there exists the concept of an iterator; this is orthogonal to the concept of an enumerator in the world of COM. Anyone who has had the pleasure of implementing the IEnumVARIANT interface will appreciate the ease of implementing the IEnumerable interface along with providing an IEnumerator interface available in the .NET framework.

```
foreach( element_type variable in expression )
    statement;
```

Looking at the syntax of the foreach statement, the *element_type* is the data type to be used as the variable declaration. The expression can be an array or a collection class that contains elements of type *element_type*. Listing 2.1.15 uses the foreach statement to iterate over the contents of an integer array.

LISTING 2.1.15   The foreach Statement

```
 1: //File    :part02_15.cs
 2: //Author :Richard Weeks
 3: //Purpose:Using the foreach statement
 4:
 5:
 6: using System;
 7: public class ArrayListing {
 8:
 9:     public static void Main( ) {
10:
11:         int[] whole_numbers = {1,2,3,4,5,6,7,8,9,10};
12:
13:
14:         //Display each element in the whole_numbers array
15:         foreach( int value in whole_numbers )
16:             Console.WriteLine( "value = {0}", value );
17:     }
18: }
```

There is not a lot of code in Listing 2.1.15 because the focus is on putting the foreach statement to work. When you look under the covers of the foreach statement, lines 15 and 16 of Listing 2.1.15 are equivalent to the following code segment in Listing 2.1.16.

LISTING 2.1.16   Expanding the `foreach` Statement

```
1: IEnumerator iterator = whole_numbers.GetEnumerator( );
2: while( iterator.MoveNext( ) ) {
3:     int value = (int)iterator.Current;
4:     Console.WriteLine( "value = {0}", value );
5: }
```

As you can see, the expanded code makes use of the `IEnumerator` interface and the `GetEnumerator()` method provided by the `System.Array` type. Next, a `while` statement is used to enumerate the elements of the array. The current element is accessed and cast to the proper type. When the type requested is a primitive type, this step requires unboxing the element from the object type and placing the value into the appropriate primitive type.

Operators

Operators are actions that can be applied to primitive types and object types that provide the operator implementation. Unary operators are operations that only act on a single entity. Binary operators require both a left and right side value on which to operate. The relational operators evaluate to Boolean expressions that can be used to form conditional expressions. Table 2.1.2 contains the available operators found in C#.

TABLE 2.1.2   C# Operators

Operator Category	Operator
Arithmetic	+, -, *, /, %,
Logical (Boolean and Bitwise)	&, |, ^, !, ~, &&, ||, true, false
Increment, Decrement	++, —
Shift	>>, <<
Relational	==, !=, <, >, <=, >=
Assignment	=, +=, -=, *=, /=, %=, !=, ^=, <<=, >>=
Type Information	is
Casting	(Type)Variable, as

The C# reference contains a full listing of not only unary and binary operators, but also indexing, member access, indirect access, expanded type information, and casting. The operators in Table 2.1.2 will be familiar to programmers of most languages with the exception of `is` and `as`.

These two operators need some further explanation; each operator accomplishes similar, but slightly different tasks.

The `is` operator

The `is` operator is used to test if an entity is of a certain type. C# supports a very robust run-time type information and the `is` operator uses this type information to determine if the given entity is of the requested type.

```
expression is type
```

The `is` operator evaluates to a Boolean result and can be used as a conditional expression. The `is` operator will return `true` if the following conditions are met:

- The expression is not null.
- The expression can be safely cast to the type. The cast assumes an explicit cast in the form of (*type*)(*expression*).

If both of these conditions are satisfied, the `is` operator will return a Boolean `true`; otherwise, the `is` operator will return `false`. Listing 2.1.17 demonstrates the use of the `is` operator.

LISTING 2.1.17 The is Operator

```csharp
 1: //File       :part02_16.cs
 2: //Author     :Richard L. Weeks
 3: //Purpose    :Demonstrate the 'is' operator
 4:
 5:
 6: using System;
 7:
 8: //Create two empty classes.  We only need their declaration for
 9: //the purpose of demonstrating the is keyword
10:
11: class Dog {
12: }
13:
14: class Cat {
15: }
16:
17:
18: public class IsDemo {
19:
20:     public static void Main( ) {
21:
22:         Dog myDog = new Dog( );
23:         Cat myCat = new Cat( );
```

2.1

C# BASICS

LISTING 2.1.17   Continued

```
24:         int i = 10;
25:
26:         WhatIsIt(myDog);
27:         WhatIsIt(myCat);
28:         WhatIsIt(i);
29:     }
30:
31:     public static void WhatIsIt( object o ) {
32:
33:         if( o is Dog )
34:             Console.WriteLine("It is a dog");
35:         else if( o is Cat )
36:             Console.WriteLine("It is a cat");
37:         else
38:             Console.WriteLine("I don't know what it is");
39:     }
40: }
```

The is example in Listing 2.1.17 actually introduces two concepts not yet discussed. The first is the creation of a static method WhatIsIt in the IsDemo class. A static method can be used like a standalone function because no object instance is required. Static methods will be covered in detail when classes are covered later in this section.

The next item of interest is the parameter being passed to the static WhatIsIt method. Notice that the formal parameter is object. In C#, all classes implicitly inherit from the base class object and all value types can be boxed as object. Because this is the case, object can be used as a generic type that accepts anything.

The actual use of the is operator is fairly straightforward. Within each if statement, the is operator is used to determine the runtime type information of the object passed in. Depending on the results of the is expression, the appropriate response will be displayed to the console.

The following is the output of Listing 2.1.16.

```
It is a dog
It is a cat
I don't know what it is
```

The as Operator

Like the is operator, the as operator makes use of runtime type information in an attempt to cast a given expression to the requested type. The normal casting operator—$(T)e$, where T is the type and e is the expression—generates an InvalidCastException when there is no valid cast. The as operator does not throw an exception; instead, the result returned is null.

The as operator uses the same syntax as the is operator:

```
expression as type
```

The as syntax can be formally expanded into the following:

```
expression is type ? (type)expression : (type)null
```

The as operator is therefore merely shorthand notation for using both the is operator and the conditional operator. The benefit of the as operator is its ease of use and the fact that no exception is thrown in the event that a type safe cast does not exist.

Arrays

In C#, arrays are a special entity. All arrays implicitly inherit from the System.Array type. The System.Array base class provides various methods used during the manipulation of arrays. Arrays are also index checked; that is, any attempt to access an invalid index, such as an index out of range, will generate an exception. In C and C++, simple arrays were not ranged checked and it was possible to overwrite the stack space or the heap; not so in C#.

The declaration of an array might seem slightly odd at first, but when you analyze the syntax, it actually makes much more sense than the C and C++ declaration for arrays.

The following syntax is used to allocate an array of Rank 1.

```
array-type[] var = new array-type[size]
```

Notice that the array brackets are next to the array type and not the variable name. This syntax actually makes more sense than placing the brackets next to the variable name. After all, the array is the type and type declarations precede the variable name.

Arrays in C# use zero-based indexing. Languages, such as COBOL and Visual Basic, use one based indexing, although Visual Basic allows you to define the default array indexing base value. Listing 2.1.18 makes use of a single dimension array and some of the methods the System.Array type provides.

LISTING 2.1.18 Single Dimension Array

```
1: //File    :part02_17.cs
2: //Author  :Richard L. Weeks
3: //Purpose :Demonstrate C# arrays
4:
5: using System;
6:
7: public class ArrayTest {
8:
9:     public static void Main( ) {
```

LISTING 2.1.18   Continued

```
10:
11:           //Declare a single dim array of ints
12:           int[] array_1 = new int[5];
13:
14:           //Fill the array
15:           for( int i = array_1.GetLowerBound(0);
➥i <= array_1.GetUpperBound(0); i++)
16:                array_1[i] = i+1;
17:
18:           //Display the contents of the array
19:           for( int j = array_1.GetLowerBound(0);
➥j <= array_1.GetUpperBound(0); j++)
20:                Console.WriteLine("array_1[{0}] = {1}", j, array_1[j]);
21:
22:           Console.WriteLine("\n****** Phase II ******\n");
23:
24:           //Declare an array and initialize the values
25:           int[] array_2 = new int[] { 25, 10, 4, 7, 15, 2, 1 };
26:
27:           //Sort the array
28:           System.Array.Sort( array_2 );
29:
30:           //Display the sorted values
31:           for( int k = array_2.GetLowerBound(0);
➥k <= array_2.GetUpperBound(0); k++)
32:                Console.WriteLine("array_2[{0}] = {1}", k, array_2[k] );
33:
34:
35:     }
36: }
37:
```

Listing 2.1.18 makes use of the System.Array methods GetLowerBound and GetUpperBound. The method GetLowerBound takes an integer argument that specifies the Rank for which to get the lower index value. GetUpperBound also takes an integer argument that specifies the Rank to get the largest index value. Notice that the for statement on lines 15, 19, and 31 all make use of these methods.

Lines 12 through 16 declare an array and use a for statement to initialize the values. On line 25, the declaration and initialization is done with a single statement.

The System.Array class also provides the static method Sort. The Sort method can be used to sort intrinsic types or any type that implements the IComparable interface. Interface implementation will be covered later in Chapter 2.2, "Advanced C#."

C# arrays are not restricted to a single dimension. Declaring arrays of rank greater than one merely requires specifying the lengths of each rank. It is also important to note that arrays do not have to be rectangular. Each rank can have a different upper bound (see Listing 2.1.19).

LISTING 2.1.19 Multi-Dimensional Arrays

```
1: //File     :part02_18.cs
2: //Author   :Richard L. Weeks
3: //Purpose  :Arrays with a Rank greater than 1
4:
5:
6: using System;
7:
8: public class ArrayTest {
9:     public static void Main( ) {
10:
11:         int[,] grid = new int[3,3] { {1,2,3}, {4,5,6}, {7,8,9} };
12:
13:     //Display the contents of the grid
14:         for( int i = 0; i < 3; i++ ) {
15:             for( int j = 0; j < 3; j++ ) {
16:                 Console.Write("{0} ", grid[i,j] );
17:             }
18:             Console.WriteLine("");
19:         }
20:     }
21: }
```

The declaration for the array variable grid on line 11 follows the same syntax and initialization as an array of rank 1. The only difference in the number of dimensions is now 2; the rank of the array is 2. Notice that the indexers for the array are separated with a comma. This syntax will be familiar to Visual Basic programmers, but to C and C++ developers, the syntax is different from what you are use to seeing.

Listing 2.1.19 also makes use of an initialization list when declaring the grid array.

struct

Early on in this section, there was a discussion of value types and reference types. In C#, a struct is considered a value type and, as such, is managed on the stack rather than the heap. C# implements primitive types such as int and char as structs.

structs are best used for simple data types or mementos for object serialization and object state. structs can contain data members, methods, properties, and constructors. In most ways, a struct is similar to a class. However, a struct cannot inherit from a class or another struct, but can implement one or more interfaces. structs cannot contain constructors without parameters, and the compiler will issue an error if you attempt to define one.

The default protection level for struct members is private. In C++, the only real difference between a struct and a class was the default protection level. Not so in C#. It is important to know that in C#, structs and classes are not interchangeable. Remember that a struct is considered a value type and a class is considered a reference type. Listing 2.1.20 implements a simple struct to represent a Point.

LISTING 2.1.20   Declaring and Using a struct

```
 1: using System;
 2:
 3: public struct Point {
 4:     public int x;
 5:     public int y;
 6: }
 7:
 8: public class StructTest {
 9:
10:     public static void Main( ) {
11:         Point p;
12:         p.x = 5;
13:         p.y = 10;
14:         Point p2 = p;
15:         PrintPoint( p );
16:         PrintPoint( p2 );
17:     }
18:
19:     public static void PrintPoint( Point p ) {
20:         Console.WriteLine( "x = {0}, y = {1}", p.x, p.y );
21:     }
22: }
```

Listing 2.1.20 demonstrates how to define and use a C# struct. The struct Point contains two public data members—x and y. Notice that on line 14 the variable p2 is assigned the value of variable p. When dealing with value types, the default assignment operator will copy the contents of the right side to the variable on the left side. This is in sharp contrast to the way in which reference types work. Remember that when dealing with reference types, the assignment operator will act as a reference and not a copy, as with value types.

There are some interesting points to note when dealing with structs. A struct cannot be used until all the values within the struct have been initialized. Every struct has a synthesized default constructor that initializes the data members to their respective default values. However, when a `struct` contains a private data member, the default constructor will not initialize it without an explicit invocation of the default constructor. To accomplish this, the `struct` must be created using the new operator. This is a bit confusing because the `struct` is still created on the stack and not on the heap, as would be expected by the use of the new operator. Listing 2.1.21 demonstrates the warning issued by the compiler when attempting to use a `struct` that contains un-initialized members.

LISTING 2.1.21   `struct` Member Initialization

```
 1: using System;
 2:
 3: public struct Simple {
 4:
 5:     public  int i;
 6:     private string s;
 7:
 8:     public void init( ) {
 9:         i = 10;
10:         s = "Hello";
11:     }
12:
13: }
14:
15:
16:
17: public class T {
18:
19:     public static void Main( ) {
20:
21:         Simple simple;
22:
23:         simple.init( );
24:
25:     }
26: }
```

When Listing 2.1.21 is compiled, the C# compiler will issue the following error.

```
Microsoft (R) Visual C# Compiler Version 7.00.9030 [CLR version 1.00.2204.21]
Copyright (C) Microsoft Corp 2000. All rights reserved.
struct_02.cs(25,3): error CS0165: Use of unassigned local variable 'simple'
```

The error issued by the C# compiler is somewhat misleading at first because it complains about the use of an unassigned local variable simple. This error is due to the fact that the private data member *s* is un-initialized. To have private data members initialized, an instance of the `struct` must be declared using the `new` operator (see Listing 2.1.22).

LISTING 2.1.22   Revision of Listing 2.1.21

```
 1: using System;
 2:
 3: public struct Simple {
 4:
 5:     public  int i;
 6:     private string s;
 7:
 8:     public void init( ) {
 9:         i = 10;
10:         s = "Hello";
11:     }
12:
13:     public void show( ) {
14:
15:         Console.WriteLine("i = {0}", i);
16:         Console.WriteLine("s = {0}", s);
17:     }
18:
19: }
20:
21: public class T {
22:
23:     public static void Main( ) {
24:
25:         Simple simple = new Simple( );
26:
27:         simple.init( );
28:
29:     }
30: }
```

Revising the previous listing and making two changes now allows for a clean compile and the expected behavior. The first change involves the addition of the show method, which makes use of the data member *s*. This change satisfies the compilers complaint about the unused private data member.

Notice that the declaration on line 25 now makes use of the `new` operator. Again, it is important to understand that a `struct` is a value type and, as such, will still exist on the stack. The usage of the new operator forces the invocation of the default constructor and initializes the private data members.

Because C# provides a synthesized parameter less constructor, any attempt to implement such a construct for a value type will cause the compiler to issue an error.

Classes

A class represents the encapsulation of data and methods that act on that data. In C#, classes are considered reference types and, as such, instances of classes are allocated on the heap and managed by the GC. When an instance of a class is created, memory is allocated on the heap and the object is referenced counted. When the reference count for the object reaches zero, the GC will reclaim the memory area being used by the object and return that memory to the available memory pool.

Classes can contain fields, methods, events, properties, and nested classes. Classes also have the ability to inherit from another class and implement multiple interfaces.

Like structs, the default protection level for class members is private. Classes can declare members to be public, protected, private, internal, or protected internal.

Declaring a class consists of specifying the following:

```
[attributes] [access modifier] class class-name [: [base-class], [interface]*]
{
    body
}
```

The square brackets indicate optional specifiers and are not required to declare a class. Listing 2.1.23 presents a simple class representation for a Dog type.

LISTING 2.1.23 A Simple Class

```
1: using System;
2:
3: public class Dog {
4:
5:     //Fields
6:     private string Name;
7:
8:     //Constructor
9:     public Dog( string name ) {
10:     Name = name;
11:     }
12:
13:     //Methods
14:     public void Speak( ) {
15:         Console.WriteLine( "Hello. My name is {0}", Name );
16:     }
```

LISTING 2.1.23   Continued

```
17: }
18:
19: public class Simple {
20:
21:     public static void Main( ) {
22:
23:         Dog spot = new Dog( "spot" );
24:         spot.Speak( );
25:     }
26: }
```

The Dog class in Listing 2.1.23 demonstrates the basics of defining and implementing a class in C#. The class contains a private field, a parameter-based constructor, and a single method. Unlike a struct, the new operator must be used to create an instance of the class. Line 23 shows the creating of a new instance of the Dog class and uses the parameter constructor to initialize the object.

As a brief note on access modifiers, Table 2.1.3 presents the access modifiers and how they affect class members.

TABLE 2.1.3   Member Access Modifiers

Access Modifier	Definition
public	Visible to all code
protected	Visible to current class and derived classes
private	Visible only to current class
internal	Visible to current assembly only
protected internal	Visible to current assembly or types derived from the class

Object

Every class in C# implicitly derives from the base class System.Object. Because all classes derive from a common base class, the ability to create generic collection classes becomes a trivial point. Every instance of a class can be treated as if it were a System.Object instance.

The System.Object class also provides a few basic services that other classes in the .NET framework use. For example, the Console.Write method will use the ToString method of a class to display the class to the console. Any C# class can thus override the behavior of ToString and provide a custom implementation specific to the class. Table 2.1.4 lists some of the basic Object methods.

TABLE 2.1.4 The `System.Object` Class

Method	Purpose
Equals(*Object*)	Boolean comparison
Finalize	Similar to a C++ destructor
ToString	Convert class to string representation

The `System.Object` base class also provides additional methods for type information, reflection, and cloning. These topics are outside the scope of this conversation, but their exploration is well worth the time spent.

Methods

In OO terminology, a method represents an object message. Methods can be either instance or static in nature. An instance method requires an instance of the object and generally acts on the data members of the current object. Static methods do not require an instance of an object and, therefore, cannot access the data members of the current class.

Methods, like data members, can also have an access modifier applied to them. Public methods allow any user of the object to invoke that method; it is the public contract, so to speak. Protected methods are only to be used by the object itself or any object that derives from the object. Private methods can only be accessed by the class declaring the method. Derived classes cannot make use of any private methods found in the base class.

Listing 2.1.24 demonstrates the use of instance verses `static` methods.

LISTING 2.1.24 Instance and Static Methods

```
 1: using System;
 2:
 3: public class MyMath {
 4:
 5:     //instance method
 6:     public long Factorial( long l ) {
 7:         return l <= 0 ? 1 : l * Factorial( l - 1 );
 8:     }
 9:
10:     //static method
11:     public static long SFactorial( long l ) {
12:         return l <= 0 ? 1 : l * SFactorial( l - 1 );
13:     }
14: }
15:
```

LISTING 2.1.24 Continued

```
16: public class Methods {
17:
18:     public static void Main ( ) {
19:
20:         //Use the static method
21:         Console.WriteLine("5 Factorial = {0}", MyMath.SFactorial( 5 ) );
22:
23:         //Use the instance method
24:         MyMath m = new MyMath( );
25:         Console.WriteLine("5 Factorial = {0}", m.Factorial( 5 ) );
26:     }
27: }
```

To access a static method, the method name needs to be qualified with the name of the class. Line 21 of Listing 2.1.24 invokes the SFactorial method of the MyMath class by making use of the dot operator. C# has unified member, method, and scooping access to the dot operator. In C++, it was necessary to use the pointer access operator, the dot operator or the scope resolution operator, depending on the situation. Not so in C#; only the dot operator is necessary to perform all access.

Instance methods require an object to invoke them. The Factorial method is such a method because the static modifier has not been applied to the method. Line 24 creates an instance of the MyMath class to invoke it. Notice that the same dot operator is used to access the instance method the same way that access to the static method is specified.

Parameter Passing

Depending on the language you are familiar with, there exists specific syntax for defining whether a parameter is passed by-value—a copy of the parameter is placed on the call stack— or by-reference—an alias to the variable is placed on the call stack. In C and C++, you can pass a parameter by value, by reference, pass a pointer, and so on. Users of Visual Basic know that parameters are passed by reference by default and need to specify by value otherwise.

C# offers not only supports by-value and by-reference parameter passing, but it also allows for additional marshaling instructions, such as in and out. These modifiers are orthogonal to the in and out directives used in COM.

In C#, value types, such as primitive types and structs, are passed by value unless otherwise specified. When a parameter is passed by value, a copy of the value type is created. The method receiving the parameter can make use of the copy and even modify its value. However, the parameter is not in any way related to the outside world. If a method modifies a value passed by value, the effects of that modification only exist within the scope of that method.

Reference types—any class or interface—are passed by reference and cannot be passed by value. To pass a value type by reference, the `ref` keyword must be used. When a parameter is passed by reference to a method, the method can modify the parameter, and the modifications will affect the actual parameter, thus producing a side effect. Listing 2.1.25 demonstrates parameter passing available in C#.

LISTING 2.1.25 Parameter Passing

```
 1:
 2: using System;
 3:
 4: //Create a value type
 5: public struct Point {
 6:
 7:     public int x;
 8:     public int y;
 9: }
10:
11: //Create a Reference type
12: public class MyObject {
13:     public int i;
14: }
15:
16:
17:
18: public class Pass {
19:
20:     public static void Main( ) {
21:
22:
23:         //Create a primitive type and pass to the various methods
24:         int i = 100;
25:
26:         Console.WriteLine(
➥"Value of i before PassByValue Method is {0}", i );
27:         PassByValue( i );
28:         Console.WriteLine(
➥"Value of i after PassByValue Method is {0}", i );
29:
30:         Console.WriteLine("");
31:
32:         Console.WriteLine(
➥"Value of i before PassByRef Method is {0}", i );
33:         PassByRef( ref i );
34:         Console.WriteLine(
➥"Value of i before PassByRef Method is {0}", i );
```

LISTING 2.1.25   Continued

```
35:
36:
37:          Console.WriteLine("");
38:
39:          //Create an the Point type
40:          Point p; p.x = 10; p.y = 15;
41:          Console.WriteLine(
➥"Value of p before PassByValue is x={0}, y={1}", p.x,p.y);
42:          PassByValue( p );
43:          Console.WriteLine(
➥"Value of p after PassByValue is x={0}, y={1}", p.x,p.y);
44:
45:          Console.WriteLine("");
46:
47:          Console.WriteLine(
➥"Value of p before PassByRef is x={0}, y={1}", p.x,p.y);
48:          PassByRef( ref p );
49:          Console.WriteLine(
➥"Value of p after PassByRef is x={0}, y={1}", p.x,p.y);
50:
51:
52:          Console.WriteLine("");
53:
54:          //Create an object instance
55:          MyObject o = new MyObject( );
56:          o.i = 10;
57:
58:          Console.WriteLine(
➥"Value of o.i before PassReferenceType is {0}", o.i );
59:          PassReferenceType( o );
60:          Console.WriteLine(
➥"Value of o.i after PassReferenceType is {0}", o.i );
61:
62:
63:      }
64:
65:
66:
67:     public static void PassByValue( Point p )  {
68:          Console.WriteLine(
➥"Entering public static void PassByvalue( Point p )" );
69:
70:          Console.WriteLine(
➥"Value of Point.x = {0} : Point.y = {1}", p.x, p.y );
71:          p.x++; p.y++;
```

LISTING 2.1.25 Continued

```
72:         Console.WriteLine(
➥"New Value of Point.x = {0} : Point.y = {1}", p.x, p.y );
73:
74:         Console.WriteLine(
➥ "Exiting public static void PassByvalue( Point p )" );
75:     }
76:
77:
78:     public static void PassByValue( int i ) {
79:         Console.WriteLine(
➥"Entering public static void PassByValue( int i )" );
80:
81:         Console.WriteLine("Value of i = {0}", i );
82:         i++;
83:         Console.WriteLine("New Value of i = {0}", i );
84:
85:         Console.WriteLine(
➥"Exiting public static void PassByValue( int i )" );
86:     }
87:
88:     public static void PassByRef( ref Point p ) {
89:         Console.WriteLine(
➥"Entering public static void PassByRef( ref Point p )" );
90:
91:         Console.WriteLine(
➥"Value of Point.x = {0} : Point.y = {1}", p.x, p.y );
92:         p.x++; p.y++;
93:         Console.WriteLine(
➥"New Value of Point.x = {0} : Point.y = {1}", p.x, p.y );
94:
95:         Console.WriteLine(
➥"Exiting public static void PassByRef( ref Point p )" );
96:     }
97:
98:     public static void PassByRef( ref int i ) {
99:         Console.WriteLine(
➥"Entering public static void PassByRef( ref int i )" );
100:
101:         Console.WriteLine("Value of i = {0}", i );
102:         i++;
103:         Console.WriteLine("New Value of i = {0}", i );
104:
105:         Console.WriteLine(
➥"Exiting public static void PassByRef( ref int i )" );
106:     }
```

LISTING 2.1.25   Continued

```
107:
108:    public static void PassReferenceType( MyObject o ) {
109:        Console.WriteLine(
➥"Entering public static void PassReferenceType( MyObject o )" );
110:
111:        Console.WriteLine("Value of MyObject.i = {0}", o.i);
112:        o.i++;
113:        Console.WriteLine("New Value of MyObject.i = {0}", o.i);
114:
115:        Console.WriteLine(
➥"Exiting public static void PassReferenceType( MyObject o )" );
116:    }
117: }
```

The parameter passing Listing 2.1.25 presents cases for passing primitive types, structs, and reference types to methods by value and by reference.

Output of Listing 2.1.25

```
Value of i before PassByValue Method is 100
Entering public static void PassByValue( int i )
Value of i = 100
New Value of i = 101
Exiting public static void PassByValue( int i )
Value of i after PassByValue Method is 100

Value of i before PassByRef Method is 100
Entering public static void PassByRef( ref int i )
Value of i = 100
New Value of i = 101
Exiting public static void PassByRef( ref int i )
Value of i before PassByRef Method is 101

Value of p before PassByValue is x=10, y=15
Entering public static void PassByvalue( Point p )
Value of Point.x = 10 : Point.y = 15
New Value of Point.x = 11 : Point.y = 16
Exiting public static void PassByvalue( Point p )
Value of p after PassByValue is x=10, y=15

Value of p before PassByRef is x=10, y=15
Entering public static void PassByRef( ref Point p )
Value of Point.x = 10 : Point.y = 15
```

```
New Value of Point.x = 11 : Point.y = 16
Exiting public static void PassByRef( ref Point p )
Value of p after PassByRef is x=11, y=16

Value of o.i before PassReferenceType is 10
Entering public static void PassReferenceType( MyObject o )
Value of MyObject.i = 10
New Value of MyObject.i = 11
Exiting public static void PassReferenceType( MyObject o )
Value of o.i after PassReferenceType is 11
```

Properties

In the C++ and COM world, properties are nothing more than a simple semantic for assessor and setter methods. In COM, the methods would be put_*T* and get_*T* where *T* is the property name. Visual Basic programmers will be immediately familiar with the concept of properties, because there exists a parallel among the entities.

C# allows for properties to be either read only, write only, or read/write, although a write-only property doesn't really have much use.

The property construct has the following syntax:

```
access-modifier return-type PropertyName {
    [ get { statement; } ]
    [ set { statement; } ]
}
```

Properties provide a simple syntax for accessing elements within a class while still allowing for a level of abstraction as to the actual property implementation. Listing 2.1.26 revisits Newton's method for square roots and implements two properties: Value and Result.

LISTING 2.1.26 Using Properties

```
 1: using System;
 2:
 3:
 4: public class Newton {
 5:
 6:     private double m_dblValue;
 7:     private double m_dblResult;
 8:
 9:
10:     public Newton( ) {
11:         m_dblValue  = 1.0;
```

LISTING 2.1.26 Continued

```
12:              m_dblResult = 0.0;
13:              }
14:
15:      //Properties
16:
17:      //Value is set/get
18:      public double Value {
19:          set {
20:              if( value <= 0 ) {
21:                  Console.WriteLine("Value must be greater than Zero");
22:                  return;
23:              }
24:              m_dblValue = value;     //the rhs is value
25:          }
26:
27:          get { return m_dblValue; }
28:      }
29:
30:      //The result is get only.
31:      public double Result {
32:          get { return m_dblResult; }
33:      }
34:
35:      //Find the Square Root of m_dblValue
36:      public void FindSqrt( ) {
37:          const double Epsilon = 1.0e-9;
38:          double        Guess   = 11;
39:
40:          m_dblResult = ((m_dblValue / Guess) + Guess) / 2;
41:
42:          while( Math.Abs( m_dblResult - Guess ) > Epsilon) {
43:              Guess  = m_dblResult;
44:              m_dblResult = ((m_dblValue / Guess) + Guess) / 2;
45:          }
46:      }
47: }
48:
49:
50:
51:
52: public class PropertyTest {
53:
54:      public static void Main( ) {
55:
56:          Newton n = new Newton( );
```

LISTING 2.1.26   Continued

```
57:
58:            //set the requested value
59:            n.Value = 100;
60:
61:            //Find the Sqrt of 100
62:            n.FindSqrt( );
63:
64:            //display the result
65:            Console.WriteLine("The Sqrt of {0} is {1}", n.Value, n.Result );
66:      }
67: }
```

Returning to the Newton example, Listing 2.1.26 presents a class that implements Newton's method for approximating the square root of a number. The Newton class implements two properties, Value and Result. The Value property implements both the set and get methods. This allows the property to be read and written to. The Result property only implements the get method, effectively creating a read-only property.

The purpose of properties is to allow for a natural semantic for accessing data members but still allowing for a layer of abstraction. Within the implementation of the property accessor or setter, the developer is free to implement validation, conversion, and any other logic necessary. From the user's point of view, all the implementation detail has been abstracted away, and a clean semantic for accessing data elements is provided.

Operators

C# provides the facility for user-defined operators. Any struct or class can provide a specific implementation of a given operator, such as addition, subtraction, or casting from one type to another. The ability to create a new type and define operator semantics for it allows for the development of new value types as well as reference types.

In earlier discussions, the assignment operator was discussed and how it differs from value types and reference types. C# does not allow for the implementation of an assignment operator. C++ developers can scream now. This restriction is due to reference counting verses coping. Another consideration is the .NET platform is meant for languages to interoperate with each other in ways never before possible. To make a copy of a reference type, most reference types provide a Copy method. When developing classes, you should follow the same guidelines.

C# requires that all operators be static methods. Again, this makes sense to a language purist. Operators pertain to a type and not an instance, just one of the details that was not overlooked in the design of C#.

To gain an understanding of operator overloading, the Fraction class, Listing 2.1.27 demonstrates implementing the arithmetic operators + and -.

LISTING 2.1.27 Operator Overloading

```
 1: //File       :part02_26.cs
 2: //Author     :Richard L. Weeks
 3: //Purpose    :Demonstrate operator overloading
 4:
 5: using System;
 6:
 7: public class Fraction {
 8:
 9:     //data members
10:     private int     m_numerator;
11:     private int     m_denominator;
12:
13:     //Properties
14:     public int Numerator {
15:         get { return m_numerator; }
16:         set { m_numerator = value; }
17:     }
18:     public int Denominator {
19:         get { return m_denominator; }
20:         set { m_denominator = value; }
21:     }
22:
23:
24:     //Constructors
25:     public Fraction( ) { m_numerator = 0; m_denominator = 0; }
26:
27:     public Fraction( int iNumerator, int iDenominator ) {
28:             m_numerator = iNumerator;
29:             m_denominator = iDenominator;
30:     }
31:
32:     //Arithmetic operators +,-,/,*
33:
34:     public static Fraction operator+(Fraction f1, Fraction f2) {
35:         Fraction Result = new Fraction( );
36:         //In order to add fractions, the denominators need to be the same
37:         //the fastest way is to multiply
➥them together and adjust the numerators
38:             if( f1.Denominator != f2.Denominator ) {
39:                 Result.Denominator = f1.Denominator * f2.Denominator;
```

LISTING 2.1.27 Continued

```
40:               Result.Numerator    =
➡ (f1.Numerator * f2.Denominator) + (f2.Numerator * f1.Denominator);
41:          } else {
42:               Result.Denominator = f1.Denominator;
43:               Result.Numerator   = f1.Numerator + f2.Numerator;
44:          }
45:          return Result;
46:      }
47:
48:
49:      public static Fraction operator-(Fraction f1, Fraction f2) {
50:          Fraction Result = new Fraction( );
51:          //In order to subtract fractions,
➡the denominators need to be the same
52:          //the fastest way is to multiply them together and adjust the
numerators
53:          if( f1.Denominator != f2.Denominator ) {
54:               Result.Denominator = f1.Denominator * f2.Denominator;
55:               Result.Numerator    =
➡ (f1.Numerator * f2.Denominator) - (f2.Numerator * f1.Denominator);
56:          } else {
57:               Result.Denominator = f1.Denominator;
58:               Result.Numerator    = f1.Numerator - f2.Numerator;
59:          }
60:          return Result;
61:      }
62:
63: }
64:
65:
66: public class OperatorTest {
67:
68:      public static void Main( ) {
69:
70:          Fraction f1 = new Fraction( 1, 5 );
71:          Fraction f2 = new Fraction( 2, 5 );
72:
73:          //Add the Fractions
74:          Fraction f3 = f1 + f2;
75:
76:          //Display the result
77:          Console.WriteLine("f1 + f2 = {0}/{1}",
➡ f3.Numerator, f3.Denominator );
78:
79:          //Subtract f2 from f3 should get f1
```

LISTING 2.1.27 Continued

```
80:          f3 = f3 - f2;
81:          Console.WriteLine("f3 - f2 = {0}/{1}",
➥f3.Numerator, f3.Denominator );
82:      }
83: }
```

The Fraction class presented in Listing 2.1.27 implements both the + and – operators. The addition operator is implemented on line 34 and the subtraction operator on line 49. The general form for overloading an operator can be expressed as follows:

```
public static return-type operator T(param p [,param p1])
```

where the return-type specifies the result of the operator, T is the actual operator to overload, and the number of parameters is dependant on the operator being overloaded.

In addition to standard arithmetic operators, C# provides the ability to overload relational operators and casting operators. Relational operators often come in pairs. For example, when overloading the equality operator ==, the inequality operator != must also be defined. Relational operators have the same semantic for overloading as the operators presented so far.

Casting operators have a slightly different semantic than regular operators. When implementing a casting operator, the decision of implicit or explicit must be made. Remember, an implicit cast does not require the type to be specified, whereas an explicit cast does.

```
Fraction f = new Fraction( 1, 5 );
double d = f;               //implicit cast
double dd = (double)f;      //explicit cast
```

The decision about implicit verses explicit will need to be determined by the use case in mind. The syntax for overloading a casting operator is as follows:

```
public static [implicit|explicit] operator Return-Type( Type T )
```

Again, the Return-Type denotes to what the Type T is being cast or converted. Extending the previous operator example, the Fraction class in Listing 2.1.28 has been extended to implement an explicit cast to double and the relational operators == and !=. When compiling the code in Listing 2.1.28, the compiler will issue two warnings CS660 and CS661. The warning stems from the overloaded operators == and != and the requirement that any class overloading these operators must also provide an implementation of Object.Equals and Object.GetHashCode. For now you can dismiss the warnings. However when creating production code be sure to implement the necessary Equals and GetHashCode methods in order to satisfy the rule that says any two objects that are considered equal by Equals or by the overloaded == and != operators should have the same hash code.

LISTING 2.1.28 Extend the Fraction Class

```
 1: //File         :part02_27.cs
 2: //Author       :Richard L. Weeks
 3: //Purpose       :Demonstrate operator overloading
 4:
 5:
 6: using System;
 7:
 8:
 9:
10: public class Fraction {
11:
12:     //data members
13:     private int    m_numerator;
14:     private int    m_denominator;
15:
16:
17:     //Properties
18:     public int Numerator {
19:         get { return m_numerator; }
20:         set { m_numerator = value; }
21:     }
22:     public int Denominator {
23:         get { return m_denominator; }
24:         set { m_denominator = value; }
25:     }
26:
27:
28:     //Constructors
29:     public Fraction( ) { m_numerator = 0; m_denominator = 0; }
30:
31:     public Fraction( int iNumerator, int iDenominator ) {
32:             m_numerator = iNumerator;
33:             m_denominator = iDenominator;
34:     }
35:
36:     //Arithmetic operators +,-,/,*
37:
38:     public static Fraction operator+(Fraction f1, Fraotion f2) {
39:         Fraction Result = new Fraction( );
40:         //In order to add fractions, the denominators need to be the same
41:         //the fastest way is to multiply
them together and adjust the numerators
42:             if( f1.Denominator != f2.Denominator ) {
43:                 Result.Denominator = f1.Denominator * f2.Denominator;
```

LISTING 2.1.28   Continued

```
44:              Result.Numerator  =
➡ (f1.Numerator * f2.Denominator) + (f2.Numerator * f1.Denominator);
45:          } else {
46:              Result.Denominator = f1.Denominator;
47:              Result.Numerator  = f1.Numerator + f2.Numerator;
48:          }
49:          return Result;
50:      }
51:
52:
53:      public static Fraction operator-(Fraction f1, Fraction f2) {
54:          Fraction Result = new Fraction( );
55:          //To subtract fractions, the denominators need to be the same
56:          //the fastest way is to
➡ multiply them together and adjust the numerators
57:          if( f1.Denominator != f2.Denominator ) {
58:              Result.Denominator = f1.Denominator * f2.Denominator;
59:              Result.Numerator  =
➡ (f1.Numerator * f2.Denominator) - (f2.Numerator * f1.Denominator);
60:          } else {
61:              Result.Denominator = f1.Denominator;
62:              Result.Numerator  = f1.Numerator - f2.Numerator;
63:          }
64:          return Result;
65:      }
66:
67:      //add an explicit casting operator from fraction to double
68:      public static explicit operator double(Fraction f) {
69:          double dResult = ((double)f.Numerator / (double)f.Denominator);
70:          return dResult;
71:      }
72:
73:
74:      public static bool operator==(Fraction f1, Fraction f2) {
75:          //TODO: Implement comparison of f1 to f2
76:          return true;
77:      }
78:
79:      public static bool operator!=(Fraction f1, Fraction f2) {
80:          return !(f1 == f2);
```

LISTING 2.1.28   Continued

```
81:      }
82:
83:
84: }
85:
86:
87: public class OperatorTest {
88:
89:     public static void Main( ) {
90:
91:          Fraction f1 = new Fraction( 1, 5 );
92:          Fraction f2 = new Fraction( 2, 5 );
93:
94:          //Add the Fractions
95:          Fraction f3 = f1 + f2;
96:
97:          //Display the result
98:          Console.WriteLine("f1 + f2 = {0}/{1}",
➥ f3.Numerator, f3.Denominator );
99:
100:         //Substract f2 from f3 should get f1
101:         f3 = f3 - f2;
102:         Console.WriteLine("f3 - f2 = {0}/{1}",
➥f3.Numerator, f3.Denominator );
103:
104:         //Print f3 as a double
105:         Console.WriteLine("f3 as a double = {0}", (double)f3);
106:     }
107: }
```

Inheritance

Inheritance is a key concept in OO design and languages. Inheritance allows for common functionality and attributes to reside in a base class, and specialized classes can inherit the functionality provided by the base class. C# only supports single inheritance. C++ provides for multiple inheritances and, when used correctly, is a truly powerful paradigm. However, multiple inheritance has proven to be difficult to maintain and somewhat hard to follow. This is one reason that C# only implements single inheritance.

Figure 2.1.1 illustrates a common case of inheritance.

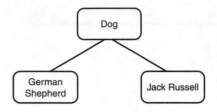

FIGURE 2.1.1

Basic Inheritance

The base class Dog would contain attributes and methods common to all canines. Each derived class can then specialize the implementation as necessary. It is also important to note that C# only provides public inheritance (see Listing 2.1.29). Again, C++ developers may scream now.

LISTING 2.1.29   Inheritance

```
 1: //File        :part02_28.cs
 2: //Purpose     :Demonstrate basic inheritance
 3: //
 4:
 5: using System;
 6:
 7: public class Dog {
 8:
 9:     //Common attributes
10:     public string Name;
11:     public int    Weight;
12:
13:
14:     //Common methods
15:     public void Speak( ) { Console.WriteLine("ruff!"); }
16:     public void DrinkWater( ) { Console.WriteLine("Gulp"); }
17:
18: }
19:
20:
21: //A specialized version of a Dog
22: public class GermanShepard: Dog {
23:     public void OnGuard( ) { Console.WriteLine("In Guard Mode"); }
24: }
25:
26:
27: public class JackRussell : Dog {
28:     public void Chew( ) {
➥Console.WriteLine("I'm chewing your favorite shoes!"); }
```

LISTING 2.1.29 Continued

```
29: }
30:
31:
32:
33:
34:
35: public class Inherit {
36:
37:     public static void Main( ) {
38:
39:         GermanShepard Simon = new GermanShepard( );
40:         JackRussell Daisy    = new JackRussell( );
41:
42:         //Both Simon and Daisy have a name and weight
43:         Simon.Name = "Simon"; Simon.Weight = 85;
44:         Daisy.Name = "Daisy"; Daisy.Weight = 25;
45:
46:         //Both Simon and Daisy have the speak and DrinkWater methods
47:         Simon.Speak( ); Simon.DrinkWater( );
48:         Daisy.Speak( ); Daisy.DrinkWater( );
49:
50:
51:         //Only Simon has the OnGuard Method
52:         Simon.OnGuard( );
53:
54:         //Only Daisy has the Chew method
55:         Daisy.Chew( );
56:     }
57: }
```

Figure 2.1.1 has been implemented in C# and presented in Listing 2.1.29. Remember that C# only supports single inheritance, so it is not possible to create a derived class that specifies more than one base class. The syntax to inherit from a base class is to place the name of the base class to the right of a colon following the name of the derived class, as shown in the following:

```
class Bar : Foo { }
```

In this case, Bar is the derived class and Foo is the base class.

Polymorphism

The term *polymorphism* translates to "many forms." In OO terminology, the ability to override a base class method and provide a different implementation in a derived class is a basic form of polymorphism.

Consider the previous example where GermanShepard and JackRussell were derived from the common base class Dog. The base class Dog provides a method Speak that all derived classes inherit. However, if you've ever heard a German Shepard bark and a Jack Russell bark, they don't sound the same. Therefore, the base class Dog should allow for derived classes to provide their own implementation of the Speak method.

C# provides the keyword virtual to denote a method that can be overridden by a derived class. A derived class can override the virtual method by using the override keyword.

```
class Dog {
    public virtual void Speak( ) {...}
}
class JackRussell : Dog {
    public override void Speak( ) {...}
}
```

The true power of polymorphism comes into play when the object type is unknown at compile time. This allows for runtime type information to be used to determine the actual method to be invoked. Listing 2.1.30 updates the Dog base class and provides for the virtual method Speak.

LISTING 2.1.30   Virtual Methods

```
 1: //File        :part02_28.cs
 2: //Purpose     :Demonstrate basic inheritance
 3: //
 4:
 5: using System;
 6:
 7: public class Dog {
 8:
 9:     //Common attributes
10:     public string Name;
11:     public int    Weight;
12:
13:
14:     //Common methods
15:     public virtual void Speak( ) { Console.WriteLine("ruff!"); }
16:     public void DrinkWater( ) { Console.WriteLine("Gulp"); }
17:
18: }
19:
20:
21: //A specialized version of a Dog
22: public class GermanShepard : Dog {
23:
24:     public void OnGuard( ) { Console.WriteLine("In Guard Mode"); }
25:
```

LISTING 2.1.30   Continued

```
26:     //override the Dog.Speak() method
27:     public override void Speak( ) { Console.WriteLine("RUFF,RUFF,RUFF"); }
28: }
29:
30:
31: public class JackRussell : Dog {
32:     public void Chew( ) {
➥Console.WriteLine("I'm chewing your favorite shoes!"); }
33:
34:     //override the Dog.Speak() method
35:     public override void Speak( ) { Console.WriteLine("yap,yap,yap"); }
36:
37: }
38:
39:
40:
41:
42:
43: public class Inherit {
44:
45:     public static void Main( ) {
46:
47:         GermanShepard Simon = new GermanShepard( );
48:         JackRussell Daisy   = new JackRussell( );
49:
50:         //Both Simon and Daisy have a name and weight
51:         Simon.Name = "Simon"; Simon.Weight = 85;
52:         Daisy.Name = "Daisy"; Daisy.Weight = 25;
53:
54:         //Polymorphism allows for the proper method to be called
55:         //based on runtime type information
56:         Dog d = Simon;
57:         d.Speak( );         //calls GermanShepard.Speak( );
58:
59:         d = Daisy;
60:         d.Speak( );         //calls JackRussell.Speak( );
61:
62:     }
63: }
```

The revised inheritance example now makes use of a virtual method Speak. Both
GermanShepard and JackRussell derived classes provide a specialized implementation of the
base class Dog.Speak method.

Nothing real exciting happens until line 56. Notice the declaration of a variable of type Dog and its initialization with a reference to Simon. Now is when things get interesting. When the Speak method is invoked, the runtime type of the object is determined and, based on that information, the proper implementation of Speak is invoked—in this case, GermanShepard.Speak(). Following the invocation of d.Speak(), the variable d is set to reference Daisy. Again, d.Speak() is invoked and the runtime type information is accessed to determine the proper Speak method to invoke.

Polymorphism represents a powerful paradigm in the OO world. When applied properly, components can interact with each other without having intimate knowledge of each other.

Interfaces

Interfaces provide a powerful abstraction to component-based development. Interfaces provide a public contract that allows components to work together. Consider an electrical wall outlet to be a receptor of a specific interface. An appliance that provides the proper plug type, the proper interface, can be used in the electrical wall outlet. The wall outlet implements one interface and the appliance implements another. Essentially, the wall outlet states that it can use any device that implements the 110-plug interface. The appliance states that it can make use of any wall outlet that implements the 110-outlet interface.

In more concrete terms, the alarm clock next to your bed implements several interfaces—the Alarm interface, the Clock interface, and possibly the Radio interface.

Figure 2.1.2 depicts an AlarmClock component that supports an Alarm interface, a Clock interface, and a Radio interface. Figure 2.1.2 is known as a box-spoon diagram, the spoons are the lines with circles at the end sticking out of the box.

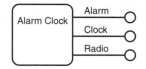

FIGURE 2.1.2
The AlarmClock component and supported interfaces.

An interface is not a class and, as such, does not contain any implementation code. An interface contains members and method signatures, all of which must be public. C# allows for both a struct and a class to implement one or more interfaces. This is different from inheritance. Inheritance involves implementation from a base class, interface implementation only states that the class implementing a particular interface guarantees to fulfill the interface contract.

C# uses the `interface` keyword to denote the declaration of an interface, as follows:

```
interface name {
    body;
}
```

A class or `struct` can implement an interface by declaring the interface during declaration, as shown in the following:

```
public class AlarmClock : IAlarm, IClock, IRadio {
//implementation
}
```

> **NOTE**
>
> A standard naming convention for interfaces states that an interface name should begin with the capital letter I. This naming convention allows for consistency and makes it easy to spot an interface with respect to a class or `struct` definition.

The .NET framework makes heavy use of interfaces. In fact, to take full advantage of the services provided by .NET, understanding interface development and implementation is a must. Listing 2.1.31 implements an `AlarmClock` class that fulfills the interface contract shown in Figure 2.1.2.

LISTING 2.1.31   The AlarmClock

```
 1: //File        :part02_30.cs
 2: //Author      :Richard L. Weeks
 3: //Purpose     :Interfaces
 4:
 5: using System;
 6:
 7: //Define the IAlarm interface
 8: interface IAlarm {
 9:     bool On { get; set; }
10:     void Snooze( );
11: }
12:
13: //Define the IClock interface
14: interface IClock {
15:     void SetTime( );
16: }
17:
18:
```

LISTING 2.1.31   Continued

```
19: //Define the IRadio interface
20: interface IRadio {
21:     void SetStation( double station_id );
22: }
23:
24:
25:
26: //Create an alarm clock that implements IAlarm, IClock and IRadio
27: public class AlarmClock : IAlarm, IClock, IRadio {
28:
29:     //Data members
30:     private bool    m_bOnOff;
31:
32:
33:     //The IAlarm interface implementation
34:     public bool On { get { return m_bOnOff; } set { m_bOnOff = value; } }
35:     public    void Snooze( ) { Console.WriteLine("IAlarm.Snooze"); }
36:
37:     //The IClock Interface
38:     public    void SetTime( ) { Console.WriteLine("IClock.SetTime"); }
39:
40:     //The IRadio interface
41:     public    void SetStation( double station_id )
➥{ Console.WriteLine("IRadio.SetStation( {0} )", station_id ); }
42: }
43:
44:
45:
46: public class InterfaceTest {
47:     public static void Main( ) {
48:
49:         AlarmClock a = new AlarmClock( );
50:
51:         //Get the IAlarm Interface
52:         IAlarm ialarm = (IAlarm)a;
53:         ialarm.On = false;
54:         ialarm.Snooze( );
55:
56:         //Get the IClock interface
57:         IClock iclock = (IClock)a;
58:         iclock.SetTime( );
59:
60:         //Get the IRadio interface
61:         IRadio iradio = (IRadio)a;
```

LISTING 2.1.31 Continued

```
62:            iradio.SetStation( 98.1 );
63:    }
64: }
```

Figure 2.1.2 has been implemented in Listing 2.1.31. The casting operator is used to obtain a requested interface, see line 52 of Listing 2.1.31. The IAlarm interface is requested from the AlarmClock instance. In the event that the AlarmClock does not support the IAlarm interface, an InvalidCastException will be thrown. If the interface does exist, a reference to the interface will be returned. As a quick aside, there are now two references to the alarm clock—one reference for the AlarmClock variable and one reference for the IAlarm interface. Both of these references must be released before the GC will collect the AlarmClock instance.

Delegates

Delegates are the ultimate function pointer. Developers familiar with C and C++ are very familiar with function pointers and their lack of instance-based knowledge. A delegate can be thought of as a call back mechanism, essentially saying, "Please invoke this method for me when the time is right."

Consider the following scenario: Your department has just hired a new employee. Human Resources needs to be notified when a new employee is hired so they can put them to sleep with endless paper work and boring drivel about company policies and practices. This type of interaction is a perfect example of a delegate. Basically, Human Resources is requesting a notification when a new employee is hired and provides a method to be invoked. Listing 2.1.32 shows the basic use of delegates.

LISTING 2.1.32 Using Delegates

```
1: //File        :part02_31.cs
2: //Author      :Richard L. Weeks
3: //Purpose     :Demonstrate the use of delegates
4:
5: using System;
6:
7: //Define a person struct
8: public struct Person {
9:     public string FName;
10:     public string LName;
11: }
12:
13: //Define a delegate
```

LISTING 2.1.32 Continued

```
14: public delegate void OnNewHire( Person person );
15:
16: //The HR Class
17: public class HR {
18:
19:     //Implement the delegate to be called when a new person is hired
20:     public void OnNewHire( Person person ) {
21:         Console.WriteLine(
➥"HR is in the process of putting {0} to sleep", person.FName );
22:     }
23: }
24:
25: //Create a department
26: public class Department {
27:
28:     //Who to notify
29:     private OnNewHire    m_OnNewHireDelegate = null;
30:
31:     //set the OnNewHire delegate
32:     public void AddOnNewHireDelegate( OnNewHire onh ) {
33:         m_OnNewHireDelegate = onh;
34:     }
35:
36:
37:     public void HirePerson( Person p ) {
38:         //do we need to notify someone?
39:         if( m_OnNewHireDelegate != null )
40:             m_OnNewHireDelegate( p );
41:     }
42: }
43:
44:
45: public class DelegateTest {
46:
47:     public static void Main( ) {
48:
49:         HR hr = new HR( );
50:         Department dept = new Department( );
51:
52:         //Register the OnNewHire Delegate
53:         dept.AddOnNewHireDelegate( new OnNewHire( hr.OnNewHire ) );
54:
55:         //Create a person
56:         Person me; me.FName = "Richard"; me.LName = "Weeks";
```

LISTING 2.1.32   Continued

```
57:
58:           //Hire ME!!!
59:           dept.HirePerson( me );
60:       }
61: }
```

Listing 2.1.32 implements the HR scenario and makes use of a delegate to notify HR when a new person has been hired. The delegate `OnNewHire` is defined on line 14. Notice the use of the `delegate` keyword to denote what is being declared. Remember that C# does not allow for global methods, so C# would issue an error without the `delegate` keyword.

The HR class provides a handler for the delegate. The method name does not have to be the same as the name of the delegate; this was done to make it easier to follow. The `Department` class provides a method `AddOnNewHireDelegate` to handle the "hooking-up" of the delegate with the intended handler. Notice the call on line 53 that actually adds the HR handler to the `Department`. A delegate is a type in C# and requires an instance, hence the use of the new keyword to create a new delegate.

I would encourage any developer to explore delegates in detail because their use in .NET is prolific, especially in Windows Forms development.

Summary

By now you should have an idea of the power and simplicity that C# offers. Interface-based development has been a prominent theme in recent years, and C# delivers on this theme with a simple and consistent model of development. With the addition of instance-based delegates, a powerful subject/observer model is built into the language. The next chapter cover such topics as collections, attributes, and XML support.

Advanced C#

CHAPTER

2.2

IN THIS CHAPTER

.NET Collections

A general problem is the need to deal with several objects at once and to somehow keep track of them. There is never one employee, or one car, or generally one of anything. To this end, .NET provides several generic collections in the System.Collections namespace.

Collections in C# implement the IEnumerable interface. The IEnumerable interface allows for traversal over the elements contained with a given collection. The following collections will be covered in brief: stack, queue, and hashtable. Along with these basic collections, an implementation of a linked list that implements the IEnumerable interface and provides an IEnumerator for the elements is also presented.

For detailed information about generic collections, data structures, and algorithms, I suggest either *Algorithms in C++* by Sedgewick or *The Art of Computer Programming, Volume 3* by Donald Knuth.

Stack

A stack represents a basic FILO, First-in-Last-Out, container. The basic premise of a stack is to push elements onto the top of the stack and to pop elements off the top of the stack. In C#, the System.Collections.Stack (see Listing 2.2.1) also implements the IEnumerable interface, which allows for enumerating the contents of the stack.

LISTING 2.2.1   System.Collections.Stack

```
 1: using System;
 2: using System.Collections;
 3:
 4: public class StackTest {
 5:
 6:     public static void Main( ) {
 7:
 8:         Stack myStack = new Stack( );
 9:
10:         for( int i = 0; i < 10; i++ )
11:             myStack.Push(i);
12:
13:         for( int i = 0; i < 10; i++ )
14:             Console.WriteLine( "{0}", myStack.Pop( ) );
15:
16:
17:         //Refill the stack and use an enumerator to list the elements
18:         for( int i = 0; i < 10; i++ )
19:             myStack.Push(i);
20:
```

LISTING 2.2.1 Continued

```
21:          foreach( int i in myStack )
22:              Console.WriteLine( "{0}", i );
23:      }
24: }
```

The code in Listing 2.2.1 shows the basic use of a stack. Elements are pushed onto the stack
and popped off in reverse order. Stacks are useful for recursive algorithms and can serve as
place holders.

Queue

A queue represents a FIFO, first in first out, collection. Queues provide an `Enqueue` and
`Dequeue` methods to add and remove elements to the queue. As with all .NET collections, the
`Queue` collection also provides an `IEnumerator` interface. Listing 2.2.2 uses the `Queue` provided
by .NET to demonstrate its basic use.

LISTING 2.2.2 Queue

```
 1: using System;
 2: using System.Collections;
 3:
 4: public class QueueTest {
 5:
 6:     public static void Main( ) {
 7:
 8:         Queue myQueue = new Queue( );
 9:
10:         //Fill the queue
11:         for( int i = 0; i < 10; i++ )
12:             myQueue.Enqueue( i );
13:
14:         //Empty the queue
15:         for( int i = 0; i < 10; i++ )
16:             Console.WriteLine( "{0}", myQueue.Dequeue( ) );
17:
18:
19:         //Fill the queue again
20:         for( int i = 0; i < 10; i++ )
21:             myQueue.Enqueue( i );
22:
23:         foreach( int i in myQueue )
24:             Console.WriteLine( "{0}", i );
25:     }
26: }
```

Hashtable

A hashtable is useful when you need to store objects and access them with a given key. The seek time for a hashtable is O(1). Each key is used to generate a hash value that acts as an index for the item. When access to a specific element is required, the hash value of the key is computed and the element is accessed. A hashtable generally trades off memory space for speed and, depending on the use, a hashtable may fit the bill (see Listing 2.2.3).

LISTING 2.2.3   Hashtable

```
 1: using System;
 2: using System.Collections;
 3:
 4: struct Person {
 5:     public Person( string f, string l ) { FName = f; LName = l; }
 6:     public string LName;
 7:     public string FName;
 8: }
 9:
10: public class HashtableTest {
11:
12:     public static void Main( ) {
13:
14:         Hashtable People = new Hashtable( );
15:
16:         //Add some people
17:         People.Add( "Smith", new Person( "Jim", "Smith" ) );
18:         People.Add( "Jones", new Person( "Dawn", "Jones" ) );
19:         People.Add( "Powell", new Person( "Bob", "Powell" ) );
20:
21:         //Locate Jim Smith
22:         Person p = (Person)People["Smith"];
23:         Console.WriteLine("{0} {1}", p.FName, p.LName );
24:     }
25: }
```

It is important to note that a hashtable will not allow for more than one item to share a key value. Doing so will cause the hashtable to throw an `ArgumentException`.

Roll Your Own: Linked List

To drive home the importance of interfaces and the extensibility of the .NET framework, a linked list collection is presented that implements the `IEnumerable` interface and provides an `IEnumerator` object. By providing the necessary interfaces, the `foreach` construct can be used to iterate through the contents of the linked list.

Although the linked list presented in Listing 2.2.4 is not by any means complete, the basic plumbing is in place. As an exercise, you should extend the functionality of the linked list. Example extensions include the ability to provide a method to add items at the end of the list or at any point in the list. It would also be of interest to locate a particular object within the list. (Hint: IComparable interface will come in handy.)

LISTING 2.2.4 Linked List

```
 1: //File           :part02_35.cs
 2: //Author  :Richard L. Weeks
 3: //Purpose :Implement a linked list that supports the IEnumerable interface
 4:
 5:
 6:
 7: using System;
 8: using System.Collections;
 9:
10:
11:
12: public class _node {
13:
14:    public _node    next;
15:    public _node    prev;
16:    public object   value;
17:
18:    public _node( ) { next = prev = null; value = null; }
19:    public _node( object o ) {
20:           value = o;
21:           next = prev = null;
22:    }
23:
24:    public _node( _node n ) {
25:           next = n.next;
26:           prev = n.prev;
27:           value = n.value;
28:    }
29: }
30:
31:
32: //Linked list enumerator
33: public class LinkedListEnumerator : IEnumerator {
34:
35:    private _node m_current = null;
36:    private _node m_begin   = null;
37:    private bool  m_last  = false;
38:
```

LISTING 2.2.4   Continued

```csharp
39:    public LinkedListEnumerator( _node n ) { m_current = m_begin = n; }
40:
41:
42:    //Implement the IEnumerator interface
43:    public object Current {
44:           get { return m_current.value; }
45:           set { m_current.value = value; }
46:    }
47:
48:    public bool MoveNext( ) {
49:           if( m_last )
50:                   return false;
51:           else {
52:                   m_current = m_current.next;
53:                   m_last = m_current == m_begin ? true : false;
54:                   return true;
55:           }
56:    }
57:
58:    public void Reset( ) {
59:           m_current = m_begin;
60:           m_last = false;
61:    }
62: }
63:
64: public class LinkedList : IEnumerable {
65:
66:    private _node  m_root = null;
67:
68:
69:    //Implement the IEnumerable interface method GetEnumerator( )
70:    public IEnumerator GetEnumerator( ) {
71:           return (IEnumerator)new LinkedListEnumerator( m_root.prev );
72:    }
73:
74:
75:    //Implement some basic methods
76:    public void AddHead( object o ) {
77:           _node newNode = new _node( o );
78:           if( m_root == null ) {
79:                   m_root = newNode;
80:                   m_root.next = m_root;
81:                   m_root.prev = m_root;
```

LISTING 2.2.4   Continued

```
82:                } else {
83:                        newNode.next = m_root;
84:                        newNode.prev = m_root.prev;
85:                        m_root.prev.next = newNode;
86:                        m_root.prev = newNode;
87:                        m_root = newNode;
88:                }
89:        }
90: }
91:
92:
93:
94:
95: public class LinkedListTest {
96:
97:     public static void Main( ) {
98:
99:
100:            LinkedList l = new LinkedList( );
101:
102:            for(int i = 0; i < 10; i++ )
103:                    l.AddHead( i );
104:
105:            foreach( int i in l )
106:                    Console.WriteLine( i );
107:    }
108: }
```

The linked list example demonstrates the basic concepts of implementing interfaces and how C# can use those interfaces seamlessly. Because the LinkedList class implements the IEnumerable interface and provides an IEnumerator entity, the foreach statement can be used to iterate through the contents of the linked list.

Attributes

New to .NET is the concept of attributes. *Attributes* are declarative tags that can be applied to various members and methods. That information can then be viewed using the System.Reflection API. The details of reflection are beyond the scope of discussion for our purposes, but the importance of attributes necessitates a brief tour. Listing 2.2.5 demonstrates the use of the Conditional attribute provided by the .NET framework classes.

LISTING 2.2.5 The Conditional Attribute

```
 1: //File        :part02_36.cs
 2: //Author    :Richard L. weeks
 3: //Purpose     :The Conditional attribute
 4: //
 5: //Compile instructions:
 6: // csc /define:DEBUG part02_36.cs
 7: // csc part02_36.cs
 8:
 9: using System;
10: using System.Diagnostics;    //The ConditionalAttribute lives here
11:
12: public class Foo {
13:
14:     [Conditional("DEBUG")]
15:     public void OnlyWhenDebugIsDefined( ) {
16:         Console.WriteLine("DEBUG is defined");
17:     }
18: }
19:
20: public class AttributeTest {
21:     public static void Main( ) {
22:         Foo f = new Foo( );
23:         f.OnlyWhenDebugIsDefined( );
24:     }
25: }
```

The best way to get a quick understanding of attributes is to look at one up close. Listing 2.2.5 makes use of the Conditional attribute. As the name implies, the Conditional attribute is used during conditional compilation. Take a look at line 14. The Conditional attribute is applied to the OnlyWhenDebugIsDefined method. In essence, the OnlyWhenDebugIsDefined will only be available when DEBUG is defined during the compilation process. Notice that line 23 makes a call to the OnlyWhenDebugIsDefined method and yet does not have any conditional markers. This is an added benefit of the Conditional attribute. There is no need to wrap code up in conditional #ifdef types of preprocessor statements.

As a point of interest, methods marked with the Conditional attribute are still included in the compiled assembly. However, all calls to the method are removed. In a final release build, all conditional code should be excluded from the compilation process by making use of #if style preprocessor statements.

.NET makes use of attributes not only for conditional compilation, but also for WebServices, XML, and Windows Services, just to name a few. Attributes are not limited to C#; they can also be found in ATL Server, the next generation of ATL from Microsoft.

Like all aspects of the .NET framework, the ability to create custom attributes exists. All attributes inherit from the System.Attribute base class. Creating and using custom attributes could easily fill a small book, so its exploration is left to you.

XML Serialization

Object serialization has been a major topic in the OO world for a number of years. The ability to persist an object and aggregate objects has never been trivial and often has required the development of specialized code to handle specific cases. The ability to provide a generalized framework for serialization often required objects to take an active role in their persistence.

XML has become an important part of doing business today. With an open standard for B2B communication, the necessity of XML now plays a major role in software development. Because XML defines not only the data but also the metadata, it is well suited for object persistence.

C# XML Serialization Support

C# makes use of attributes to support XML serialization. Attributes exist for defining the root element(s), attributes, and elements within the XML document. There are, of course, some basic requirements to support serialization. Any member of a class or struct that needs to be serialized must be either public or have an assessor property. If a member needs to be deserialized, a corresponding setter property is required. There is also a limitation regarding the serialization of collection classes. Currently, only typed arrays can be serialized and deserialized. This, of course, requires the programmer to provide a property that transforms the collection being used into an array, and from an array into the proper collection.

To define the root element, there is the XmlRootAttribute that can be applied to a class or struct. The XmlRootAttribute constructor takes a string that defines the name of the root element within the XML document. Only the top level element, the root element, requires the XmlRoot attribute. All sub elements only need to define the members that will be persisted.

```
[XmlRoot("purchase-order")]
public class PurchaseOrder {
    //PurchaseOrder members
}
```

The PurchaseOrder class represents the root element for the XML document. Each member within the PurchaseOrder class in Listing 2.2.6 to be serialized will need to be attributed with the XmlElement attribute or XmlAttribute, depending on how the element itself should be persisted.

2.2

ADVANCED C#

LISTING 2.2.6   Using XML Attributes for Serialization

```
1: //File     :PurchaseOrder.cs
2: //Author   :Richard L. Weeks
3: //Purpose :Demonstrate the basics of XML serialization
4: //
5: //Compilation instructions
6: // csc PurchaseOrder.cs /r:System.dll,System.Xml.dll
7:
8:
9: using System;
10: using System.Xml;
11: using System.Xml.Serialization;
12: using System.Collections;
13: using System.IO;
14:
15:
16: ////////////////////////////
17: //Define the Purchase Order
18: [XmlRoot("purchase-order")]
19: public class PurchaseOrder {
20:
21:     //private data
22:     private ArrayList     m_Items;
23:
24:     public PurchaseOrder( ) {
25:         m_Items = new ArrayList();
26:     }
27:
28:     //Properties
29:     [XmlElement("item")]
30:     public Item[] Items {
31:         get {
32:             Item[] items = new Item[ m_Items.Count ];
33:             m_Items.CopyTo( items );
34:             return items;
35:         }
36:         set {
37:             if( value == null ) return;
38:             Item[] items = (Item[])value;
39:             m_Items.Clear();
40:             foreach( Item i in items )
41:                 m_Items.Add( i );
42:         }
43:     }
44:
```

LISTING 2.2.6 Continued

```csharp
45:     //methods
46:     public void AddItem( Item item ) {
47:             m_Items.Add( item );
48:     }
49:
50:     //indexer
51:     public Item this[string sku] {
52:             get {
53:                     //locate the item by sku
54:                     foreach( Item i in m_Items )
55:                             if( i.sku == sku )
56:                                     return i;
57:                     throw( new Exception("Item not found") );
58:             }
59:     }
60:
61:     public void DisplayItems( ) {
62:             foreach( Item i in m_Items )
63:                     Console.WriteLine( i );
64:     }
65:
66: }
67:
68: ////////////////////
69: //Define an item entity
70: public class Item {
71:
72:     //item data
73:     [XmlAttribute("sku")]   public string  sku;
74:     [XmlAttribute("desc")]  public string  desc;
75:     [XmlAttribute("price")] public double  price;
76:     [XmlAttribute("qty")]   public int     qty;
77:
78:
79:     //Default constructor required for XML serialization
80:     public Item( ) {   }
81:
82:     public Item( string Sku, string Desc, double Price, int Qty ) {
83:             sku = Sku;
84:             desc = Desc;
85:             price = Price;
86:             qty = Qty;
87:
88:     }
89:
```

LISTING 2.2.6 Continued

```
90:    public override string ToString( ) {
91:           object[] o = new object[] { sku, desc, price, qty };
92:           return string.Format("{0,-5} {1,-10} ${2,5:#,###.00} {3,3}", o);
93:    }
94: }
95:
96:
97:
98:
99: ///
100: ///Test the XML Serialization and Deserialization
101: //
102: public class POExample {
103:
104:
105:    public static void Main( ) {
106:
107:           PurchaseOrder po = new PurchaseOrder( );
108:
109:           po.AddItem( new Item("123","pencil",.15,100) );
110:           po.AddItem( new Item("321","copy paper", 7.50, 25) );
111:           po.AddItem( new Item("111","white out", 1.35, 10) );
112:
113:           po.DisplayItems( );
114:           Console.WriteLine("Serialization in progress");
115:           //Serialize the Current Purchase Order
116:           XmlSerializer s = new XmlSerializer( typeof( PurchaseOrder ) );
117:           TextWriter w = new StreamWriter("po.xml");
118:           s.Serialize( w, po );
119:           w.Close();
120:           Console.WriteLine("Serialization complete\n\n");
121:
122:           Console.WriteLine("Deserialization in progress");
123:           //Deserialize to a new PO
124:           PurchaseOrder po2;// = new PurchaseOrder( );
125:           TextReader r = new StreamReader( "po.xml" );
126:           po2 = (PurchaseOrder)s.Deserialize( r );
127:           r.Close( );
128:           Console.WriteLine("Deserialization complete");
129:           po2.DisplayItems();
130:    }
131:
132: }
```

Listing 2.2.6 puts the C# XML serialization support to work. Again, the PurchaseOrder class represents the top level element for the XML document. The PurchaseOrder class contains an ArrayList to contain the added items. Because there is currently no support for serializing container classes, it is necessary to provide a property that transforms the ArrayList into an array and vise-versa. Line 27 defines an XmlElement for item. The property is implemented such that the ArrayList is converted to any array of type Item[]. This allows for the XML serialization implemented by the XmlSerializer to persist the items.

To deserialize an object, the class or struct must provide a default constructor. In the case of the Item class, because we've defined a parameter-based constructor, there also needs to be a default constructor without parameters so that the object can be created dynamically at run-time. The override ToString method of the Item class plays no role in the XML serialization. Its existence is only to allow for output to the Console stream.

To serialize the PurchaseOrder, an instance is created and items are added to it. Next is the creation of an instance of the XmlSerializer object. The XmlSerializer supports several constructors that allow for extra XML element information—the default namespace and the root element name. For this example, only the object type is passed in.

For those of you familiar ith COM serialization, the notion of a stream should not be a foreign concept. A *stream* allows for a generalized view of persistence storage. This notion allows the stream to be connected to a database, file system, or even a network socket.

When the PurchaseOrder sample is executed, the following XML is the result of the serialization.

```xml
<?xml version="1.0" encoding="utf-8"?>
<purchase-order xmlns:xsi="http://www.w3.org/2001/XMLSchema-instance"
xmlns:xsd="http://www.w3.org/2001/XMLSchema">
  <item sku="123" desc="pencil" price="0.15" qty="100" />
  <item sku="321" desc="copy paper" price="7.5" qty="25" />
  <item sku="111" desc="white out" price="1.35" qty="10" />
</purchase-order>
```

The process of deserialization works in basically the same way. The XmlSerializer makes use of the Reflection API to construct the necessary objects and assign the attributes and elements to those items.

Now for something a bit more interesting, instead of the standard boring serialization of objects, we will create a Finite State Machine from an XML representation. Based on the states and productions that are defined for the machine, we can then enter a token string for processing. Figure 2.2.1 depicts a small FSM that will be represented in code using the XML Serialization support provided by .NET.

2.2

ADVANCED C#

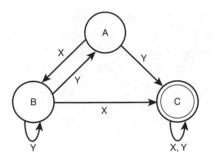

FIGURE 2.2.1

3 State FSM.

The XML description for the State Machine in Figure 2.2.1 is as follows:

```xml
<?xml version="1.0"?>
<fsm
➥xmlns:xsi="http://www.w3.org/1999/XMLSchema-instance"
➥xmlns:xsd="http://www.w3.org/1999/XMLSchema" state_count="3">
  <state name="a" is_start="true" is_final="false" production_count="2">
    <production token="x" state="b"/>
    <production token="y" state="c"/>
  </state>
  <state name="b" is_start="false" is_final="false" production_count="2">
    <production token="x" state="c"/>
    <production token="y" state="b"/>
  </state>
  <state name="c" is_start="false" is_final="true" production_count="2">
    <production token="x" state="c"/>
    <production token="y" state="c"/>
  </state>
</fsm>
```

The root element `fsm` defines the `FiniteStateMachine` to be deserialized. The `fsm` contains various states, and each state contains the productions that it supports.

The code to process the State Machine has been kept to a minimum to demonstrate the capability of XML serialization. When the sample code is executed, it will prompt the user for a token string to process. For example, the token string xyxyxxy results in a valid string, where as the token string xyxy does not. Only token strings that terminate within the final state are considered valid. Listing 2.2.7 implements the FSM depicted in Figure 2.2.1.

LISTING 2.2.7 Implementing an FSM with XML Serialization

```
 1: //////////////////////////////////////////////
 2: //File     :part02_38.cs
 3: //Author   :Richard L. Weeks
 4: //Purpose :Make use of XML Serialization to implement
 5: //           a finite state machine
 6: //
 7: //
 8: //
 9:
10: using System;
11: using System.Xml;
12: using System.Xml.Serialization;
13: using System.IO;
14:
15:
16: ///////////////////////////////
17: //The FSM class
18: [XmlRoot("fsm")]
19: public class FSM {
20:
21:     //data members
22:     private int m_StateCount;
23:
24:     [XmlAttribute("state_count")]
25:     public int StateCount {
26:         get { return m_StateCount; }
27:         set {
28:       m_StateCount = value;
29:       States = new State[m_StateCount];
30:         }
31:     }
32:
33:     [XmlElement("state")]
34:     public State[] States = null;
35:
36:
37:     public bool ProcessString( string s ) {
38:
39:        State CurrentState = GetStartState( );
40:        Console.WriteLine("Start state is {0}",CurrentState.Name);
41:        //Process the token string
```

LISTING 2.2.7   Continued

```
42:          for( int i = 0; i < s.Length; i++ ) {
43:            string next_state =
➥CurrentState.ProcessToken( string.Format("{0}",s[i]) );
44:            if( next_state != "" )
45:             CurrentState = GetState( next_state );
46:            else {
47:                        Console.WriteLine(
➥"No production from {0} with token {1}",
➥CurrentState.Name, s[i]);
48:                  return false;
49:                }
50:            Console.WriteLine(
➥"Current State => {0}", CurrentState.Name );
51:              }
52:
53:        return CurrentState.IsFinal;
54:      }
55:
56:      private State GetState( string state_name ) {
57:        //Locate the state name
58:        for( int i = 0; i < States.Length; i++ )
59:            if( States[i].Name == state_name )
60:                return States[i];
61:        return null;
62:      }
63:
64:      private State GetStartState( ) {
65:        for( int i = 0; i < States.Length; i++ )
66:            if( States[i].IsStart )
67:                return States[i];
68:        return null;
69:      }
70: }
71:
72: ////////////////////////////
73: //State class
74: [XmlRoot("state")]
75: public class State {
76:
77:     private string        m_Name;
78:     private bool          m_IsStart;
79:     private bool          m_IsFinal;
80:     private int         m_ProductionCount;
81:
82:
83:     [XmlAttribute("name")]
```

LISTING 2.2.7 Continued

```
84:     public string Name {
85:         get { return m_Name; }
86:         set { m_Name = value; }
87:     }
88:
89:     [XmlAttribute("is_start")]
90:     public bool IsStart {
91:         get { return m_IsStart; }
92:         set { m_IsStart = value; }
93:     }
94:
95:     [XmlAttribute("is_final")]
96:     public bool IsFinal {
97:         get { return m_IsFinal; }
98:         set { m_IsFinal = value; }
99:     }
100:
101:     [XmlAttribute("production_count")]
102:     public int ProductionCount {
103:         get { return m_ProductionCount; }
104:         set {
105:             Productions = new Production[value];
106:             m_ProductionCount = value;
107:         }
108:     }
109:
110:     [XmlElement("production")]
111:     public Production[] Productions = null;
112:
113:
114:     public string ProcessToken( string token ) {
115:         //loop through the productions and
➥return the name of the next state
116:         for( int i = 0;
➥i < Productions.Length; i++ ) {
117:             Console.WriteLine("State {0} is evaluating token {1}",
➥m_Name, token );
118:             Console.WriteLine("Testing Production {0} : {1}",
➥Productions[i].token, Productions[i].state);
119:             if( Productions[i].token == token )
120:                 return Productions[i].state;
121:             }
122:         return "";
123:     }
124:
125: }
```

LISTING 2.2.7   Continued

```
126:
127: /////////////////////////////
128: //Production struct
129: [XmlRoot("production")]
130: public struct Production {
131:
132:     [XmlAttribute("token")]
133:     public string token;
134:
135:     [XmlAttribute("state")]
136:     public string state;
137: }
138:
139:
140:
141:
142: public class FiniteStateMachine {
143:
144:     public static void Main( ) {
145:
146:         //Deserialize the FSM from the xml file
147:         XmlSerializer s = new XmlSerializer( typeof( FSM ) );
148:         TextReader tr = new StreamReader( "fsm.xml" );
149:         FSM fsm = (FSM)s.Deserialize( tr );
150:         tr.Close( );
151:
152:         //Get the token string to process
153:         Console.Write("Enter token string to process: ");
154:         string tokens = Console.ReadLine( );
155:         string result = fsm.ProcessString( tokens ) ? "valid" : "invalid";
156:
157:         Console.WriteLine("The token string {0} is {1}", tokens, result );
158:
159:     }
160: }
```

Summary

In this section, we've explored various aspects of C# and the .NET framework. Microsoft has put considerable resources and effort into making the .NET platform language agnostic and extremely extensible. The shear size of the .NET framework seems overwhelming at first glance, but peeling back the layers piece by piece allows for a thorough understanding of what .NET has to offer.

Windows Forms

IN THIS PART

Introduction to Windows Forms

IN THIS CHAPTER

Windows Forms is the .NET replacement for MFC. Unlike the MFC library, which was a thin(ish) wrapper on the Win32 API, Windows Forms is a totally object-oriented, hierarchical answer to Windows development under .NET.

Despite its "Forms" epithet, the layout of components is not done with a resource file as is the case in MFC dialogs and form windows. Every component is a concrete instance of a class. Placement of the components and control of their properties are accomplished by programming them via their methods and accessors. The drag-and-drop tools used to define a Windows Form are actually maintaining the source code that initializes, places, and allows interaction with a target application.

Resource files are used by Windows Forms for tasks such as placing images on the form or storing localized text, but not in the familiar format that has been used by Windows since the 1980s. As you might expect, the new resource file format is an XML file. We'll examine resources in more detail in Chapter 3.4, "Windows Forms Example Application (Scribble .NET)."

Windows Forms layout can be done by dragging components from a tool palette onto a form. You can use VS.NET for this or alternatively, if you really want the whole hands-on experience, you can lay out your forms by coding the objects directly in C#, VB, managed C++, or any of the .NET languages. To give you the benefit of understanding what really goes on in a Windows Form, we won't be dealing with any of the design tools early in this section. Rather, we will do as much as possible by hand and then, when you understand the basics, move on to using the drag-and-drop tools.

User interaction in Windows Forms is accomplished through events. The components provide event sources, such as mouse movement, position, and button clicks, and then you wire the events to handlers. These are functions called by a standard form of delegate, which means there are no message maps of which to keep track.

The Hello Windows Forms Application

Listing 3.1.1 is a simple Windows Forms application that displays the text "Hello Windows Forms!" in a label on the main form.

LISTING 3.1.1 HWF.cs: The Hello Windows Forms Application

```
// HWF.cs
namespace HelloWindowsFormsNamespace {

    using System;
    using System.Drawing;
    using System.ComponentModel;
    using System.WinForms;
```

LISTING 3.1.1   Continued

```
public class HelloWindowsForms : System.WinForms.Form
{
    //Label 1 displays the text message "Hello Windows Forms!"
    private System.WinForms.Label label1;

    //The constructor is where all initialization happens.
    //Forms created with the designer have an InitializeComponent() method.
    public HelloWindowsForms()
    {

        this.label1 = new System.WinForms.Label();

        label1.Location = new System.Drawing.Point(8, 8);
        label1.Text = "Hello Windows Forms!";
        label1.Size = new System.Drawing.Size(408, 48);
        label1.Font = new System.Drawing.Font("Microsoft Sans Serif", 24f);
        label1.TabIndex = 0;
        label1.TextAlign = System.WinForms.HorizontalAlignment.Center;

        this.Text = "Hello World";
        this.MaximizeBox = false;
        this.AutoScaleBaseSize = new System.Drawing.Size(5, 13);
        this.BorderStyle = System.WinForms.FormBorderStyle.FixedDialog;
        this.MinimizeBox = false;
        this.ClientSize = new System.Drawing.Size(426, 55);
        this.Controls.Add(label1);
    }

    // This main function instantiates a new form and runs it.
    public static void Main(string[] args)
    {
        Application.Run(new HelloWindowsForms());
    }
}

} // end of namespace
```

You can see that the class HelloWindowsForms contains a simple label component, label1. It has only two methods: a static Main method that creates and runs an instance of the HelloWindowsForms class and a constructor in which all of the component initialization occurs.

This shows the minimum functionality and minimum complication of the Windows Forms system. Programs designed and maintained by VS.NET or WinDes.exe have some added functions and data members that detract from the simplicity of this example, but are necessary for the RAD environments to keep track of the form design.

To build the executable, we have prepared a small batch file that creates a Windows executable and references all the correct library DLLs. Using this batch file will allow you to stay away from the Visual Studio build environment for a while—because it hides too much of the important information—and concentrate on the actual functionality. Listing 3.1.2 shows build.bat.

LISTING 3.1.2 build.bat

```
csc /t:winexe /r:Microsoft.win32.Interop.dll, system.dll,
➥system.configuration.dll, system.data.dll,
➥system.diagnostics.dll, system.drawing.dll,
➥ system.winforms.dll /out:%1.exe %1.cs
➥ %2 %3 %4 %5 %6 %7 %8 %9
```

build.bat is available with the software that accompanies this book, but if you want to type it in yourself, make sure that it's all on the same line and there are no spaces between the libraries named in the /r: reference directive. To use build.bat, simply type **build** followed by the name of the .cs file to compile. For example

```
build HWF
```

will compile the HWF.cs file and create HWF.exe.

Running the hwf.exe program will produce a form shown in Figure 3.1.1.

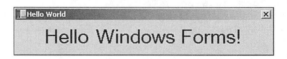

FIGURE 3.1.1
The Hello Windows Forms Application.

Creating and Using an Event Handler

If you're familiar with Windows C development, you will understand the idea of handling messages as they arrive by the action of the WndProc switch statement. If you have been working with MFC, you will know that messages are routed through the message map of your application. Under .NET the message routing system is provided by delegates. Your application will define event handlers that are called through a delegate whenever a message arrives. Button clicks for example, can be handled by using a generic EventHandler delegate. Other types of events, such as mouse events or timer events, are serviced through specific handlers that have their own delegate signatures.

Adding a button to the Windows Forms application is simple. You can add a button member to the class, initialize it in the constructor, and place it in the controls collection.

When this is done, you can wire up an event that is trapped whenever the button is clicked. Events sent through the system are hooked to event handlers of a specific signature by a multi-cast delegate that is declared especially for this purpose. Your event handlers must all have the following method signature:

```
void EventMethodName(Object sender, EventArgs e);
```

Event handlers are added to the control's event sources with the += operator and removed with the -= operator, so events can be modified dynamically at runtime. Because events are multi-cast, you can add more than one handler at a time to the same event.

Listing 3.1.3 shows the modified file HWFButton.cs.

LISTING 3.1.3   HWFButton.cs: Hello Windows Forms with a Simple Button Handler

```
// HWFButton.cs
namespace HelloWindowsFormsNamespace {

    using System;
    using System.Drawing;
    using System.ComponentModel;
    using System.WinForms;

public class HelloWindowsForms : System.WinForms.Form
{

    //Label 1 displays the text message "Hello Windows Forms!"
    private System.WinForms.Label label1;

    //Adding a button member allows us to place a button on the panel.
    private System.WinForms.Button button1;

    //The constructor is where all initialization happens.
    //Forms created with the designer have an InitializeComponent() method.
    public HelloWindowsForms()
    {

        this.label1 = new System.WinForms.Label();

        label1.Location = new System.Drawing.Point(8, 8);
        label1.Text = "Hello Windows Forms!";
        label1.Size = new System.Drawing.Size(408, 48);
```

LISTING 3.1.3 Continued

```
        label1.Font = new System.Drawing.Font("Microsoft Sans Serif", 24f);
        label1.TabIndex = 0;
        label1.TextAlign = System.WinForms.HorizontalAlignment.Center;

    this.button1=new System.WinForms.Button();

    button1.Location=new System.Drawing.Point(8,58);
    button1.Size = new System.Drawing.Size(408,25);
    button1.Text = "Click Me!";
    button1.TabIndex = 1;
    button1.Click += new EventHandler(OnButton1Clicked);

        this.Text = "Hello World";
        this.MaximizeBox = false;
        this.AutoScaleBaseSize = new System.Drawing.Size(5, 13);
        this.BorderStyle = System.WinForms.FormBorderStyle.FixedDialog;
        this.MinimizeBox = false;
        this.ClientSize = new System.Drawing.Size(426, 85);

        this.Controls.Add(label1);
    this.Controls.Add(button1);
    }

    void OnButton1Clicked(Object sender,EventArgs e)
    {
    if(this.label1.Text == "Hello Windows Forms!")
        this.label1.Text = "You Clicked?";
    else
        this.label1.Text = "Hello Windows Forms!";
    }


    // This main function instantiates a new form and runs it.
    public static void Main(string[] args)
    {
            Application.Run(new HelloWindowsForms());
    }
}

} // end of namespace
```

Type in Listing 3.1.3 and build it with the build batch file. Running the sample will show a
window that has the same message and a clickable button. The button handler simply swaps
the text in the label control to verify that the handler worked.

> **NOTE**
>
> Note that the code in Listing 3.1.3 uses the fully qualified name for the components and methods:
>
>   button1.Size = new System.Drawing.Size(408,25);
>
> This longhand form is not always necessary. You could abbreviate the line above to
>
>   button1.Size = new Size(408,25);
>
> Layout tools will always give you the longhand version because they never get tired of typing.
>
> Generally, if the object you're creating is in a namespace you declared you were using, you can use the shorthand.

When you run the file, you will see the application shown in Figure 3.1.2.

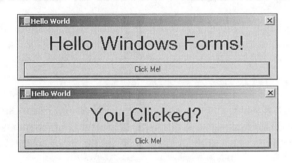

FIGURE 3.1.2
Using a simple Click Handler.

Defining the Border Style of the Form

The previous examples are both simple, fixed-size forms that have no minimize or restore button. The border style of the form object controls how a form is shown and if it can be resized.

Listing 3.1.4 shows a very simple Windows Forms application with a sizable client area.

LISTING 3.1.4   `resize.cs`: A Simple Resizable Windows Forms Application

```
using System;
using System.Drawing;
using System.ComponentModel;
using System.WinForms;
```

LISTING 3.1.4 Continued

```
public class SizeApp : System.WinForms.Form
{

    public      SizeApp()
    {
        this.Text = "SizeApp";
        this.MaximizeBox = true;
        this.BorderStyle = FormBorderStyle.Sizable;
    }

    static void Main()
    {
        Application.Run(new SizeApp());
    }

}
```

Building and running this application will result in a resizable application that can also be min-imized to the taskbar and restored in the normal way.

Adding a Menu

A Windows application without a menu is a rare thing. A Windows Forms application is no exception. Like the button and label you saw earlier, the menu component can be added to the Menu member of the main application, and events from the menu items can be hooked to han-dlers.

Menus under .NET come in two forms. MainMenu is applied to a form to provide the main user interface menu, and ContextMenu is used to respond to right mouse clicks. In both cases, the individual items within the menus are objects of type MenuItem. A menu is constructed as a hierarchy of parent and child objects. The main menu owns the individual drop-downs, which in turn own their menu items.

A typical menu creation sequence is seen in Listing 3.1.5.

LISTING 3.1.5 Constructing a Menu

```
MainMenu menu = new MainMenu();

    MenuItem filemenu = new MenuItem();
    filemenu.Text = "File";
    menu.MenuItems.Add(filemenu);
        MenuItem open = new MenuItem();
        open.Text = "Open";
        filemenu.MenuItems.Add(open);
```

LISTING 3.1.5   Continued

```
        MenuItem save= new MenuItem();
        save.Text = "Save";
        filemenu.MenuItems.Add(save);

        MenuItem exit= new MenuItem();
        exit.Text = "Exit";
        filemenu.MenuItems.Add(exit);

        MenuItem editmenu = new MenuItem();
        editmenu.Text = "Edit";
    menu.MenuItems.Add(editmenu);

        MenuItem cut= new MenuItem();
        cut.Text = "Cut";
        editmenu.MenuItems.Add(cut);

        MenuItem copy = new MenuItem();
        copy.Text = "Copy";
        editmenu.MenuItems.Add(copy);

        MenuItem paste = new MenuItem();
        paste.Text = "Paste";
        editmenu.MenuItems.Add(paste);

this.Menu = menu;
```

The indentation in Listing 3.1.5 illustrates the hierarchy of the menus.

Figure 3.1.3 shows a simple resizable application with a menu added.

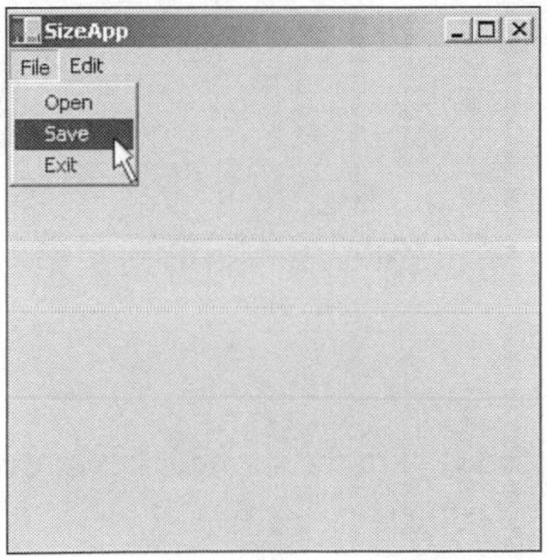

FIGURE 3.1.3

A simple resizable application with a menu.

Adding a Menu Shortcut

Placing an ampersand before a character in the menu text will automatically give the menu item an underscore when the Alt key is pressed. The key combination of Alt+F followed by O can be used to invoke the menu handler as if the menu were selected with the mouse.

A direct key combination might also be added to the menu item by using one of the predefined Shortcut enumerations. The File, Open menu item handler can be made to fire in response to a Ctrl+O keypress by adding the shortcut, as shown in Listing 3.1.6.

LISTING 3.1.6   Adding a Shortcut to the File, Open MenuItem

```
MenuItem filemenu = new MenuItem();
filemenu.Text = "&File";
menu.MenuItems.Add(filemenu);
    MenuItem open = new MenuItem();
    open.Text = "&Open";
    filemenu.MenuItems.Add(open);
    open.Shortcut = Shortcut.CtrlO;
    open.ShowShortcut = true;
```

When you press the Alt key, the F in the File menu is underlined. You can press **F** to pop up the menu and press **O** to invoke the menu's function, as shown in Figure 3.1.4.

FIGURE 3.1.4
Menu shortcuts in action.

Note how the Open menu is appended with the shortcut key press combination Ctrl+O by the MenuItem.ShowShortcut property setting.

Handling Events from Menus

There are several events that you can handle from a `MenuItem`. The most important is the one that you defined the item for in the first place. Remember from our button click example earlier that the events are hooked to the `Click` event source by a delegate defined by the system. In Listing 3.1.7, a handler that pops up a message box is defined and added to the methods of the `SizeApp` class.

LISTING 3.1.7   A Simple Event Handler

```
public class SizeApp : System.WinForms.Form
{

    public void OnFileOpen(Object sender, EventArgs e)
    {
        MessageBox.Show("You selected File-Open!");
    }
}
```

The event handler has the standard method signature for events `void_function(Object, EventArgs)` and can be added to the File, Open `MenuItem`'s `Click` event source like this:

```
open.Click += new EventHandler(OnFileOpen);
```

This line is added to the menu setup code after the shortcut initialization.

Whenever the menu item is selected with the mouse, the Alt+F+O key sequence, or the Ctrl+O shortcut, the menu handler will fire and the message box will pop up.

The complete C# file for the modified `resize.cs` program is available as `resize2.cs` on this book's Web site. You can find this at `http://www.samspublishing.com/`. Type in the ISBN **067232153X** for this book.

User Interface Control Events for `MenuItems`

Other events are fired by `MenuItems` to enable you to give better feedback to the user or to customize the user experience. MFC had the `CCmdUI` class for this purpose. Windows Forms provides the `Popup` event source.

Just before a `MenuItem` is shown, the `Popup` event is fired to give you time to decide whether to show, check, or change the appearance of a menu item. You can trap this event by adding an event handler to the `Popup` event source:

```
filemenu.Popup += new EventHandler(OnPopupFilemenu);
```

The handler for this event is defined in Listing 3.1.8. It shows some of the standard things you can do, checking, enabling, hiding, and so on, with MenuItems. The class has a Boolean variable called m_bPopupChecked. Every time the File menu is expanded, the program toggles this variable to true or false depending on its previous state. The Sender object is known to be a MenuItem, so it's possible to cast to that type safely. The three menu entries in the File menu are then checked, disabled, or hidden entirely, depending on the state of the variable. The image (seen in Figure 3.1.5) shows the menus in their two states.

LISTING 3.1.8 The Popup Event Handler

```
bool m_bPopupChecked;

public void OnPopupFilemenu(Object Sender, EventArgs e)
{
    // this handler illustrates the Popup event and the MenuItem UI properties.
    m_bPopupChecked = !m_bPopupChecked;
    MenuItem item = (MenuItem)Sender;
    item.MenuItems[0].Checked = m_bPopupChecked;
    item.MenuItems[1].Enabled = m_bPopupChecked;
    item.MenuItems[2].Visible = m_bPopupChecked;
}
```

FIGURE 3.1.5
The menu after the Popup *event.*

Defining a MenuItem as a Separator

Very often a group of menu entries will be strongly associated with one another, or one menu item will be separated from another by strategic placement of a menu separator. Under Windows Forms the menu separator is a menu item that does nothing but draw a line across the menu. This is very simple; just set the text of a menu item to a single dash:

```
MenuItem dummymenu = new MenuItem();
dummymenu.Text = "Separator";
menu.MenuItems.Add(dummymenu);
    dummymenu.MenuItems.Add(new MenuItem("Above"));
    dummymenu.MenuItems.Add(new MenuItem("-"));
    dummymenu.MenuItems.Add(new MenuItem("Below"));
```

Handling the `Select` Event

Once a menu item has been popped up, all of its visible members can be selected by positioning the mouse over them or using the arrows keys. When this selection takes place, an event is fired. The event source for this is called `Select`, and it is handled in much the same way as the `Popup` event.

The `Select` event is used primarily to update a status bar or other control with a help string that explains an otherwise cryptic menu entry. It could also be used for other user-interface customization.

The demonstration in Listing 3.1.9 uses the `Select` event to display a string in a label control on the client area.

LISTING 3.1.9   menus.cs: Handling the `Select` Event

```
using System;
using System.Drawing;
using System.ComponentModel;
using System.WinForms;


public class menuapp : System.WinForms.Form
{

    Label label;

    void ShowInfo(Object Sender,EventArgs e)
    {
        MenuItem item=(MenuItem)Sender;
        switch(item.Text)
        {
            case "&Open":
                label.Text = "Open a file from disk";
            break;
            case "&Save":
                label.Text = "Save a file onto disk";
            break;
```

LISTING 3.1.9 Continued

```csharp
                    case "E&xit":
                        label.Text = "Exit MenuApp";
                    break;
            }
        }

        public  menuapp()
        {
            this.Text = "MenuApp";
            this.MaximizeBox = true;
            this.BorderStyle = FormBorderStyle.Sizable;

            this.label = new Label();
            label.Location = new Point(8,100);
            label.Size = new Size(200,25);

            this.Controls.Add(label);

            MainMenu menu = new MainMenu();

            MenuItem filemenu = new MenuItem();
            filemenu.Text = "&File";
            menu.MenuItems.Add(filemenu);

                MenuItem open = new MenuItem();
                open.Text = "&Open";
                open.Select += new EventHandler(ShowInfo);
                filemenu.MenuItems.Add(open);

                MenuItem save= new MenuItem();
                save.Text = "&Save";
                save.Select += new EventHandler(ShowInfo);
                filemenu.MenuItems.Add(save);

                MenuItem exit= new MenuItem();
                exit.Text = "E&xit";
                exit.Select += new EventHandler(ShowInfo);
                filemenu.MenuItems.Add(exit);

            this.Menu = menu;

        }

        static void Main()
```

LISTING 3.1.9 Continued

```
{
    Application.Run(new menuapp());
}

}
```

Figure 3.1.6 shows the `menus.cs` program in action.

FIGURE 3.1.6
The Select *event handler in action.*

Menu Layout

Menus are built up from `MenuItem` components. These can be arranged across the screen on the menu bar, and are most often arranged vertically in drop-down menus. You can change the default layout of `MenuItems` to give a different UI style.

The `Break` and `BarBreak` methods are used to create menus that are arranged horizontally rather than vertically. Setting the `BarBreak` property in a `MenuItem` causes the item to be drawn in a new column. `BarBreak` adds a vertical separator bar to the menu between the columns. `Break` makes a new column but doesn't add the vertical bar. The modifications to the `menus.cs` code on lines 14 and 20 in the following result in the change seen in Figure 3.1.7.

```
1:      MenuItem filemenu = new MenuItem();
2:      filemenu.Text = "&File";
3:      menu.MenuItems.Add(filemenu);
4:
5:          MenuItem open = new MenuItem();
6:          open.Text = "&Open";
7:          open.Select += new EventHandler(ShowInfo);
8:          filemenu.MenuItems.Add(open);
```

```
 9:
10:          MenuItem save= new MenuItem();
11:          save.Text = "&Save";
12:          save.Select += new EventHandler(ShowInfo);
13:          filemenu.MenuItems.Add(save);
14:          save.BarBreak=true;
15:
16:          MenuItem exit= new MenuItem();
17:          exit.Text = "E&xit";
18:          exit.Select += new EventHandler(ShowInfo);
19:          filemenu.MenuItems.Add(exit);
20:          exit.Break=true;
21:
```

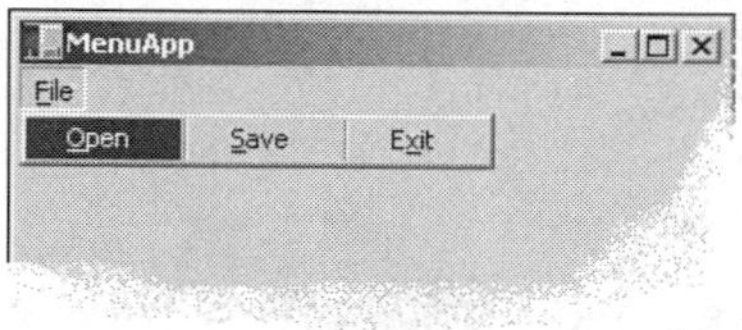

FIGURE 3.1.7

The BarBreak *property.*

Similarly, the code changes to lines 14 and 20 in the following result in the menu style shown in Figure 3.1.8.

```
 1:     MenuItem filemenu = new MenuItem();
 2:     filemenu.Text = "&File";
 3:     menu.MenuItems.Add(filemenu);
 4:
 5:          MenuItem open = new MenuItem();
 6:          open.Text = "&Open";
 7:          open.Select += new EventHandler(ShowInfo);
 8:          filemenu.MenuItems.Add(open);
 9:
10:          MenuItem save= new MenuItem();
11:          save.Text = "&Save";
12:          save.Select += new EventHandler(ShowInfo);
13:          filemenu.MenuItems.Add(save);
14:          //save.BarBreak=true;
15:
16:          MenuItem exit= new MenuItem();
17:          exit.Text = "E&xit";
18:          exit.Select += new EventHandler(ShowInfo);
19:          filemenu.MenuItems.Add(exit);
20:          exit.Break=true;
21:
```

FIGURE 3.1.8
The Break *Property in use.*

Each time you set the Break property, the MenuItem is placed in a new column.

Right-to-Left Menus

To cater to cultures that read right-to-left or to add an unconventional style to your menus, you can modify the menu's RightToLeft property.

```
1: MainMenu menu = new MainMenu();
2: menu.RightToLeft=RightToLeft.Yes;
3: MenuItem filemenu = new MenuItem();
4: filemenu.Text = "&File";
```

Adding line 2 to resize.cs results in the effect seen in Figure 3.1.9.

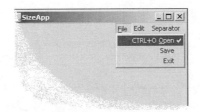

FIGURE 3.1.9
Right-to-left reading menus.

Creating and Using a Context Menu

A context menu is a floating menu that can pop up wherever it's needed for selections in a particular editing or user interface context. The convention is for the context menu to appear in response to a right-mouse button click.

Windows Forms follows this convention. The application has a ContextMenu property that, like its MainMenu counterpart, is available from the top-level application form.

Adding, showing, or modifying the appearance of a context menu and specifying its handler are largely the same as the main menu. The following adds a context menu with three items to the main window of the resize.cs form:

```
ContextMenu cmenu = new ContextMenu();
cmenu.MenuItems.Add(new MenuItem("&First"));
cmenu.MenuItems.Add(new MenuItem("&Second"));
cmenu.MenuItems.Add(new MenuItem("-"));
cmenu.MenuItems.Add(new MenuItem("&Third"));
this.ContextMenu=cmenu;
```

A simple right mouse click will bring up the context menu.

Replacing, Cloning, and Merging Menus

A common practice in Windows applications is to change menus according to the data displayed in the client window. To save you from having to create and destroy menus on-the-fly, .NET allows you to swap out menus and create new ones by merging one or more predefined menu hierarchies.

Listing 3.1.10 shows a simple application that constructs several menus and then combines them in different ways according to selections made by the user.

LISTING 3.1.10   `menuswop.cs`: Manipulating, Cloning, and Merging Menus

```
 1: using System;
 2: using System.Drawing;
 3: using System.ComponentModel;
 4: using System.WinForms;
 5:
 6: namespace Sams {
 7:
 8: class menuswop : System.WinForms.Form
 9: {
10:     MainMenu m_menu;
11:     MenuItem m_editmenu,m_menumenu,m_switchitem,m_showsecond,m_merge;
12:     MenuItem m_playmenu;
13:
14:     bool m_bswop;
15:     bool m_bshowsecond;
16:     bool m_bmerge;
17:
18:     // private helper function for the BuildMenu function.
19:     void addmenuitem(MenuItem menu, string s)
20:     {
21:         MenuItem temp=new MenuItem(s);
22:         temp.Enabled= false;
23:         menu.MenuItems.Add(temp);
24:     }
25:
```

LISTING 3.1.10 Continued

```
26:     // This builds a menu structure from copies
27:     // of the originals using CloneMenu.
28:     void BuildMenu()
29:     {
30:         m_menu=new MainMenu();
31:         m_menu.MenuItems.Add(m_menumenu.CloneMenu());
32:
33:         if(m_bmerge) // when we merge...
34:         {
35:             MenuItem temp=new MenuItem();
36:
37:             if(!m_bswop)
38:             {
39:                 addmenuitem(temp,"Edit");
40:                 temp.MergeMenu(m_editmenu.CloneMenu());
41:             }
42:             else
43:             {
44:                 addmenuitem(temp,"Play");
45:                 temp.MergeMenu(m_playmenu.CloneMenu());
46:             }
47:
48:             temp.MenuItems.Add(new MenuItem("-"));
49:
50:             if(m_bshowsecond)
51:             {
52:                 if(!m_bswop)
53:                 {
54:                     addmenuitem(temp,"Play");
55:                     temp.MergeMenu(m_playmenu.CloneMenu());
56:                 }
57:                 else
58:                 {
59:                     addmenuitem(temp,"Edit");
60:                     temp.MergeMenu(m_editmenu.CloneMenu());
61:                 }
62:             }
63:
64:             temp.Text = "&Merged";
65:             m_menu.MenuItems.Add(temp);
66:
67:         }
68:         else // when we dont merge...
69:         {
```

Listing 3.1.10   Continued

```
70:                if(!m_bswop)
71:                {
72:                    if(m_bshowsecond)
73:                    {
74:                        m_menu.MenuItems.Add(m_editmenu.CloneMenu());
75:                    }
76:                    m_menu.MenuItems.Add(m_playmenu.CloneMenu());
77:                }
78:                else
79:                {
80:                    if(m_bshowsecond)
81:                    {
82:                        m_menu.MenuItems.Add(m_playmenu.CloneMenu());
83:                    }
84:                    m_menu.MenuItems.Add(m_editmenu.CloneMenu());
85:                }
86:            }
87:
88:        this.Menu = m_menu;
89:    }
90:
91:    //This method sets or resets the checks on menu items
92:    //note how the MenuItem collection is accessible as an array.
93:    void PopupMenuMenu(Object sender, EventArgs e)
94:    {
95:        m_menu.MenuItems[0].MenuItems[0].Checked = m_bswop;
96:        m_menu.MenuItems[0].MenuItems[1].Checked = m_bshowsecond;
97:        m_menu.MenuItems[0].MenuItems[2].Checked = m_bmerge;
98:    }
99:
100:    // The event handler for the switch menu entry
101:    void OnSwitchMenu(Object sender, EventArgs e)
102:    {
103:        m_bswop = !m_bswop;
104:        BuildMenu();
105:    }
106:
107:    //The event handler for the show menu entry
108:    void Onshowsecond(Object sender, EventArgs e)
109:    {
110:        m_bshowsecond = !m_bshowsecond;
111:        BuildMenu();
112:    }
113:
```

LISTING 3.1.10   Continued

```
114:      //The event handler for the merge menu entry
115:      void OnMerge(Object sender, EventArgs e)
116:      {
117:          m_bmerge = !m_bmerge;
118:          BuildMenu();
119:      }
120:
121:      public menuswop()
122:      {
123:          // setup a main menu
124:          m_menumenu = new MenuItem("&Menu");
125:          m_menumenu.Popup += new EventHandler(PopupMenuMenu);
126:
127:          //Create the switch item.
128:          m_switchitem=new MenuItem("&Switch");
129:          m_switchitem.Click+=new EventHandler(OnSwitchMenu);
130:          m_menumenu.MenuItems.Add(m_switchitem);
131:
132:          m_showsecond = new MenuItem("&Show");
133:          m_showsecond.Click+= new EventHandler(Onshowsecond);
134:          m_menumenu.MenuItems.Add(m_showsecond);
135:
136:          m_merge = new MenuItem("&Merge");
137:          m_merge.Click += new EventHandler(OnMerge);
138:          m_menumenu.MenuItems.Add(m_merge);
139:
140:          // create a second menu
141:          m_editmenu=new MenuItem("&Edit");
142:          m_editmenu.MenuItems.Add(new MenuItem("Cut"));
143:          m_editmenu.MenuItems.Add(new MenuItem("Copy"));
144:          m_editmenu.MenuItems.Add(new MenuItem("Paste"));
145:
146:          // and an alternative.
147:          m_playmenu=new MenuItem("&Play");
148:          m_playmenu.MenuItems.Add(new MenuItem("Normal"));
149:          m_playmenu.MenuItems.Add(new MenuItem("Fast Forward"));
150:          m_playmenu.MenuItems.Add(new MenuItem("Reverse"));
151:
152:          m_bshowsecond=true;
153:
154:          //Now build the menu from its parts.
155:          BuildMenu();
156:
157:      }
```

Listing 3.1.10   Continued

```
158:
159:    public static void Main()
160:    {
161:        Application.Run(new menuswop());
162:    }
163: }
164:
165: }// end of Sams namespace
```

In this listing you can see that initially the menu creation process is normal, but that no menus are actually added to the `MenuItem` lists of a parent. The Edit and Play menus are kept separate.

The `BuildMenu` function on line 28 creates a new main menu and assigns it to the application's main menu. This will cause the GC to delete all of the submenus and entries from the main menu. `BuildMenu` then goes on to create the menu order or merge the two submenus into one, depending on the settings of the class member variables.

This technique allows you to create an initial set of menu items with all their handlers and settings in place, and then use them in many combinations without having to keep track of them or reset them to default values.

In Listing 3.1.10 the merge is very simple. There are however, more complex ways that `MenuItems` can be combined. The `MenuItem` has a merge order property so that when they are merged into another menu, they will sort themselves into a specific sequence. For example, you might want to have a File menu on which functionality is grouped according to the file type or system resources. With the menu merge order, you can ensure that common functions are first in the menu and less common ones are last. To illustrate the merge order functionality, Listing 3.1.11 shows a program in which the menu sorts itself according to the popularity of the selections.

Listing 3.1.11   menuorder.cs: On-the-Fly Menu Reordering and Merging

```
1: using System;
2: using System.Drawing;
3: using System.ComponentModel;
4: using System.WinForms;
5:
6: namespace Sams {
7: class menuorder : System.WinForms.Form
8: {
9:     MainMenu m_menu;
10:    MenuItem m_workingmenu;
11:    MenuItem m_menuentry;
```

LISTING 3.1.11   Continued

```
12:
13:      // this event handler is called whenever an item is used
14:      void OnUsed(Object sender, EventArgs e)
15:      {
16:          for(int i=0;i<m_menuentry.MenuItems.Count;i++)
17:              m_menuentry.MenuItems[i].MergeOrder ++;
18:
19:          MenuItem m=(MenuItem)sender;
20:
21:          m.MergeOrder--;
22:
23:          if(m.MergeOrder < 0)
24:              m.MergeOrder = 0;
25:
26:      }
27:
28:      // this event handler is also invoked. You could have
29:      // many event handlers attached to the Click sources
30:      void OnClicked(Object sender, EventArgs e)
31:      {
32:          MenuItem m=(MenuItem)sender;
33:          MessageBox.Show("You clicked "+m.Text);
34:      }
35:
36:      //As a menu is popped up it is constructed on the fly.
37:      void OnPopup(Object sender, EventArgs e)
38:      {
39:          m_menu.MenuItems.Clear();
40:          m_workingmenu.MenuItems.Clear();
41:          m_workingmenu.MergeMenu(m_menuentry);
42:          m_menu.MenuItems.Add(m_workingmenu);
43:      }
44:
45:      // Sets up the initial menu text and orders.
46:      public menuorder()
47:      {
48:
49:          string[] s=new string[8]{"Cats","Dogs","Elephants","Geese",
➥"Mooses","Rats","Giunea-pigs","Horses"};
50:
51:          m_menu = new MainMenu();
52:          m_menuentry = new MenuItem("&Menu");
53:          m_menuentry.Popup += new EventHandler(OnPopup);
54:
55:          m_workingmenu = new MenuItem();
```

LISTING 3.1.11 Continued

```
56:
57:            for(int i=0;i<8;i++)
58:            {
59:                MenuItem temp = new MenuItem(s[i]);
60:                temp.MergeOrder=i;
61:                temp.Click+=new EventHandler(OnUsed);
62:                temp.Click+=new EventHandler(OnClicked);
63:                m_menuentry.MenuItems.Add(temp);
64:            }
65:
66:        m_workingmenu.MergeMenu(m_menuentry);
67:        m_menu.MenuItems.Add(m_workingmenu);
68:        this.Menu = m_menu;
69:    }
70:
71:    // instantiates and runs the application.
72:    public static void Main()
73:    {
74:        Application.Run(new menuorder());
75:    }
76: }
77:
78: }
```

This listing also illustrates how you can add more than one event handler to a Windows Forms `Click`. The same is true for the `Select`, `Popup`, and all other events.

Adding Sub Menus

`MenuItem` objects in Windows Forms have their own `MenuItem` collections. This allows you to create a hierarchical structure of menus that have their own cascading child menus within them. The following listing illustrates this process.

```
MenuItem filemenu = new MenuItem();
filemenu.Text = "&File";
menu.MenuItems.Add(filemenu);

    MenuItem open = new MenuItem();
    open.Text = "&Open";
    filemenu.MenuItems.Add(open);

    MenuItem print= new MenuItem();
    print.Text = "Print...";
    filemenu.MenuItems.Add(print);
```

```
              MenuItem temp= new MenuItem();
              temp.Text = "Pre&view";
              print.MenuItems.Add(temp);

              temp= new MenuItem();
              temp.Text = "To &File";
              print.MenuItems.Add(temp);

          MenuItem exit= new MenuItem();
          exit.Text = "E&xit";
          filemenu.MenuItems.Add(exit);
```

As before, the indentation shows the menu level. Figure 3.1.10 shows the menu in action.

FIGURE 3.1.10
Submenus in action.

Summary

In this chapter you have progressed from the simplest Windows Forms application to relatively complex menu and event handler operations. You've seen how the Delegate system replaces the message map or the WndProc for message routing in your application, and you've seen a little of the basic .NET framework for GUI components. Coming up in Chapter 3.2 "User Interface Components," we'll deal with a selection of the more commonly used Windows Forms components and show you how to lay these items out for use in your forms and dialogs.

User Interface Components

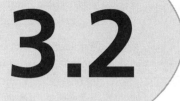
IN THIS CHAPTER

In this chapter, we will be showing you a good selection of the standard controls available, how to place and use them, how to add handlers for some of the more useful events, and how to create an application with some nice user interface features.

Windows Forms has a lot of standard user interface components that can be used in your applications. As you might expect, many of them are far more advanced through evolution than their Win32 counterparts. There are dialogs, list boxes, tree controls, panels, labels, toolbars, and many more. There is a large selection of common dialog controls including file selection, color picker, font style, and print dialogs. After a menu format, the dialog box is probably the most widely employed user interface item. Let's examine them more closely now.

Dialogs

Dialogs come in two styles. The *modal* style requires that the user complete the actions on the dialog before returning to the normal flow of the application. *Modeless*, which is a simple fixed size window that can be used to perform some action, but leaves the user free to work on the main application too.

> **NOTE**
>
> Dialogs are best when they are simple. The design of a dialog is crucial to the usability of the application. Too many small dialogs can be annoying, especially if there is no choice of seeing them or not. Large dialogs, especially modal ones, are annoying because they require a lot of interaction that can break the flow of the application.

Dialogs under MFC were the usual odd mixture of Win32 API and object-oriented wrapper code, particularly in the Dialog Data eXchange or DDX system. This represented data in the dialog as data members of the dialog class, but used these members as a staging area for the real information that is edited or selected by the Windows controls on the dialog surface. This meant that there was no instant update mechanism for dialogs because data needed to be transferred to and from the dialog's child windows by the use of Windows messages. Dialogs under Windows Forms are different. They are, like the applications that host them, fully object-oriented components that work in a more logical manner.

Under .NET, dialogs are essentially Windows Forms. Controls are placed on them in the same way that you would build a form application—with a tool or by coding directly.

Using the Common Dialogs

Common dialogs are simple to use and provide a consistent interaction with the underlying operating system. Dialogs are displayed with the ShowDialog function. All common dialogs are derived from the `System.Windows.Forms.CommonDialog` class. You can use this as a base class for custom dialogs that you might create.

The `FileDialog` Family

The most used of the common dialogs must be the file dialogs. Windows Forms defines a file-open and file-save dialog. To use these in your application, you need to put a member of type `OpenFileDialog` or `SaveFileDialog` in your application. Incidentally, both these dialogs are derived from `System.Windows.Forms.FileDialog`.

Listing 3.2.1 shows a simple application with a file-open dialog.

LISTING 3.2.1   fileopen.cs:OpenFileDialog in Action

```
 1: using System;
 2: using System.Drawing;
 3: using System.ComponentModel;
 4: using System.Windows.Forms;
 5:
 6:
 7: namespace Sams
 8: {
 9:
10: class fileopenapp : System.Windows.Forms.Form
11: {
12:
13:     MainMenu m_menu;
14:     MenuItem m_filemenu;
15:
16:     void OnOpenFile(Object sender, EventArgs e)
17:     {
18:         OpenFileDialog dlg=new OpenFileDialog();
19:
20:         if(dlg.ShowDialog() == DialogResult.OK)
21:         {
22:             MessageBox.Show("You selected the file "+dlg.FileName);
23:         }
24:     }
25:
26:     void OnExit(Object sender, EventArgs e)
27:     {
28:         Application.Exit();
29:     }
30:
31:     fileopenapp()
32:     {
```

LISTING 3.2.1 Continued

```
33:          m_menu = new MainMenu();
34:          m_filemenu=new MenuItem("&File");
35:          m_menu.MenuItems.Add(m_filemenu);
36:          MenuItem t;
37:
38:          t=new MenuItem("&Open");
39:          t.Click += new EventHandler(OnOpenFile);
40:          m_filemenu.MenuItems.Add(t);
41:
42:          t=new MenuItem("-");
43:          m_filemenu.MenuItems.Add(t);
44:
45:          t=new MenuItem("E&xit");
46:          t.Click += new EventHandler(OnExit);
47:          m_filemenu.MenuItems.Add(t);
48:
49:          this.Menu = m_menu;
50:      }
51:
52:      public static void Main()
53:      {
54:          Application.Run(new fileopenapp());
55:      }
56: }
57:
58: }// end of Sams namespace
```

This example is the very simplest use of the dialog. Common dialogs provide much more functionality and are used in more complex ways.

A common dialog control is used differently when the application is constructed by Visual Studio.NET for example. In this instance, the application will instantiate a copy of the dialog when the application is run and attach an event source called FileOK to a button click handler in the form that uses the dialog. The delegate for this event handler is a little different from that of menu events. The signature for the CancelEventHandler is as follows:

void FN(object sender, System.ComponentModel.CancelEventArgs e)

Listing 3.2.2 shows the equivalent to this approach in a hand-built form.

LISTING 3.2.2 fileopenevent.cs: Event-driven Common Dialog Response

```
1: using System;
2: using System.Drawing;
```

LISTING 3.2.2   Continued

```
 3: using System.ComponentModel;
 4: using System.Windows.Forms;
 5: using System.IO;
 6:
 7:
 8: namespace Sams
 9: {
10:
11: class fileopenapp : System.Windows.Forms.Form
12: {
13:
14:     MainMenu m_menu;
15:     MenuItem m_filemenu;
16:
17:     OpenFileDialog openfiledlg1;
18:
19:     void OnOpenFile(Object sender, EventArgs e)
20:     {
21:         openfiledlg1.Filter = "C# files (*.cs)|"+
22:             "*.cs|Bitmap files (*.bmp)|*.bmp";
23:         openfiledlg1.FilterIndex = 1;
24:         openfiledlg1.ShowDialog();
25:     }
26:
27:     void OnExit(Object sender, EventArgs e)
28:     {
29:         Dispose();
30:     }
31:
32:     fileopenapp()
33:     {
34:         m_menu = new MainMenu();
35:         m_filemenu=new MenuItem("&File");
36:         m_menu.MenuItems.Add(m_filemenu);
37:         MenuItem t;
38:
39:         t=new MenuItem("&Open");
40:         t.Click += new EventHandler(OnOpenFile);
41:         m_filemenu.MenuItems.Add(t);
42:
43:         t=new MenuItem("-");
44:         m_filemenu.MenuItems.Add(t);
45:
46:         t=new MenuItem("E&xit");
```

LISTING 3.2.2 Continued

```
47:            t.Click += new EventHandler(OnExit);
48:            m_filemenu.MenuItems.Add(t);
49:
50:            this.Menu = m_menu;
51:
52:            openfiledlg1 = new OpenFileDialog();
53:            openfiledlg1.FileOk += new CancelEventHandler(OnFileOpenOK);
54:        }
55:
56:    void OnFileOpenOK(Object sender, CancelEventArgs e)
57:    {
58:        //MessageBox.Show("You selected the file "+openfiledlg1.FileName);
59:        // remember to add "using System.IO;" to the top of this file.
60:        OpenFileDialog dlg = (OpenFileDialog)sender;
61:
62:        Stream FileStream;
63:        if((FileStream = dlg.OpenFile())!=null)
64:        {
65:            //perform the read from FileStream here...
66:            FileStream.Close(); //and tidy up...
67:        }
68:    }
69:
70:    public static void Main()
71:    {
72:        Application.Run(new fileopenapp());
73:    }
74: }
75:
76: }// end of Sams namespace
```

The event in Listing 3.2.2 will only fire if the OK button has been clicked. There is also a HelpRequested event that will fire if the Help button in the dialog is chosen.

A file dialog can be made to present only a particular set of files by specifying a filter or even to open a file and return a file-stream for you. Lines 19–25 of the listing show how a filter is set for a particular selection of file types.

Lines 56–68 define the event handler that is triggered when a file is selected and opened using the dialog box.

Figure 3.2.1 shows a screen shot of FileOpenDialog as defined by this code.

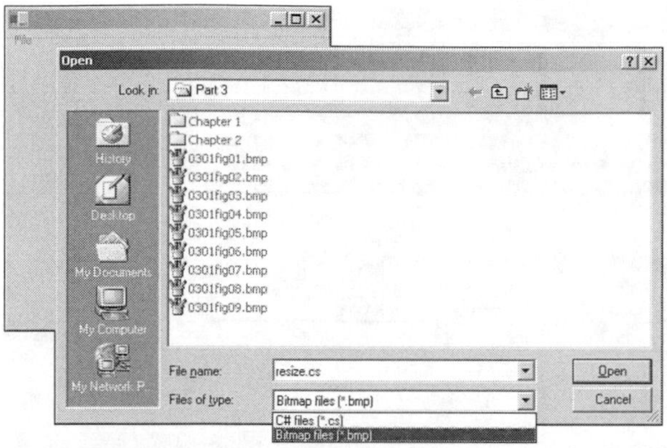

FIGURE 3.2.1
The FileOpenDialog *showing file filtering.*

SaveFileDialog works in a similar manner because it inherits most of its functionality from
FileDialog. If you use the OpenFile function, a chosen file will be created or opened for
writing.

> **NOTE**
>
> Note that FileDialog, OpenFileDialog, and SaveFileDialogs support properties that
> allow you to change the way files are displayed, checked, or selected. The .NET SDK
> help files should be consulted for details

The ColorDialog

Selecting color is a common function. Many people try to write color pickers themselves for
reasons of aesthetics, but the Windows ColorDialog is simple to use and effective. What's
more, it's consistent and familiar to most users.

Invoking ColorDialog is the same as other common dialogs by virtue of its base class. Create
an instance of the class and call the ShowDialog method.

Figure 3.2.2 shows the ColorDialog in its various modes.

The ColorDialog class returns color information in the form of a Color object. This contains
the alpha, or transparency, and the red, green, and blue values of the color. There are also
methods for ascertaining a color's hue, brightness, and saturation values.

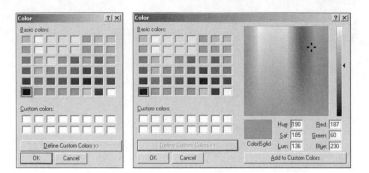

FIGURE 3.2.2

The ColorDialog in all its glory.

There is a property called AllowFullOpen in the ColorDialog that allows you to decide if the Define Custom Colors button is enabled. You can also use the FullOpen property to force the complex color picker to appear. The CustomColors property is an array of color values that can be set or interrogated and that fill the custom color boxes on the control.

Listing 3.2.3 shows the ColorDialog in a selection of modes.

LISTING 3.2.3   colordlgs.cs: Various Incarnations of the ColorDialog

```
 1: using System;
 2: using System.Drawing;
 3: using System.ComponentModel;
 4: using System.Windows.Forms;
 5:
 6:
 7: namespace Sams {
 8:
 9:
10: class ColorStretcher : System.Windows.Forms.Form
11: {
12:
13:     void OnFull(Object sender, EventArgs e)
14:     {
15:         ColorDialog dlg=new ColorDialog();
16:         dlg.FullOpen = true;
17:
18:         dlg.ShowDialog();
19:     }
20:
21:     void OnNoCustom(Object sender, EventArgs e)
```

LISTING 3.2.3   Continued

```
22:       {
23:           ColorDialog dlg=new ColorDialog();
24:           dlg.AllowFullOpen = false;
25:
26:           dlg.ShowDialog();
27:       }
28:
29:       void OnNormal(Object sender, EventArgs e)
30:       {
31:           ColorDialog dlg=new ColorDialog();
32:           dlg.Color = Color.PaleGoldenrod;
33:           dlg.ShowDialog();
34:       }
35:
36:       void OnWithColours(Object sender, EventArgs e)
37:       {
38:           ColorDialog dlg=new ColorDialog();
39:           dlg.FullOpen = true;
40:           // this statement defines the first five of the
41:           // custom color settings as ints the data is
42:           // 0xAARRGGBB where AA is alpha, RR is red,
43:           // GG is green and BB is blue expressed as the
44:           // hexadecimal byte equivalent
45:           dlg.CustomColors = new int[5]{0x00ff8040, 0x00c256fe,
46:                             0x00aa2005, 0x0004f002, 0x002194b5};
47:
48:           dlg.ShowDialog();
49:       }
50:
51:       ColorStretcher()
52:       {
53:           // first a menu for the choices
54:
55:           MainMenu m=new MainMenu();
56:           MenuItem top,temp;
57:
58:           top=new MenuItem("ColorDialog");
59:           m.MenuItems.Add(top);
60:
61:           temp=new MenuItem("Full");
62:           temp.Click+=new EventHandler(OnFull);
63:           top.MenuItems.Add(temp);
64:
65:           temp=new MenuItem("No custom");
```

LISTING 3.2.3   Continued

```
66:            temp.Click+=new EventHandler(OnNoCustom);
67:            top.MenuItems.Add(temp);
68:
69:            temp=new MenuItem("With Colours");
70:            temp.Click+=new EventHandler(OnWithColours);
71:            top.MenuItems.Add(temp);
72:
73:            temp=new MenuItem("Normal");
74:            temp.Click+=new EventHandler(OnNormal);
75:            top.MenuItems.Add(temp);
76:
77:            this.Menu = m;
78:
79:        }
80:
81:     public static void Main()
82:     {
83:            Application.Run(new ColorStretcher());
84:     }
85:
86: }
87: }
```

Notice how the custom colors are defined as integer values in the OnWithColours event handler (lines 36–49).

To get the chosen color from the ColorDialog, simply read the contents of the Color property. Setting this property before invoking the ShowDialog method will pre-select a color. This is useful for changing colors that are already set in an application. This is shown in the OnNormal handler. To see the color selection, you must click the Define Custom Colors button. The color selected in the palette is the one that is programmed.

FontDialog

The font you choose for text is very important. Times Roman conveys a sense of solidity and reliability. Tahoma shows technical competence, Shotgun proves that you spent too much of your youth before 1975, and nothing says "I love you" better than 72-point Gigi.

The plethora of fonts available to the modern wordsmith is truly phenomenal, so there is nothing more important than a quick, simple method for choosing the face, size, and weight of a font. The standard font dialog is available to .Net programmers through the FontDialog class which, like its FileDialog and ColorDialog cousins, is derived from the CommonDialog class.

The technique for invoking the font dialog is the same as we have seen before. The properties of the dialog and the return data is uniquely dedicated to type face selection.

Listing 3.2.4 shows a simple application with a label and a font selection button. The button is wired to an event that invokes the font dialog. The font dialog itself has many options, set through its properties, that allow you to select the operations the dialog can perform. In the following example, we have enabled the Apply button and attached an event that updates the label text each time the Apply button is clicked.

LISTING 3.2.4   `fontdlg.cs`: Using the Font Selection Dialog

```
using System;
using System.ComponentModel;
using System.Drawing;
using System.Windows.Forms;


namespace Sams {

class FontPicker : System.Windows.Forms.Form
{

  Button b;
  Label l;

  void OnApply(Object sender,System.EventArgs e)
  {
    FontDialog dlg = (FontDialog)sender;
    l.Font=dlg.Font;
  }

  void OnClickedb(Object sender,EventArgs e)
  {
    // Create a new Font Dialog
    FontDialog dlg=new FontDialog();

    //Initialize it with the existing font in the label
    dlg.Font = l.Font;

    //Set the property to allow an "Apply button on the form"
    dlg.ShowApply = true;

    //attach an OnApply event handler
    dlg.Apply += new EventHandler(OnApply);

    if(dlg.ShowDialog() != DialogResult.Cancel)
    {
      l.Font = dlg.Font;
    }
  }
```

LISTING 3.2.4 Continued

```
public FontPicker()
  {
    this.Size=new Size(416,320);

    l=new Label();
    l.Location = new Point(8,8);
    l.Size = new Size(400,200);
    l.Text = "0 1 2 3 4 5 6 7 8 9 \nabcdefghijklmnopqrstuvwxyz"+
    "\nABCDEFGHIJKLMNOPQRSTUVWXYZ";
    l.Font = new Font("Microsoft Sans Serif", 18f);
    this.Controls.Add(l);

    b=new Button();
    b.Text = "Choose Font";
    b.Click += new EventHandler(OnClickedb);
    b.Location = new Point(8,250);
    b.Size = new Size(400,32);
    this.Controls.Add(b);

  }


  static void Main()
  {
    Application.Run(new FontPicker());
  }
}

}
```

Build this file with the command line:

```
csc /t:winexe fontdlg.cs
```

The Print and Print Preview Dialogs

Rendering a document onscreen or to the printer requires graphics knowledge that we will cover more in depth later in this book, so we wont go into great detail on that subject at this stage. Just to give you a feel for print and print preview. In Listing 3.2.5 we have created a very simple application that enables you to perform print and print preview.

LISTING 3.2.5 `printpreview.cs` Printing and Print Preview in Action

```
Totally re-written…  1: namespace Sams
  2: {
  3:     using System;
  4:     using System.Drawing;
  5:     using System.Drawing.Printing;
  6:     using System.Collections;
  7:     using System.ComponentModel;
  8:     using System.Windows.Forms;
  9:
 10:
 11:     /// <summary>
 12:     ///the ppView is a simple control window that uses a common draw
 13:     ///method for both painting on screen and printing or print preview
 14:     /// </summary>
 15:     public class ppView : System.Windows.Forms.Panel
 16:     {
 17:     private ArrayList points;
 18:
 19:     Point mousePoint;
 20:
 21:
 22:     void OnClick(Object sender, MouseEventArgs e)
 23:     {
 24:       if(points == null)
 25:       {
 26:         points=new ArrayList();
 27:       }
 28:
 29:       points.Add(mousePoint);
 30:       Invalidate();
 31:     }
 32:
 33:     void OnMouseMove(Object sender,MouseEventArgs e)
 34:     {
 35:       mousePoint = new Point(e.X,e.Y);
 36:     }
 37:
 38:     public ppView()
 39:         {
 40:       this.MouseDown+=new MouseEventHandler(OnClick);
 41:       this.MouseMove+=new MouseEventHandler(OnMouseMove);
```

3.2

USER INTERFACE
COMPONENTS

LISTING 3.2.5   Continued

```
42:        this.BackColor=Color.White;
43:          }
44:
45:    private void DrawSmiley(Point pt, Graphics g)
46:    {
47:      g.FillEllipse(Brushes.Black,pt.X-52,pt.Y-52,104,104);
48:      g.FillEllipse(Brushes.Yellow,pt.X-50,pt.Y-50,100,100);
49:      g.FillEllipse(Brushes.Black,pt.X-30,pt.Y-10,60,40);
50:      g.FillEllipse(Brushes.Yellow,pt.X-35,pt.Y-10,70,35);
51:      g.FillEllipse(Brushes.Black,pt.X-25,pt.Y-15,10,10);
52:      g.FillEllipse(Brushes.Black,pt.X+10,pt.Y-15,10,10);
53:    }
54:
55:    private void DoDraw(Graphics g)
56:    {
57:      if(points == null)
58:      {
59:        return;
60:      }
61:      foreach(Point p in points)
62:      {
63:        DrawSmiley(p,g);
64:      }
65:    }
66:
67:    protected override void OnPaint(PaintEventArgs e)
68:    {
69:      if(points == null)
70:      {
71:        return;
72:      }
73:      DoDraw(e.Graphics);
74:    }
75:
76:    public void OnPrintPage(Object sender,PrintPageEventArgs e)
77:    {
78:      if(points == null)
79:      {
80:        return;
81:      }
82:      DoDraw(e.Graphics);
83:    }
84:    }
85:
86:
```

LISTING 3.2.5   Continued

```
87:     /// <summary>
88:     ///     This is the application that hosts the MainApps.
89:     /// </summary>
90:     public class MDIChildForm : System.Windows.Forms.Form
91:     {
92:         /// <summary>
93:         ///     Required designer variable.
94:         /// </summary>
95:         private System.ComponentModel.Container components;
96:     private ppView vw;
97:
98:     // Accessor for private data
99:     public ppView View {
100:       get
101:       {
102:         return vw;
103:       }
104:     }
105:
106:     public MDIChildForm()
107:         {
108:
109:
110:             //
111:             // Required for Windows Form Designer support
112:             //
113:             InitializeComponent();
114:
115:     vw=new ppView();
116:     vw.Location = new Point(3,3);
117:     vw.Size = new Size(this.Size.Width-6,this.Size.Height-6);
118:     vw.Anchor=AnchorStyles.Left|
119:             AnchorStyles.Top|
120:             AnchorStyles.Right|
121:             AnchorStyles.Bottom;
122:
123:     this.Controls.Add(vw);
124:
125:         //
126:         // TODO: Add any constructor code after InitializeComponent call
127:         //
128:         }
129:
130:         /// <summary>
131:         ///     Clean up any resources being used.
```

LISTING 3.2.5 Continued

```
132:        /// </summary>
133:        public override void Dispose()
134:        {
135:            base.Dispose();
136:            components.Dispose();
137:        }
138:
139:        /// <summary>
140:        ///     Required method for Designer support - do not modify
141:        ///     the contents of this method with the code editor.
142:        /// </summary>
143:        private void InitializeComponent()
144:    {
145:      this.components = new System.ComponentModel.Container ();
146:      this.Text = "MDIChildForm";
147:      this.AutoScaleBaseSize = new System.Drawing.Size (5, 13);
148:      this.ClientSize = new System.Drawing.Size (328, 277);
149:    }
150:    }
151:
152:    /// <summary>
153:    ///     Summary description for MainApp.
154:    /// </summary>
155:    public class MainApp : System.Windows.Forms.Form
156:    {
157:        /// <summary>
158:        ///     Required designer variable.
159:        /// </summary>
160:        private System.ComponentModel.Container components;
161:    private System.Windows.Forms.MenuItem FileExit;
162:    private System.Windows.Forms.MenuItem FilePrintPreview;
163:    private System.Windows.Forms.MenuItem FilePrint;
164:    private System.Windows.Forms.MenuItem FileNew;
165:    private System.Windows.Forms.MenuItem menuItem1;
166:    private System.Windows.Forms.MainMenu mainMenu1;
167:
168:        public MainApp()
169:        {
170:            //
171:            // Required for Windows Form Designer support
172:            //
173:            InitializeComponent();
174:
175:            //
```

LISTING 3.2.5 Continued

```
176:            // Add any constructor code after InitializeComponent call
177:            //
178:        }
179:
180:        /// <summary>
181:        ///     Clean up any resources being used.
182:        /// </summary>
183:        public override void Dispose()
184:        {
185:            base.Dispose();
186:            components.Dispose();
187:        }
188:
189:        /// <summary>
190:        ///     Required method for Designer support - do not modify
191:        ///     the contents of this method with the code editor.
192:        /// </summary>
193:        private void InitializeComponent()
194:    {
195:      this.components = new System.ComponentModel.Container ();
196:      this.mainMenu1 = new System.Windows.Forms.MainMenu ();
197:      this.FilePrintPreview = new System.Windows.Forms.MenuItem ();
198:      this.FileExit = new System.Windows.Forms.MenuItem ();
199:      this.menuItem1 = new System.Windows.Forms.MenuItem ();
200:      this.FileNew = new System.Windows.Forms.MenuItem ();
201:      this.FilePrint = new System.Windows.Forms.MenuItem ();
202:      mainMenu1.MenuItems.AddRange(
203:        new System.Windows.Forms.MenuItem[1] {this.menuItem1});
204:      FilePrintPreview.Text = "P&review...";
205:      FilePrintPreview.Index = 2;
206:      FilePrintPreview.Click +=
207:        new System.EventHandler (this.FilePrintPreview_Click);
208:      FileExit.Text = "&Exit";
209:      FileExit.Index = 3;
210:      FileExit.Click += new System.EventHandler (this.FileExit_Click);
211:      menuItem1.Text = "&File";
212:      menuItem1.Index = 0;
213:      menuItem1.MenuItems.AddRange(new System.Windows.Forms.MenuItem[4]
214:                {this.FileNew,
215:         this.FilePrint,
216:         this.FilePrintPreview,
217:         this.FileExit});
218:      FileNew.Text = "&New";
219:      FileNew.Index = 0;
```

LISTING 3.2.5 Continued

```
220:        FileNew.Click += new System.EventHandler (this.FileNew_Click);
221:        FilePrint.Text = "&Print...";
222:        FilePrint.Index = 1;
223:        FilePrint.Click += new System.EventHandler (this.FilePrint_Click);
224:        this.Text = "MainApp";
225:        this.AutoScaleBaseSize = new System.Drawing.Size (5, 13);
226:        this.IsMdiContainer = true;
227:        this.Menu = this.mainMenu1;
228:        this.ClientSize = new System.Drawing.Size (368, 289);
229:    }
230:
231:    protected void FileExit_Click (object sender, System.EventArgs e)
232:    {
233:        Application.Exit();
234:    }
235:
236:    protected void FilePrintPreview_Click(object sender,
➥System.EventArgs e)
237:    {
238:        PrintPreviewDialog d=new PrintPreviewDialog();
239:        PrintDocument doc = new PrintDocument();
240:
241:        MDIChildForm f = (MDIChildForm)this.ActiveMdiChild;
242:        ppView vw = f.View;
243:        doc.PrintPage += new PrintPageEventHandler(vw.OnPrintPage);
244:
245:        d.Document=doc;
246:
247:        d.ShowDialog();
248:
249:        doc.PrintPage -= new PrintPageEventHandler(vw.OnPrintPage);
250:    }
251:
252:    protected void FilePrint_Click (object sender, System.EventArgs e)
253:    {
254:        PrintDialog dlg = new PrintDialog();
255:        PrintDocument doc = new PrintDocument();
256:
257:        MDIChildForm f = (MDIChildForm)this.ActiveMdiChild;
258:        ppView vw = f.View;
259:        doc.PrintPage += new PrintPageEventHandler(vw.OnPrintPage);
260:
261:        dlg.Document=doc;
262:
```

LISTING 3.2.5 Continued

```
263:        dlg.ShowDialog();
264:
265:        doc.PrintPage -= new PrintPageEventHandler(vw.OnPrintPage);
266:
267:    }
268:
269:    protected void FileNew_Click (object sender, System.EventArgs e)
270:    {
271:      MDIChildForm f = new MDIChildForm();
272:      f.MdiParent=this;
273:      f.Show();
274:    }
275:
276:        /// <summary>
277:        /// The main entry point for the application.
278:        /// </summary>
279:        public static void Main(string[] args)
280:        {
281:            Application.Run(new MainApp());
282:        }
283:    }
284: }
```

This application has three components. The form, called MainApp, is a Multiple Document Interface (MDI) application and hosts a number of MDIChildForm objects. These, in turn, host a simple control called ppView.

The ppView does all the work of tracking the mouse, adding simple points to an array list, and drawing smiley faces at every stored point. It also employs the technique of a single, simple draw routine that takes a Graphics object as an argument.

The print and print preview mechanism uses a PrintDocument that fires an event for each printed page. To use the print preview and print facilities, the simple draw routine is used by the OnPaint, line 67, and the OnPrintPage, line 76, events that call the DoDraw method with whatever drawing device context they have been given by the screen or printer drivers. The Graphics context passed to the DoDraw routine when drawing onscreen is different than when printing. The drawing system knows that it needs to change scales and pixel resolution for you, depending on the device.

If you're interested in the graphics used, lines 47–52 draw the smileys.

Creating Dialogs

Under .NET, the interpretation of what is and is not a dialog is largely dependant on the user interface you choose to use on it. As was mentioned before, a modal dialog is something that requires the user to finish his or her interaction before continuing with the rest of the application. Therefore, dialogs become less and less useful as they get more complex. You must make very careful decisions about what functionality goes into the application's forms and what goes in its dialogs.

Modal and Modeless Dialogs

A dialog can be created in the same way as a form, by dragging tools from a tool palette or by laying out components by hand. The Form class has a property called Modal that will cause the form to be displayed modally when set to true. The Form method ShowDialog sets this property for you and allows you to display forms in a modal fashion. Listing 3.2.6 shows the same dialog form employed in these two different modes.

LISTING 3.2.6 Modes.cs: Creating Modal and Modeless Dialogs

```
 1: using System;
 2: using System.ComponentModel;
 3: using System.Drawing;
 4: using System.Windows.Forms;
 5: using System.Collections;
 6:
 7: class ADialog : Form
 8: {
 9:
10:     private Button ok,can;
11:
12:     public bool Modeless
13:     {
14:         set
15:         {
16:             if(value)
17:             {
18:                 ok.Click += new EventHandler(OnCloseModeless);
19:                 can.Click += new EventHandler(OnCloseModeless);
20:             }
21:         }
22:     }
23:
24:     void OnCloseModeless(Object sender, EventArgs e)
25:     {
```

LISTING 3.2.6 Continued

```
26:            this.Close();
27:        }
28:
29:     public ADialog()
30:        {
31:            this.Location = new Point(100,100);
32:            this.Size=new Size(200,100);
33:            this.BorderStyle = FormBorderStyle.FixedDialog;
34:
35:            ok = new Button();
36:            ok.Text = "OK";
37:            ok.DialogResult = DialogResult.OK;
38:            ok.Location = new Point(20,10);
39:            ok.Size = new Size(80,25);
40:            this.Controls.Add(ok);
41:
42:            can = new Button();
43:            can.Text = "Cancel";
44:            can.DialogResult = DialogResult.OK;
45:            can.Location = new Point(110,10);
46:            can.Size = new Size(80,25);
47:            this.Controls.Add(can);
48:        }
49: }
50:
51:
52: class AnApp : Form
53: {
54:     void OnModeless(Object sender, EventArgs e)
55:        {
56:            ADialog dlg = new ADialog();
57:            dlg.Text = "Modeless";
58:            dlg.Modeless = true;
59:            dlg.Show();
60:        }
61:
62:
63:     void OnModal(Object sender, EventArgs e)
64:        {
65:            ADialog dlg = new ADialog();
66:            dlg.Text = "Modal";
67:            dlg.ShowDialog();
68:        }
69:
```

LISTING 3.2.6   Continued

```
70:     public AnApp()
71:     {
72:         this.Size=new Size(400,100);
73:         this.BorderStyle = FormBorderStyle.FixedDialog;
74:         this.Text = "Dialog Mode Tester";
75:
76:         Button modal = new Button();
77:         modal.Text = "New Modal dialog";
78:         modal.Location = new Point(10,10);
79:         modal.Size = new Size(180,25);
80:         modal.Click += new EventHandler(OnModal);
81:         this.Controls.Add(modal);
82:
83:         Button modeless = new Button();
84:         modeless.Text = "New Modeless dialog";
85:         modeless.Location = new Point(210,10);
86:         modeless.Size = new Size(180,25);
87:         modeless.Click += new EventHandler(OnModeless);
88:         this.Controls.Add(modeless);
89:     }
90:
91:     static void Main()
92:     {
93:     Application.Run( new AnApp());
94:     }
95: }
```

In Listing 3.2.6, the main application is a simple form with two buttons. One button instantiates a new modeless dialog. The other button instantiates a modal dialog.

Lines 70–89 set up the main application window and tie the buttons to the click handlers on lines 52–60 and lines 63–68.

Lines 7–49 define a dialog box that also has two buttons. When running from the ShowDialog command, this form will automatically put the dialog return value in the right place and close the form. When running as a modeless dialog, there is an extra setup property on lines 12–22 that ties a click handler to the dialog buttons. Without this handler (defined on lines 24–27), the dialog would not close in response to a button click, only by choosing the Close button on the main window bar.

Notice that you can bring up as many modeless forms as you want, but as soon as a modal dialog is shown, interaction with the main application and all the other modeless forms is blocked.

Closing the main application will close all of the modeless dialogs that are open.

Data Transfer to and from Dialog Members

In its simplest form, a dialog might only transfer data about which button was clicked to exit
the dialog. A more complex dialog might make properties available to the programmer that
have other information about more complex controls in the dialog. A form run with the
ShowDialog method is closed by setting the DialogResult property of the form. This value is
then returned to the code that invoked the dialog.

Listing 3.2.7 shows a simple dialog form with this type of behavior.

LISTING 3.2.7   simpledialog.cs: A simple Dialog

```
 1: using System;
 2: using System.Drawing;
 3: using System.ComponentModel;
 4: using System.Windows.Forms;
 5:
 6: namespace Sams {
 7:
 8: class SimpleDialog : Form
 9: {
10:     public SimpleDialog()
11:     {
12:         // Create two buttons.
13:         Button OkButton=new Button();
14:         OkButton.Text = "Ok";
15:         OkButton.DialogResult = DialogResult.OK;
16:         OkButton.Location = new Point(8,20);
17:         OkButton.Size = new Size(50,24);
18:         this.Controls.Add(OkButton);
19:
20:         Button CancelButton=new Button();
21:         CancelButton.Text = "Cancel";
22:         CancelButton.DialogResult = DialogResult.Cancel;
23:         CancelButton.Location = new Point(64,20);
24:         CancelButton.Size = new Size(50,24);
25:         this.Controls.Add(CancelButton);
26:
27:         this.Text="Dialog";
28:         this.Size = new Size(130,90);
29:         this.BorderStyle = FormBorderStyle.FixedDialog;
30:         this.StartPosition = FormStartPosition.CenterParent;
31:         this.ControlBox = false;
```

3.2

USER INTERFACE
COMPONENTS

LISTING 3.2.7 Continued

```
32:      }
33: }
34:
35:
36: class AnApp : Form
37: {
38:     void OnTest(Object sender, EventArgs e)
39:     {
40:         SimpleDialog dlg = new SimpleDialog();
41:         dlg.Owner = this;
42:
43:         if(dlg.ShowDialog() == DialogResult.OK)
44:             MessageBox.Show("You clicked Ok");
45:         else
46:             MessageBox.Show("You clicked Cancel");
47:
48:     }
49:
50:     public AnApp()
51:     {
52:         this.Menu = new MainMenu();
53:         this.Menu.MenuItems.Add(new MenuItem("Dialog"));
54:         this.Menu.MenuItems[0].MenuItems.Add(new MenuItem("Test"));
55:         this.Menu.MenuItems[0].MenuItems[0].Click +=
➡           new EventHandler(OnTest);
56:     }
57:
58:     static void Main()
59:     {
60:         Application.Run(new AnApp());
61:     }
62: }
63: }
```

Dialogs, because they are forms, can host all the Windows Forms controls. Dialogs can be used to return simple information from check boxes, radio buttons, edit controls, and other components. To do this, you need to be able to return more than the simple dialog result seen in the previous example.

Data from dialogs can be accessed via public data members or through methods and properties that you add especially for the task. If you are a veteran MFC programmer, you might want to change your habits from the former method to the latter. Accessor properties play a big role in .NET object interaction.

The interaction between the user and the dialog can be quite complex. A button click, check box selection, or other action may generate events that are trapped by your dialog box code and acted on before the OK button is finally clicked. The design of a dialog can be as exacting as the design of the form that hosts the dialog.

Validation

Some controls, such as the NumericUpDown control, have specific behavior for validation. This control has a Minimum and Maximum property that can be used to define a numeric range for the control. The control will also fire an event when it is validating itself and again when it is validated. You can trap these events, but really the Windows Forms user interface experience is a little rough-and-ready when compared to the ease of using MFC because there is no specific DDX behavior. The validation events are inherited from System.Windows.Forms.Control and, in the case of forms shown with the ShowDialog method, are generated whenever the control loses focus. This means that validation will take place as you move from control to control within a dialog. This includes clicking a button that sets the DialogResult property and closes the dialog. An invalid condition will prevent the dialog box from closing.

Listing 3.2.8 shows a simple application that uses validation to ensure that a numeric value is correct.

LISTING 3.2.8 dialogValid.cs: Retrieving validated Data from the Dialog

```
 1: using System;
 2: using System.ComponentModel;
 3: using System.Drawing;
 4: using System.Windows.Forms;
 5: using System.IO;
 6: using System.Text;
 7:
 8: namespace Sams {
 9:
10: class DialogValid : System.Windows.Forms.Form
11: {
12:
13:     private Button okButton;
14:     private Button cancelButton;
15:     private NumericUpDown num;
16:
17:     public decimal Num {
18:         get { return num.Value; }
19:         set { num.Value = value;    }
20:         }
21:
```

LISTING 3.2.8   Continued

```
22:      void OnValidating(Object sender, CancelEventArgs e)
23:      {
24:          MessageBox.Show("NumericUpDown is validating");
25:      }
26:
27:      void OnValid(Object sender,EventArgs e)
28:      {
29:          MessageBox.Show("NumericUpDown is valid");
30:      }
31:
32:      public DialogValid()
33:      {
34:
35:          Size = new Size(400,100);
36:          FormBorderStyle = FormBorderStyle.FixedDialog;
37:          Text = "Dialog test";
38:
39:          //place the buttons on the form
40:          okButton = new Button();
41:          okButton.DialogResult = DialogResult.OK;
42:          okButton.Location = new Point(20,28);
43:          okButton.Size = new Size(80,25);
44:          okButton.Text = "OK";
45:          Controls.Add(okButton);
46:
47:          cancelButton = new Button();
48:          cancelButton.Location = new Point(300,28);
49:          cancelButton.Size = new Size(80,25);
50:          cancelButton.Text = "Cancel";
51:          cancelButton.DialogResult = DialogResult.Cancel;
52:          Controls.Add(cancelButton);
53:
54:          // place a label on the form.
55:          Label l = new Label();
56:          l.Text = "NumericUpDown";
57:          l.Location = new Point(20,5);
58:          l.Size = new Size(120,25);
59:          Controls.Add(l);
60:
61:          // finally the numeric control;
62:          num = new NumericUpDown();
63:          num.Location = new Point(140,5);
64:          num.Size = new Size(80,25);
65:          num.Minimum = (decimal)10.0;
```

Listing 3.2.8   Continued

```
66:             num.Maximum = (decimal)100.0;
67:             num.Value = (decimal)10.0;
68:
69:             //here we add event handlers to show the validating process.
70:             num.Validating+=new CancelEventHandler(OnValidating);
71:             num.Validated+=new EventHandler(OnValid);
72:
73:             Controls.Add(num);
74:
75:         }
76:
77:     }
78:
79:     class ddApp : System.Windows.Forms.Form
80:     {
81:
82:         void OnExit(Object sender, EventArgs e)
83:         {
84:             Application.Exit();
85:         }
86:
87:         void OnDialogTest(Object sender, EventArgs e)
88:         {
89:             DialogValid dlg = new DialogValid();
90:
91:             DialogResult r=dlg.ShowDialog();
92:
93:
94:             StringWriter sw=new StringWriter(new StringBuilder());
95:
96:             sw.WriteLine("Dialog return value = {0}"+
97:             "\nNumericUpDown = {1}",r,dlg.Num);
98:
99:             MessageBox.Show(sw.ToString());
100:
101:         }
102:
103:         public ddApp()
104:         {
105:             MainMenu mm=new MainMenu();
106:             mm.MenuItems.Add(new MenuItem("&Dialog"));
107:             mm.MenuItems[0].MenuItems.Add(new MenuItem("&Test",
108:                 new EventHandler(OnDialogTest)));
109:             mm.MenuItems[0].MenuItems.Add(new MenuItem("-"));
```

Listing 3.2.8   Continued

```
110:              mm.MenuItems[0].MenuItems.Add(new MenuItem("E&xit",
111:                 new EventHandler(OnExit)));
112:              Menu = mm;
113:        }
114:
115:        static void Main()
116:        {
117:              Application.Run(new ddApp());
118:        }
119:   }
120:
121:   }
```

When you derive your own controls, you can use the CausesValidation property to make the Validating and Validated events fire on your control when the focus changes within the form.

Using Controls

So far, we have seen the Button controls and the NumericUpDown in action. Let's take a closer look at some of the more commonly used form controls.

Check Boxes and Radio Buttons

Check box and radio button behavior is essentially the same as that of their MFC counterparts. However, the Windows Forms versions do not have any of the nice DDX traits we are all so used to, so reading them and reacting to them is a little more time consuming.

Check boxes can be placed on the form or within other panels or group boxes but, because they don't generally rely on the state of other check boxes around them, their setup is relatively simple.

Radio buttons that are associated with one another should be children of another object, such as a panel or group box, for their automatic radio-button selection to work.

Retrieving the state of these controls is simply a matter of interrogating them directly or using their click methods to keep a record of the user's choices.

Listing 3.2.9 shows a dialog with both check boxes and radio buttons. The code shows several methods for reading the button states or trapping events.

LISTING 3.2.9 dialogtest.cs: Using Check Boxes and Radio Buttons

```
 1: using System;
 2: using System.ComponentModel;
 3: using System.Drawing;
 4: using System.Windows.Forms;
 5: using System.IO;
 6: using System.Text;
 7:
 8: namespace Sams {
 9:
10: class DialogTest : System.Windows.Forms.Form
11: {
12:
13:     private Button okButton;
14:     private Button cancelButton;
15:     private CheckBox checkbox;
16:     private GroupBox radiogroup;
17:     private RadioButton radio1,radio2,radio3;
18:
19:     public int Radio;
20:
21:     public bool Check {
22:         get { return checkbox.Checked; }
23:         set { checkbox.Checked = value;}
24:         }
25:
26:     void OnRadio(Object sender,EventArgs e)
27:     {
28:         int n=0;
29:         foreach(Object o in radiogroup.Controls)
30:         {
31:             if(o is RadioButton)
32:             {
33:                 RadioButton r=(RadioButton)o;
34:                 if(r.Checked)
35:                     Radio=n;
36:                 n++;
37:             }
38:         }
39:     }
40:
41:     public DialogTest()
42:     {
43:
44:         Size = new Size(400,300);
```

LISTING 3.2.9   Continued

```
45:         BorderStyle = FormBorderStyle.FixedDialog;
46:         Text = "Dialog test";
47:
48:         //place the buttons on the form
49:         okButton = new Button();
50:         okButton.DialogResult = DialogResult.OK;
51:         okButton.Location = new Point(20,230);
52:         okButton.Size = new Size(80,25);
53:         okButton.Text = "OK";
54:         Controls.Add(okButton);
55:
56:         cancelButton = new Button();
57:         cancelButton.Location = new Point(300,230);
58:         cancelButton.Size = new Size(80,25);
59:         cancelButton.Text = "Cancel";
60:         cancelButton.DialogResult = DialogResult.Cancel;
61:         Controls.Add(cancelButton);
62:
63:         //place the check box
64:         checkbox = new CheckBox();
65:         checkbox.Location = new Point(20,30);
66:         checkbox.Size = new Size(300,25);
67:         checkbox.Text = "CheckBox";
68:         Controls.Add(checkbox);
69:
70:         //place the radiobuttons
71:         //they need to go into a a group box or a panel...
72:         radiogroup = new GroupBox();
73:         radiogroup.Text = "Radio Buttons";
74:         radiogroup.Location = new Point(10,60);
75:         radiogroup.Size = new Size(380,110);
76:         Controls.Add(radiogroup);
77:
78:         radio1 = new RadioButton();
79:         radio1.Location = new Point(10,15);
80:         // remember this is relative to the group box...
81:         radio1.Size = new Size(360,25);
82:         radio1.Click += new EventHandler(OnRadio);
83:         radio1.Text = "Radio Button #1";
84:         radiogroup.Controls.Add(radio1);
85:
86:
87:         radio2 = new RadioButton();
88:         radio2.Location = new Point(10,40);
```

LISTING 3.2.9   Continued

```
89:          // remember this is relative to the group box...
90:          radio2.Size = new Size(360,25);
91:          radio2.Click += new EventHandler(OnRadio);
92:          radio2.Text = "Radio Button #2";
93:          radiogroup.Controls.Add(radio2);
94:
95:
96:          radio3 = new RadioButton();
97:          radio3.Location = new Point(10,70);
98:          // remember this is relative to the group box...
99:          radio3.Size = new Size(360,25);
100:         radio3.Click += new EventHandler(OnRadio);
101:         radio3.Text = "Radio Button #3";
102:         radiogroup.Controls.Add(radio3);
103:
104:     }
105:
106: }
107:
108: class dtApp : System.Windows.Forms.Form
109: {
110:
111:     void OnExit(Object sender, EventArgs e)
112:     {
113:         Application.Exit();
114:     }
115:
116:     void OnDialogTest(Object sender, EventArgs e)
117:     {
118:         DialogTest dlg = new DialogTest();
119:
120:         DialogResult r=dlg.ShowDialog();
121:
122:
123:         StringWriter sw=new StringWriter(new StringBuilder());
124:
125:         sw.WriteLine("Dialog return value = {0}"+
126:                     "\nRadio Buttons = {1}\nCheck box = {2}",
127:                     r,dlg.Radio,dlg.Check);
128:
129:         MessageBox.Show(sw.ToString());
130:
131:     }
132:
```

LISTING 3.2.9 Continued

```
133:     public dtApp()
134:     {
135:         MainMenu mm=new MainMenu();
136:         mm.MenuItems.Add(new MenuItem("&Dialog"));
137:         mm.MenuItems[0].MenuItems.Add(new MenuItem("&Test",
138:             new EventHandler(OnDialogTest)));
139:         mm.MenuItems[0].MenuItems.Add(new MenuItem("-"));
140:         mm.MenuItems[0].MenuItems.Add(new MenuItem("E&xit",
141:             new EventHandler(OnExit)));
142:         Menu = mm;
143:     }
144:
145:     static void Main()
146:     {
147:         Application.Run(new dtApp());
148:     }
149: }
150:
151: }
```

Looking more closely at the code in Listing 3.2.9, you can see that the radio buttons are, in fact, children of the group box control (lines 70–103), and that they all use the same click handler (lines 26–39). This radiobutton handler reads through the child controls of the group box one at a time. When it finds a radio button, it looks to see if it's checked. If it is, the corresponding value is set in the forms member data. This is one of many techniques you can use to read radio buttons. You could just as easily define one handler per button and set a specific value for each of them.

In the case of radio buttons, the dialog data is stored in a public data member. This can be read directly by external objects. The check box data is read by a public property that accesses the actual check box control.

Simple Edit Controls

There is a simple text box that handles multiline editing and password display for entering text into your forms. The TextBox class can also allow the user to use the Tab key and press Enter so multiline editing is more flexible.

Text edit boxes are illustrated later in the chapter in Listing 3.2.10.

List Boxes

Windows Forms list boxes can be used to display information in vertical or horizontal lists.

List box usage is illustrated in Listing 3.2.10, shown later in this chapter.

Tree Views

The tree view has become a standard for displaying the hierarchical structures of disk directories and other information, such as XML data. Naturally, Windows Forms has a very good tree view class that has great capabilities.

Tree views hold tree nodes. Each node can have a text label associated with it and have other properties such as images that denote the state of the node. Nodes themselves have a `Nodes` collection in which they store their child nodes and so on.

Think of structure of a `TreeView` class as being similar to that of the menu and menu-item relationship.

Tree views support many events for detecting changes in the nodes. The `Beforexxxxx` events will allow you to trap a change before it is effected and cancel it. The `Afterxxxxx` events inform you of the changes that have been made.

Tree views support three event types aside from the ones associated with `RichControl` from which it derives. These event types are `TreeViewEventHandler`, `TreeViewCancelEventHandler`, and `NodeLabelEditEventHandler`. There are also `EventArg` derivatives to go along with these event types

The `TreeView` class, some node operations, and the events associated with them are illustrated shortly in Listing 3.2.10.

Tab Controls

Tab controls can be used to create forms with tabbed pages. They consist of a tab bar that can be selected by the user and a collection of `TabPage` objects that can host other form controls. Listing 3.2.10, later in this chapter, shows tab controls and a host of other controls.

Dynamic Control Management

As you have seen from all of the previous demonstrations in this chapter, the addition, placement, and programming of controls is all performed at runtime, with no reference to layout resources. This implies that Windows Forms controls are easier to use when it comes to creating forms and dialogs that morph and reshape themselves in reaction to the user's commands. Probably everyone who is familiar with MFC will have tried, at one time or another, to create a dynamically changing dialog and have been frustrated by the difficulty of adding and removing controls and handling the messages they generate. Listing 3.2.10, later in this chapter, shows an application with all of the elements shown previously plus some dynamic control features.

About the MungoTabApp

The application laid out in Listing 3.2.10 is rather large but illustrates many of the important principles of Windows Forms development. The code listing is numbered but is interspersed with comments in the form of notes in addition to the code comments we have added. For your own sanity, do not try typing this application. It's supplied with this book or available for download from the Sams Publishing Web site. (See the Appendixes in this book for information.)

> **NOTE**
>
> At this point, it is important to note that the application shown in Listing 3.2.10 has nothing like the structure of an application built with VisualStudio.NET. To use such an application for educational purposes is an almost impossible task. The form layout engine puts code into a routine called InitializeComponent and does not make any effort to order it in a logical manner. The following application has been laid out as logically as possible for your benefit.

LISTING 3.2.10   MungoTabApp.cs: Tabbed Windows and Controls

```
 1: namespace Sams
 2: {
 3:     using System;
 4:     using System.ComponentModel;
 5:     using System.Drawing;
 6:     using System.Windows.Forms;
 7:     using System.Text;
 8:
 9:
10:     /// <summary>
11:     ///     The MungoTabApp is to show off many of the capabilities and
12:     ///     ease of use of the Windows Forms system. The application
13:     ///     is contructed as a form with a tab control along the bottom.
14:     ///     Each page in the tab control shows off a different aspect of
15:     ///     Windows Forms usage
16:     /// </summary>
17:     public class MungoTabApp : Form
18:     {
```

> **NOTE**
>
> The variables and members in the application are all private. This is good practice for encapsulation. First, all the components are declared.

LISTING 3.2.10   Continued

```
19:
20:         // basic parts
21:         private Timer timer1;
22:         private MainMenu mainMenu1;
23:         private TabControl MainTabControl;
24:         private TabPage WelcomeTabPage;
25:         private TabPage SimpleTabPage;
26:         private TabPage DynamicTabPage;
27:         private TabPage ListBoxTabPage;
28:         private TabPage MouseTabPage;
29:         private TabPage TreeTabPage;
30:
31:
32:         //Welcome page.
33:         private RichTextBox WelcomeTextBox;
34:
35:         //Controls for the Simple Controls page
36:         private Label label1;
37:         private Label label2;
38:         private LinkLabel linkLabel1;
39:         private TextBox ClearTextBox;
40:         private TextBox PasswordTextBox;
41:         private GroupBox groupBox1;
42:         private RadioButton radioButton1;
43:         private RadioButton radioButton2;
44:         private Panel panel1;
45:         private RadioButton radioButton3;
46:         private RadioButton radioButton4;
47:         private Button button1;
48:         private CheckBox checkBox1;
49:         private CheckBox checkBox2;
50:
51:         // the listbox page
52:         private ListBox listBox1;
53:         private CheckedListBox checkedListBox1;
54:         private Label label3;
55:         private Label label4;
56:         private Label PickAWord;
57:         private ComboBox comboBox1;
58:         private ListView listView1;
59:         private DateTimePicker dateTimePicker1;
60:         private Label label6;
61:         private Label label7;
62:         private MonthCalendar monthCalendar1;
```

LISTING 3.2.10 Continued

```
63:          private Label label10;
64:          private TrackBar trackBar1;
65:          private ProgressBar progressBar1;
66:          private Label label8;
67:          private DomainUpDown domainUpDown1;
68:          private NumericUpDown numericUpDown1;
69:          private Label label9;
70:          private Label label11;
71:
72:
73:          //Mouse movement and dynamic placement
74:          private Button ClickMeButton;
75:
76:          // Dynamic controls
77:          private CheckBox ShowDynamic;
78:          private CheckBox UseAlternates;
79:          private CheckBox HideChecks;
80:          private GroupBox DynGroup;
81:          private RadioButton DynRadioButtn1;
82:          private RadioButton DynRadioButtn2;
83:          private RadioButton DynRadioButtn3;
84:          private RadioButton DynRadioButtn4;
85:          private ListBox EventList1;
86:          private ListBox EventList2;
87:          private Button ClearEvents1;
88:          private Button ClearEvents2;
89:          //TreeView tab
90:          private TreeView treeView1;
91:          private ListBox tvlistBox;
92:          private Button button4;
93:          private Button button5;
94:
95:
96:          private bool ShowingRadioGroup;
97:
```

> **NOTE**
>
> The next section initializes the Welcome page. Sections initializing each of the Tab control pages follow.

LISTING 3.2.10   Continued

```
 98:         private void InitWelcome()
 99:         {
100:             WelcomeTextBox=new RichTextBox();
101:             WelcomeTabPage = new TabPage();
102:             WelcomeTabPage.Text = "Welcome";
103:             WelcomeTabPage.Size = new System.Drawing.Size(576, 422);
104:             WelcomeTabPage.TabIndex = 0;
105:             WelcomeTextBox.Text = "Welcome to the Mungo Tab App.\n"+
106:                 "This Windows Forms demonstration" +
107:                 " application accompanies the
➥Sams C# and the .NET framework"+
108:                 " book by Bob Powell and Richard Weeks.\n\nThis tab hosts a"+
109:                 " RichTextBox. You can edit this text if you wish."+
110:                 "\n\nThe tabs in this form will show you"+
111:                 " some of the more complex controls that
➥ you can use in your "+
112:                 "Windows Forms application.\n\nPlease
➥examine the source code"+
113:                 " for this application carefully.\n\nBob Powell.\n";
114:             WelcomeTextBox.Size = new System.Drawing.Size(576, 424);
115:             WelcomeTextBox.TabIndex = 0;
116:             WelcomeTextBox.Anchor = AnchorStyles.Top |
117:                 AnchorStyles.Left |
118:                 AnchorStyles.Right |
119:                 AnchorStyles.Bottom;
120:             WelcomeTextBox.Visible = true;
121:             WelcomeTabPage.Controls.Add(WelcomeTextBox);
122:             MainTabControl.Controls.Add(WelcomeTabPage);
123:         }
124:
```

3.2

NOTE

The handlers dedicated to the simple page are in the next section.

```
125:         // Handlers for the simple page
126:
127:         private void OnClickedSimple1(Object sender, EventArgs e)
128:         {
```

LISTING 3.2.10 Continued

```
129:            // This is one of two handlers that may be attached
➡ to the button
130:            string message = "You clicked the big button";
131:            if(this.checkBox1.Checked)
132:            {
133:                message = "And the password is....
➡"+this.PasswordTextBox.Text;
134:            }
135:
136:            MessageBox.Show(message);
137:        }
138:
139:        private void OnCheckColorEdit(Object sender,EventArgs e)
140:        {
141:            // this handler add or removes a second
➡click handler to the button.
142:
143:            if(this.checkBox2.Checked)
144:            {
145:                this.button1.Click += new EventHandler(OnColorEdit);
146:            }
147:            else
148:            {
149:                this.button1.Click -= new EventHandler(OnColorEdit);
150:            }
151:        }
152:
153:        private void OnColorEdit(Object sender, EventArgs e)
154:        {
155:            // This second handler is added to the
➡click event of the button
156:            // when the check box is checked.
157:            ColorDialog dlg = new ColorDialog();
158:            if(dlg.ShowDialog() == DialogResult.OK)
159:            {
160:                this.panel1.BackColor=dlg.Color;
161:            }
162:        }
163:
164:        //This handler is invoked by clicking the link label
165:        //it will take you to a web site.
166:        private void LinkClick(Object sender, EventArgs e)
167:        {
168:            this.linkLabel1.LinkVisited=true;
```

LISTING 3.2.10 Continued

```
169:                if(this.ClearTextBox.Text=="This is an editable text box")
170:                {
171:                    System.Diagnostics.Process.Start("IExplore.exe ",
172:                        "http://www.bobpowell.net/");
173:                }
174:                else
175:                {
176:                    try
177:                    {
178:                        System.Diagnostics.Process.Start(ClearTextBox.Text);
179:                    }
180:                    catch(Exception)
181:                    {
182:                        MessageBox.Show("Cannot start
➥process "+ClearTextBox.Text);
183:                    }
184:                }
185:                this.linkLabel1.Text = "Been there, Done that!";
186:            }
187:
188:            //This handler is invoked each time the text in the clear text box
189:            // is modified. It transfers the text to the link button.
190:            // but only if the link has been visited.
191:            private new void TextChanged(Object sender, EventArgs e)
192:            {
193:                if(linkLabel1.LinkVisited )
194:                {
195:                    linkLabel1.Text = ClearTextBox.Text;
196:                }
197:
198:            }
199:
```

3.2

USER INTERFACE
COMPONENTS

NOTE

The simple controls page is initialized here.

Just before the actual initialization, we have placed the handlers that are associated with the events on this page. This structure is repeated throughout the application.

LISTING 3.2.10   Continued

```
200:          // initializes the simple page.
201:          private void InitSimple()
202:          {
203:              SimpleTabPage = new TabPage();
204:              SimpleTabPage.Size = new System.Drawing.Size(576, 422);
205:              SimpleTabPage.TabIndex = 1;
206:              SimpleTabPage.Text = "Simple controls";
207:
208:              button1 = new Button();
209:              button1.Location = new System.Drawing.Point(32, 240);
210:              button1.Size = new System.Drawing.Size(520, 32);
211:              button1.TabIndex = 7;
212:              button1.Text = "Buttons can be clicked...";
213:              button1.Click+=new EventHandler(OnClickedSimple1);
214:              checkBox1 = new CheckBox();
215:              checkBox1.Location = new System.Drawing.Point(32, 288);
216:              checkBox1.Size = new System.Drawing.Size(520, 16);
217:              checkBox1.TabIndex = 8;
218:              checkBox1.Text =
219:                  "Checking this box will make the button "+
220:                  "above say whats in the password box";
221:              checkBox2 = new CheckBox();
222:              checkBox2.Location = new System.Drawing.Point(32, 327);
223:              checkBox2.Size = new System.Drawing.Size(520, 16);
224:              checkBox2.TabIndex = 9;
225:              checkBox2.Text = "Checking this box will make the button" +
226:                  " above edit the colour of the text panel";
227:              checkBox2.Click += new EventHandler(OnCheckColorEdit);
228:
229:              ClearTextBox = new TextBox();
230:              ClearTextBox.Location = new System.Drawing.Point(344, 8);
231:              ClearTextBox.Size = new System.Drawing.Size(216, 20);
232:              ClearTextBox.TabIndex = 2;
233:              ClearTextBox.Text = "This is an editable text box";
234:
235:              domainUpDown1 = new DomainUpDown();
236:              domainUpDown1.AccessibleName = "DomainUpDown";
237:              domainUpDown1.AccessibleRole = AccessibleRole.ComboBox;
238:              domainUpDown1.Location = new System.Drawing.Point(128, 368);
239:              domainUpDown1.Size = new System.Drawing.Size(144, 20);
240:              domainUpDown1.TabIndex = 10;
241:              domainUpDown1.Text = "domainUpDown1";
242:              domainUpDown1.Items.AddRange(new object [])("England",
243:                                                  "Africa",
244:                                                  "Mongolia",
245:                                                  "Japan"});
```

LISTING 3.2.10   Continued

```
246:
247:             groupBox1 = new GroupBox();
248:             groupBox1.Location = new System.Drawing.Point(8, 80);
249:             groupBox1.Size = new System.Drawing.Size(560, 80);
250:             groupBox1.TabIndex = 5;
251:             groupBox1.TabStop = false;
252:             groupBox1.Text = "A GroupBox";
253:
254:             label1 = new Label();
255:             label1.Location = new System.Drawing.Point(8, 8);
256:             label1.Size = new System.Drawing.Size(144, 24);
257:             label1.TabIndex = 0;
258:             label1.Text = "This is a label control";
259:
260:             label2 = new Label();
261:             label2.Location = new System.Drawing.Point(8, 41);
262:             label2.Size = new System.Drawing.Size(328, 24);
263:             label2.TabIndex = 4;
264:             label2.Text = "The edit box to the right has a
➥password character";
265:
266:             label9 = new Label();
267:             label9.Location = new System.Drawing.Point(16, 368);
268:             label9.Size = new System.Drawing.Size(104, 24);
269:             label9.TabIndex = 12;
270:             label9.Text = "DomainUpDown";
271:
272:             label10 = new Label();
273:             label10.Location = new System.Drawing.Point(276, 370);
274:             label10.Size = new System.Drawing.Size(104, 24);
275:             label10.TabIndex = 13;
276:             label10.Text = "NumericUpDown";
277:
278:             linkLabel1 = new LinkLabel();
279:             linkLabel1.Location = new System.Drawing.Point(152, 8);
280:             linkLabel1.Size = new System.Drawing.Size(176, 24);
281:             linkLabel1.TabIndex = 1;
282:             linkLabel1.TabStop = true;
283:             linkLabel1.Text = "Link labels are like hypertext links";
284:             linkLabel1.Click += new EventHandler(LinkClick);
285:
286:             numericUpDown1 = new NumericUpDown();
287:             numericUpDown1.BeginInit();
288:             numericUpDown1.EndInit();
289:             numericUpDown1.Location = new System.Drawing.Point(392, 368);
290:             numericUpDown1.Size = new System.Drawing.Size(176, 20);
```

LISTING 3.2.10   Continued

```
291:              numericUpDown1.TabIndex = 11;
292:
293:              panel1 = new Panel();
294:              panel1.BackColor =
295:                  (System.Drawing.Color)System.Drawing.
➥Color.FromArgb((byte)255,
296:                  (byte)255,
297:                  (byte)128);
298:              panel1.BorderStyle = (BorderStyle)FormBorderStyle.Fixed3D;
299:              panel1.Location = new System.Drawing.Point(8, 168);
300:              panel1.Size = new System.Drawing.Size(560, 64);
301:              panel1.TabIndex = 6;
302:
303:              radioButton1 = new RadioButton();
304:              radioButton1.Location = new System.Drawing.Point(16, 24);
305:              radioButton1.Size = new System.Drawing.Size(504, 16);
306:              radioButton1.TabIndex = 0;
307:              radioButton1.Text = "RadioButtons";
308:
309:              radioButton2 = new RadioButton();
310:              radioButton2.Location = new System.Drawing.Point(16, 48);
311:              radioButton2.Size = new System.Drawing.Size(504, 16);
312:              radioButton2.TabIndex = 1;
313:              radioButton2.Text = "In a groupBox are used to isolate";
314:
315:              radioButton3 = new RadioButton();
316:              radioButton3.Location = new System.Drawing.Point(16, 8);
317:              radioButton3.Size = new System.Drawing.Size(536, 16);
318:              radioButton3.TabIndex = 0;
319:              radioButton3.Text = "Other radio buttons";
320:
321:              radioButton4 = new RadioButton();
322:              radioButton4.Location = new System.Drawing.Point(16, 32);
323:              radioButton4.Size = new System.Drawing.Size(536, 16);
324:              radioButton4.TabIndex = 1;
325:              radioButton4.Text = "in other GroupBoxes,
➥or in this case, Panels.";
326:
327:              panel1.Controls.Add(radioButton3);
328:              panel1.Controls.Add(radioButton4);
329:
330:              groupBox1.Controls.Add(radioButton1);
331:              groupBox1.Controls.Add(radioButton2);
332:
```

LISTING 3.2.10   Continued

```
333:             PasswordTextBox = new TextBox();
334:             PasswordTextBox.Location = new System.Drawing.Point(344, 40);
335:             PasswordTextBox.PasswordChar = '*';
336:             PasswordTextBox.Size = new System.Drawing.Size(216, 20);
337:             PasswordTextBox.TabIndex = 3;
338:             PasswordTextBox.Text = "Password";
339:
340:             ClearTextBox.TextChanged += new EventHandler(TextChanged);
341:
342:             SimpleTabPage.Controls.Add(button1);
343:             SimpleTabPage.Controls.Add(checkBox1);
344:             SimpleTabPage.Controls.Add(checkBox2);
345:             SimpleTabPage.Controls.Add(ClearTextBox);
346:             SimpleTabPage.Controls.Add(domainUpDown1);
347:             SimpleTabPage.Controls.Add(groupBox1);
348:             SimpleTabPage.Controls.Add(label1);
349:             SimpleTabPage.Controls.Add(label10);
350:             SimpleTabPage.Controls.Add(label2);
351:             SimpleTabPage.Controls.Add(label9);
352:             SimpleTabPage.Controls.Add(linkLabel1);
353:             SimpleTabPage.Controls.Add(numericUpDown1);
354:             SimpleTabPage.Controls.Add(panel1);
355:             SimpleTabPage.Controls.Add(PasswordTextBox);
356:         }
357:
```

NOTE

Event handlers for the list box tab are in the following section.

```
358:         // List box tab event handlers.
359:         // This handler transfers the value of the trackbar
➥to the progress bar.
360:         private void OnTrack(Object sender, EventArgs e)
361:         {
362:             TrackBar b=(TrackBar)sender;
363:             this.progressBar1.Value = b.Value;
364:         }
365:
366:         // This handler constructs a sentence from the
➥checked items in the list
367:         // and displays it in a label to the right of the control.
```

LISTING 3.2.10 Continued

```
368:          private void CheckedListHandler(Object sender,
➥ItemCheckEventArgs e)
369:          {
370:              StringBuilder sb=new StringBuilder();
371:              int ni=-1;
372:              if(e.NewValue==CheckState.Checked)
373:                  ni=e.Index;
374:              for(int i=0;i<checkedListBox1.Items.Count;i++)
375:              {
376:                  if(i==ni || (i!=e.Index && checkedListBox1.
➥GetItemChecked(i)))
377:                      sb.Append(checkedListBox1.Items[i].ToString()+" ");
378:              }
379:              PickAWord.Text = sb.ToString();
380:          }
381:
382:          // this handler gets the items from the list box
➥and changes their case
383:          // as the mouse passes over them.
384:          private void ListBoxMouseOver(Object sender, MouseEventArgs e)
385:          {
386:              string s;
387:              int i=0;
388:              // first we reset the case of all the strings
389:              foreach(object o in listBox1.Items)
390:              {
391:                  s=(string)o;
392:                  listBox1.Items[i++]=s.ToLower();
393:              }
394:              i = listBox1.IndexFromPoint(e.X,e.Y);
395:              if(i>-1)
396:              {
397:                  s=(string)listBox1.Items[i];
398:                  listBox1.Items[i]=s.ToUpper();
399:              }
400:          }
401:
402:          // Right clicking the combo box invokes this handler
403:          // it sorts the contents of the dropdown.
404:          private void SortComboboxHandler(Object sender, EventArgs e)
405:          {
406:              this.comboBox1.Sorted=true;
407:          }
408:
```

LISTING 3.2.10 Continued

> **NOTE**
>
> The next section illustrates how the list box classes are used. There is also a track bar control and a progress bar with which you can experiment.

```
409:            // List box tab initialization.
410:            private void InitLists()
411:            {
412:                ListBoxTabPage = new TabPage();
413:                ListBoxTabPage.Size = new System.Drawing.Size(576, 422);
414:                ListBoxTabPage.TabIndex = 2;
415:                ListBoxTabPage.Text = "List boxes";
416:
417:                checkedListBox1 = new CheckedListBox();
418:                checkedListBox1.Items.AddRange(new object[] {"The",
419:                          "These","All","Words","Men","Are","Can","Be",
420:                          "Might","Not","Be","Made","As","Happy","Equal",
421:                          "Stupid","Lost"});
422:                checkedListBox1.Location = new System.Drawing.Point(216, 8);
423:                checkedListBox1.Size = new System.Drawing.Size(192, 94);
424:                checkedListBox1.TabIndex = 1;
425:                checkedListBox1.CheckOnClick=true;
426:                checkedListBox1.ItemCheck +=
427:                    new ItemCheckEventHandler(CheckedListHandler);
428:
429:                comboBox1 = new ComboBox();
430:                comboBox1.Items.AddRange(new object[] {"A",
431:                          "Little","aardvark","Never","Hurt",
432:                          "Anyone","5 ","9 ","7 ","1","0 ",
433:                          "2","4","3","6","8"});
434:                comboBox1.Location = new System.Drawing.Point(8, 144);
435:                comboBox1.Size = new System.Drawing.Size(184, 21);
436:                comboBox1.TabIndex = 5;
437:                comboBox1.Text = "Context menu sorts";
438:                ContextMenu m=new ContextMenu();
439:                MenuItem t=new MenuItem("Sort",new EventHandler
➥(SortComboboxHandler));
440:                m.MenuItems.Add(t);
441:                comboBox1.ContextMenu = m;
442:
443:                dateTimePicker1 = new DateTimePicker();
444:                dateTimePicker1.Location = new System.Drawing.Point(216, 272);
```

LISTING 3.2.10   Continued

```
445:               dateTimePicker1.Size = new System.Drawing.Size(344, 20);
446:               dateTimePicker1.TabIndex = 7;
447:
448:               label3 = new Label();
449:               label3.Location = new System.Drawing.Point(8, 112);
450:               label3.Size = new System.Drawing.Size(184, 16);
451:               label3.TabIndex = 2;
452:               label3.Text = "A Simple list box";
453:               label4 = new Label();
454:               label4.Location = new System.Drawing.Point(224, 112);
455:               label4.Size = new System.Drawing.Size(184, 16);
456:               label4.TabIndex = 3;
457:               label4.Text = "A Checked list box";
458:               label6 = new Label();
459:               label6.Location = new System.Drawing.Point(216, 248);
460:               label6.Size = new System.Drawing.Size(184, 16);
461:               label6.TabIndex = 8;
462:               label6.Text = "A list view";
463:               label7 = new Label();
464:               label7.Location = new System.Drawing.Point(214, 303);
465:               label7.Size = new System.Drawing.Size(184, 16);
466:               label7.TabIndex = 9;
467:               label7.Text = "A DateTimePicker";
468:               label8 = new Label();
469:               label8.Location = new System.Drawing.Point(7, 341);
470:               label8.Size = new System.Drawing.Size(184, 16);
471:               label8.TabIndex = 11;
472:               label8.Text = "The MonthCalender control";
473:
474:               label11 = new Label();
475:               label11.Location = new System.Drawing.Point(7, 384);
476:               label11.Size = new System.Drawing.Size(184, 16);
477:               label11.TabIndex = 14;
478:               label11.Text = "Trackbar and progress bar (Right)";
479:
480:               listBox1 = new ListBox();
481:               listBox1.Items.AddRange( new object[] {"Fish",
482:                       "Chips","Vinegar","Marmite","Cream Crackers",
483:                       "Marmalade","Stilton","Mushy Peas",
484:                       "Sherbert Lemons","Wellie boots","Spanners"});
485:               listBox1.Location = new System.Drawing.Point(8, 8);
486:               listBox1.Size = new System.Drawing.Size(184, 95);
487:               listBox1.TabIndex = 0;
488:               listBox1.MouseMove += new MouseEventHandler(ListBoxMouseOver);
489:
```

LISTING 3.2.10 Continued

```
490:                listView1 = new ListView();
491:                listView1.ForeColor = System.Drawing.SystemColors.WindowText;
492:                listView1.Items.Add(new ListViewItem("knives"));
493:                listView1.Items.Add(new ListViewItem("forks"));
494:                listView1.Items.Add(new ListViewItem("spoons"));
495:                listView1.Items.Add(new ListViewItem("dogs"));
496:                listView1.Items.Add(new ListViewItem("fish"));
497:                listView1.Location = new System.Drawing.Point(216, 136);
498:                listView1.Size = new System.Drawing.Size(352, 96);
499:                listView1.TabIndex = 6;
500:
501:                monthCalendar1 = new MonthCalendar();
502:                monthCalendar1.Location = new System.Drawing.Point(8, 184);
503:                monthCalendar1.TabIndex = 10;
504:                monthCalendar1.TabStop = true;
505:
506:                progressBar1 = new ProgressBar();
507:                progressBar1.Location = new System.Drawing.Point(216, 344);
508:                progressBar1.Size = new System.Drawing.Size(336, 24);
509:                progressBar1.TabIndex = 13;
510:
511:                PickAWord = new Label();
512:                PickAWord.Location = new System.Drawing.Point(416, 8);
513:                PickAWord.Size = new System.Drawing.Size(152, 96);
514:                PickAWord.TabIndex = 4;
515:
516:                trackBar1 = new TrackBar();
517:                trackBar1.BeginInit();
518:                trackBar1.Location = new System.Drawing.Point(272, 376);
519:                trackBar1.Maximum = 100;
520:                trackBar1.Size = new System.Drawing.Size(184, 42);
521:                trackBar1.TabIndex = 12;
522:                trackBar1.ValueChanged += new EventHandler(OnTrack);
523:                trackBar1.EndInit();
524:
525:
526:
527:                ListBoxTabPage.Controls.Add(checkedListBox1);
528:                ListBoxTabPage.Controls.Add(comboBox1);
529:                ListBoxTabPage.Controls.Add(dateTimePicker1);
530:                ListBoxTabPage.Controls.Add(label11);
531:                ListBoxTabPage.Controls.Add(label3);
532:                ListBoxTabPage.Controls.Add(label4);
533:                ListBoxTabPage.Controls.Add(label6);
```

3.2

USER INTERFACE
COMPONENTS

LISTING 3.2.10   Continued

```
534:                ListBoxTabPage.Controls.Add(label7);
535:                ListBoxTabPage.Controls.Add(label8);
536:                ListBoxTabPage.Controls.Add(listBox1);
537:                ListBoxTabPage.Controls.Add(listView1);
538:                ListBoxTabPage.Controls.Add(monthCalendar1);
539:                ListBoxTabPage.Controls.Add(PickAWord);
540:                ListBoxTabPage.Controls.Add(progressBar1);
541:                ListBoxTabPage.Controls.Add(trackBar1);
542:            }
```

NOTE

The event handlers for the Dynamic `RadioButtons` tab are a little complex. A group of buttons is added or destroyed as needed, and a set of events are added or re-directed according to the user's choice.

```
543:
544:            // This is the first of two possible events fired by the
545:            // dynamic radio buttons. It adds to a list box.
546:            private void RadioEvent1(Object sender, EventArgs e)
547:            {
548:                RadioButton r = (RadioButton)sender;
549:                this.EventList1.Items.Add("Event #1 from: "+r.Text);
550:            }
551:
552:            // This is the second of two possible events fired by the
553:            // dynamic radio buttons. It adds to a list box.
554:            private void RadioEvent2(Object sender, EventArgs e)
555:            {
556:                RadioButton r = (RadioButton)sender;
557:                this.EventList2.Items.Add("Event #2 from: "+r.Text);
558:            }
559:
560:            // This handler clears the first list box out
561:            private void Clear1(Object sender,EventArgs e)
562:            {
563:                this.EventList1.Items.Clear();
564:            }
565:
566:            // This handler clears the second list box out
567:            private void Clear2(Object sender,EventArgs e)
```

LISTING 3.2.10   Continued

```
568:          {
569:                this.EventList2.Items.Clear();
570:          }
571:
572:          // This routine removes all events from all radio buttons
573:          // in the dynamic page.
574:          private void RemoveEvents()
575:          {
576:              DynRadioButtn4.Click -= new EventHandler(RadioEvent1);
577:              DynRadioButtn3.Click -= new EventHandler(RadioEvent1);
578:              DynRadioButtn2.Click -= new EventHandler(RadioEvent1);
579:              DynRadioButtn1.Click -= new EventHandler(RadioEvent1);
580:              DynRadioButtn4.Click -= new EventHandler(RadioEvent2);
581:              DynRadioButtn3.Click -= new EventHandler(RadioEvent2);
582:              DynRadioButtn2.Click -= new EventHandler(RadioEvent2);
583:              DynRadioButtn1.Click -= new EventHandler(RadioEvent2);
584:          }
585:
586:          // This method add the correct event handler alternative
587:          // to the radiobuttons on the dynamic page
588:          private void AddEvents()
589:          {
590:
591:              if(!this.UseAlternates.Checked )
592:              {
593:                  DynRadioButtn4.Click += new EventHandler(RadioEvent1);
594:                  DynRadioButtn3.Click += new EventHandler(RadioEvent1);
595:                  DynRadioButtn2.Click += new EventHandler(RadioEvent1);
596:                  DynRadioButtn1.Click += new EventHandler(RadioEvent1);
597:              }
598:              else
599:              {
600:                  DynRadioButtn4.Click += new EventHandler(RadioEvent2);
601:                  DynRadioButtn3.Click += new EventHandler(RadioEvent2);
602:                  DynRadioButtn2.Click += new EventHandler(RadioEvent2);
603:                  DynRadioButtn1.Click += new EventHandler(RadioEvent2);
604:              }
605:          }
606:
607:          // This event handler swops the dynamic radio
    ➥button event handlers
608:          public void OnUseAlternates(Object sender, EventArgs e)
609:          {
610:              if(ShowingRadioGroup)
```

3.2

USER INTERFACE
COMPONENTS

LISTING 3.2.10   Continued

```
611:                  {
612:                      RemoveEvents();
613:                      AddEvents();
614:                  }
615:          }
616:
617:          // This method removes the whole dynamic radiobutton
618:          // panel, clears the event list and destroys the items
619:          public void RemoveRadio()
620:          {
621:              if(ShowingRadioGroup)
622:              {
623:                  DynGroup.Controls.Remove(DynRadioButtn4);
624:                  DynGroup.Controls.Remove(DynRadioButtn3);
625:                  DynGroup.Controls.Remove(DynRadioButtn2);
626:                  DynGroup.Controls.Remove(DynRadioButtn1);
627:                  DynamicTabPage.Controls.Remove(DynGroup);
628:
629:                  RemoveEvents();
630:                  DynamicTabPage.Controls.Remove(DynGroup);
631:
632:                  DynRadioButtn4.Dispose();
633:                  DynRadioButtn3.Dispose();
634:                  DynRadioButtn2.Dispose();
635:                  DynRadioButtn1.Dispose();
636:                  DynGroup.Dispose();
637:
638:                  ShowingRadioGroup = false;
639:
640:              }
641:          }
642:
643:          //This method adds the dynamic radio button group and
644:          //wires up the event handlers.
645:          private void AddRadio()
646:          {
647:              if(!ShowingRadioGroup)
648:              {
649:                  DynGroup = new GroupBox();
650:                  DynGroup.Location = new System.Drawing.Point(240, 16);
651:                  DynGroup.Size = new System.Drawing.Size(312, 120);
652:                  DynGroup.TabIndex = 3;
653:                  DynGroup.TabStop = false;
654:                  DynGroup.Text = "Dynamic radiobuttons";
655:
```

LISTING 3.2.10 Continued

```
656:                    DynRadioButtn1 = new RadioButton();
657:                    DynRadioButtn1.Location = new
➥System.Drawing.Point(8, 24);
658:                    DynRadioButtn1.Size = new System.Drawing.Size(296, 16);
659:                    DynRadioButtn1.TabIndex = 0;
660:                    DynRadioButtn1.Text = "Choice 1";
661:
662:                    DynRadioButtn2 = new RadioButton();
663:                    DynRadioButtn2.Location = new
➥System.Drawing.Point(8, 41);
664:                    DynRadioButtn2.Size = new System.Drawing.Size(296, 16);
665:                    DynRadioButtn2.TabIndex = 1;
666:                    DynRadioButtn2.Text = "Choice 2";
667:
668:                    DynRadioButtn3 = new RadioButton();
669:                    DynRadioButtn3.Location =
➥new System.Drawing.Point(8, 64);
670:                    DynRadioButtn3.Size = new System.Drawing.Size(296, 16);
671:                    DynRadioButtn3.TabIndex = 2;
672:                    DynRadioButtn3.Text = "Choice 3";
673:
674:                    DynRadioButtn4 = new RadioButton();
675:                    DynRadioButtn4.Location =
➥new System.Drawing.Point(8, 88);
676:                    DynRadioButtn4.Size = new System.Drawing.Size(296, 16);
677:                    DynRadioButtn4.TabIndex = 3;
678:                    DynRadioButtn4.Text = "Choice 4";
679:
680:                    AddEvents();
681:
682:                    DynGroup.Controls.Add(DynRadioButtn4);
683:                    DynGroup.Controls.Add(DynRadioButtn3);
684:                    DynGroup.Controls.Add(DynRadioButtn2);
685:                    DynGroup.Controls.Add(DynRadioButtn1);
686:                    DynamicTabPage.Controls.Add(DynGroup);
687:
688:                    ShowingRadioGroup = true;
689:                }
690:            }
691:
692:        //This event handler uses helper methods to manage
➥the presence of the
693:        //dynamic radiobutton group and the handlers that they use
694:        private void ShowDynamicEvent(Object sender, EventArgs e)
```

LISTING 3.2.10 Continued

```
695:              {
696:                  CheckBox b=(CheckBox) sender;
697:
698:                  if(b.Checked)
699:                  {
700:                      AddRadio();
701:                  }
702:                  else
703:                  {
704:                      RemoveRadio();
705:                  }
706:
707:              }
708:
709:          // This event handler adds or removes the dynamic
➡check buttons and
710:          // repositions the control to make it look neat and tidy.
711:          private void AddChecks(Object sender, EventArgs e)
712:          {
713:              CheckBox c=(CheckBox)sender;
714:
715:              if(this.HideChecks.Checked)
716:              {
717:                  RemoveRadio();
718:                  c.Location = new Point(8,16);
719:                  DynamicTabPage.Controls.Remove(UseAlternates);
720:                  DynamicTabPage.Controls.Remove(ShowDynamic);
721:                  ShowDynamic.Click -= new EventHandler(ShowDynamicEvent);
722:                  UseAlternates.Dispose();
723:                  ShowDynamic.Dispose();
724:              }
725:              else
726:              {
727:                  c.Location = new Point(8,64);
728:
729:                  ShowDynamic = new CheckBox();
730:                  ShowDynamic.Location = new System.Drawing.Point(8, 16);
731:                  ShowDynamic.Size = new System.Drawing.Size(168, 16);
732:                  ShowDynamic.TabIndex = 0;
733:                  ShowDynamic.Text = "Show dynamic RadioRuttons";
734:                  ShowDynamic.Click += new EventHandler(ShowDynamicEvent);
735:
736:                  UseAlternates = new CheckBox();
737:                  UseAlternates.Location = new System.Drawing.Point(8, 40);
```

LISTING 3.2.10 Continued

```
738:                        UseAlternates.Size = new System.Drawing.Size(168, 16);
739:                        UseAlternates.TabIndex = 1;
740:                        UseAlternates.Text = "Use alternate handlers";
741:                        UseAlternates.Click += new EventHandler(OnUseAlternates);
742:
743:                        DynamicTabPage.Controls.Add(UseAlternates);
744:                        DynamicTabPage.Controls.Add(ShowDynamic);
745:                }
746:        }
747:
```

> **NOTE**
>
> Initialization for the Dynamic Controls tab follows in the next section.

```
748:                // This method initializes the dynamic buttons tab
749:                private void InitDynamic()
750:                {
751:
752:                        DynamicTabPage = new TabPage();
753:                        DynamicTabPage.Size = new System.Drawing.Size(576, 422);
754:                        DynamicTabPage.TabIndex = 3;
755:                        DynamicTabPage.Text = "Dynamic controls";
756:
757:                        ClearEvents1 = new Button();
758:                        ClearEvents1.Location = new System.Drawing.Point(48, 328);
759:                        ClearEvents1.Size = new System.Drawing.Size(128, 24);
760:                        ClearEvents1.TabIndex = 6;
761:                        ClearEvents1.Text = "Clear the events";
762:                        ClearEvents1.Click += new EventHandler(Clear1);
763:
764:                        ClearEvents2 = new Button();
765:                        ClearEvents2.Location = new System.Drawing.Point(340, 330);
766:                        ClearEvents2.Size = new System.Drawing.Size(128, 24);
767:                        ClearEvents2.TabIndex = 7;
768:                        ClearEvents2.Text = "Clear the events";
769:                        ClearEvents2.Click += new EventHandler(Clear2);
770:
771:                        EventList1 = new ListBox();
772:                        EventList1.Location = new System.Drawing.Point(16, 176);
773:                        EventList1.Size = new System.Drawing.Size(200, 121);
774:                        EventList1.TabIndex = 4;
```

LISTING 3.2.10   Continued

```
775:                EventList2 = new ListBox();
776:                EventList2.Location = new System.Drawing.Point(308, 180);
777:                EventList2.Size = new System.Drawing.Size(200, 121);
778:                EventList2.TabIndex = 5;
779:
780:                HideChecks = new CheckBox();
781:                HideChecks.Location = new System.Drawing.Point(8, 64);
782:                HideChecks.Size = new System.Drawing.Size(168, 16);
783:                HideChecks.TabIndex = 2;
784:                HideChecks.Text = "Hide checkboxes";
785:                HideChecks.Click += new EventHandler(AddChecks);
786:                AddChecks(HideChecks,new EventArgs());
787:
788:                DynamicTabPage.Controls.Add(ClearEvents1);
789:                DynamicTabPage.Controls.Add(ClearEvents2);
790:                DynamicTabPage.Controls.Add(EventList2);
791:                DynamicTabPage.Controls.Add(EventList1);
792:                DynamicTabPage.Controls.Add(HideChecks);
793:            }
794:
```

NOTE

Now come the handlers for the mouse interaction tab.

```
795:            //
796:            // Handlers for the mouse tab
797:            //
798:
799:
800:            // This handler moves the button to the
➡opposite side of the tab-page
801:            // from the mouse cursor
802:            private void OnMouseMoved(Object sender, MouseEventArgs e)
803:            {
804:                Point center =
805:                    new Point(MouseTabPage.Width/2,MouseTabPage.Height/2);
806:                ClickMeButton.Location =
807:                    new Point(center.X-
➡(ClickMeButton.Size.Width/2)-(e.X-center.X),
808:                    center.Y-(ClickMeButton.Size.Height/2)-(e.Y-center.Y));
809:            }
```

LISTING 3.2.10 Continued

```
810:
811:        //This handler shows when the button is caught and clicked.
812:        private void OnClickedClickme(Object sender, EventArgs e)
813:        {
814:            MessageBox.Show("Caught me!!");
815:        }
816:
```

> **NOTE**
>
> The Mouse Interaction tab initialization is in the following section.

```
817:        // This method initializes the mouse page.
818:        private void InitMouse()
819:        {
820:            MouseTabPage = new TabPage();
821:            MouseTabPage.Controls.Add(ClickMeButton);
822:            MouseTabPage.Size = new System.Drawing.Size(576, 422);
823:            MouseTabPage.TabIndex = 4;
824:            MouseTabPage.Text = "Mouse interaction";
825:
826:            ClickMeButton = new Button();
827:            ClickMeButton.Location = new System.Drawing.Point(200, 128);
828:            ClickMeButton.Size = new System.Drawing.Size(184, 112);
829:            ClickMeButton.TabIndex = 0;
830:            ClickMeButton.Text = "Click me!";
831:            ClickMeButton.Click += new EventHandler(OnClickedClickme);
832:
833:            MouseTabPage.Controls.Add(ClickMeButton);
834:
835:            MouseTabPage.MouseMove +=
➥new MouseEventHandler(OnMouseMoved);
836:        }
837:
```

3.2

> **NOTE**
>
> The handlers for the tree tab follow in this section. Note how the Beforexxx and
> Afterxxx action handlers are used to create the list of actions taking place.

LISTING 3.2.10   Continued

```
838:            //Handlers for the tree tab....
839:
840:
841:            //The overloaded list function shows the treee
➡view events in a list
842:
843:        private void List(string s, TreeNode n)
844:        {
845:            string o=s+" "+n.Text;
846:            tvlistBox.Items.Add(o);
847:        }
848:
849:        private void List(string s, string l, TreeNode n)
850:        {
851:            string o=s+" (new = "+l+") current = "+n.Text;
852:            tvlistBox.Items.Add(o);
853:        }
854:
855:            // These handlers simply reflect the event
➡type and a little bit of
856:            // node data to the list box on the right of
➡the treeView1 control.
857:        private void OnAfterCheck(Object sender,TreeViewEventArgs e)
858:        {
859:            List("AfterCheck", e.Node);
860:        }
861:
862:        private void OnAfterCollapse(Object sender,TreeViewEventArgs e)
863:        {
864:            List("AfterCollapse", e.Node);
865:        }
866:
867:        private void OnAfterExpand(Object sender,TreeViewEventArgs e)
868:        {
869:            List("AfterExpand", e.Node);
870:        }
871:
872:        private void OnAfterSelect(Object sender,TreeViewEventArgs e)
873:        {
874:            List("AfterSelect", e.Node);
875:        }
876:        private void OnBeforeCheck(Object
➡sender,TreeViewCancelEventArgs e)
877:        {
```

LISTING 3.2.10   Continued

```
878:                 List("AfterCollapse", e.Node);
879:           }
880:           private void OnBeforeCollapse(Object
➥sender,TreeViewCancelEventArgs e)
881:           {
882:                 List("BeforeCollapse", e.Node);
883:           }
884:           private void OnBeforeExpand(Object
➥sender,TreeViewCancelEventArgs e)
885:           {
886:                 List("BeforeExpand", e.Node);
887:           }
888:           private void OnBeforeLabelEdit
➥(Object sender,NodeLabelEditEventArgs e)
889:           {
890:                 List("BeforeEdit", e.Label, e.Node);
891:           }
892:
893:           private void OnAfterLabelEdit(Object
➥sender,NodeLabelEditEventArgs e)
894:           {
895:                 List("AfterEdit", e.Label, e.Node);
896:           }
897:
898:
899:           private void OnBeforeSelect(Object
➥sender,TreeViewCancelEventArgs e)
900:           {
901:                 List("BeforeSelect", e.Node);
902:           }
903:
904:           private void OnAddRoot(Object sender, EventArgs e)
905:           {
906:               button5.Enabled=true;
907:
908:               if(treeView1.Nodes.Count==0)
909:               {
910:                   treeView1.Nodes.Add(new TreeNode("Root node"));
911:               }
912:               else
913:               {
914:                   treeView1.Nodes.Add(new TreeNode("Sibling node"));
915:               }
916:           }
```

LISTING 3.2.10   Continued

```
917:
918:        private void OnAddChild(Object sender, EventArgs e)
919:        {
920:            if(treeView1.SelectedNode==null)
921:                return;
922:            treeView1.SelectedNode.Nodes.Add(new TreeNode("Child"));
923:        }
924:
```

> **NOTE**
>
> The following section initializes the tree control test tab.

```
925:        //Initializes the tree control.
926:        private void InitTree()
927:        {
928:            TreeTabPage = new TabPage();
929:            TreeTabPage.Text = "TreeView";
930:            TreeTabPage.Size = new System.Drawing.Size(576, 422);
931:            TreeTabPage.TabIndex = 5;
932:
933:            treeView1 = new TreeView();
934:            treeView1.Anchor = AnchorStyles.Left |
935:                AnchorStyles.Top |
936:                AnchorStyles.Right |
937:                AnchorStyles.Bottom;
938:            treeView1.Size = new System.Drawing.Size(264, 360);
939:            treeView1.TabIndex = 0;
940:            treeView1.ShowLines=true;
941:            treeView1.ShowPlusMinus=true;
942:            treeView1.ShowRootLines=true;
943:            treeView1.LabelEdit=true;
944:
945:            treeView1.AfterCheck +=
946:                new  TreeViewEventHandler(OnAfterCheck);
947:            treeView1.AfterCollapse +=
948:                new  TreeViewEventHandler(OnAfterCollapse);
949:            treeView1.AfterExpand +=
950:                new  TreeViewEventHandler(OnAfterExpand);
951:            treeView1.AfterSelect +=
952:                new  TreeViewEventHandler(OnAfterSelect);
```

LISTING 3.2.10 Continued

```
953:                 treeView1.AfterLabelEdit +=
954:                     new  NodeLabelEditEventHandler(OnAfterLabelEdit);
955:                 treeView1.BeforeCheck +=
956:                     new  TreeViewCancelEventHandler(OnBeforeCheck);
957:                 treeView1.BeforeCollapse +=
958:                     new  TreeViewCancelEventHandler(OnBeforeCollapse);
959:                 treeView1.BeforeExpand +=
960:                     new  TreeViewCancelEventHandler(OnBeforeExpand);
961:                 treeView1.BeforeSelect +=
962:                     new  TreeViewCancelEventHandler(OnBeforeSelect);
963:                 treeView1.BeforeLabelEdit +=
964:                     new  NodeLabelEditEventHandler(OnBeforeLabelEdit);
965:
966:
967:                 tvlistBox = new ListBox();
968:                 tvlistBox.Location = new System.Drawing.Point(272, 0);
969:                 tvlistBox.Size = new System.Drawing.Size(304, 424);
970:                 tvlistBox.ForeColor = System.Drawing.SystemColors.WindowText;
971:                 tvlistBox.TabIndex = 1;
972:
973:
974:                 button4 = new Button();
975:                 button4.Location = new System.Drawing.Point(16, 376);
976:                 button4.Size = new System.Drawing.Size(96, 24);
977:                 button4.TabIndex = 2;
978:                 button4.Text = "Add Root";
979:                 button4.Click += new EventHandler(OnAddRoot);
980:
981:                 button5 = new Button();
982:                 button5.Location = new System.Drawing.Point(138, 376);
983:                 button5.Size = new System.Drawing.Size(96, 24);
984:                 button5.TabIndex = 3;
985:                 button5.Text = "Add Child";
986:                 button5.Click += new EventHandler(OnAddChild);
987:                 button5.Enabled=false;
988:
989:                 TreeTabPage.Controls.Add(button4);
990:                 TreeTabPage.Controls.Add(button5);
991:                 TreeTabPage.Controls.Add(tvlistBox);
992:                 TreeTabPage.Controls.Add(treeView1);
993:             }
994:
995:
996:
```

3.2

USER INTERFACE
COMPONENTS

LISTING 3.2.10   Continued

> **NOTE**
>
> The application puts it all together by calling all the initializers and adding all the
> tabs to the main page.

```
997:          public MungoTabApp()
998:          {
999:              //          components = new System.ComponentModel.Container();
1000:             AutoScaleBaseSize = new System.Drawing.Size(5, 13);
1001:             ClientSize = new System.Drawing.Size(600, 477);
1002:
1003:             MainTabControl = new TabControl();
1004:
1005:             MainTabControl.Location = new System.Drawing.Point(8, 8);
1006:             MainTabControl.SelectedIndex = 0;
1007:             MainTabControl.Size = new System.Drawing.Size(584, 448);
1008:             MainTabControl.TabIndex = 0;
1009:
1010:             InitWelcome();
1011:             InitSimple();
1012:             InitLists();
1013:             InitDynamic();
1014:             InitMouse();
1015:             InitTree();
1016:
1017:             mainMenu1 = new MainMenu();
1018:             Menu = mainMenu1;
1019:             Text = "Mungo Tab App";
1020:             timer1 = new Timer();
1021:
1022:             MainTabControl.Controls.Add(SimpleTabPage);
1023:             MainTabControl.Controls.Add(ListBoxTabPage);
1024:             MainTabControl.Controls.Add(DynamicTabPage);
1025:             MainTabControl.Controls.Add(MouseTabPage);
1026:             MainTabControl.Controls.Add(TreeTabPage);
1027:
1028:             Controls.Add(MainTabControl);
1029:
1030:          }
1031:
```

LISTING 3.2.10   Continued

> **NOTE**
>
> Finally, we add the Main static function that bootstraps the whole process.

```
1032:        public static int Main(string[] args)
1033:        {
1034:            Application.Run(new MungoTabApp());
1035:            return 0;
1036:        }
1037:    }
1038: }
```

Summary

This chapter has seen you progress from the simple Windows Forms Hello World application to the tabbed application shown in Listing 3.2.10. We've covered a lot of ground but have really only just begun with Windows Forms. The basic information in this chapter will allow you to place forms and controls, add handlers, and understand the dynamic nature of the new Windows framework.

Data Bound Controls

IN THIS CHAPTER

In the previous chapter, we looked at some of the more common user interface elements and how to place and interact with them. The user interfaces presented in Windows Forms are not so different from the familiar MFC ones with which we are familiar. However, the MFC controls can require a lot of programming to make them useful. Some of the Windows Forms elements, such as the `TreeView` and `ListView` controls, are very complex and look as if they require a lot of coding to populate and use. This is not always the case, especially when controls are tied to database tables through data binding.

Data Binding Strategies

Data is generally held in tables that have one or more rows and one or more columns. *Data Binding* is the technique of tying user interface controls directly to individual elements, whole rows, whole columns, or entire tables for the purpose of viewing, manipulating, or editing them.

There are two types of data binding. *Simple Binding* ties a simple data viewer such as a text box or a numeric edit box to a single data item in a data table. *Complex Binding* presents a view of a whole table or many tables.

Data Binding Sources

Suitable sources for data binding include any object that exposes the `IList` interface. Most of the .NET collections implement this interface. Data objects provided by ADO.NET also expose `Ilist`, and you can also write your own objects that expose data through this interface.

The `IList` Interface

The `Ilist` interface has only a few methods. They are as follows:

- `Add` adds an item to the list.
- `Clear` removes all items from a list.
- `Contains` searches a list for a certain value.
- `IndexOf` determines the index of a particular value within the list.
- `Insert` places a value into the list before a given index. This moves all following indexes up one and makes the list longer.
- `Remove` takes an item out of the list.
- `RemoveAt` removes one item from a specific index.

Accessing items within the list is done by index. For example, `Item x = MyList[n]` items are assumed to be objects so any data can be stored in a list if it's a boxed value type or if it's a .NET object.

Some .NET Objects That Implement `IList`

There are a lot of classes in the framework that implement `IList`. Some of them are just for accessing data. The `Array`, `ArrayList`, and `StringCollection` classes are very commonly used. More complex classes include `DataSetView` and `DataView`, which work in conjunction with ADO to provide data table access.

The less mundane classes that support the interface are used extensively by the .NET developer tools for looking at the metadata associated with classes. These include the `CodeClassCollection` and the `CodeStatementCollection` classes and other objects that use the code Document Object Model or DOM.

Simple Binding

As previously mentioned, simple binding is the business of taking a simple chunk of data and tying it to a user control. When the data changes, the control reflects that change. When the control's display is edited, the data changes if write access is enabled.

Each Windows Forms control maintains a `BindingContext` object that, in turn, has a collection of `CurrencyManager` objects. By the way, the `CurrencyManager` has nothing to do with financial exchanges. It simply maintains a current position within a particular data object for you. Child controls, such as the `GroupBox`, can also have their own independent `BindingContexts` and `CurrencyManagers`.

The illustration in Figure 3.3.1 shows the relationships between Form, Control, `BindingContext` and `CurrencyManager`.

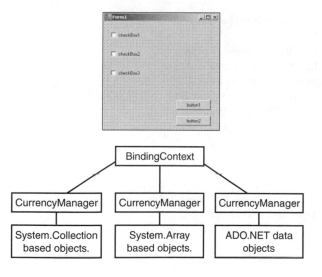

3.3

DATA BOUND CONTROLS

FIGURE 3.3.1

The relationship between form, BindingManager, *and* CurrencyManager.

Let's take a look at using the `BindingManager` and `CurrencyManager` with a simple application that binds a text box's `Text` property to a collection of strings. Listing 3.3.1 shows the `DataBound` application source code.

LISTING 3.3.1   `databound.cs`: Simple Binding of Controls to Data

```
 1: namespace Sams
 2: {
 3:     using System;
 4:     using System.Drawing;
 5:     using System.Collections;
 6:   using System.Collections.Specialized;
 7:     using System.ComponentModel;
 8:     using System.Windows.Forms;
 9:
10:     /// <summary>
11:     ///     Summary description for databound.
12:     /// </summary>
13:     public class databound : System.Windows.Forms.Form
14:     {
15:     private Button RightButton;
16:     private Button LeftButton;
17:     private TextBox textBox2;
18:     private TextBox textBox1;
19:     private Button DoneButton;
20:
21:     private StringCollection sa;
22:
23:        public databound()
24:        {
25:     this.textBox2 = new TextBox();
26:     this.RightButton = new Button();
27:     this.textBox1 = new TextBox();
28:     this.DoneButton = new Button();
29:     this.LeftButton = new Button();
30:     this.SuspendLayout();
31:     //
32:     // textBox2
33:     //
34:     this.textBox2.Location = new Point(184, 16);
35:     this.textBox2.Name = "textBox2";
36:     this.textBox2.TabIndex = 2;
37:     this.textBox2.Text = "textBox2";
38:     //
39:     // RightButton
```

LISTING 3.3.1 Continued

```
40:        //
41:        this.RightButton.Location = new Point(192, 64);
42:        this.RightButton.Name = "RightButton";
43:        this.RightButton.TabIndex = 4;
44:        this.RightButton.Text = ">>";
45:        this.RightButton.Click += new EventHandler(this.RightButton_Click);
46:        //
47:        // textBox1
48:        //
49:        this.textBox1.Location = new Point(8, 16);
50:        this.textBox1.Name = "textBox1";
51:        this.textBox1.TabIndex = 1;
52:        this.textBox1.Text = "textBox1";
53:        //
54:        // DoneButton
55:        //
56:        this.DoneButton.Location = new Point(104, 64);
57:        this.DoneButton.Name = "DoneButton";
58:        this.DoneButton.TabIndex = 0;
59:        this.DoneButton.Text = "Done";
60:        this.DoneButton.Click += new EventHandler(this.DoneButton_Click);
61:        //
62:        // LeftButton
63:        //
64:        this.LeftButton.Location = new Point(16, 64);
65:        this.LeftButton.Name = "LeftButton";
66:        this.LeftButton.TabIndex = 3;
67:        this.LeftButton.Text = "<<";
68:        this.LeftButton.Click += new EventHandler(this.LeftButton_Click);
69:        //
70:        // databound
71:        //
72:        this.AutoScaleBaseSize = new System.Drawing.Size(5, 13);
73:        this.ClientSize = new System.Drawing.Size(294, 111);
74:        this.ControlBox = false;
75:        this.Controls.AddRange(new Control[] {
76:                    this.RightButton,
77:                    this.LeftButton,
78:                    this.textBox2,
79:                    this.textBox1,
80:                    this.DoneButton});
81:        this.FormBorderStyle = FormBorderStyle.FixedDialog;
82:        this.Name = "databound";
83:        this.ShowInTaskbar = false;
```

3.3

DATA BOUND CONTROLS

LISTING 3.3.1 Continued

```
84:        this.Text = "databound";
85:        this.ResumeLayout(false);
86:
87:        //This is the setup code for the simple binding example
88:        //We have bound two text controls to the same StringCollection
89:
90:        // This is setting up the "database" (an IList thing)
91:        sa=new StringCollection();
92:        sa.Add("Hello databinding");
93:        sa.Add("Sams publishing");
94:        sa.Add("C# example");
95:        sa.Add("By Bob Powell");
96:
97:        //This binds the controls to that database.
98:        this.textBox1.DataBindings.Add("Text",sa,"");
99:        this.textBox2.DataBindings.Add("Text",sa,"");
100:       //See the button handlers below for details
101:       //on how to move through the data.
102:         }
103:
104:      /// <summary>
105:      ///     Clean up any resources being used.
106:      /// </summary>
107:      public override void Dispose()
108:      {
109:          base.Dispose();
110:        }
111:
112:
113:    //Very simply increments the Position property of the CurrencyManager
114:    protected void RightButton_Click (object sender, System.EventArgs e)
115:    {
116:      //Note how updating one position affects all
117:      //controls bound to this data
118:      this.BindingContext[sa].Position++;
119:    }
120:
121:    //Very simply decrements the Position property of the CurrencyManager
122:    protected void LeftButton_Click (object sender, System.EventArgs e)
123:    {
124:      //Note how updating one position affects all
125:      //controls bound to this data
126:      this.BindingContext[sa].Position--;
127:    }
```

LISTING 3.3.1 Continued

```
128:
129:    protected void DoneButton_Click (object sender, System.EventArgs e)
130:    {
131:      Application.Exit();
132:    }
133:
134:    public static void Main()
135:    {
136:      Application.Run(new databound());
137:    }
138:    }
139: }
```

Compile this program with the command line:

```
csc t:/winexe databound.cs
```

The setup of the objects on the form will be familiar to you so we don't need to re-iterate those principles. The interesting parts are on lines 91–95 which creates and populates a simple `StringCollection`. Remember that the .NET collections all implement the `IList` interface, making them candidates for databinding. Lines 98 and 99 perform the actual binding of the data to the textboxes. Finally, the click handlers on lines 114–119 and 122–127 move forward or backward through the data by moving the position, analogous to the cursor in a database, through the data.

Simple Binding to a DataSet

Binding of all sorts of controls is an important feature of .NET. Databound controls are available in Windows Forms, WebForms, and ASP.NET. All these controls can use ADO.NET to bind to database tables either on the local machine or somewhere else on the network. The vehicle for database binding is the `DataSet`. This class represents a set of cached data that is held in memory. The data cache can be created manually or populated with data drawn from a database using ADO.NET's database connection system. After the information is in that memory store on your machine, you can bind controls to individual columns of data and select rows for editing or viewing.

The easiest way to understand a DataSet is to use it. Listing 3.3.2 shows an application that generates and manipulates a simple DataSet on your machine using simple binding to controls.

LISTING 3.3.2   `datasetapp.cs`: Simple Binding of Multiple Controls

```
 1: namespace Sams
 2: {
 3:     using System;
 4:     using System.Drawing;
 5:     using System.Collections;
 6:     using System.Data;
 7:     using System.ComponentModel;
 8:     using System.Windows.Forms;
 9:
10:     //This application shows simple data binding to a
11:     //programatically created dataset.
12:     public class datasetapp : System.Windows.Forms.Form
13:     {
14:         private System.ComponentModel.Container components;
15:
16:         //Component declarations
17:         private Label lbl_first,lbl_name,lbl_title,lbl_company,lbl_phone;
18:         private TextBox FirstName,SurName,Title,Company,Phone;
19:         private Button btnNext, btnPrev, btnNew, btnEnd;
20:
21:         //The dataset used to store the table
22:         private DataSet dataset;
23:
24:         //Button handler to navigate backwards through the table records
25:         private void OnPrev(Object sender,EventArgs e)
26:         {
27:             this.BindingContext[dataset.Tables["Contacts"]].Position--;
28:         }
29:
30:         //Button handler to navigate forward through the table records
31:         private void OnNext(Object sender,EventArgs e)
32:         {
33:             this.BindingContext[dataset.Tables["Contacts"]].Position++;
34:         }
35:
36:         //Button handler to create a new row
37:         private void OnNew(Object sender, EventArgs e)
38:         {
39:             NewEntry();
40:         }
41:
42:     //Button handler to exit the application
43:     private void OnEnd(Object sender, EventArgs e)
44:     {
```

LISTING 3.3.2   Continued

```
45:          Application.Exit();
46:      }
47:
48:          //Method to move to the last record. Used when adding a row.
49:          private void MoveToEnd()
50:          {
51:            this.BindingContext[dataset.Tables["Contacts"]].Position=
52:              dataset.Tables["Contacts"].Rows.Count-1;
53:          }
54:
55:          //Method to add a new row to the table. Called at initialization
56:          //and by the "New" button handler.
57:          private void NewEntry()
58:          {
59:              DataRow row = dataset.Tables["Contacts"].NewRow();
60:              //set up row data with new entries of your choice
61:              row["First"]="Blank";
62:              row["Name"]="";
63:              row["Company"]="";
64:              row["Title"]="";
65:              row["Phone"]="";
66:              dataset.Tables[0].Rows.Add(row);
67:              dataset.AcceptChanges();
68:              MoveToEnd();
69:          }
70:
71:          //Called at creation to initialize the
72:          //dataset and create an empty table
73:          private void InitDataSet()
74:          {
75:              dataset = new DataSet("ContactData");
76:
77:              DataTable t=new DataTable("Contacts");
78:
79:              t.Columns.Add("First",typeof(System.String));
80:              t.Columns.Add("Name",typeof(System.String));
81:              t.Columns.Add("Company",typeof(System.String));
82:              t.Columns.Add("Title",typeof(System.String));
83:              t.Columns.Add("Phone",typeof(System.String));
84:
85:              t.MinimumCapacity=100;
86:
87:              dataset.Tables.Add(t);
88:          }
```

3.3

**DATA BOUND
CONTROLS**

LISTING 3.3.2   Continued

```
 89:
 90:        //Called at initialization to do simple binding of the edit
 91:        //controls on the form to the dataset's "Contacts" table entries
 92:        private void BindControls()
 93:        {
 94:            FirstName.DataBindings.Add("Text",dataset.Tables["Contacts"],
➥"First");
 95:            SurName.DataBindings.Add("Text",dataset.Tables["Contacts"],
➥"Name");
 96:            Title.DataBindings.Add("Text",dataset.Tables["Contacts"],
➥"Title");
 97:            Company.DataBindings.Add("Text",dataset.Tables["Contacts"],
➥"Company");
 98:            Phone.DataBindings.Add("Text",dataset.Tables["Contacts"],
➥"Phone");
 99:        }
100:
101:        //Constructor. Positions the form controls,
102:        //Ininitializes the dataset, binds the controls and
103:        //wires up the handlers.
104:        public datasetapp()
105:        {
106:            this.components = new System.ComponentModel.Container ();
107:            this.Text = "datasetapp";
108:            this.AutoScaleBaseSize = new System.Drawing.Size (5, 13);
109:            this.ClientSize = new System.Drawing.Size (250, 200);
110:            this.FormBorderStyle = FormBorderStyle.Fixed3D;
111:
112:            lbl_first = new Label();
113:            lbl_first.Text="First name";
114:            lbl_first.Location = new Point(5,5);
115:            lbl_first.Size = new Size(120,28);
116:            lbl_first.Anchor = AnchorStyles.Left | AnchorStyles.Right;
117:            Controls.Add(lbl_first);
118:
119:            FirstName = new TextBox();
120:            FirstName.Location = new Point(125,5);
121:            FirstName.Size = new Size(120,28);
122:            FirstName.Anchor = AnchorStyles.Left | AnchorStyles.Right;
123:            Controls.Add(FirstName);
124:
125:            lbl_name = new Label();
126:            lbl_name.Text="Surname";
127:            lbl_name.Location = new Point(5,35);
```

LISTING 3.3.2   Continued

```
128:            lbl_name.Size = new Size(120,28);
129:            lbl_name.Anchor = AnchorStyles.Left|AnchorStyles.Right;
130:            Controls.Add(lbl_name);
131:
132:            SurName = new TextBox();
133:            SurName.Location = new Point(125,35);
134:            SurName.Size = new Size(120,28);
135:            SurName.Anchor = AnchorStyles.Left | AnchorStyles.Right;
136:            Controls.Add(SurName);
137:
138:            lbl_company = new Label();
139:            lbl_company.Text="Company";
140:            lbl_company.Location = new Point(5,65);
141:            lbl_company.Size = new Size(120,28);
142:            Controls.Add(lbl_company);
143:
144:            Company = new TextBox();
145:            Company.Location = new Point(125,65);
146:            Company.Size = new Size(120,28);
147:            Controls.Add(Company);
148:
149:            lbl_title = new Label();
150:            lbl_title.Text="Title";
151:            lbl_title.Location = new Point(5,95);
152:            lbl_title.Size = new Size(120,28);
153:            Controls.Add(lbl_title);
154:
155:            Title = new TextBox();
156:            Title.Location = new Point(125,95);
157:            Title.Size = new Size(120,28);
158:            Controls.Add(Title);
159:
160:            lbl_phone = new Label();
161:            lbl_phone.Text="Telephone";
162:            lbl_phone.Location = new Point(5,125);
163:            lbl_phone.Size = new Size(120,28);
164:            Controls.Add(lbl_phone);
165:
166:            Phone = new TextBox();
167:            Phone.Location = new Point(125,125);
168:            Phone.Size = new Size(120,28);
169:            Controls.Add(Phone);
170:
171:            btnNew = new Button();
```

LISTING 3.3.2   Continued

```
172:              btnNew.Location = new Point(5,155);
173:              btnNew.Size = new Size(70,28);
174:              btnNew.Text="New";
175:              btnNew.Click+=new EventHandler(OnNew);
176:              Controls.Add(btnNew);
177:
178:              btnPrev = new Button();
179:              btnPrev.Location = new Point(80,155);
180:              btnPrev.Size = new Size(35,28);
181:              btnPrev.Text="<<";
182:              btnPrev.Click += new EventHandler(OnPrev);
183:              Controls.Add(btnPrev);
184:
185:              btnEnd = new Button();
186:              btnEnd.Location = new Point(120,155);
187:              btnEnd.Size = new Size(70,28);
188:              btnEnd.Text="End";
189:              btnEnd.Click += new EventHandler(OnEnd);
190:              Controls.Add(btnEnd);
191:
192:              btnNext = new Button();
193:              btnNext.Location = new Point(200,155);
194:              btnNext.Size = new Size(35,28);
195:              btnNext.Text=">>";
196:              btnNext.Click += new EventHandler(OnNext);
197:              Controls.Add(btnNext);
198:
199:              InitDataSet();
200:
201:              NewEntry();
202:
203:              BindControls();
204:
205:          }
206:
207:          //Cleans up the Form
208:          public override void Dispose()
209:          {
210:              base.Dispose();
211:              components.Dispose();
212:          }
213:
214:          //Main method to instantiate and run the application.
215:          static void Main()
```

LISTING 3.3.2   Continued

```
216:          {
217:              Application.Run(new datasetapp());
218:          }
219:      }
220: }
```

Let's examine Listing 3.3.2 in more detail. The main initialization of the DataSet takes place on lines 73–88. Here, a DataSet is created and a new table placed in its tables collection. The table is given a set of columns that are identified by the strings "First", "Name", and so on.

Adding data to a table is done one row at a time. The method on lines 57–69 adds a new row to the end of the table and optionally fills it with text. You could also create a table with numeric values or other types.

Lines 92–99 do the binding of the data in the table to the Text property of the identified controls. These controls can now be used to edit the information in the table, and they will display each entry automatically as you navigate through the database.

The button handlers that do the navigation are on lines 24–37. These use the ContextManager.Position property to index the rows in the table.

Figure 3.3.2 shows a screenshot of the application.

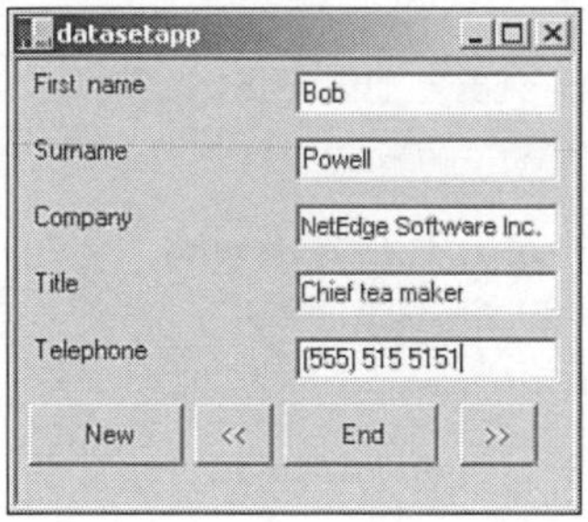

FIGURE 3.3.2
The DataSet simple binding application.

Complex Binding of Controls to Data

Simple binding is the process of tying a single control to a single data item. Complex binding ties a single control to many data items. Controls that are often used for complex data binding include DataGrid which has the appearance of a simple spreadsheet. This control can display, edit, or add and delete records from a table. A single databinding operation is used to attach the control to a `DataTable`. The `DataGrid` can only be used to show one table at a time, but it can be used to show relationships between tables.

Listing 3.3.3 shows a modified version of the simple binding example demonstrated in Listing 3.3.2. This listing removes all the controls associated with the `DataSet` and replaces them with a complex bound grid control. Don't be put off by the title. Complex data binding is complex only in its function, not its usage.

LISTING 3.3.3   gridbind.cs: An Example of Complex Data Binding

```
 1: namespace Sams
 2: {
 3:   using System;
 4:   using System.Drawing;
 5:   using System.Collections;
 6:   using System.Data;
 7:   using System.ComponentModel;
 8:   using System.Windows.Forms;
 9:
10:   //This application shows simple data binding to a
11:   //programatically created dataset.
12:   public class GridBind : System.Windows.Forms.Form
13:   {
14:     private System.ComponentModel.Container components;
15:     private System.Windows.Forms.DataGrid dataGrid1;
16:
17:     //The dataset used to store the table
18:     private DataSet dataset;
19:
20:     //Called at creation to initialize the
21:     //dataset and create an empty table
22:     private void InitDataSet()
23:     {
24:       dataset = new DataSet("ContactData");
25:
26:       DataTable t=new DataTable("Contacts");
27:
28:       t.Columns.Add("First",typeof(System.String));
29:       t.Columns.Add("Name",typeof(System.String));
30:       t.Columns.Add("Company",typeof(System.String));
31:       t.Columns.Add("Title",typeof(System.String));
32:       t.Columns.Add("Phone",typeof(System.String));
33:
34:       t.MinimumCapacity=100;
35:
```

LISTING 3.3.3   Continued

```
36:        dataset.Tables.Add(t);
37:    }
38:
39:    //Called at initialization to do complex binding of the DataGrid
40:    //to the dataset's "Contacts" table entries
41:    private void BindGrid()
42:    {
43:      this.dataGrid1.SetDataBinding(dataset.Tables["Contacts"],"");
44:    }
45:
46:    //Constructor. Positions the form controls,
47:    //Ininitializes the dataset, binds the controls and
48:    //wires up the handlers.
49:    public GridBind()
50:    {
51:      InitializeComponent();
52:
53:      InitDataSet();
54:
55:      BindGrid();
56:
57:    }
58:
59:    //Cleans up the Form
60:    public override void Dispose()
61:    {
62:      base.Dispose();
63:      components.Dispose();
64:    }
65:
66:    //Method added by the form designer
67:    private void InitializeComponent()
68:    {
69:      this.components = new System.ComponentModel.Container ();
70:      this.dataGrid1 = new System.Windows.Forms.DataGrid ();
71:      dataGrid1.BeginInit ();
72:      dataGrid1.Location = new System.Drawing.Point (8, 16);
73:      dataGrid1.Size = new System.Drawing.Size (472, 224);
74:      dataGrid1.DataMember = "";
75:      dataGrid1.TabIndex = 0;
76:      this.Text = "GridBind";
77:      this.AutoScaleBaseSize = new System.Drawing.Size (5, 13);
78:      this.FormBorderStyle = System.Windows.Forms.FormBorderStyle.Fixed3D;
79:      this.ClientSize = new System.Drawing.Size (486, 251);
```

LISTING 3.3.3   Continued

```
80:        this.Controls.Add (this.dataGrid1);
81:        dataGrid1.EndInit ();
82:    }
83:
84:
85:
86:    //Main method to instantiate and run the application.
87:    static void Main()
88:    {
89:      Application.Run(new GridBind());
90:    }
91:  }
92: }
```

Compile this program with the following command line:

```
csc /t:winexe gridbind.cs
```

Looking at the information in Listing 3.3.3, you can see that the code used to navigate the data set is no longer needed. The method to add a new row of data is not needed either. The DataGrid control does all that for you. Binding the data to the grid takes place on line 43. Initialization of the data set is identical to the previous example; it is shown on lines 22–37. Figure 3.3.3 shows the GridBind application in action. Notice that the grid provides column and row headers that allow you to select a whole row or order the table according to column alphabetic order.

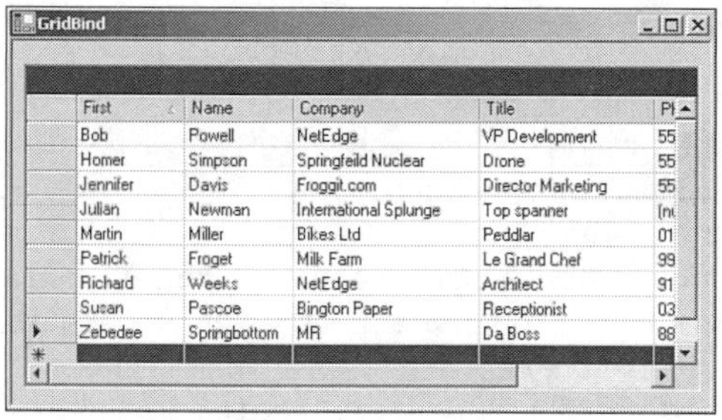

FIGURE 3.3.3
Complex binding to a DataGrid.

The DataGrid control can also be used to show hierarchical relationships between multiple data tables. Perhaps a Customer Resource Management application would want to show the relationship between a customer and his or her orders or a client and his or her technical support incidents. Complex binding of data makes this otherwise difficult process painless.

So far, you have seen data binding to `DataSets` and `DataTables` created on-the-fly by the listing examples. A good real world example will be to show complex binding to an existing database.

The objects we have been using to store and manipulate the data are parts of the ADO.NET framework. This system allows high level interaction with database tables from many different database providers. ADO.NET can be used in conjunction with OleDB, SQL, and other database drivers. Take a look now at an example of complex bound database usage.

Binding Controls to Databases Using ADO.NET

ADO.NET employs a disconnected database model that uses data tables on the client machine to cache information while it is viewed or manipulated. Even when the database is stored on the same machine as the editing program, ADO.NET will copy a snapshot of data into a `DataSet` and pass changes back to the database later.

This model is used to allow better scaling of the database application over a network because it obviates the need for many, simultaneous, open connections to the database.

Data tables are very structured and hierarchical. This makes XML an ideal medium for transmitting and storing data. Indeed, when ADO makes a connection to a database, the information will be transported as XML. This means that your software can take advantage of intranet and Internet data stores just as easily as it can local databases.

It is important to note that transporting large amounts of data to and from databases becomes more demanding as the database becomes more disconnected from the client. Modern n-tier systems often employ many databases in different geographical locations and Web services to provide data on demand to many clients. This means that your client application should try to use small chunks of data that can be refreshed quickly and with as little strain as possible on network bandwidth. For this reason, many modern data systems employ a messaging architecture that deals with data transactions at a very granular level. It often has been the responsibility of the application programmer to devise and manage schemes for such transactions, but the high level abilities of ADO.NET hide much of that pain from you and allow you to be more productive with data.

Visual StudioVisual StudioData is copied to or from DataSet by a `DataAdapter`. ADO.NET provides two main `DataAdapter` types, the `OleDBDataAdapter` that connects DataSets to OLE DB data providers and the `SqlDataAdapter`, targeting SQL server connections. Both of these data adapter classes use a set of `Command` objects to perform selects, updates, inserts, and deletes in the databases to which they connect. The `Select` command gets data from the data source. The `Update`, `Delete`, and `Insert` commands all change the data source based on changes made to the DataSet.

Filling a DataSet with information from a database is fairly simple. The steps to perform are shown in the code snippet that follows:

```
 1: System.Data.OleDb.OleDbConnection connection =
 2:   new System.Data.OleDb.OleDbConnection();
 3: connection.ConnectionString=
 4: @"Provider=Microsoft.Jet.OLEDB.4.0;"+
 5: @"Data Source=northwind.mdb; ";
 6: System.Data.OleDb.OleDbCommand SelectCommand=
 7:   new System.Data.OleDb.OleDbCommand("SELECT * FROM Customers");
 8: SelectCommand.Connection=connection;
 9: System.Data.DataSet ds=new System.Data.DataSet("Customer Table");
10: ds.Tables.Add("Customers");
11: System.Data.OleDb.OleDbDataAdapter adapter =
12:    new System.Data.OleDb.OleDbDataAdapter(SelectCommand);
13: adapter.Fill(ds);
14: Console.WriteLine(ds.GetXml());
```

This snippet assumes that the NortWind database `northwind.mdb` is available in the local directory.

Lines 1–5 create an OleDbConnection and set the connection string.

Lines 6 and 7 create the SelectCommand and populate the select string with a valid query.

Line 8 associates the database connection with the select command, while lines 9 and 10 create a DataSet object and add one table to it.

Lines 11 and 12 create a data adapter and add the select command. Line 13 fills the data set from the adapter and finally, to prove it actually did something, the last line dumps the whole northwing customer table from the DataSet as XML.

From the point of view of your own productivity, you will most likely perform such an operation using the Visual Studio.NET IDE to create the application. Databinding using Visual Studio generates some enormous blocks of code and does a very comprehensive job of connecting up your database. We have generally avoided using Visual Studio until now because the layout of applications created in this manner is not easily read and there are sometimes dire consequences when you edit the code generated by the studio. In this case, however, a good exercise will be to do a complete walk through of a database viewer using the IDE and then examine the resulting application to see what it does.

Creating a Database Viewer with Visual Studio and ADO.NET

Follow these steps carefully to create the application.

1. Create a new Windows Forms project, and call it **DBBind**.

2. Drag a DataGrid from the toolbox and position it on the form. Select the DataGrid properties and set the Dock property to Fill by clicking the center button in the UI editor that pops up for the Dock property.

3. From the toolbar, select an OleDbDataAdapter from the Data tab. When you place it on the form, you'll see the Data Adapter Configuration Wizard dialog.

4. On the first page of the wizard, select the Northwind database. You may need to click New Connection, select Microsoft Jet 4.0 OLE DB Provider in the Provider tab, press Next, and then browse for northwind.mdb. When you find it, or another database with which you are familiar, press the Test Connection button to ensure that the database is useable. Press OK on the New Connection dialog and press Next on the wizard.

5. Select the radio button marked Use SQL Statements. Press Next.

6. Type in a query that you know or select the query builder to create querys from the tables in the connected database. For our example, we used the query builder, added the Customers table from NorthWind, selected the check box marked All Columns on the table shown, and pressed OK on the query builder dialog.

7. Pressing Next shows you the successful creation of the adapter and the connection, and you can click the Finish button. At this point, you will have a form with two objects, an OleDbDataAdapter and an OleDbConnection in the icon tray.

8. Select the OleDbDataAdapter in the icon tray. Below the property browser, you will see a link that reads Generate DataSet. Click this link to create a dataset. Simply click OK on the following dialog; the default values are good. Now you'll have three icons in the tray.

9. Select the DataGrid on the form again and edit the DataSource property using the drop-down combo box provided. You will see several data sources. If you have followed along and used the NorthWind database, select the dataSet11.Customers choice. When you do this, you'll see the DataGrid on the form begin to display all the column headers for the database.

10. The final step is a manual one. You need to edit the constructor of the class to add the Fill command. Add the following line of code after the InitializeComponent call in the class constructor;

    ```
    this.oleDbDataAdapter1.Fill(this.dataSet11);
    ```

    Now you can build and run the program by pressing F5.

You will see the application shown in Figure 3.3.4, which will allow you to browse, order, edit, and generally muck-about with the NorthWind Customers table.

Address	City	CompanyNa	ContactName	ContactTitle	Country	CustomerID	Fax	Phone	Posta
Obere Str. 57	Berlin	Alfreds Futter	Maria Anders	Sales Repres	Germany	ALFKI	030-0076545	030-0074321	12209
Avda. de la C	México D.F.	Ana Trujillo E	Ana Trujillo	Owner	Mexico	ANATR	(5) 555-3745	(5) 555-4729	05021
Mataderos 2	México D.F.	Antonio More	Antonio More	Owner	Mexico	ANTON	(null)	(5) 555-3932	05023
120 Hanover	London	Around the H	Thomas Hard	Sales Repres	UK	AROUT	(171) 555-67	(171) 555-77	WA1
Berguvsväge	Luleå	Berglunds sn	Christina Ber	Order Admini	Sweden	BERGS	0921-12 34 6	0921-12 34 6	S-958
Forsterstr. 57	Mannheim	Blauer See D	Hanna Moos	Sales Repres	Germany	BLAUS	0621-08924	0621-08460	68306
24, place Klé	Strasbourg	Blondel père	Frédérique Ci	Marketing Ma	France	BLONP	88.60.15.32	88.60.15.31	67000
C/ Araquil, 67	Madrid	Bólido Comid	Martín Somm	Owner	Spain	BOLID	(91) 555 91 9	(91) 555 22 8	28023
12, rue des B	Marseille	Bon app'	Laurence Leb	Owner	France	BONAP	91.24.45.41	91.24.45.40	13008
23 Tsawasse	Tsawassen	Bottom-Dollar	Elizabeth Lin	Accounting M	Canada	BOTTM	(604) 555-37	(604) 555-47	T2F 8J
Fauntleroy Ci	London	B's Beverage	Victoria Ashw	Sales Repres	UK	BSBEV	(null)	(171) 555-12	EC2 5
Cerrito 333	Buenos Aires	Cactus Comi	Patricio Simp	Sales Agent	Argentina	CACTU	(1) 135-4892	(1) 135-5555	1010
Sierras de Gr	México D.F.	Centro comer	Francisco Ch	Marketing Ma	Mexico	CENTC	(5) 555-7293	(5) 555-3392	05022
Hauptstr. 29	Bern	Chop-suey C	Yang Wang	Owner	Switzerland	CHOPS	(null)	0452-076545	3012
Av. dos Lusía	São Paulo	Comércio Min	Pedro Afonso	Sales Associ	Brazil	COMMI	(null)	(11) 555-764	05432
Berkeley Gar	London	Consolidated	Elizabeth Bro	Sales Repres	UK	CONSH	(171) 555-91	(171) 555-22	WX1
Walserweg 2	Aachen	Drachenblut	Sven Ottlieb	Order Admini	Germany	DRACD	0241-059428	0241-039123	52066
67, rue des Ci	Nantes	Du monde en	Janine Labru	Owner	France	DUMON	40.67.89.89	40.67.88.88	44000
35 King Geor	London	Eastern Conn	Ann Devon	Sales Agent	UK	EASTC	(171) 555-33	(171) 555-02	WX3
Kirchgasse 6	Graz	Ernst Handel	Roland Mend	Sales Manag	Austria	ERNSH	7675-3426	7675-3425	8010
Rua Orós, 92	São Paulo	Familia Arqui	Aria Cruz	Marketing As	Brazil	FAMIA	(null)	(11) 555-985	05442
C/ Moralzarz	Madrid	FISSA Fabric	Diego Roel	Accounting M	Spain	FISSA	(91) 555 55 9	(91) 555 94 4	28034
184, chaussé	Lille	Folies gourm	Martine Ranc	Assistant Sal	France	FOLIG	20.16.10.17	20.16.10.16	59000
Åkergatan 24	Bräcke	Folk och fä H	Maria Larsso	Owner	Sweden	FOLKO	(null)	0695-34 67 2	S-844
Berliner Platz	München	Frankenwersa	Peter Franke	Marketing Ma	Germany	FRANK	089-0877451	089-0877310	80805
54, rue Royal	Nantes	France restau	Carine Schmi	Marketing Ma	France	FRANR	40.32.21.20	40.32.21.21	44000

FIGURE 3.3.4

Complex DataBinding of the DataGrid to a database.

As an education, go back into the Visual Studio editor again and find the `InitializeComponent` method. It will probably be folded away in a little region and you'll have to expand it. Take a look at the code added by the DataAdapter wizard to set up the `OleDataAdapter` connection and the four datbase command objects.

As performing the walk through will generate the code for you, we won't list it here and save a small forest or two. You can clearly see that the wizards and helpers in ADO.NET really save your fingers.

Summary

In this chapter, we looked at the basic principals of data binding in .NET and saw how the power of the .NET controls can work for us to create a very productive environment. We saw how simple binding works for single data items and single controls. We then saw how complex binding works for the DataGrid both in isolation with a locally created data table and using a full database through ADO.NET.

We're keeping the focus on Windows Forms now as we continue with Chapter 3.4, "Windows Forms Example Application (Scribble. NET)," which deals with more component usage, including the use of resources as a means of decorating your GUI elements.

Windows Forms Example Application (Scribble .NET)

IN THIS CHAPTER

In this chapter, we will be looking at some more of the features of Windows Forms that you will need to be familiar with when writing applications for the .NET framework.

Specifically, we'll deal with resources, including text, bitmap images, and icons. We'll also be looking at globalization, the process of making your applications friendly to an international audience.

Resources in .NET

Unlike Win32 and MFC, .NET applications do not rely heavily on resources for dialog and form layout. However, resources are required for localization of applications, integration of images and icons, and for custom data that can be easily modified without needing to recompile an application.

The resource model under .NET is that of a default resource for an application and an optional set of additional resources that provide localization, or more properly internationalization, data for a specific culture. For example, an application might have a default resource culture of US—English but require localization for the UK—English, where the currency symbol would be different, or for French, where the text strings associated with menus and dialogs would be in the correct language.

The default resource is usually contained within the assembly that holds the application code. Other assemblies, called *satellite assemblies*, have resources that can be loaded and used when needed. This approach is similar to the idea of an application using a resource DLL under Win32 or MFC.

A good "global citizen" application should always be localizable and should always provide a resource for any culture in which that the software is used. It is also true that not every application needs to be a global citizen, so you must choose your level of culture—friendliness— according to your distribution and target audience needs.

Localization Nuts and Bolts

It's good practice to build your applications with localization in mind. The most important thing you can do to prepare for this is to not embed any strings in your code that the user will see. For example you would never use:

```
MessageBox.Show("Hello World!");
```

because it embeds the "Hello World!" string in the source code. To make this program a good global citizen, you would create a default resource where the string was identified by a value. For example,

```
MessageBox.Show((String)resources.GetObject("MyHelloworldResourceString"));
```

In this line, the actual text of the message is not placed in the code but retrieved from a resource that has a string identified as `"MyHelloWorldResourceString"`.

If your default culture is US-English, the string would say "Hello World!" If the application needed to be used in France, a satellite assembly with the French resources would have a string with the same `"MyHelloWorldResourceString"` ID, except that this string would have the value of "Bonjour Le Monde!"

.NET Resource Management Classes

The .NET framework provides a family of classes that are designed to make resource management consistent and easy. These classes are as follows:

- `ResourceManager` is used to manage all resources in an application.
- `ResourceSet` represents a collection of all the resources for a particular culture.
- `ResourceReader` is an implementation class for the `IResourceReader` interface. This is used to read resources from a stream.
- `ResourceWriter` is an implementation of the `IResourceWriter` interface. This are used to write resources to a stream.

Your application must use a `ResourceManager` to load the resource assemblies and make them available to the rest of the program. The `ResourceManager` will return a `ResourceSet` for a given culture.

Got Culture?

Different cultures and languages are identified through the `CultureInfo` class. This class is a simple information store that contains data about the culture selected by the user when he or she installed the operating system. It contains information about the language, calendar, currency, and other preferences that the user might have chosen. Your software will have access to this information so that it can determine whether it has the ability to offer culture-specific resources or must choose the neutral default value.

Being culture specific might be very important in the message you are trying to deliver. There is an anecdote that illustrates why.

A Little Bit of Culture

A large soap manufacturer created a printed advertisement for display on billboards that showed dirty clothes being loaded into a washing machine. A second picture showed the washing powder being poured into the machine and a third image depicted these clothes being taken out of the washer all clean and fresh. They couldn't understand why the sales of the product dropped dramatically in certain countries until it was pointed out that the places that had low sales were right-to-left reading cultures. Their advertisement, created by American's, had shown clean clothes washed in this soap powder emerging all dirty and stained from the machine. Never underestimate the power of assumption.

Culture information about languages is provided by a two-letter code and an optional region identifier that accompanies the two letter code. For example, the neutral English language is represented by the two letter code en, but the different flavors of English—English from England, Canada, the United States and other places—is identified by the sub-codes GB, CA, US, and so on.

Listing 3.4.1 shows a program that will get the CultureInfo for your computer and display the language and region that applies to your computer. It also shows the full name of the culture and which calendar your current culture is using.

LISTING 3.4.1   culture.cs: Displaying the Current Culture Information

```
 1: namespace Sams
 2: {
 3:     using System;
 4:     using System.Drawing;
 5:     using System.Collections;
 6:     using System.ComponentModel;
 7:     using System.Globalization;
 8:     using System.Windows.Forms;
 9:     using System.Data;
10:
11: class CultureInfoTest : Form
12: {
13:
14:     public CultureInfoTest()
15:     {
```

LISTING 3.4.1   Continued

```
16:        this.Size = new Size(300,200);
17:
18:        Label l = new Label();
19:        l.Location = new Point(3,5);
20:        l.Size = new Size(294,190);
21:
22:        InputLanguage inL = InputLanguage.CurrentInputLanguage;
23:
24:        CultureInfo info = inL.Culture;
25:
26:        l.Text = String.Format("Culture identifier = {0}\n"+
27:                    "Display name = {1}\n"+
28:                    "Calender = {2}\n",
29:                    info.ToString(),
30:                    info.DisplayName,
31:                    info.Calendar.ToString());
32:        this.Controls.Add(l);
33:
34:    }
35:    static void Main()
36:    {
37:        Application.Run(new CultureInfoTest());
38:    }
39: }
40:
41: }
```

Creating Text Resources

There are several ways you can create text resources for your programs. The simplest is by creating a text file that has a set of name-value pairs. These specify a name that you can use in your code to find the resource and the text to associate with that name.

When you've finished making your basic string resource file, you must turn it into a `.resx` or `.resource` file using the .NET tool RESGEN.EXE. The following example shows this process.

The String Resource Text

The following simple text file shows a set of name/-value pairs for a resource that will be used to provide the default strings for an application. Note that quotation marks are not required on strings. If you use quotes, they will be embedded in the resource string.

```
#Default culture resources
WindowText = Internationalization example
LabelText = Hello World!!!
```

The text file can be converted into one of two forms—an XML-based form that is stored as a
.resx file or directly to its compiled .resource form. The .resx file is an XML dataset that is
used to serialize resource information during development. Conversion of resources from one
form to another is accomplished using the Resgen utility. Type in the previous simple resource
text and save it as **firstresource.txt**, and then create a .resx file using the following command line:

```
resgen firstresource.txt firstresource.resx
```

The utility will compile the file and tell you that two resources have been converted.
Listing 3.4.2 shows the resulting XML file.

LISTING 3.4.2   firstresource.resx: The Converted Resource File in XML Form

```xml
<?xml version="1.0" encoding="utf-8"?>
<root>
  <xsd:schema id="root" targetNamespace="" xmlns=""
➥ xmlns:xsd="http://www.w3.org/2001/XMLSchema"
➥xmlns:msdata="urn:schemas-microsoft-com:xml-msdata">
    <xsd:element name="root" msdata:IsDataSet="true">
      <xsd:complexType>
        <xsd:choice maxOccurs="unbounded">
          <xsd:element name="data">
            <xsd:complexType>
              <xsd:sequence>
                <xsd:element name="value" type="xsd:string" minOccurs="0"
➥msdata:Ordinal="1" />
                <xsd:element name="comment" type="xsd:string" minOccurs="0"
➥msdata:Ordinal="2" />
              </xsd:sequence>
              <xsd:attribute name="name" type="xsd:string" />
              <xsd:attribute name="type" type="xsd:string" />
              <xsd:attribute name="mimetype" type="xsd:string" />
            </xsd:complexType>
          </xsd:element>
          <xsd:element name="resheader">
            <xsd:complexType>
              <xsd:sequence>
                <xsd:element name="value" type="xsd:string" minOccurs="0"
➥msdata:Ordinal="1" />
```

LISTING 3.4.2   Continued

```xml
            </xsd:sequence>
            <xsd:attribute name="name" type="xsd:string" use="required" />
          </xsd:complexType>
        </xsd:element>
      </xsd:choice>
    </xsd:complexType>
  </xsd:element>
</xsd:schema>
<data name="WindowText">
  <value>Internationalization example</value>
</data>
<data name="LabelText">
  <value>Hello World!!!</value>
</data>
<resheader name="ResMimeType">
  <value>text/microsoft-resx</value>
</resheader>
<resheader name="Version">
  <value>1.0.0.0</value>
</resheader>
<resheader name="Reader">
  <value>System.Resources.ResXResourceReader</value>
</resheader>
<resheader name="Writer">
  <value>System.Resources.ResXResourceWriter</value>
</resheader>
</root>
```

You can see from Listing 3.4.2 that this is probably not a file you will want to type in by hand. The first part of the file is the schema that defines XML content of the file. Each element is contained within an XML node tagged <data name="some-name">. If you look through the file, you will see the two resources that were specified in the text file and their respective values. It is this .resx form of the resources that Visual Studio maintains when you create resources in your applications.

To use the resource file in a sample program, you will need to convert it to its compiled form. You can do this from either the text format or the XML format by using one of the following command lines:

```
Resgen firstresource.txt firstresource.resources
```

or

```
Resgen firstresource.resx firstresource.resources
```

A Simple Winforms Application That Relies on a Resource

To test the resource file shown in Listing 3.4.2, you can create a simple "Hello World"-type application as shown in Listing 3.4.3. This program relies on the `firstresource.resources` file created previously to provide the text for the label and the window title bar.

LISTING 3.4.3 `hellores.cs`: Using Simple String Resources

```
1: namespace Sams
2: {
3:    using System;
4:    using System.Drawing;
5:    using System.Collections;
6:    using System.ComponentModel;
7:    using System.Globalization;
8:    using System.Windows.Forms;
9:    using System.Data;
10:    using System.Resources;
11:
12:    class hellores: Form
13:    {
14:
15:      public hellores()
16:      {
17:         ResourceManager rm=new ResourceManager(
       ➥"firstresource",this.GetType().Assembly);
18:
19:         this.Size = new Size(400,100);
20:         this.Text=rm.GetString("WindowText");
21:
22:         Label l = new Label();
23:         l.Location = new Point(3,5);
24:         l.Size = new Size(394,90);
25:         l.Font = new Font("Tahoma",36F,FontStyle.Bold);
26:         l.Text=rm.GetString("LabelText");
27:         this.Controls.Add(l);
28:
29:      }
30:
31:      static void Main()
32:      {
33:         Application.Run(new hellores());
34:      }
35:    }
36:
37: }
```

The code in Listing 3.4.3 is a good global citizen application. It embeds no strings, and draws all of its text from the resource set provided. Line 17 of the listing shows how a resource manager is created, and lines 20 and 26 show how the named strings are retrieved from the resources in the assembly and applied to the Windows Forms elements.

To build this file and run it, you will need to use the following command line:

```
csc /out:hellores.exe /t:winexe /res:firstresource.resources hellores.cs
```

Notice how the command line option /res: is used to embed the compiled form of the resources created earlier.

Running the program now will produce the result shown in Figure 3.4.1.

FIGURE 3.4.1
The hellores program in operation.

Creating and Using a Satellite Assembly

The globalization example is not much use without an alternative resource set from which to draw. In the following example, we'll add a satellite assembly containing a French resource set.

> **NOTE**
>
> A satellite assembly is a DLL, containing code or data, that is used by an application's main assembly.

A satellite assembly, in this case, is analogous to a resource-only DLL. Satellite assemblies for localization are normally private to a particular application. They are stored in a specially named subdirectory below the main application directory. In this case, you'll need to create a directory called fr so that the resource manager can find it.

First, create the resource text using the same names but different values for every string that needs to be displayed. Notice that only the label text changes here. This will be explained shortly.

```
#Version Francaise.
LabelText = Bonjour le monde!!!
```

Call this file **firstresource.fr.txt**. After this file is complete, you can create the satellite assembly using the following command lines:

```
resgen firstresource.fr.txt firstresource.fr.resources
al /out:fr/hellores2.Resources.DLL /c:fr /embed:firstresource.fr.resources
```

The utility program invoked in the second line is the Assembly Linker (AL). AL can be used for creating assemblies of all sorts, but here we're only interested in its resource packaging abilities. Notice that the /out: command line option places the assembly DLL into the fr directory.

Now you can build the hellores2.exe program. It's very similar to the original but has a command line option that allows you to select the culture by typing in the culture identification string. Listing 3.4.4 shows the source.

LISTING 3.4.4   hellores2.cs: The Localized Hello World Example

```
 1: namespace Sams
 2: {
 3:    using System;
 4:    using System.Drawing;
 5:    using System.Collections;
 6:    using System.ComponentModel;
 7:    using System.Globalization;
 8:    using System.Windows.Forms;
 9:    using System.Data;
10:    using System.Resources;
11:    using System.Threading;
12:
13:    class hellores: Form
14:    {
15:
16:      private Label l;
17:      private ResourceManager rm;
18:
19:
20:      public hellores(string culture)
21:      {
22:         Thread.CurrentThread.CurrentUICulture =
         ➥new CultureInfo(culture);
23:
24:         rm=new ResourceManager("firstresource",
         ➥this.GetType().Assembly);
25:
26:         this.Size = new Size(400,100);
27:         this.Text=rm.GetString("WindowText");
```

LISTING 3.4.4 Continued

```
28:
29:            l = new Label();
30:            l.Location = new Point(3,5);
31:            l.Size = new Size(394,90);
32:            l.Font = new Font("Tahoma",36F,FontStyle.Bold);
33:            l.Text=rm.GetString("LabelText");
34:            l.Anchor = (AnchorStyles.Top |
35:                    AnchorStyles.Left |
36:                    AnchorStyles.Bottom |
37:                    AnchorStyles.Right);
38:            this.Controls.Add(l);
39:
40:        }
41:
42:        static void Main(string[] args)
43:        {
44:            string culture ="";
45:            if(args.Length == 1)
46:                culture = args[0];
47:            Application.Run(new hellores(culture));
48:        }
49:    }
50:
51: }
```

There are a few simple changes to the program in Listing 3.4.4. Line 22 forces a setting for the current user interface culture based on the input from the command line. The properties of the label are modified on lines 34–37 so that the label changes size with the form. In this example, you will need to resize the form to see the whole label text. This shows another aspect of internationalization that you have to contend with, the possibility that physical resource sizes might be different across cultures. It is possible to store the size and placement information of your resources in the satellite assembly also. Visual Studio does this for you, and we'll look at that in a moment. Otherwise, the use of the string resources is identical.

The application can be compiled with the following command line:

```
csc /out:hellores2.exe /t:winexe /res:firstresource.resources hellores2.cs
```

Now the program can be run and an fr culture selected by invoking it as follows:

```
hellores2 fr
```

In this circumstance, you'll see the application displaying the French resource string, as shown in Figure 3.4.2.

Bonjour le monde!!!

FIGURE 3.4.2
The French connection to resources.

There was a reason for only modifying one of the resources in the French satellite assembly. This illustrates that the resource manager will use strings and other resources from the correct locale or culture if they exist, but it will fall back to the default information in the main assembly if they do not. The `"WindowText"` string is not in the satellite assembly, so the default was used.

Using Visual Studio.NET for Internationalization

Visual Studio.NET will manage resources for you and help you to create localized forms and components. Figure 3.4.3 shows the `Localizable` property being set for a form. Setting this property to `true` will cause the design time environment to store all the relevant information in the resource file for you.

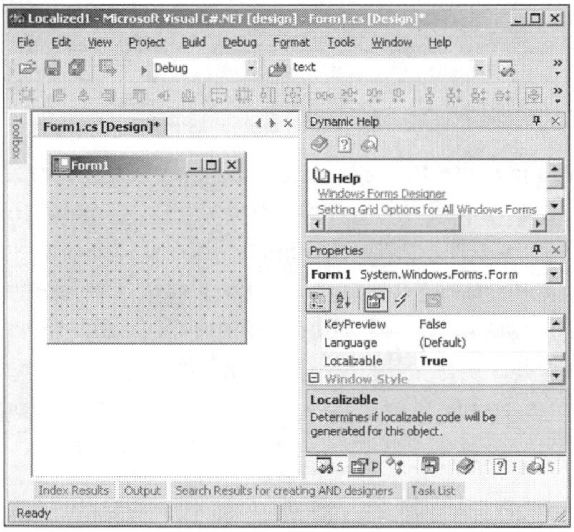

FIGURE 3.4.3
Setting the `Localizale` property.

The `InitializeComponent` method for Form1 will now contain code to initialize a resource manager and retrieve any information that might change as the application is transferred between locales from the resources.

As you saw with the handmade example shown in Figure 3.4.2, the physical extents of text strings could change as they are translated, so as well as the text itself, you will find position and size information stored in the resources. InitializeComponent method for Form1 is shown in Listing 3.4.5.

LISTING 3.4.5   Form1.cs: InitializeComponent Method

```
1: private void InitializeComponent()
2: {
3:     System.Resources.ResourceManager resources =
4:       new System.Resources.ResourceManager(typeof(Form1));
5:     this.AutoScaleBaseSize = new System.Drawing.Size(5, 13);
6:     this.ClientSize = ((System.Drawing.Size)(resources.GetObject(
    ➥"$this.ClientSize")));
7:     this.Text = resources.GetString("$this.Text");
8:
9: }
```

You can see that the IDE has created a new resource manager on line 3, and lines 6 and 7 retrieve text and client size information from the resources.

When a form is made localizable in this way, all the components you put on the form will also save their text, size, and position information to a resource file. Listing 3.4.4 shows the InitializeComponent method after the addition of a label to Form1.

LISTING 3.4.4   Form1.cs: InitializeComponent after Adding a Label

```
 1: private void InitializeComponent()
 2: {
 3:   System.Resources.ResourceManager resources =
 4:     new System.Resources.ResourceManager(typeof(Form1));
 5:   this.label1 = new System.Windows.Forms.Label();
 6:   this.label1.Location =
 7:     ((System.Drawing.Point)(resources.GetObject("label1.Location")));
 8:   this.label1.Size =
 9:     ((System.Drawing.Size)(resources.GetObject("label1.Size")));
10:   this.label1.TabIndex =
11:     ((int)(resources.GetObject("label1.TabIndex")));
12:   this.label1.Text = resources.GetString("label1.Text");
13:   this.AutoScaleBaseSize = new System.Drawing.Size(5, 13);
14:   this.ClientSize =
15:     ((System.Drawing.Size)(resources.GetObject("$this.ClientSize")));
16:   this.Controls.AddRange(new System.Windows.Forms.Control[]{this.label1});
17:   this.Text = resources.GetString("$this.Text");
18: }
```

Now the label child component of the form stores its location, size, tab-index, and text in the resources.

Image Resources

So far, we have dealt with string resources but, like Win32 programs, .NET applications store images in resources for icons, backgrounds, and other things. Ultimately, the images get stored in the compiled .resource form, but, when you create them in Visual Studio or by hand, they are converted to the XML-based .resx form. Obviously, editing an image file as text in XML form is going to be no fun at all. The prescribed method for placing images in the resources is with the tools, such as VS.NET, provided by Microsoft.

A component, for example, might have an image as a background. You would place the component on the form and edit the component's background image property. The editor will allow you to select an image that is then placed into the resource for you. Figure 3.4.4 shows an image used on a form in this way.

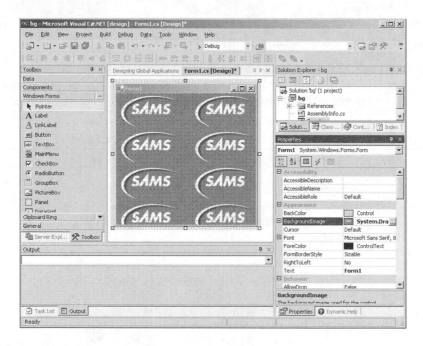

FIGURE 3.4.4

Placing a background image on a form.

Using Image Lists

Many components require images for their user interface. The ListView and TreeView classes can use images to enhance their appearances. Image lists are collections of bitmap images held in a single file. These images can have a transparent background keyed from a chosen color so that only the chosen portion of the image is shown.

The demo code for this section will be created as we go. Using Visual Studio, create a new C# application and call it **imagelistdemo**. Follow along for the rest of the chapter to complete the job.

To create an image list with Visual Studio, you should first drag an ImageList component from the toolbox onto the form. Now create some images. MS Paint is suitable for this task, just remember to save the images into a common directory. Figure 3.4.5 shows a 16×16 icon being edited in MS Paint.

> **NOTE**
>
> For the purposes of this example, we have prepared four small icons, icon1.bmp through icon4.bmp, available from the Web site.

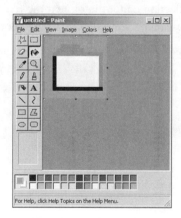

FIGURE 3.4.5

Editing an icon image.

The background of the icon is filled with magenta. This is a color that does not appear anywhere on the actual icon image, so it is safe to use it as the transparency key. To add a collection of images to the ImageList object, you can select the Images collection in the object properties and click the Browse button. This brings up a dialog, as shown in Figure 3.4.6, that can be used to add as many images as you need to the list. Note that it is important to keep all images in an image list the same size—in this instance, 16×16.

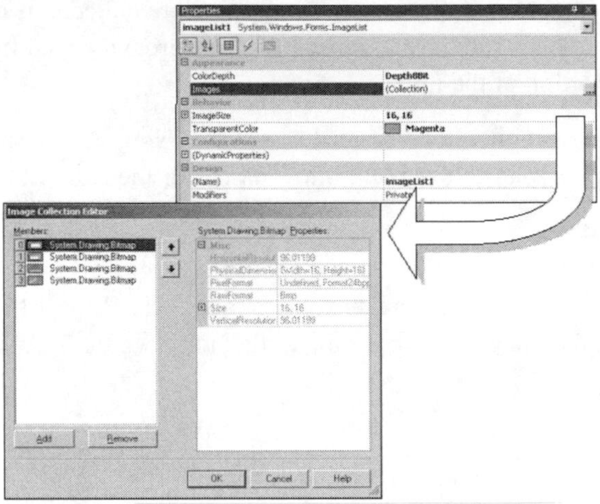

FIGURE 3.4.6
Adding images to an image list.

You can see from the image collection editor dialog that the four images are numbered from 0–3, and each has properties that can be viewed within the editor.

Now, to use these images in your `ListView` object, from the toolbox, drag a `ListView` object onto the form. For the moment, we'll simply get the `ListView` to display small icons. So select the `listView1` object and show its properties. The property called `SmallImageList` can now be set to use the `imageList1` that we just created.

Let's take a sneak peek at the `InitializeComponent` code (see Listing 3.4.5) right away to see how these tasks have affected the code.

LISTING 3.4.5   Form1.cs: InitializeComponent

```
 1: private void InitializeComponent()
 2: {
 3:   this.components = new System.ComponentModel.Container();
 4:   System.Resources.ResourceManager resources =
 5:       ➥new System.Resources.ResourceManager(typeof(Form1));
 6:   this.listView1 = new System.Windows.Forms.ListView();
 7:   this.imageList1 = new System.Windows.Forms.ImageList(this.components);
 8:   this.SuspendLayout();
 9:   //
10:   // listView1
```

LISTING 3.4.5   Continued

```
11:     //
12:     this.listView1.Location = new System.Drawing.Point(8, 8);
13:     this.listView1.Name = "listView1";
14:     this.listView1.Size = new System.Drawing.Size(272, 200);
15:     this.listView1.SmallImageList = this.imageList1;
16:     this.listView1.TabIndex = 0;
17:     //
18:     // imageList1
19:     //
20:     this.imageList1.ColorDepth = System.Windows.Forms.ColorDepth.Depth8Bit;
21:     this.imageList1.ImageSize = new System.Drawing.Size(16, 16);
22:     this.imageList1.ImageStream ((System.Windows.Forms.ImageListStreamer)
➥(resources.GetObject("imageList1.ImageStream")));
23:     this.imageList1.TransparentColor = System.Drawing.Color.Magenta;
24:     //
25:     // Form1
26:     //
27:     this.AutoScaleBaseSize = new System.Drawing.Size(5, 13);
28:     this.ClientSize = new System.Drawing.Size(292, 273);
29:     this.Controls.AddRange(new System.Windows.Forms.Control[] {
30:   this.listView1});
31:     this.Name = "Form1";
32:     this.Text = "Form1";
33:     this.ResumeLayout(false);
34: }
```

Lines 4 and 5 created the ResourceManager for the form. Lines 12–16 create the ListView and sets up the SmallImageList property to use the imageList1 component. Lines 20–24 initialize the image list by getting the image list streamer, setting the transparent color and the image size.

To use the resources in the ListView, select the properties for the ListView object, select the Items collection property, and click the button marked with ellipsis (…). This brings up the dialog shown in Figure 3.4.7 that lets you add and edit items in the list box.

NOTE

Note that your programs can also accomplish adding items to components dynamically. Visual Studio provides an additional RAD way of doing things.

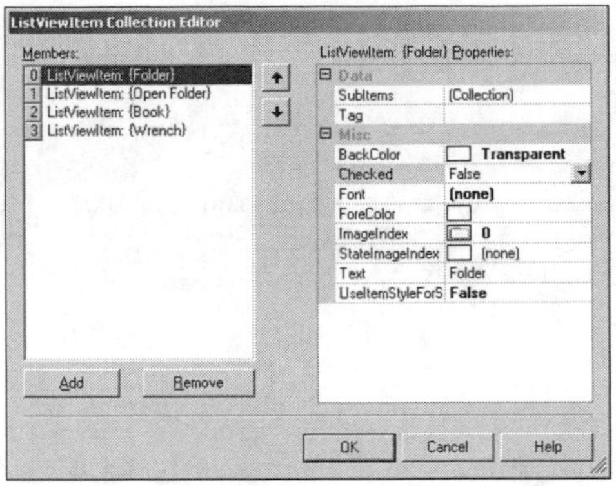

FIGURE 3.4.7

Using resource-based images in ListViewItem *objects.*

Each of the items added to the tree can be given some text and an image to display. The ListView also provides events similar to those seen in the tree view demonstration from Chapter 3.2, "User Interface Components," when list items are selected, edited, and so on. Handling these events allows you to interact with the list.

Let's take a look now at the final InitializeComponent listing for the example shown (see Listing 3.4.6).

LISTING 3.4.6 Form1.cs: InitializeComponent

```
 1:  private void InitializeComponent()
 2:  {
 3:    this.components = new System.ComponentModel.Container();
 4:    System.Resources.ResourceManager resources = new
 5:      ➥System.Resources.ResourceManager(typeof(Form1));
 6:    System.Windows.Forms.ListViewItem listViewItem1 = new
 7:      ➥System.Windows.Forms.ListViewItem("Folder",0);
 8:    System.Windows.Forms.ListViewItem listViewItem2 = new
 9:      ➥System.Windows.Forms.ListViewItem("Open Folder", 1);
10:    System.Windows.Forms.ListViewItem listViewItem3 = new
11:      ➥System.Windows.Forms.ListViewItem("Book", 2);
12:    System.Windows.Forms.ListViewItem listViewItem4 = new
13:      ➥System.Windows.Forms.ListViewItem("Wrench", 3);
14:    this.imageList1 = new System.Windows.Forms.ImageList(this.components);
15:    this.listView1 = new System.Windows.Forms.ListView();
16:    this.SuspendLayout();
17:    //
18:    // imageList1
19:    //
```

Listing 3.4.6 Continued

```
20:     this.imageList1.ColorDepth = System.Windows.Forms.ColorDepth.Depth8Bit;
21:     this.imageList1.ImageSize = new System.Drawing.Size(16, 16);
22:     this.imageList1.ImageStream = ((System.Windows.Forms.ImageListStreamer)
23:        ➥ (resources.GetObject("imageList1.ImageStream")));
24:     this.imageList1.TransparentColor = System.Drawing.Color.Magenta;
25:     //
26:     // listView1
27:     //
28:     listViewItem1.UseItemStyleForSubItems = false;
29:     listViewItem2.UseItemStyleForSubItems = false;
30:     listViewItem3.UseItemStyleForSubItems = false;
31:     listViewItem4.UseItemStyleForSubItems = false;
32:     this.listView1.Items.AddRange(new System.Windows.Forms.ListViewItem[] {
33:         listViewItem1,
34:         listViewItem2,
35:         listViewItem3,
36:         listViewItem4});
37:     this.listView1.Location = new System.Drawing.Point(8, 8);
38:     this.listView1.Name = "listView1";
39:     this.listView1.Size = new System.Drawing.Size(272, 200);
40:     this.listView1.SmallImageList = this.imageList1;
41:     this.listView1.TabIndex = 0;
42:     this.listView1.View = System.Windows.Forms.View.SmallIcon;
43:     //
44:     // Form1
45:     //
46:     this.AutoScaleBaseSize = new System.Drawing.Size(5, 13);
47:     this.ClientSize = new System.Drawing.Size(292, 273);
48:     this.Controls.AddRange(new System.Windows.Forms.Control[]
49:        {➥this.listView1});
50:     this.Name = "Form1";
51:     this.Text = "Form1";
52:     this.ResumeLayout(false);
53:  }
```

Now, lines 6–13 create the ListViewItem objects and set the text and image offset within the ImageList to use. Lines 32–36 add the items to the ListView.

Programmatic Access to Resources

In addition to creating resources with Visual Studio or the other tools provided, you can create, manage, and use resources easily through code. An example of this application of resources would be to store some custom data for your application (for example, window sizes and positions) to be retrieved when the program was run again.

Reading and writing resources are performed with the `ResourceReader` and `ResourceWriter` classes. These objects let you deal with resources stored in streams or in files.

In the example that follows, we have prepared a simple Windows Forms application that displays a red and yellow ball on the form's surface. You can pick these balls up with the mouse and move them about. When the application is closed, it creates and writes a resource called `ball_locations.resources`. This resource stores the positions onscreen of the two balls so that the next time it is loaded, the application replaces the balls where you left them.

As a bonus, this application shows some simple mouse handling and the use of the `ImageList` to draw images on the form surface.

LISTING 3.4.7   `Resourcerw.cs`: The Resource Read/Write Application

```
 1: using System;
 2: using System.Drawing;
 3: using System.Collections;
 4: using System.ComponentModel;
 5: using System.Windows.Forms;
 6: using System.Data;
 7: using System.Resources;
 8: using System.Globalization;
 9:
10:
11:
12: namespace resourcerw
13: {
14:    /// <summary>
15:    /// Summary description for Form1.
16:    /// </summary>
17:    public class Form1 : System.Windows.Forms.Form
18:    {
19:      private System.Windows.Forms.ImageList imageList1;
20:      private System.ComponentModel.IContainer components;
21:      private System.Drawing.Point[] BallLocations;
22:
23:      private bool _mousedown;
24:      private int _grabbed;
25:
26:      public Form1()
27:      {
28:        //
29:        // Required for Windows Form Designer support
30:        //
31:        InitializeComponent();
32:
```

LISTING 3.4.7 Continued

```
33:     //
34:     // TODO: Add any constructor code after InitializeComponent call
35:     //
36:
37:     this.BallLocations=new System.Drawing.Point[2];
38:
39:   }
40:
41:   /// <summary>
42:   /// Clean up any resources being used.
43:   /// </summary>
44:   protected override void Dispose( bool disposing )
45:   {
46:     if( disposing )
47:     {
48:       if (components != null)
49:       {
50:         components.Dispose();
51:       }
52:     }
53:     base.Dispose( disposing );
54:   }
55:
56:   #region Windows Form Designer generated code
57:   /// <summary>
58:   /// Required method for Designer support - do not modify
59:   /// the contents of this method with the code editor.
60:   /// </summary>
61:   private void InitializeComponent()
62:   {
63:     this.components = new System.ComponentModel.Container();
64:     System.Resources.ResourceManager resources =
65:         new System.Resources.ResourceManager(typeof(Form1));
66:     this.imageList1 =
67:         new System.Windows.Forms.ImageList(this.components);
68:     //
69:     // imageList1
70:     //
71:     this.imageList1.ColorDepth =
72:         System.Windows.Forms.ColorDepth.Depth8Bit;
73:     this.imageList1.ImageSize = new System.Drawing.Size(64, 64);
74:     this.imageList1.ImageStream =
75:         ((System.Windows.Forms.ImageListStreamer)
76:         (resources.GetObject("imageList1.ImageStream")));
77:     this.imageList1.TransparentColor = System.Drawing.Color.Magenta;
```

LISTING 3.4.7 Continued

```
 78:        //
 79:        // Form1
 80:        //
 81:        this.AutoScaleBaseSize = new System.Drawing.Size(5, 13);
 82:        this.BackColor = System.Drawing.Color.Green;
 83:        this.ClientSize = new System.Drawing.Size(376, 301);
 84:        this.Name = "Form1";
 85:        this.Text = "Resource read-write";
 86:        this.MouseDown +=
 87:          new System.Windows.Forms.MouseEventHandler(this.Form1_MouseDown);
 88:        this.Closing +=
 89:          new System.ComponentModel.CancelEventHandler(this.Form1_Closing);
 90:        this.Load +=
 91:          new System.EventHandler(this.Form1_Load);
 92:        this.MouseUp +=
 93:          new System.Windows.Forms.MouseEventHandler(this.Form1_MouseUp);
 94:        this.Paint +=
 95:          new System.Windows.Forms.PaintEventHandler(this.Form1_Paint);
 96:        this.MouseMove +=
 97:          new System.Windows.Forms.MouseEventHandler(this.Form1_MouseMove);
 98:
 99:      }
100:    #endregion
101:
102:    /// <summary>
103:    /// The main entry point for the application.
104:    /// </summary>
105:    [STAThread]
106:    static void Main()
107:    {
108:      Application.Run(new Form1());
109:    }
110:
111:
112:    private void Form1_MouseMove(object sender,
113:        ➥System.Windows.Forms.MouseEventArgs e)
114:    {
115:      if(_mousedown && (_grabbed!=-1))
116:      {
117:        if(e.X>31 && e.Y>31 && e.X<(this.Size.Width-32) &&
118:          e.Y<(this.Size.Height-32))
119:        {
120:          BallLocations[_grabbed].X=e.X;
121:          BallLocations[_grabbed].Y=e.Y;
122:
```

LISTING 3.4.7 Continued

```
123:            this.Invalidate();
124:        }
125:      }
126:    }
127:
128:    private void Form1_MouseUp(object sender,
129:        ➥System.Windows.Forms.MouseEventArgs e)
130:    {
131:      _mousedown=false;
132:    }
133:
134:    private void Form1_MouseDown(object sender,
135:          ➥System.Windows.Forms.MouseEventArgs e)
136:    {
137:      _mousedown=true;
138:      int index=0;
139:      _grabbed=-1;
140:      foreach(Point p in this.BallLocations)
141:      {
142:        if(Math.Abs(e.X-p.X)<32 && Math.Abs(e.Y-p.Y)<32)
143:          _grabbed=index;
144:        index++;
145:      }
146:    }
147:
148:    private void Form1_Paint(object sender,
149:          ➥System.Windows.Forms.PaintEventArgs e)
150:    {
151:      int index=0;
152:      foreach(Point p in this.BallLocations)
153:      {
154:        this.imageList1.Draw(e.Graphics,p.X-32,p.Y-32,64,64,index++);
155:      }
156:    }
157:
158:    private void Form1_Load(object sender, System.EventArgs e)
159:    {
160:
161:      ResourceSet rs;
162:
163:      try
164:      {
165:        rs = new ResourceSet("ball_locations.resources");
166:        BallLocations[0] = (Point)rs.GetObject("RedBall",false);
167:        BallLocations[1] = (Point)rs.GetObject("YellowBall",false);
```

3.4

WINDOWS FORMS
EXAMPLE
APPLICATION

LISTING 3.4.7 Continued

```
168:            rs.Close();
169:        }
170:        catch(System.Exception)
171:        {
172:            // Any old exception will do, probably file not yet created...
173:            BallLocations[0]=new Point(100,100);
174:            BallLocations[1]=new Point(200,200);
175:        }
176:
177:    }
178:
179:    private void Form1_Closing(object sender,
180:            ➥System.ComponentModel.CancelEventArgs e)
181:    {
182:        // Write the ball positions to the custom resource
183:        // note you can just write objects.
184:        ResourceWriter rw = new ResourceWriter("ball_locations.resources");
185:        rw.AddResource("RedBall",this.BallLocations[0]);
186:        rw.AddResource("YellowBall",this.BallLocations[1]);
187:        rw.Generate();
188:        rw.Close();
189:    }
190:
191:
192:  }
193: }
```

Lines 61–99 show the InitializeComponent method required by Visual Studio. Lines 63–65 open the image resources used by the ImageList object, and lines 66–77 initialize the ImageList by loading in the image stream and setting the parameters for size and transparent color. Lines 86–97 add the mouse and paint other handlers.

Now for the event handlers themselves. The two important ones are the form loading and form closing events. Lines 158–175 are the form load event handler. This attempts to open a resource and get the ball positions from it. If this fails for any reason, an exception handler simply assumes that the file doesn't exist and initializes both balls to their default positions. Lines 179–188 are invoked when the form is ready to close. Here, the code creates a resource file and stores all the ball positions in it. The next time the program is run, this file will exist and the load event handler will successfully find the stored positions.

The MouseUp handler (lines 128–132) simply resets a semaphore that signifies no dragging is taking place. The MouseDown handler (lines 134–146) decides which of the two balls, if any, the mouse is in, and flags the correct one to grab.

The MouseMove handler checks to see if a ball is grabbed and if the mouse is inside the client area, so that you cannot drag a ball off the screen. All being correct, it updates the position of the currently active ball. This method is found on lines 112–126.

Lastly, on lines 148–156 the Paint handler paints the balls on the surface of the form.

Reading and Writing RESX XML Files

Resource files, as we mentioned at the beginning of this chapter, come in several flavors—
.resources files and .resx files. Resx files are the raw, uncompiled XML used as a basic source form for resources. In the previous example, we showed the ResourceReader and ResourceWriter classes. There are corresponding ResXResourceReader and ResXResourceWriter classes that can be used to maintain the XML forms of the resources.

In our last example for this chapter, we've created a simple application that lets you load chosen bitmap, text, and icon files and convert these to a .RESX resource file (see Listing 3.4.8). The complexity of the task and the simplicity of this application show off some of the raw power of the Windows Forms architecture.

LISTING 3.4.8 ResXUtilForm.cs: The RESX Writer Utility

```
 1: using System;
 2: using System.Drawing;
 3: using System.Collections;
 4: using System.ComponentModel;
 5: using System.Windows.Forms;
 6: using System.Data;
 7: using System.IO;
 8:
 9: /*
10:  * NOTES: A bug in an early version of the .NET framework caused
11:  * the program to raise an exception when the resource name is
12:  * edited. In this file there are two sections of commented code
13:  * that are designed to work around this problem
14:  * If this code fails, simply uncomment the sections marked
15:  * BUGFIXER and re-compile
16:  *
17:  */
18:
19: namespace ResxUtil
20: {
21:     /// <summary>
22:     /// Summary description for Form1.
23:     /// </summary>
24:     public class ResXUtilForm : System.Windows.Forms.Form
```

LISTING 3.4.8   Continued

```
25:   {
26:     private System.Windows.Forms.ListView listView1;
27:     private System.Windows.Forms.Button button1;
28:     private System.Windows.Forms.Button button2;
29:     private System.Windows.Forms.ImageList imageList1;
30:     private System.Windows.Forms.ColumnHeader columnHeader2;
31:     private System.Windows.Forms.ColumnHeader columnHeader1;
32:     private System.ComponentModel.IContainer components;
33:
34:     public ResXUtilForm()
35:     {
36:       //
37:       // Required for Windows Form Designer support
38:       //
39:       InitializeComponent();
40:
41:       //BUGFIXER uncomment the line below
42:       //this.listView1.LabelEdit=false;
43:     }
44:
45:     /// <summary>
46:     /// Clean up any resources being used.
47:     /// </summary>
48:     protected override void Dispose( bool disposing )
49:     {
50:       if( disposing )
51:       {
52:         if (components != null)
53:         {
54:           components.Dispose();
55:         }
56:       }
57:       base.Dispose( disposing );
58:     }
59:
60:     #region Windows Form Designer generated code
61:     /// <summary>
62:     /// Required method for Designer support - do not modify
63:     /// the contents of this method with the code editor.
64:     /// </summary>
65:     private void InitializeComponent()
66:     {
67:       this.components = new System.ComponentModel.Container();
68:       System.Resources.ResourceManager resources =
➥new System.Resources.ResourceManager(typeof(ResXUtilForm));
```

LISTING 3.4.8   Continued

```
69:        this.columnHeader2 = new System.Windows.Forms.ColumnHeader();
70:        this.columnHeader1 = new System.Windows.Forms.ColumnHeader();
71:        this.imageList1 =
➥new System.Windows.Forms.ImageList(this.components);
72:        this.listView1 = new System.Windows.Forms.ListView();
73:        this.button1 = new System.Windows.Forms.Button();
74:        this.button2 = new System.Windows.Forms.Button();
75:        this.SuspendLayout();
76:        //
77:        // columnHeader2
78:        //
79:        this.columnHeader2.Text = "File name";
80:        this.columnHeader2.Width = 545;
81:        //
82:        // columnHeader1
83:        //
84:        this.columnHeader1.Text = "Resource name";
85:        this.columnHeader1.Width = 220;
86:        //
87:        // imageList1
88:        //
89:        this.imageList1.ColorDepth =
➥System.Windows.Forms.ColorDepth.Depth8Bit;
90:        this.imageList1.ImageSize = new System.Drawing.Size(16, 16);
91:        this.imageList1.ImageStream =
➥ ((System.Windows.Forms.ImageListStreamer)
➥(resources.GetObject("imageList1.ImageStream")));
92:        this.imageList1.TransparentColor = System.Drawing.Color.Magenta;
93:        //
94:        // listView1
95:        //
96:        this.listView1.Anchor = ((System.Windows.Forms.AnchorStyles.Top |
➥System.Windows.Forms.AnchorStyles.Left)
97:            | System.Windows.Forms.AnchorStyles.Right);
98:        this.listView1.Columns.AddRange(
➥new System.Windows.Forms.ColumnHeader[] {
99:                                               this.columnHeader1,
100:                                              this.columnHeader2});
101:       this.listView1.FullRowSelect = true;
102:       this.listView1.Location = new System.Drawing.Point(8, 8);
103:       this.listView1.Name = "listView1";
104:       this.listView1.Size = new System.Drawing.Size(792, 304);
105:       this.listView1.SmallImageList = this.imageList1;
106:       this.listView1.TabIndex = 0;
107:       this.listView1.View = System.Windows.Forms.View.Details;
```

LISTING 3.4.8 Continued

```
108:        this.listView1.KeyDown +=
➥new System.Windows.Forms.KeyEventHandler(this.listView1_KeyDown);
109:        this.listView1.LabelEdit=true;
110:        //
111:        // button1
112:        //
113:        this.button1.Location = new System.Drawing.Point(696, 328);
114:        this.button1.Name = "button1";
115:        this.button1.Size = new System.Drawing.Size(104, 32);
116:        this.button1.TabIndex = 1;
117:        this.button1.Text = "Save";
118:        this.button1.Click += new System.EventHandler(this.button1_Click);
119:        //
120:        // button2
121:        //
122:        this.button2.Location = new System.Drawing.Point(8, 328);
123:        this.button2.Name = "button2";
124:        this.button2.Size = new System.Drawing.Size(88, 32);
125:        this.button2.TabIndex = 2;
126:        this.button2.Text = "Add...";
127:        this.button2.Click += new System.EventHandler(this.button2_Click);
128:        //
129:        // ResXUtilForm
130:        //
131:        this.AllowDrop = true;
132:        this.AutoScaleBaseSize = new System.Drawing.Size(5, 13);
133:        this.ClientSize = new System.Drawing.Size(816, 373);
134:        this.Controls.AddRange(new System.Windows.Forms.Control[] {
135:                                        this.button2,
136:                                        this.button1,
137:                                        this.listView1});
138:        this.FormBorderStyle =
➥System.Windows.Forms.FormBorderStyle.FixedDialog;
139:        this.Name = "ResXUtilForm";
140:        this.Text = "ResX Utility";
141:        this.ResumeLayout(false);
142:
143:    }
144:    #endregion
145:
146:    /// <summary>
147:    /// The main entry point for the application.
148:    /// </summary>
149:    [STAThread]
150:    static void Main()
```

LISTING 3.4.8   Continued

```
151:    {
152:      Application.Run(new ResXUtilForm());
153:    }
154:
155:    private void button2_Click(object sender, System.EventArgs e)
156:    {
157:      int icon=-1;
158:      OpenFileDialog dlg=new OpenFileDialog();
159:      if(dlg.ShowDialog()==DialogResult.OK)
160:      {
161:        string s=dlg.FileName;
162:        string[] d=s.Split(new char[]{'.'});
163:        string resname="Unidentified";
164:
165:        if(d.Length<2)
166:          return;
167:
168:        switch(d[d.Length-1].ToLower())
169:        {
170:          case "bmp":
171:            icon=0;
172:            break;
173:          case "txt":
174:            icon=1;
175:            break;
176:          case "ico":
177:            icon=2;
178:            break;
179:        }
180:
181:
182:        //BUGFIXER remove comment block tags from the
183:        //code below.
184:        /*Form f=new Form();
185:        f.Size=new Size(350,110);
186:        f.Text="Resource name";
187:        f.FormBorderStyle=FormBorderStyle.FixedDialog;
188:        Button ok=new Button();
189:        ok.DialogResult=DialogResult.OK;
190:        ok.Location=new Point(5,32);
191:        ok.Size=new Size(75,22);
192:        ok.Text="Ok";
193:        f.Controls.Add(ok);
194:        Button can=new Button();
```

LISTING 3.4.8   Continued

```
195:          can.DialogResult=DialogResult.Cancel;
196:          can.Location=new Point(260,32);
197:          can.Size=new Size(75,22);
198:          can.Text="Cancel";
199:          f.Controls.Add(can);
200:          TextBox tb=new TextBox();
201:          tb.Location=new Point(5,5);
202:          tb.Size=new Size(330,25);
203:          tb.Text="Resource"+
204:            ((object)(this.listView1.Items.Count+1)).ToString();
205:          f.Controls.Add(tb);
206:          if(f.ShowDialog()==DialogResult.Cancel || tb.Text.Trim() == "")
207:            return;
208:          resname=tb.Text.Trim();
209:          */
210:
211:
212:          if(icon>=0)
213:          {
214:            ListViewItem item=new ListViewItem(resname,icon);
215:            item.SubItems.Add(s);
216:            this.listView1.Items.Add(item);
217:          }
218:        }
219:      }
220:
221:      private void button1_Click(object sender, System.EventArgs e)
222:      {
223:        if(this.listView1.Items.Count>0)
224:        {
225:          //Check that all resources have a name
226:          foreach(ListViewItem item in this.listView1.Items)
227:          {
228:            if(item.Text=="Undefined")
229:            {
230:              MessageBox.Show("All resources must have names");
231:              return;
232:            }
233:          }
234:
235:          //Fetch the filename for the resx file
236:          SaveFileDialog dlg=new SaveFileDialog();
237:          dlg.Title="Save .resx file";
238:          dlg.Filter="XML resource files|.resx";
```

LISTING 3.4.8   Continued

```
239:            if(dlg.ShowDialog()==DialogResult.Cancel)
240:              return;
241:
242:            //Create a resource writer
243:            System.Resources.ResXResourceWriter rw=
244:              new System.Resources.ResXResourceWriter(dlg.FileName);
245:
246:            //Step through the items on the list
247:            foreach(ListViewItem item in this.listView1.Items)
248:            {
249:              switch(item.ImageIndex)
250:              {
251:                case 0: // bitmap images
252:                  goto case 2;
253:                case 1: // text files
254:                  System.IO.StreamReader sr=
255:                    new System.IO.StreamReader(
256:                      item.SubItems[1].Text);
257:                  string inputline;
258:                  do
259:                  {
260:                    inputline = sr.ReadLine();
261:                    if(inputline != null)
262:                    {
263:                      string[] splitline=
264:                        inputline.Split(new char[]{'='},2);
265:                      if(splitline.Length==2)
266:                      {
267:                        rw.AddResource(
268:                        item.Text.TrimEnd().TrimStart()+
269:                        "."+
270:                        splitline[0].TrimEnd().TrimStart(),
271:                        splitline[1]);
272:                      }
273:                    }
274:                  }
275:                  while(inputline!=null);
276:                  break;
277:                case 2: // icons
278:                  System.Drawing.Image im=
279:                    System.Drawing.Image.FromFile(
280:                    item.SubItems[1].Text);
281:                  rw.AddResource(item.Text,im);
282:                  break;
```

LISTING 3.4.8   Continued

```
283:              }
284:          }
285:
286:          rw.Generate();
287:          rw.Close();
288:        }
289:      }
290:
291:
292:      private void listView1_KeyDown(object sender,
293:              System.Windows.Forms.KeyEventArgs e)
294:      {
295:        if(this.listView1.SelectedIndices.Count==0)
296:          return;
297:        if(e.KeyCode.Equals(Keys.Delete))
298:          this.listView1.Items.RemoveAt(
299:            this.listView1.SelectedIndices[0]);
300:      }
301:    }
302:
303: }
```

> **NOTE**
>
> Be aware that the style of layout in this and other listings has been modified to fit an 80 column format. In particular, the InitializeComponent method has been modified from its original form. If you download the file from the Sams Web site, it might differ slightly in layout, but it will be functionally identical.

By now, you should be able to go through the InitializeComponent and understand what's happening, so we'll just pick out highlights of the application.

Lines 79–80 create a set of column headers used when the ListView is in Detail mode to provide headers for each column of information. We have chosen to display the item icon from an ImageList plus the name of the resource, which you must choose, along with the full filename of the source resource.

Lines 89–92 set up the ImageList, bringing in the image stream and setting up sizes and transparent color and so on.

Lines 98–100 add the column headers to the list view control. Lines 93–104 set the properties of the `ListView` to enable row selection (so you can delete an object from the list), label editing (which lets you name your resource, locations, and sizes for the control), and finally, the `KeyDown` handler (which only responds to the Delete key).

Lines 110–128 are the buttons. One adds a resource, the other saves the RESX file.

Lines 155–219 handle the Add button. This allows you to browse files (lines 154 and 155) for bitmaps, text, or icons. After you find a resource candidate, lines 168–179 decide whether it's a file we care about and select the correct icon. Finally, lines 212–217 use the icon selection to create a `ListViewItem` that has a label (at first "Undefined") and a sub-item that populates the second column of the list control with the filename.

The Save button on lines 221–284 does a quick check to see if all the resources have been named (lines 226–233) and then gets a filename for the target file (lines 236–240). Lines 243–244 make a new `ResXResourceWriter` and then pass it into a `foreach` loop that goes through item by item and creates the resources.

The switch statement (line 249) has three cases. Cases 0 and 2 are handled the same way because, for the XML format, there is no distinction between a bitmap and an icon. Case 1 (lines 254–276) reads in the text file one line at a time and separates the lines into the name-value pairs used to create each text resource. The name is prefixed with the name you chose for the text file in the listbox. Note that this demonstration only understands text files with the "*<name string>*=*<value string>*" syntax. Other files are likely to give errors. After processing is done, lines 286 and 287 write and close the RESX file.

Finally, lines 292–300 handle the Delete key presses and remove items from the list if you want.

A Note about Bugs

Line 42 and the block of code on lines 184–208 are a contingency plan that solves a potential problem with an early version of the .NET framework. If you edit the resource name and the program crashes, uncomment the two sections of code in the lines marked "BUGFIXER" and recompile the program. It will work in a slightly different way, and it will not crash.

Notice also how the `bugfix` code creates a dialog box on-the-fly for you.

NOTE

For applications built with Visual Studio, the complete solution is included as a zip archive on the Sams Web site (http://www.samspublishing.com).

Summary

In this chapter, you have seen how to create text resources by hand, how to internationalize applications using satellite assemblies, how to use Visual Studio to create applications with image and other resources, and how to dynamically create and use resource files in your programs. In the next chapter, we'll be looking at the powerful graphics options available to you with GDI+.

GDI+: The .NET Graphics Interface

IN THIS CHAPTER

In this chapter, we'll look at the Graphical Device Interface (GDI) used by Windows Forms to create graphics. Notice the name is GDI+ not GDI.NET. This is because GDI+ is not solely a .NET Framework API. It can also be used by unmanaged code. For the purposes of this chapter however, we'll use it exclusively from Windows Forms.

The Basic Principles of GDI+

Like its predecessor GDI, GDI+ is an immediate mode graphics system. This means that as you send commands to the graphic interface, effects are seen on the device surface or in the display memory immediately. The other kind of graphics system, retained mode graphics, usually maintain hierarchies of objects that know how to paint themselves.

GDI+ uses brushes and pens to paint on the graphics surface, just like GDI did. Unlike GDI, though, you can use any graphical object on any surface at any time. GDI required you to create a graphics object, select it for use in a Device Context (DC), use the object, deselect it from the DC, and then destroy the object. If you didn't do it in that order, you could get system resource leaks that would eventually cause all the memory in your system to be allocated away and the system would need a reboot. GDI+ is altogether friendlier to use because you don't have to worry about selecting and deselecting objects in the right order.

As you might expect, the evolution of GDI+ reflects many of the recent changes in graphics card capabilities. Additions to your graphics arsenal include Alpha Blending or image transparency, antialiasing, transformations like rotation and scaling, plus many new innovations in the areas of color correction and region manipulation.

The Graphics Object

The root of all GDI+ graphics capabilities for .NET is the Graphics object. This is analogous to the Win32 DC and can be obtained explicitly from a window handle or is passed to your application from, say, the OnPaint event. To obtain a Graphics object in Managed C++, for example, you would write the following code:

```
HDC dc;
PAINTSTRUCT ps;
Graphics *pGraphics;

Dc=BeginPaint(hWnd,&ps)
pGraphics=new Graphics(dc);
// use the Graphics...
EndPaint(hWnd,&ps);
```

For the purposes of this chapter, we'll assume that GDI+ operations will take place in the context of a Windows Forms application and that the `Graphics` object is handed to you in an event delegate. For example, we see the `Graphics` object that's supplied in the `PaintEventArgs` in the following:

```
public void OnPaint(object sender, PaintEventArgs e)
{
    // use e.Graphics.SomeMethod(...) here
```

Graphics Coordinates

Objects are painted onto the screen using coordinates that are mapped to no less than three systems. The World Coordinate system, which is an abstract concept of space within the graphics system, the Page Coordinate system, which is another abstract concept of physical dimension on a hypothetical page, and the Device Coordinate system, which is tied to the physical properties of the screen or printer upon which the graphics are rendered. To display anything onscreen, the graphical data that you write to the GDI+ graphics object has to be transformed several times. The reason for this is to allow you to deal with graphics in a device-independent way. For example, if you place a shape or some text in World Coordinates, you might want to ensure that the resulting graphic is displayed as though it were on a standard A4 sheet of paper. The image must look as if it's on A4 both on the monitor and on any printer of any resolution. The World Coordinate is, therefore, mapped to a Page Coordinate that represents an 8 1/2" by 11" physical measurement. When the system comes to display the A4 page, the monitor might have a resolution of 72 dots per inch (DPI)—printer A has a resolution of 300 DPI and printer B has a resolution of 1200 by 400 DPI. Page space, a physical measurement, then needs to be mapped to Device Space so that, in reality, the monitor maps 8.5 inches across the page to 612 pixels on the monitor—2550 pixels on printer A and 10200 pixels on printer B.

GDI+ allows you to set the way that objects are transformed from the world to the page using the `PageUnit`, `PageUnit`, `PageScale`, and `PageScale` properties. You have no control over the transformation to device space. That all happens in the device drivers themselves. You can, however, read the device's DPI with the `DpiX` and `DpiY` properties.

We'll examine coordinate transformations in detail later in this chapter.

Drawing Lines and Simple Shapes

Drawing lines or the outline of a shape requires the use of a pen. Filling an area, particularly the interior of a shape, is accomplished with a brush. The simple Windows Forms example in Listing 3.5.1 shows these operations. This is a self-contained, hand-edited example, so Visual Studio.Net is not needed.

> **NOTE**
>
> A word about graphics object management under GDI+ for Windows Forms. The garbage collection heap, as you know by now, does memory management under .NET for you. Technically, there is no need to worry about reclaiming your objects by deleting them because the garbage collector will do it for you eventually.
>
> This is also true for graphical operations that create pens and brushes. However, an intense graphics routing could create many thousands of pens or brushes during each draw cycle and, in circumstances such as this, the garbage collector might not be quick enough to reclaim all the objects, causing a large number of dead items to be left on the heap for a considerable period of time.
>
> To minimize the amount of work the garbage collector does, you should, wherever possible, explicitly invoke the `Dispose()` method on pens, brushes, and other such objects. This reclaims the memory in the object and tells the garbage collector not to bother with them.
>
> In certain examples, you will see the declaration of the object inline, for example, `DrawRectangle(new Pen(Color.Red),....` This will not cause a memory leak of the pen, it simply defers reclamation of the object when it's no longer in scope. In other examples, you will see explicit use of, for example, `myPen.Dispose()`. This is the recommended method for highest memory performance.

LISTING 3.5.1   `DrawLines.cs`: Drawing Lines and Filling Rectangles

```
 1: using System;
 2: using System.Drawing;
 3: using System.Windows.Forms;
 4:
 5: class drawlines : System.Windows.Forms.Form
 6: {
 7:     Timer t;
 8:     bool BackgroundDirty;
 9:
10:     public void TickEventHandler(object sender, EventArgs e)
11:     {
12:         Invalidate();
13:     }
14:
15:     public void OnPaint(object sender, PaintEventArgs e)
16:     {
17:         // the current graphics object for
18:         // this window is in the PaintEventArgs
19:
```

LISTING 3.5.1 Continued

```
20:        Random r=new Random();
21:
22:        Color c=Color.FromArgb(r.Next(255),r.Next(255),r.Next(255));
23:        Pen p=new Pen(c,(float)r.NextDouble()*10);
24:        e.Graphics.DrawLine(p,r.Next(this.ClientSize.Width),
25:                            r.Next(this.ClientSize.Height),
26:                            r.Next(this.ClientSize.Width),
27:                            r.Next(this.ClientSize.Height));
28:        p.Dispose();
29:    }
30:
31:    protected override void OnPaintBackground(PaintEventArgs e)
32:    {
33:        // When we resize or on the first time run
34:        // we'll paint the background, otherwise
35:        // it will be left so the lines build up
36:        if(BackgroundDirty)
37:        {
38:            BackgroundDirty = false;
39:            // We could call base.OnPaintBackground(e);
40:            // but that doesn't show off rectangle filling
41:            e.Graphics.FillRectangle(new SolidBrush(this.BackColor),
42:                                this.ClientRectangle);
43:        }
44:
45:    }
46:
47:    public void OnSized(object sender, EventArgs e)
48:    {
49:        BackgroundDirty=true;
50:        Invalidate();
51:    }
52:
53:    public drawlines()
54:    {
55:        t=new Timer();
56:        t.Interval=300;
57:        t.Tick+=new System.EventHandler(TickEventHandler);
58:        t.Enabled=true;
59:        this.Paint+=new PaintEventHandler(OnPaint);
60:        this.SizeChanged+=new EventHandler(OnSized);
61:        this.Text="Lines and lines and lines";
62:        BackgroundDirty = true;
63:    }
```

LISTING 3.5.1   Continued

```
64:
65:    static void Main()
66:    {
67:        Application.Run(new drawlines());
68:    }
69: };
```

Compile Listing 3.5.1 by using the following command line:

`csc /t:winexe drawlines.cs`

Lines 53–62 set up the application by creating a timer and by adding the OnPaint handler to the Paint event list. It also adds an event handler for the SizeChanged event, so that we can detect when a new background needs painting.

Lines 10–13 are a simple Tick event handler that just invalidates the window. And lines 15–29 are the paint handler that creates a pen and draws a line between two random coordinates onscreen.

Lines 31–43 paint the background for us. The reason that it's done this way is so that the invalidation of the screen doesn't paint over the lines already drawn. You can take this out if you like to see what happens. It illustrates how a brush fills a rectangle.

Using Gradient Pens and Brushes

Pens and brushes have come a long way in a short time. GDI+ allows you to have lines and filled areas that show a gradient or sweep of colors. Modifying the code in Listing 3.5.1 will allow us to use the gradient pens or gradient fills instead of solid lines or colors.

To fill the background of the window is simple enough, we just need to specify a gradient fill brush. The LinearGradientBrush object is a member of the System.Drawing.Drawing2d namespace. Drawing a gradient fill on a line is very simple, because one of the overloads allows you to specify two Point objects, each at opposite corners of a rectangle.

Listing 3.5.2 is a selective listing of the two sections you need to change in the example from Listing 3.5.1. It contains only the modified routines OnPaint and OnPaintBackground. Remember, though, to add the declaration

`Using System.Drawing.Drwing2D;`

to your source also.

LISTING 3.5.2   DrawLines2.cs: The Modified Line and Fill Code for DrawLines.cs

```
 1:
 2: public void OnPaint(object sender, PaintEventArgs e)
 3: {
 4:         // the current graphics object for
 5:         // this window is in the PaintEventArgs
 6:
 7:         Random r=new Random();
 8:
 9:         Color cA=Color.FromArgb(r.Next(255),r.Next(255),r.Next(255));
10:         Color cB=Color.FromArgb(r.Next(255),r.Next(255),r.Next(255));
11:         Point pA=new Point(r.Next(this.ClientSize.Width),
12:                         r.Next(this.ClientSize.Height));
13:         Point pB=new Point(r.Next(this.ClientSize.Width),
14:                         r.Next(this.ClientSize.Height));
15:         LinearGradientBrush brush = new LinearGradientBrush(pA,pB,cA,cB);
16:         Pen p=new Pen(brush,(float)r.NextDouble()*10);
17:         e.Graphics.DrawLine(p,pA,pB);
18:         p.Dispose();
19: }
20:
21: protected override void OnPaintBackground(PaintEventArgs e)
22: {
23:         // When we resize or on the first time run
24:         // we'll paint the background, otherwise
25:         // it will be left so the lines build up
26:         if(BackgroundDirty)
27:         {
28:            BackgroundDirty = false;
29:            LinearGradientBrush gb=
30:              new LinearGradientBrush(this.ClientRectangle,
31:                                        Color.Navy,
32:                                        Color.Aquamarine,
33:                                        90);
34:            e.Graphics.FillRectangle(gb,this.ClientRectangle);
35:          gb.Dispose();
36:         }
37:
38: }
```

Figure 3.5.1 shows the application running in all it's garish glory.

FIGURE 3.5.1

The modified DrawLines program.

NOTE

You might notice that the pen itself uses a brush for filling its internal color. You can also use a hatch brush or a pattern brush to draw a line. This is very powerful indeed.

Textured Pens and Brushes

You saw in the previous example that a pen can be given a brush with which to paint the line. Brushes can be solid, gradients, textures, or hatch patterns. A textured brush can be used to draw lines that are painted with a bitmap image. To accomplish this, you can load in a bitmap from a file or a resource, create a brush with it, pass the brush to a pen, and finally draw your lines with the pen. The following snippet of code shows this process:

```
Image i=Image.FromFile("stone.bmp");
TextureBrush b= new TextureBrush(i);
Pen p=new Pen(b,10);
e.Graphics.DrawLine(p,0,0,100,100);
p.Dispose();
```

As you can see, a ridiculously simple thing to do.

Tidying up Your Lines with Endcaps

The line segments shown in Figure 3.5.1 have ends that are cut squarely and might not be good for drawing polygons. Figure 3.5.2 shows how wide lines with square ends look when used to draw a simple star.

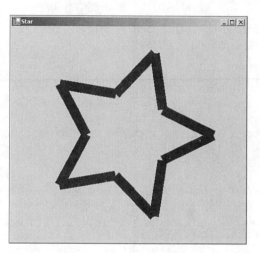

FIGURE 3.5.2
Flat end caps used in a polygon.

As you can see, the flat end caps make a mess of the shape where the lines join. To tidy this up, we can specify a rounded end cap for the lines. Pens have two properties, StartCap and EndCap, that can be set to draw specialized ends on your lines. In Listing 3.5.3, we show the program that draws the star and allows you to turn end caps on or off with a button on the form.

LISTING 3.5.3 DrawStar.cs: The Line Cap Example

```
 1: using System;
 2: using System.Drawing;
 3: using System.Drawing.Drawing2D;
 4: using System.Windows.Forms;
 5:
 6: class drawstar : System.Windows.Forms.Form
 7: {
 8:     Button button1;
 9:
10:     bool EndCap;
```

LISTING 3.5.3 Continued

```
11:
12:     public void OnPaint(object sender, PaintEventArgs e)
13:     {
14:         Pen pen=new Pen(Color.Black,(float)20.0);
15:         if(EndCap)
16:         {
17:             pen.StartCap=LineCap.Round;
18:             pen.EndCap=LineCap.Round;
19:         }
20:
21:         float r36 = (float)(36.0 * 3.1415926 / 180);
22:         Point Center=new Point(this.ClientRectangle.Width/2,
23:                             this.ClientRectangle.Height/2);
24:         float Pointsize = (float)0.8*Math.Min(Center.X,Center.Y);
25:         for(int i=0; i<10; i++)
26:         {
27:             float d1=(i & 1)==1 ? Pointsize / 2 : Pointsize;
28:             float d2=(i & 1)==0 ? Pointsize / 2 : Pointsize;
29:             e.Graphics.DrawLine(pen,
30:                 new Point((int)(d1*Math.Cos(r36*i))+Center.X,
31:                         (int)(d1*Math.Sin(r36*i))+Center.Y),
32:                 new Point((int)(d2*Math.Cos(r36*(i+1)))+Center.X,
33:                         (int)(d2*Math.Sin(r36*(i+1))+Center.Y)));
34:         }
35:         pen.Dispose();
36:     }
37:
38:     public void OnSizeChanged(object sender, EventArgs e)
39:     {
40:         Invalidate();
41:     }
42:
43:     public void OnClickedButton1(object sender, EventArgs e)
44:     {
45:         EndCap = !EndCap;
46:         Invalidate();
47:     }
48:
49:     public drawstar()
50:     {
51:         this.Paint+=new PaintEventHandler(OnPaint);
52:         this.Text="Star";
53:         this.SizeChanged+=new EventHandler(OnSizeChanged);
54:
```

LISTING 3.5.3   Continued

```
55:          button1 = new Button();
56:          button1.Location=new Point(5,5);
57:          button1.Size=new Size(50,20);
58:          button1.Text = "Caps";
59:          button1.Click+=new EventHandler(OnClickedButton1);
60:          this.Controls.Add(button1);
61:
62:      }
63:
64:      static void Main()
65:      {
66:          Application.Run(new drawstar());
67:      }
68: };
```

Compile this program with the following command line:

```
csc /t:winexe drawstar.cs
```

When you run the program, you will see a button in the top-left corner of the window, click it to change to rounded end caps. There are 11 different line cap styles altogether, including a custom style.

Already you can see that GDI+ is a great improvement over good old trusty GDI, and we've only really looked at lines and rectangles. Let's now look at curves, paths, and splines.

Curves and Paths

GDI has had Bezier curves and temporary paths for some time. GDI+ expands these capabilities by providing a rich set of functionality for curves and a persistent path object.

The simplest form is the curve drawn from an array of points. The curve is drawn so that it passes through each point on the array. The tension of the curve for any particular point is controlled by the positions of the points on either side of it in the array. The true Bezier curve has two points associated with each node—a position and a control point. Tension of the curve is determined by the relationship of the control point to the direction of the line.

Listing 3.5.4 illustrates the use of the `Graphics.DrawCurve` method by creating a set of positions that bounce around in a rectangular area onscreen. A curve, or Cardinal Spline, is drawn along this array of points, and you can select the tension of the curve with a slider.

LISTING 3.5.4   `DrawCurve.cs`: Using the `DrawCurve` Method

```
 1: using System;
 2: using System.Drawing;
 3: using System.Drawing.Drawing2D;
 4: using System.Collections;
 5: using System.ComponentModel;
 6: using System.Windows.Forms;
 7: using System.Data;
 8:
 9: namespace Curves
10: {
11:     /// <summary>
12:     /// This simple object bounces points
13:     /// around a rectangular area.
14:     /// </summary>
15:     class Bouncer
16:     {
17:         int dirx;
18:         int diry;
19:         int X;
20:         int Y;
21:
22:         Size size;
23:
24:         public Bouncer()
25:         {
26:             dirx=diry=1;
27:         }
28:
29:         public void Move()
30:         {
31:             X+=dirx;
32:             Y+=diry;
33:
34:             if(X<=0 || X>=size.Width)
35:                 dirx*=-1;
36:
37:             if(Y<=0 || Y>=size.Height)
38:                 diry*=-1;
39:         }
40:
41:         public Point Position
42:         {
43:             get{return new Point(X,Y);}
44:             set{X=value.X; Y=value.Y;}
45:         }
```

LISTING 3.5.4 Continued

```
46:
47:      public Size Size
48:      {
49:         get{ return size;}
50:         set{size = value;}
51:      }
52:    }
53:
54:    /// <summary>
55:    /// Summary description for Form1.
56:    /// </summary>
57:    public class Curves : System.Windows.Forms.Form
58:    {
59:
60:      Timer bounce,paint;
61:      TrackBar trk;
62:
63:      Bouncer[] bouncers;
64:
65:      void OnTickBounce(object sender, EventArgs e)
66:      {
67:         foreach(Bouncer b in bouncers)
68:            b.Move();
69:      }
70:
71:      void OnTickPaint(object sender, EventArgs e)
72:      {
73:         Invalidate();
74:      }
75:
76:      public void OnPaint(object sender, PaintEventArgs e)
77:      {
78:         Pen p=new Pen(Color.Red,10);
79:         SolidBrush br=new SolidBrush(Color.Blue);
80:         Point[] points = new Point[bouncers.Length];
81:         int i=0;
82:         // need to translate our bouncers to an array of points
83:         foreach(Bouncer b in bouncers)
84:            points[i++]=b.Position;
85:         //Draw the curve
86:         e.Graphics.DrawCurve(p,points,0,points.Length-
➥1,(float)trk.Value);
87:         //now draw the nodes in the curve.
88:         foreach(Point pn in points)
89:            e.Graphics.FillEllipse(br,pn.X-5,pn.Y-5,10,10);
```

LISTING 3.5.4 Continued

```
 90:          p.Dispose();
 91:          br.Dispose();
 92:      }
 93:
 94:      public Curves()
 95:      {
 96:          this.Paint+=new PaintEventHandler(OnPaint);
 97:          // A timer to manage the bouncing
 98:          bounce=new Timer();
 99:          bounce.Interval=5;
100:          bounce.Tick+=new EventHandler(OnTickBounce);
101:          // A timer to manage the painting refresh
102:          paint=new Timer();
103:          paint.Interval=100;
104:          paint.Tick+=new EventHandler(OnTickPaint);
105:          // Random number generator for initial positions
106:          Random r=new Random();
107:          // the form initial size
108:          this.Size=new Size(800,600);
109:          //iniialize an array of bouncing points
110:          bouncers = new Bouncer[6];
111:          for(int i=0;i<6;i++)
112:          {
113:              bouncers[i]=new Bouncer();
114:              bouncers[i].Position=new Point(r.Next(800),r.Next(600));
115:              bouncers[i].Size=new Size(800,600);
116:          }
117:          // turn on the timers
118:          bounce.Enabled=true;
119:          paint.Enabled=true;
120:          //create a trackbar for the line tension
121:          trk = new TrackBar();
122:          trk.Location=new Point(5,25);
123:          trk.Size=new Size(100,20);
124:          trk.Minimum=1;
125:          trk.Maximum=10;
126:          trk.Value=2;
127:          this.Controls.Add(trk);
128:          //and label it nicely for the user
129:          Label lb=new Label();
130:          lb.Location=new Point(5,5);
131:          lb.Size=new Size(100,20);
132:          lb.Text="Curve tension";
133:          this.Controls.Add(lb);
134:      }
```

LISTING 3.5.4   Continued

```
135:
136:        static void Main()
137:        {
138:            Application.Run(new Curves());
139:        }
140:    }
141: }
```

Compile Listing 3.5.4 with the following command line:

```
Csc /t:winexe drawcurve.cs
```

The work is done by two timers and a paint handler. Timer #1 (lines 98 and 65–69) makes the positions of the curve nodes bounce around the screen. Timer #2 (lines 102 and 71–74) invalidates the screen so that the painting is not done too frequently. The paint handler (lines 76–90) creates an array of points from the bounce object; sadly, Point is a sealed class so you cannot inherit from it, which would have been useful. Then line 86 draws the curve, the tension of which depends on the position of the TrackBar control. To illustrate where the individual points are, lines 88 and 89 draw them in blue. This demonstration clearly shows how line tension works for the simple curve.

Figure 3.5.3 shows the DrawCurves application running.

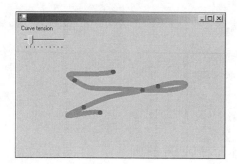

FIGURE 3.5.3
Drawing a curve with tension.

A Bezier Spline is somewhat different. For each line segment, two points define the start and end of the line, and another two determine the control points that add the line tension and curvature. Listing 3.5.5 shows how a Bezier curve is used.

LISTING 3.5.5   Beziercurves.cs: Using the Bezier Curve

```
 1: using System;
 2: using System.Drawing;
 3: using System.Drawing.Drawing2D;
 4: using System.Collections;
 5: using System.ComponentModel;
 6: using System.Windows.Forms;
 7: using System.Data;
 8:
 9: namespace Curves
10: {
11:     /// <summary>
12:     /// This simple object bounces points
13:     /// around a rectangular area.
14:     /// </summary>
15:     class Bouncer
16:     {
17:         int dirx;
18:         int diry;
19:         public int X;
20:         public int Y;
21:
22:         Size size;
23:
24:         public Bouncer()
25:         {
26:             dirx=diry=1;
27:         }
28:
29:         public void Move()
30:         {
31:             X+=dirx;
32:             Y+=diry;
33:
34:             if(X<=0 || X>=size.Width)
35:                 dirx*=-1;
36:
37:             if(Y<=0 || Y>=size.Height)
38:                 diry*=-1;
39:         }
40:
41:         public Point Position
42:         {
43:             get{return new Point(X,Y);}
44:             set{X=value.X; Y=value.Y;}
45:         }
```

LISTING 3.5.5 Continued

```
46:
47:        public Size Size
48:        {
49:            get{ return size;}
50:            set{size = value;}
51:        }
52:    }
53:
54:    /// <summary>
55:    /// Summary description for Form1.
56:    /// </summary>
57:    public class BezierCurves : System.Windows.Forms.Form
58:    {
59:
60:        Timer bounce,paint;
61:  63:        Bouncer[] bouncers;
62:
63:        void OnTickBounce(object sender, EventArgs e)
64:        {
65:            foreach(Bouncer b in bouncers)
66:                b.Move();
67:        }
68:
69:        void OnTickPaint(object sender, EventArgs e)
70:        {
71:            Invalidate();
72:        }
73:
74:        public void OnPaint(object sender, PaintEventArgs e)
75:        {
76:            Pen p=new Pen(Color.Red,10);
77:            p.StartCap=LineCap.DiamondAnchor;
78:            p.EndCap=LineCap.ArrowAnchor;
79:            SolidBrush br=new SolidBrush(Color.Blue);
80:            //Draw the curve
81:            e.Graphics.DrawBezier(p,new Point(550,300),
82:                                    bouncers[0].Position,
83:                                    bouncers[1].Position,
84:                                    new Point(50,300));
85:            //now draw the nodes in the curve.
86:            foreach(Bouncer b in bouncers)
87:                e.Graphics.FillEllipse(br,b.X-5,b.Y-5,10,10);
88:            //and show the relation between the bouncing node
89:            //and the bezier end point
```

LISTING 3.5.5   Continued

```
90:            p=new Pen(Color.Black,1);
91:            p.DashStyle=DashStyle.DashDotDot;
92:            e.Graphics.DrawLine(p,bouncers[0].Position,new Point(550,300));
93:            e.Graphics.DrawLine(p,bouncers[1].Position,new Point(50,300));
94:            p.Dispose();
95:        }
96:
97:        public BezierCurves()
98:        {
99:            this.Paint+=new PaintEventHandler(OnPaint);
100:           // A timer to manage the bouncing
101:           bounce=new Timer();
102:           bounce.Interval=5;
103:           bounce.Tick+=new EventHandler(OnTickBounce);
104:           // A timer to manage the painting refresh
105:           paint=new Timer();
106:           paint.Interval=100;
107:           paint.Tick+=new EventHandler(OnTickPaint);
108:           // Random number generator for initial positions
109:           Random r=new Random();
110:           // the form initial size
111:           this.Size=new Size(800,600);
112:           //iniialize an array of bouncing points
113:           bouncers = new Bouncer[2];
114:           for(int i=0;i<2;i++)
115:           {
116:               bouncers[i]=new Bouncer();
117:               bouncers[i].Position=new Point(r.Next(800),r.Next(600));
118:               bouncers[i].Size=new Size(800,600);
119:           }
120:           // turn on the timers
121:           bounce.Enabled=true;
122:           paint.Enabled=true;
123:        }
124:
125:        static void Main()
126:        {
127:            Application.Run(new BezierCurves());
128:        }
129:    }
130: }
```

The meat of this application is substantially similar to that shown in Listing 3.5.4. The points of interest are lines 83–86, where the Bezier is drawn, and lines 92–96, which show you how to draw dashed lines. The image shown in Figure 3.5.4 is a screenshot of the application and shows how the Bezier control points are used to add direction and tension to a particular node.

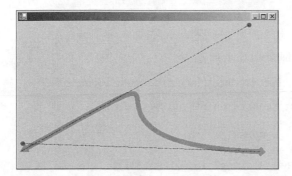

FIGURE 3.5.4
The Bezier curve in action.

An array of points can also be used to create a multi-segmented Bezier Spline. The array must have a multiple of four points and is arranged as follows:

Point[0] = Start point of line segment 1

Point[1] = Control point for the start point

Point[2] = Control point for the end point

Point[3] = End point for line segment and start point of line segment 2

Point[4] = Control point for the start point of line segment 2

And so on, giving 4 initial points plus three for each subsequent line segment.

The `GraphicsPath` Object

GDI+ Graphics Paths are a convenient way of collecting together a number of graphical shapes, or their boundaries at least, into a single unit. A path, once created, can be manipulated in its entirety, filled, stroked, or used to perform other graphical operations, such as being used to create a clipping region.

Any combination of the following graphical primitives can be placed in a `Path` object:

- Arcs
- Bezier Splines
- Cardinal splines

- Ellipses
- Lines
- Paths
- Pie segments
- Polygons
- Rectangles
- Character Glyphs from Strings

The following code snippet produces the result seen in Figure 3.5.5.

```
void OnPaint(object sender, PaintEventArgs e)
{
    GraphicsPath p=new GraphicsPath();
    p.AddEllipse(10,10,100,100);
    p.AddRectangle(new Rectangle(0,0,120,120));
    Pen pen=new Pen(Color.Black,1);
    e.Graphics.DrawPath(pen,p);
    pen.Dispose();
}
```

FIGURE 3.5.5
Two figures in a GraphicsPath.

Filling the path by substituting a suitable brush and fill command produces the following effect (see Figure 3.5.6):

```
SolidBrush brush = new SolidBrush(Color.Blue);
e.Graphics.FillPath(brush,p);
```

FIGURE 3.5.6
A filled path.

The square part of the path has been filled and the circle has not. This is because the graphics FillMode for the path is set to the default setting, Alternate.

To fill everything inside the outermost boundary of the shape, set the FillMode to Winding.

Adding Text and Other Paths

One path can be added to another quite simply by calling the AddPath method. The following code snippet creates a second path and adds it to the one shown in Figure 3.5.5.

```
void OnPaint(object sender, PaintEventArgs e)
{
    GraphicsPath p=new GraphicsPath();
    p.AddEllipse(10,10,100,100);
    p.AddRectangle(new Rectangle(0,0,120,120));
    Pen pen=new Pen(Color.Black,1);
    GraphicsPath p2=new GraphicsPath();
    Point[] tripoint=new Point[3];
    tripoint[0]=new Point(80,10);
    tripoint[1]=new Point(80,110);
    tripoint[2]=new Point(150,60);
    p2.AddClosedCurve(tripoint,(float)0);
    p2.AddPath(p,true);
    SolidBrush brush = new SolidBrush(Color.Blue);
    e.Graphics.FillPath(brush,p2);
    e.Graphics.DrawPath(pen,p2);
}
```

Now the image displayed is the sum of the two paths. Figure 3.5.7 shows the output from the modified OnPaint handler.

FIGURE 3.5.7
The combination of two paths

Placing text in a path is a great way of creating text effects. A text path only contains the glyph outlines of the letters used. These outlines can be used to create clip paths, filled with patterns or colors, scaled, rotated, or otherwise transformed to make some pretty impressive effects.

Modifying the code in our phantom `OnPaint` will illustrate again how this is accomplished.

```
void OnPaint(object sender, PaintEventArgs e)
{
   GraphicsPath p=new GraphicsPath();
   p.AddString("AYBABTU",FontFamily.GenericSansSerif,
                  0,(float)72,new Point(0,0),
                  StringFormat.GenericDefault);
   SolidBrush brush = new SolidBrush(Color.Blue);
   e.Graphics.FillPath(brush,p);
   brush.Dispose();
}
```

We'll continue this discussion in the next section because it leads nicely into that topic.

Clipping with Paths and Regions

A region is a description of some enclosed shape that can be used as a mask in which to perform graphical operations. Regions can be regular shapes, like rectangles or ellipses; they can also be irregular, perhaps created from curves or text glyphs. Because regions can be created from paths, it is possible to have very complex, clipped shapes. Going back again to our previous text path example, we can create a clipping region from it and use it for other interesting things.

In the example shown in Listing 3.5.6, we use a path, filled with a text string, as a mask for randomly positioned ellipses of color that splatter the window but are clipped by the glyph outlines of the text.

LISTING 3.5.6   `ClipToPath.cs`: Using a Path to Clip the Drawing Area

```
 1: using System;
 2: using System.Drawing;
 3: using System.Drawing.Drawing2D;
 4: using System.Collections;
 5: using System.ComponentModel;
 6: using System.Windows.Forms;
 7: using System.Data;
 8:
 9: namespace Clipping
10: {
11:     public class ClipToPath : System.Windows.Forms.Form
12:     {
13:
14:         Timer timer;
15:         GraphicsPath p;
16:         bool dirty;
```

LISTING 3.5.6 Continued

```
17:
18:          void OnPaint(object sender, PaintEventArgs e)
19:          {
20:              Random r=new Random();
21:              SolidBrush brush = new SolidBrush(
22:                  Color.FromArgb(r.Next(255),
23:                                  r.Next(255),
24:                                  r.Next(255)));
25:              e.Graphics.SetClip(p);
26:              e.Graphics.FillEllipse(brush,
27:                                  r.Next(500),
28:                                  r.Next(200),
29:                                  r.Next(20),
30:                                  r.Next(20));
31:              brush.Dispose();
32:          }
33:
34:          void OnTick(object sender, EventArgs e)
35:          {
36:              Invalidate();
37:          }
38:
39:          protected override void OnPaintBackground(PaintEventArgs e)
40:          {
41:              if(dirty)
42:              {
43:                  e.Graphics.ResetClip();
44:                  SolidBrush b=new SolidBrush(this.BackColor);
45:                  e.Graphics.FillRectangle(b, this.ClientRectangle);
46:                  dirty = false;
47:                  b.Dispose();
48:              }
49:          }
50:
51:          void OnSized(object sender, EventArgs e)
52:          {
53:              dirty=true;
54:              Invalidate();
55:          }
56:
57:          public ClipToPath()
58:          {
59:
60:              p=new GraphicsPath();
61:              p.AddString("AYBABTU",FontFamily.GenericSansSerif,
```

LISTING 3.5.6   Continued

```
62:                              0,(float)72,new Point(0,0),
63:                              StringFormat.GenericDefault);
64:              dirty=true;
65:              this.Paint+=new PaintEventHandler(OnPaint);
66:              this.SizeChanged+=new EventHandler(OnSized);
67:              timer = new Timer();
68:              timer.Interval=10;
69:              timer.Tick+=new EventHandler(OnTick);
70:              timer.Enabled=true;
71:          }
72:
73:          static void Main()
74:          {
75:              Application.Run(new ClipToPath());
76:          }
77:      }
78: }
```

The path is created once on lines 59–62 and stored for use later. Then a timer is initialized to enable the periodic refresh of the page.

Lines 39–48 handle the repaint of the background if the window is resized or on the first draw.

Finally, line 25 selects the clip-path into the Graphics object. The following lines place a random blob of color on the page; this might or might not be seen, depending on its coincidence with the clipping path.

After a while, the output from the application looks something like the image in Figure 3.5.8.

FIGURE 3.5.8

Painting clipped to a path.

Operations on regions are different from those on paths. A path specifies a set of boundaries, a region specifies an area or group of areas to be used as a mask. Regions can be combined in several ways. The operation is controlled by the CombineMode enumeration. Listing 3.5.7 illustrates the use of regions in four different modes.

LISTING 3.5.7   Regions.cs: Combining Regions in Different Ways

```
1: using System;
2: using System.Drawing;
3: using System.Drawing.Drawing2D
4: using System.Collections;
5: using System.ComponentModel;
6: using System.Windows.Forms;
7: using System.Data;
8:
9: namespace regions
10: {
11:     /// <summary>
12:     /// Summary description for Form1.
13:     /// </summary>
14:     public class RegionsTest : System.Windows.Forms.Form
15:     {
16:         void PaintRegions(Graphics g,CombineMode m,
➡Point offset,string text)
17:         {
18:             Region ra,rb;
19:             GraphicsPath p=new GraphicsPath();
20:             p.AddRectangle(new Rectangle(60,60,120,120));
21:             ra=new Region(p);
22:             p=new GraphicsPath();
23:             p.AddEllipse(0,0,120,120);
24:             rb=new Region(p);
25:             ra.Translate(offset.X,offset.Y );
26:             rb.Translate(offset.X,offset.Y);
27:             g.SetClip(ra,CombineMode.Replace);
28:             g.SetClip(rb,m);
29:             SolidBrush brush=new SolidBrush(Color.Black);
30:             g.FillRectangle(brush,this.ClientRectangle);
31:             g.ResetClip();
32:             g.DrawString(text,
33:                 new Font("Ariel",(float)16),
34:                 brush,(float)offset.X+60,(float)offset.Y+220);
35:         }
36:
37:         void OnPaint(object sender, PaintEventArgs e)
38:         {
39:             // A union of two regions...
40:             PaintRegions(e.Graphics,CombineMode.Union,
41:                 new Point(0,0),"Union");
42:             // the intersection of two regions
43:             PaintRegions(e.Graphics,CombineMode.Intersect,
44:                 new Point(250,0),"Intersect");
```

3.5

LISTING 3.5.7 Continued

```
45:              // Region exclusive or
46:              PaintRegions(e.Graphics,CombineMode.Xor,
47:                  new Point(500,0),"Xor");
48:              // The complement of the two regions
49:              PaintRegions(e.Graphics,CombineMode.Complement,
50:                  new Point(0,250),"Complement");
51:              // Exclusion.
52:              PaintRegions(e.Graphics,CombineMode.Exclude,
53:                  new Point(250,250),"Exclude");
54:          }
55:
56:          public RegionsTest()
57:          {
58:              this.Paint+=new PaintEventHandler(OnPaint);
59:              this.Size = new Size(800,800);
60:          }
61:
62:          static void Main()
63:          {
64:              Application.Run(new RegionsTest());
65:          }
66:      }
67: }
```

OnPaint (lines 37–54) repeatedly calls the PaintRegions method with a distinct CombineMode setting, some positional information, and an identifying string. The PaintRegions method (lines 16–35) begins by declaring two regions, ra and rb, and filling them with a circle and a rectangle. Lines 25 and 26 ensure that the regions are moved into position ready for display, and then line 27 selects the first clip region, replacing the one that already exists in the Graphics object. The second region is combined with the CombineMode, supplied on line 28, and the whole rectangle of the client area filled with black. Note that only the area inside the clipped region is filled. The program then removes the clipping region on line 31 to draw the information text on lines 32–34.

Output from this program is shown in Figure 3.5.9.

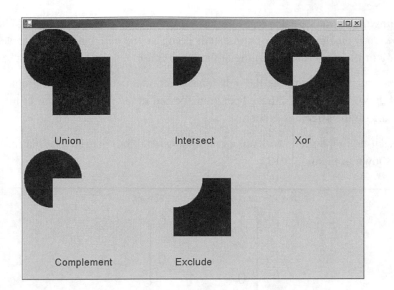

FIGURE 3.5.9
Exploring region combination modes.

Transformations

You might have noticed a couple of commands in the previous example that moved the regions into position by applying a translation to them. There are two basic ways of applying transforms to graphical objects in the Framework. You can use the methods provided, such as `Translate` or `Rotate`, or you can specify an explicit transformation matrix to be used.

By far, the easiest way for dealing with these kinds of operations is to use the methods that wrap the underlying matrix manipulations for you.

These operations allow you to do the following:

- **Translate**—Move an object in the x or y plane by an offset.
- **Rotate**—Spin an object about the origin.
- **RotateAt**—Spin an object about a point other than the origin.
- **Scale**—Magnify or reduce an object in the x and y planes.
- **Shear**—Distort an object by changing its bounding rectangle into a bounding parallelogram.

A matrix performs these operations by performing a matrix operation, such as addition, subtraction, or multiplication to the current graphics transform. We mentioned right at the beginning of this chapter that graphical commands need to go through several translations between being drawn into the graphics system and finally being seen onscreen. This is referred to as the *graphics pipeline*. Think of commands going in one end, being changed according to the plumbing of the pipes, and emerging at the other end in a somewhat different state.

The things a matrix transforms are the individual positional coordinates of a graphical object. Every pixel drawn onscreen will have been transformed in the pipeline several times before it finally appears on the screen or printer.

The matrices used in the framework are a two dimensional 3×3 matrix. The matrix is constructed as shown in Figure 3.5.10.

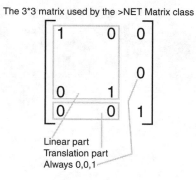

FIGURE 3.5.10

The 3×3 Identity Matrix.

The matrix shown in Figure 3.5.10 is called the Identity Matrix. An identity matrix can be applied as a transformation to an object and have no effect on it. The Identity Matrix is normally the starting point for all transformations. The matrix used by GDI+ has some fixed values in the rightmost column. The part that is always 0,0,1 in the 3×3 matrix is used to allow a compound operation (for example, a linear calculation, such as rotation or scaling) to be followed by a translation in the same multiplication. This is known as an *affined matrix calculation*. To do an affined calculation on a matrix of n dimensions, the multiplication matrix used must be n+1 by n+1. Therefore, a 2D calculation requires a 3×3 matrix. For this reason, the third column of the matrix is always set to 0,0,1, and you cannot change it.

There are lots of books on graphics but, for the sake of completeness, the operations performed by the matrix on coordinates go as follows. The following example does a simple translation by an X and Y amount.

A coordinate is turned into a vector by adding a third, z column, to it. For example,

[10,5] becomes [10,5,1]

The dX and dY, or the translation part, of the matrix shown is 10,30.

This vector is multiplied by the matrix by working down each column in the following manner.

[10 , 5 , 1]

multiply...

1 0 0

0 1 0

dX dY 1

equals...

1*x 0*x 0*x

+ + +

0*y 1*y 0*y

+ + +

1*dX 1*dY 1*1

equals...

dx+x dy+y 1

equals...

20 35 1

Take the dummy component out, and you're left with [20,35], which is [10,5] translated by [10,30].

A rotation about the origin is also performed in a similar manner. We'll use 90 degrees, because the sine and cosine of 90 are easy to compute. The matrix for rotation is initialized as follows:

cosΘ sinΘ 0

-sinΘ cosΘ 0

 0   0   1

So, cos(90)=0 and sin(90)=1 so, remembering to work down the columns, the matrix calculation looks like the following:

[10 , 5 , 1]

multiply...

```
 0  1  0
-1  0  0
 0  0  1
```

equals…

0*x 1*x 0*x

+ + +

-1*y 0*y 0*y

+ + +

1*0 1*0 1*1

equals…

[-5 , 10 , 1]

Chop off the extraneous 1, and you get [–5,10]

Taking two matrices and adding them or multiplying them together produces a resultant matrix. Successive additions or multiplications create a matrix that is the sum of all the operations performed so far. This means that you can do several operations on a matrix and they all accumulate, and then the transform in the matrix is applied to each and every pixel that the drawing command produces to obtain their resulting positions in the final output.

The order in which operations take place is very important too. For example, Rotate—Scale—Translate does not mean the same thing as Scale—Translate—Rotate. This implies that you also need to think about how the API commands apply the matrices you hand them. Do you multiply the current matrix by the one you just supplied or the one you have by the current matrix? Luckily, the calls to Rotate, Scale, and so on, have a flag that you can use to control the way matrices are worked on. MatrixOrder.Prepend, the default, applies the matrix you pass first, and then the current matrix. MatrixOrder.Append applies the requested operation after the current matrix is applied.

The following sequence illustrates the contents of a matrix as it evolves through many operations.

```
Matrix m=new Matrix() // Create an identity matrix

 1  0  0
 0  1  0
 0  0  1
```

```
m.Rotate(30,MatrixOrder.Append); //rotate 30 degrees

0.8660254 0.5  0

 -0.5 0.8660254 0

  0  0  1

m.Scale((float)1,(float)3,MatrixOrder.Append); //magnify by 3 in the Y plane

0.8660254 1.5  0

 -0.5 2.598076 0

  0  0  1

m.Translate((float)100,(float)130,MatrixOrder.Append); //move by 100 X and 130
Y

0.8660254 1.5  0

 -0.5 2.598076 0

 100 130  1
```

As this sequence progresses, you can see how the matrix accumulates the operations with each successive call.

It is important to note that keeping track of the graphics matrix is very important, especially if you want to place many different objects onscreen, each with its own transformation. It is sometimes useful to put the current matrix into a known state, perhaps with the origin in a different place or zoomed in or out by scaling, and then perform other operations. Each operation should behave itself and leave the current matrix as it was found. Saving the state of the Graphics object in a GraphicsState can do this. A GraphicsState is filled with information by the Graphics.Save() method and restored with the Graphics.Restore(state) method. For example,

```
GraphicsState gs=theGraphics.Save();
// perform operations here...
theGraphics.Restore(gs);
//Graphics are back to their original state.
```

Listing 3.5.8 demonstrates the simple transformation sequence discussed previously, as well as the use of GraphicsState and other matrix manipulations in the context of some simple graphic shapes.

LISTING 3.5.8   MatrixElements.cs: A Scene from the Matrix

```csharp
 1: using System;
 2: using System.Drawing;
 3: using System.Drawing.Drawing2D;
 4: using System.Drawing.Text;
 5: using System.Collections;
 6: using System.ComponentModel;
 7: using System.Windows.Forms;
 8: using System.Data;
 9: using System.Text;
10:
11: namespace matrixelements
12: {
13:  public class MatrixElements : System.Windows.Forms.Form
14:  {
15:    void DumpMatrix(Graphics g, Matrix m, Point p)
16:    {
17:      StringBuilder sb=new StringBuilder();
18:      sb.AppendFormat("{0},\t{1},\t0\n{2},\t{3},\t0\n{4},\t{5},\t1",
19:          m.Elements[0],m.Elements[1],m.Elements[2],
20:          m.Elements[3],m.Elements[4],m.Elements[5]);
21:      GraphicsState s=g.Save();
22:      g.ResetTransform();
23:      g.DrawString(sb.ToString(),new Font("Courier New",(float)16),
24:          new SolidBrush(Color.Black),p,StringFormat.GenericDefault);
25:      g.Restore(s);
26:    }
27:
28:    void OnSize(object sender,EventArgs e)
29:    {
30:      Invalidate();
31:    }
32:
33:    void OnPaint(object sender, PaintEventArgs e)
34:    {
35:      GraphicsState gs;
36:      Matrix m=new Matrix();
37:
38:      //position and draw the axes by translating the whole window
39:      // so that the origin is in the center of the screen
40:      e.Graphics.TranslateTransform((float)this.ClientRectangle.Width/2,
41:                                    (float)this.ClientRectangle.Height/2);
42:      e.Graphics.DrawLine(new Pen(Color.Black,(float)1),0,-1000,0,1000);
43:      e.Graphics.DrawLine(new Pen(Color.Black,(float)1),-100,0,1000,0);
44:
45:      //Draw an ordinary square about the origin.
46:      e.Graphics.DrawRectangle(new Pen(Color.Black,(float)3),
47:                               -50,-50,100,100);
```

LISTING 3.5.8 Continued

```
48:    DumpMatrix(e.Graphics,m,new Point(0,0));
49:
50:    m.Rotate(30,MatrixOrder.Append);
51:    DumpMatrix(e.Graphics,m,new Point(0,100));
52:
53:    gs=e.Graphics.Save();
54:    e.Graphics.MultiplyTransform(m);
55:    e.Graphics.DrawRectangle(new Pen(Color.Red,3),
56:                             -50,-50,100,100);
57:    e.Graphics.Restore(gs);
58:
59:    m.Scale(1,3,MatrixOrder.Append);
60:    DumpMatrix(e.Graphics,m,new Point(0,200));
61:
62:    gs=e.Graphics.Save();
63:    e.Graphics.MultiplyTransform(m);
64:    e.Graphics.DrawRectangle(new Pen(Color.Green,3),
65:                             -50,-50,100,100);
66:    e.Graphics.Restore(gs);
67:
68:    m.Translate(100,130,MatrixOrder.Append);
69:    DumpMatrix(e.Graphics,m,new Point(0,300));
70:
71:    gs=e.Graphics.Save();
72:    e.Graphics.MultiplyTransform(m);
73:    e.Graphics.DrawRectangle(new Pen(Color.Blue,3),
74:                             -50,-50,100,100);
75:    e.Graphics.Restore(gs);
76:  }
77:
78:  public MatrixElements()
79:  {
80:   this.Paint+=new PaintEventHandler(OnPaint);
81:   this.SizeChanged+=new EventHandler(OnSize);
82:  }
83:
84:  static void Main()
85:  {
86:   Application.Run(new MatrixElements());
87:  }
88: }
89: }
```

Compile the code using the following command line:

```
csc /t:winexe matrixelements.cs
```

Cutting to the chase, lines 40 and 41 create a matrix that shifts the origin to the center of the window. Lines 42 and 43 draw axis lines just to look nice and give a point of reference.

Lines 46 and 47 draw our reference square. This is the same drawing command used for all the other objects onscreen, and then line 48 dumps our identity matrix.

Line 50 rotates the matrix, which is again dumped to text, and then line 53 saves the graphics state so as not to mess up the origin. Line 54 uses the matrix, lines 55 and 56 draw our newly rotated square, and line 57 restores the world transform back to its origin-in-the-middle state.

Line 59 scales the matrix, making it 3 times taller than it is wide and stretching the output in the Y direction. Lines 62–66 use the transformation, draw the square, and return the world transform to our chosen default.

Line 68 then translates the matrix moving to the right and down. Line 69 shows the matrix settings and we round-off on lines 71–75 drawing the last, rotated, scaled, and translated square.

To draw the matrix data itself, lines 15–26 save the graphics state and reset the transform, place the text onscreen, and then returns the transform back to its original state before returning.

The final output from this program is shown in Figure 3.5.11.

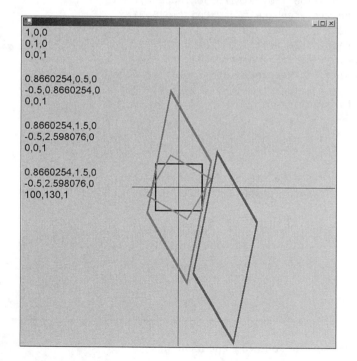

FIGURE 3.5.11

Matrix transformations of a simple square.

Alpha Blending

All colors in GDI+ have a fourth component in addition to the normal red, green, and blue values. This value is the "alpha" and it controls the amount that the background shows through the object just placed onscreen.

Alpha blending can be applied to all graphical shapes, such as lines and text. It can also be applied to images, either as a global value that affects the appearance of the whole image, or as a value for each individual pixel, which makes parts of the image more transparent than others.

To create a color with an alpha component, you can use the Color.FromARGB(…) method and supply the alpha as a value from 0, totally transparent, to 255, which is opaque.

Listing 3.5.9 demonstrates this effect by creating an array of ellipses that let the background show through according to their alpha value.

LISTING 3.5.9 AlphaBlend.cs: Using a Solid Brush with Alpha

```
 1: using System;
 2: using System.Drawing;
 3: using System.Drawing.Drawing2D;
 4: using System.Collections;
 5: using System.ComponentModel;
 6: using System.Windows.Forms;
 7: using System.Data;
 8:
 9: namespace Alphablending
10: {
11:     public class Alphablending : System.Windows.Forms.Form
12:     {
13:
14:         void OnPaint(object sender, PaintEventArgs e)
15:         {
16:             SolidBrush b=new SolidBrush(Color.Red);
17:             Rectangle r=this.ClientRectangle;
18:             GraphicsPath pth=new GraphicsPath();
19:             for(int c=1;c<10;c++)
20:             {
21:                 r.Inflate(-(this.ClientRectangle.Width/20),
22:                         -(this.ClientRectangle.Height/20));
23:                 pth.AddRectangle(r);
24:             }
25:             e.Graphics.FillPath(b,pth);
26:             Random rnd=new Random();
27:             for(int y=0;y<5;y++)
28:             {
```

LISTING 3.5.9   Continued

```
29:                for(int x=0;x<5;x++)
30:                {
31:                    b.Color=Color.FromArgb((int)((((5*x)+y)*10.63)),
32:                                    (byte)rnd.Next(255),
33:                                    (byte)rnd.Next(255),
34:                                    (byte)rnd.Next(255));
35:                    e.Graphics.FillEllipse(b,this.ClientRectangle.Width/5*x,
36:                                    this.ClientRectangle.Height/5*y,
37:                                    this.ClientRectangle.Width/5,
38:                                    this.ClientRectangle.Height/5);
39:                }
40:            }
41:        }
42:
43:        void OnSize(object sender, EventArgs e)
44:        {
45:            Invalidate();
46:        }
47:
48:        public Alphablending()
49:        {
50:            this.Paint+=new PaintEventHandler(OnPaint);
51:            this.SizeChanged+=new EventHandler(OnSize);
52:            this.BackColor=Color.White;
53:        }
54:
55:
56:        static void Main()
57:        {
58:            Application.Run(new Alphablending());
59:        }
60:    }
61: }
```

Compile Listing 3.5.9 with the following command line:

```
csc /t:winexe alphablend.cs
```

The output from Listing 3.5.9 is shown in Figure 3.5.12 and clearly shows the background scene, the dark concentric rectangles, being obscured by the graduated alpha blends of the ellipses.

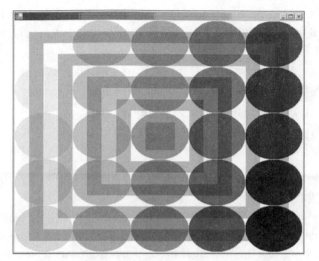

FIGURE 3.5.12
Alpha blending at work.

Alpha Blending of Images

This task is also easy to accomplish using a `ColorMatrix` object. We saw in the section on matrix manipulations that the matrix could be used to perform manipulations in 2D space for graphic objects using a 3×3 matrix. A `ColorMatrix` deals with a four dimensional concept, the color space. A color space's dimensions are R,G,B and A for Red, Green, Blue, and Alpha, respectively. Performing arbitrary matrix manipulations on a four dimensional object requires a 5×5 matrix. Like the 3×3 example for 2D space, the `ColorMatrix` maintains a dummy column that is set to 0,0,0,0,1.

The image in Figure 3.5.13 is the Identity Matrix for the `ColorMatrix` object.

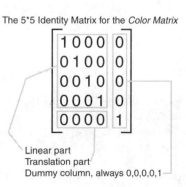

The 5*5 Identity Matrix for the *Color Matrix*

$$\begin{bmatrix} 1 & 0 & 0 & 0 & 0 \\ 0 & 1 & 0 & 0 & 0 \\ 0 & 0 & 1 & 0 & 0 \\ 0 & 0 & 0 & 1 & 0 \\ 0 & 0 & 0 & 0 & 1 \end{bmatrix}$$

Linear part
Translation part
Dummy column, always 0,0,0,0,1

FIGURE 3.5.13
The color space Identity Matrix.

3.5

GDI+: THE .NET
GRAPHICS
INTERFACE

The `ColorMatrix` class, like the matrix for 2D manipulations, has properties for its elements that can be accessed individually. To set the alpha for an image, you simply need to put the alpha value into the `Matrix33` property as follows:

```
ColorMatrix cm=new ColorMatrix(); // create an identity matrix
m.Matrix33=(float)AlphaValue;
```

This color matrix is then handed to an `ImageAttributes` class:

```
ImageAttributes ia=new ImageAttributes();
ia.SetColorMatrix(m);
```

The initialized `ImageAttributes` object is then used by the `Graphics.DrawImage()` method to paint the image with the specified alpha blend.

Listing 3.5.10 show you how to use the alpha blending features of GDI+ with any bitmap image from your machine. The program has a button to allow you to choose an image file and a track bar that lets you select the amount of transparency with which the image is displayed.

LISTING 3.5.10   `ImageAlpha.cs`: Alpha Blending an Image

```
 1: using System;
 2: using System.Drawing;
 3: using System.Drawing.Drawing2D;
 4: using System.Drawing.Imaging;
 5: using System.Collections;
 6: using System.ComponentModel;
 7: using System.Windows.Forms;
 8: using System.Data;
 9:
10: namespace ImageAlpha
11: {
12:    class Form1 : Form
13:    {
14:
15:        Button b;
16:        TrackBar t;
17:        Image i;
18:
19:        void OnPaint(object Sender,PaintEventArgs e)
20:        {
21:            SolidBrush b=new SolidBrush(Color.Red);
22:            Rectangle r=this.ClientRectangle;
23:            GraphicsPath pth=new GraphicsPath();
24:            for(int c=1;c<10;c++)
25:            {
26:                r.Inflate(-(this.ClientRectangle.Width/20),
```

LISTING 3.5.10   Continued

```
27:                    -(this.ClientRectangle.Height/20));
28:                pth.AddRectangle(r);
29:            }
30:            e.Graphics.FillPath(b,pth);
31:
32:            if(i!=null)
33:            {
34:                ColorMatrix m=new ColorMatrix();
35:                m.Matrix33=(float)(1.0/256*t.Value);
36:                ImageAttributes ia=new ImageAttributes();
37:                ia.SetColorMatrix(m);
38:                e.Graphics.DrawImage(i,this.ClientRectangle,
       ➥0,0,i.Width,i.Height,GraphicsUnit.Pixel,ia);
39:            }
40:        }
41:
42:        void OnClickB(object sender, EventArgs e)
43:        {
44:            OpenFileDialog dlg=new OpenFileDialog();
45:            dlg.Filter="Bitmap files(*.bmp)|*.bmp";
46:            if(dlg.ShowDialog()==DialogResult.OK)
47:            {
48:                i=Image.FromFile(dlg.FileName);
49:                Invalidate();
50:            }
51:        }
52:
53:        void OnTrack(object sender, EventArgs e)
54:        {
55:            Invalidate();
56:        }
57:
58:        void OnSize(object sender, EventArgs e)
59:        {
60:            Invalidate();
61:        }
62:
63:        public Form1()
64:        {
65:            this.Paint+=new PaintEventHandler(OnPaint);
66:            this.SizeChanged+=new EventHandler(OnSize);
67:
68:            b=new Button();
69:
70:            b.Click+=new EventHandler(OnClickB);
```

LISTING 3.5.10 Continued

```
71:
72:            b.Location=new Point(5,5);
73:            b.Size=new Size(60,22);
74:            b.Text="Image...";
75:
76:            this.Controls.Add(b);
77:
78:            t=new TrackBar();
79:            t.Location=new Point(100,5);
80:            t.Size=new Size(200,22);
81:            t.Maximum=255;
82:            t.Minimum=0;
83:            t.ValueChanged+=new EventHandler(OnTrack);
84:
85:            this.Controls.Add(t);
86:        }
87:
88:        static void Main()
89:        {
90:            Application.Run(new Form1());
91:        }
92:    }
93: }
```

Compile this file with the following command line:

`csc /t:winexe imagealpha.cs`

The important lines are 34–38, deceptively simple for such a powerful feature. Line 34 creates an identity matrix. Line 35 uses the value in the track bar to update the image alpha component of the matrix. Line 36 creates an `ImageAttributes` class that uses the `ColorMatrix` on line 37. Finally, line 38 paints the image onto the screen, allowing our concentric shape background to show through or not, depending on the track bar setting.

Figure 3.5.14 shows this effect with the track bar set to around 70 percent. In case you're wondering, the Bike is a 1971 Triumph Bonneville 750.

FIGURE 3.5.14
Alpha blending a bitmap image.

Other Color Space Manipulations

Having a whole huge matrix for alpha blending alone seems like overkill, until you realize that any manipulation of the color space is possible with such a tool, if only you knew what numbers to plumb in. The technique of manipulating such a matrix for the purpose of changing the color space is called *recoloring* and is also easy to do with GDI+. Once again, the tool used is the ColorMatrix and the vehicle is the ImageAttributes. Unfortunately, there are no methods on the ColorMatrix to perform color space rotations, but they would be possible, given the correct settings of the linear part of the matrix. As an exercise, you could send in a modification of Listing 3.5.10 to sams@netedgesoftware.com that does color space rotations. The best 10 correct ones within the first year of publication of this book get a free NetEdge Software Polo shirt. To get you started, Listing 3.5.11 is a modification of the previous that allows you to set the red, green, and blue component levels of your chosen image.

LISTING 3.5.11 ColorSpace1.cs: More Color Space Transformations

```
 1: using System;
 2: using System.Drawing;
 3: using System.Drawing.Drawing2D;
 4: using System.Drawing.Imaging;
 5: using System.Collections;
 6: using System.ComponentModel;
 7: using System.Windows.Forms;
 8: using System.Data;
 9:
10: namespace ColorSpace1
```

LISTING 3.5.11   Continued

```
11: {
12:     class Form1 : Form
13:     {
14:
15:         Button b;
16:         TrackBar tr,tg,tb;
17:         Image i;
18:
19:         void OnPaint(object Sender,PaintEventArgs e)
20:         {
21:             SolidBrush b=new SolidBrush(Color.Red);
22:             Rectangle r=this.ClientRectangle;
23:             GraphicsPath pth=new GraphicsPath();
24:             if(i!=null)
25:             {
26:                 ColorMatrix m=new ColorMatrix();
27:                 m.Matrix00=(float)(1.0/256*tr.Value);
28:                 m.Matrix11=(float)(1.0/256*tg.Value);
29:                 m.Matrix22=(float)(1.0/256*tb.Value);
30:                 ImageAttributes ia=new ImageAttributes();
31:                 ia.SetColorMatrix(m);
32:                 e.Graphics.DrawImage(i,this.ClientRectangle,0,
33:                     0,i.Width,i.Height,GraphicsUnit.Pixel,ia);
34:             }
35:         }
36:
37:         void OnClickB(object sender, EventArgs e)
38:         {
39:             OpenFileDialog dlg=new OpenFileDialog();
40:             dlg.Filter="Bitmap files(*.bmp)|*.bmp";
41:             if(dlg.ShowDialog()==DialogResult.OK)
42:             {
43:                 i=Image.FromFile(dlg.FileName);
44:                 Invalidate();
45:             }
46:         }
47:
48:         void OnTrack(object sender, EventArgs e)
49:         {
50:             Invalidate();
51:         }
52:
53:         void OnSize(object sender, EventArgs e)
54:         {
55:             Invalidate();
```

LISTING 3.5.11 Continued

```
56:         }
57:
58:        public Form1()
59:        {
60:            this.Paint+=new PaintEventHandler(OnPaint);
61:            this.SizeChanged+=new EventHandler(OnSize);
62:
63:            b=new Button();
64:
65:            b.Click+=new EventHandler(OnClickB);
66:
67:            b.Location=new Point(5,5);
68:            b.Size=new Size(60,22);
69:            b.Text="Image...";
70:
71:            this.Controls.Add(b);
72:
73:            tr=new TrackBar();
74:            tr.Location=new Point(100,5);
75:            tr.Size=new Size(200,22);
76:            tr.Maximum=255;
77:            tr.Minimum=0;
78:            tr.ValueChanged+=new EventHandler(OnTrack);
79:
80:
81:            this.Controls.Add(tr);
82:
83:            tg=new TrackBar();
84:            tg.Location=new Point(100,55);
85:            tg.Size=new Size(200,22);
86:            tg.Maximum=255;
87:            tg.Minimum=0;
88:            tg.ValueChanged+=new EventHandler(OnTrack);
89:
90:
91:            this.Controls.Add(tg);
92:
93:            tb=new TrackBar();
94:            tb.Location=new Point(100,105);
95:            tb.Size=new Size(200,22);
96:            tb.Maximum=255;
97:            tb.Minimum=0;
98:            tb.ValueChanged+=new EventHandler(OnTrack);
99:
100:
```

3.5

GDI+: THE .NET GRAPHICS INTERFACE

LISTING 3.5.11   Continued

```
101:          this.Controls.Add(tb);
102:      }
103:
104:      static void Main()
105:      {
106:          Application.Run(new Form1());
107:      }
108:   }
109: }
```

Compile this file with the following command line:

```
csc /t:winexe colorspace1.cs
```

This file is substantially identical to that in Listing 3.5.10 with the exception that track bars for red, green, and blue are employed, instead of for alpha. The matrix is set up on lines 27–29 to adjust the intensity of each of the R, G, and B color channels individually.

Summary

There is so much in GDI+ to explore that this chapter could go on for another hundred pages or so. We think, however, that what is here will give you the confidence to experiment further and will allow you to understand most of the conventions required to transition from the old GDI that we know and love to the exiting possibilities of GDI+. Read on now to discover more about Windows Forms applications and components in the last chapter of this section, "Practical Windows Forms Applications."

Practical Windows Forms Applications

IN THIS CHAPTER

This section of the book has covered a lot of ground, from basic Windows Forms principles to using GDI+ in your applications. In this last chapter in this section, we'll explore the practical aspects of creating applications with Windows Forms. A critical part of the .NET framework is the ability of each object to describe itself and for you, the programmer, to access its properties. This capability can be used in your own programs to assist your users and to provide a clean and consistent user interface.

In recent years, the Windows platforms have made increasing use of "properties". You can usually right-click a item and select Properties from the context menu. The idea of this is a good one but, until now, there has never been a standard and consistent way of displaying and editing these properties in your code. Usually a programmer would re-engineer a property system for every application with different dialogs or windows. Now, .NET provides a simple method for creating and using standardized property interfaces, the property attributes, and the property grid.

Using the Properties and Property Attributes

The simple class shown in Listing 3.6.1 has properties.

LISTING 3.6.1 The `SimpleObject` Class

```
1: public class SimpleObject
2: {
3:     private int _int;
4:     private string _string;
5:     private Color _color;
6:
7:     public SimpleObject()
8:     {
9:         //
10:        // TODO: Add constructor logic here
11:        //
12:     }
13:
14:     public int TheInteger
15:     {
16:         get
17:         {
18:             return _int;
19:         }
20:         set
21:         {
22:             _int=value;
23:         }
24:     }
```

LISTING 3.6.1   Continued

```
25:
26:     public string TheString
27:     {
28:         get
29:         {
30:             return _string;
31:         }
32:         set
33:         {
34:             _string=value;
35:         }
36:     }
37:
38:     public Color TheColor
39:     {
40:         get
41:         {
42:             return _color;
43:         }
44:         set
45:         {
46:             _color=value;
47:         }
48:     }
49: }
```

You can see that the class has three private data members—n integer, a string, and a color. These all have public accessor properties—TheInteger, TheString, and TheColor. This is a good strategy from a design perspective because it isolates the encapsulated data and gives a clear and unambiguous interface.

Using our object in an application is fairly simple. What follows is a walk-through sequence for Visual Studio.NET.

Create a new C# Windows application project.

NOTE

It's interesting to note that one of the most useful components in the toolbox—the property grid—isn't shown by default, you have to add it to the list manually. To update the toolbox, right-click it and select Customize Toolbox, you'll see the dialog shown in Figure 3.6.1.

Under the .NET Framework Components tab, select the Property Grid and ensure that its box is checked.

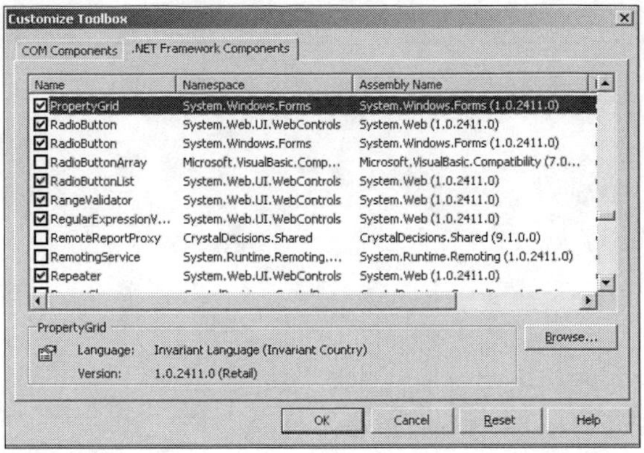

FIGURE 3.6.1

Customizing the toolbox.

Returning to the application, it's time to place some controls.

1. Drag a `ListBox` from the toolbox onto the form. Set its Dock property to Left.

2. Drag a `Splitter` onto the form, it will automatically dock to the rightmost edge of the ListBox.

3. Drag a `PropertyGrid` control to the form and place it to the right of the splitter bar. Set its Dock property to Fill.

4. Drag a `MainMenu` onto the form and place it on the toolbar, call it **Object** and make the first menu entry **New**.

At this point, you should have a form that looks like the one seen in Figure 3.6.2.

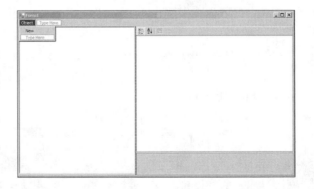

FIGURE 3.6.2

The newly created Object form with `Listbox`*,* `Splitter`*, and* `PropertyGrid`*.*

Practical Windows Forms Applications

Chapter 3.6

379

3.6

PRACTICAL
WINDOWS FORMS
APPLICATIONS

Go to the project in the Solution Explorer. Right-click it and select Add New Item. Select C# class from the wizard menu (indicated by the following icon).

Create the SimpleObject class, as shown in Listing 3.6.1. Be sure to duplicate it exactly as shown.

Now, to add a handler for the Object, New menu item, double-click the menu entry in the form designer, right where it says New. You'll be taken to the place in the code where the editor has added a handler for you. Fill out the handler as shown in Listing 3.6.2

LISTING 3.6.2 The New Object Menu Item Handler

```
1: private void menuItem2_Click(object sender, System.EventArgs e)
2: {
3:     SimpleObject o=new SimpleObject();
4:     this.listBox1.Items.Add(o);
5: }
```

Finally, create a handler for the ListBox's

SelectedIndexChanged event by selecting the ListBox in the Designer, clicking the Events icon in the Property Browser, and clicking the SelectedIndexChanged entry. Again, you'll be taken to the code where a handler entry will have been provided. Edit this handler entry so that it's the same as shown in Listing 3.6.3

LISTING 3.6.3 The SelectedIndexChanged Handler

```
1: private void listBox1_SelectedIndexChanged(object sender, System.EventArgs e)
2: {
3:     this.propertyGrid1.SelectedObject=this.listBox1.SelectedItem;
4: }
```

Now you're ready to run the program. Press F5 and wait for compilation to complete.

You can add as many SimpleObjects to the list box as you want using the menu entry. After added, selecting a menu entry in the list box will display its properties in the PropertyGrid control to the right of the form. Notice how the property grid assists you in editing the properties. The Color property is especially interesting because it allows you to select from a palette of colors, enter a known color name (for example, Red), or type in the discrete values for the red, green and blue components, such as 90,180,240. Figure 3.6.3 shows the application in action.

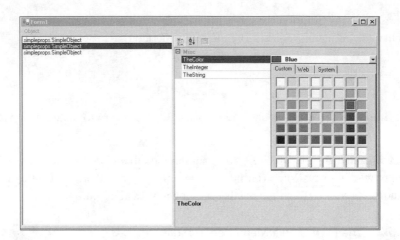

FIGURE 3.6.3

The Property browser application.

For such a small amount of work, this is a powerful application indeed.

Enhancing the Property Experience

If you look carefully at the image in Figure 3.6.3, you'll see a couple of interesting things provided by the framework and the property grid. First, the feedback box at the bottom of the property grid has some text in it. This is feedback to help the user understand what they're doing. Second, the list of properties in the panel is grouped into a category called Misc. If you look at vs.NET or other Windows Forms applications, you might see other categories, such as Behavior or Appearance.

You can arrange your properties into categories and make them provide feedback by using the attributes provided by the framework. The particular classes used are CategoryAttribute and the DescriptionAttribute. When used in your code, the name is shortened to Category or Description. The compiler will add the Attribute part for you.

Let's revisit the original SimpleObject class again. The snippet of code that follows shows these attributes added to one of the properties.

```
[Category("Appearance")]
[Description("controls the color of your moods")]
public Color TheColor
{
    get
    {
        return _color;
    }
```

```
set
{
    _color=value;
}
}
```

When this property is viewed in the Property Grid, it will be sorted into the Appearance category, and the description will be displayed in the feedback panel at the bottom of the Property Grid pane.

The class can also have attributes that help you set up the Property Grid. The [DefaultProperty("propertyname")] attribute selects which of the properties is displayed first in the Property Grid. For example, see line 12 of Listing 3.6.4.

LISTING 3.6.4 Adding Attributes to SimpleObject

```
 1: using System;
 2: using System.Drawing;
 3: using System.Drawing.Drawing2D;
 4: using System.Windows.Forms.Design;
 5: using System.ComponentModel;
 6:
 7: namespace simpleprops
 8: {
 9:     /// <summary>
10:     /// Summary description for SimpleObject.
11:     /// </summary>
12:     [DefaultProperty("TheInteger")]
13:     public class SimpleObject
14:     {
15:         private int _int;
16:         private string _string;
17:         private Color _color;
18:
19:         public SimpleObject()
20:         {
21:             //
22:             // TODO: Add constructor logic here
23:             //
24:         }
25:
26:
27:         [Category("Nothing Special")]
28:         [Description("Yes guy's 'n gal's, its an integer")]
29:         public int TheInteger
30:         {
```

LISTING 3.6.4   Continued

```
31:              get
32:              {
33:                   return _int;
34:              }
35:              set
36:              {
37:                   _int=value;
38:              }
39:         }
40:
41:         [Category("A peice of string")]
42:         [Description("This string does absolutely nothing but tie up your
➥time")]
43:         public string TheString
44:         {
45:              get
46:              {
47:                   return _string;
48:              }
49:              set
50:              {
51:                   _string=value;
52:              }
53:         }
54:
55:         [Category("Appearance")]
56:         [Description("controls the color of your moods")]
57:         public Color TheColor
58:         {
59:              get
60:              {
61:                   return _color;
62:              }
63:              set
64:              {
65:                   _color=value;
66:              }
67:         }
68:     }
69: }
```

Attributes can also be used to prevent the property from being seen in the browser. This is useful if you want to declare a public property for the programmer but keep it from the user. To do
this, use the [Browsable(false)] attribute.

Other attributes for properties are only useful if you're writing controls to be used in a design environment, such as VS.NET. The creation of such controls is not within the scope of this book.

Demonstration Application: `FormPaint.exe`

This application puts together many of the principals we've shown you in this book and shows off some of the features of Windows Forms in a complete application context.

Form Paint is a Multiple Document Interface (MDI) application that allows you to paint images with brushes and shapes. It has customized menus and shows off some of the power of GDI+ also.

Part 1: The Basic Framework

Getting started, create an application in VS.NET and immediately set the forms `IsMDIContainer` to true. This makes it a main parent window for other form-based documents that are hosted in it.

The name, `Form1`, must be changed to **MainForm** and the title of the window changed to **FormPaint**. Remember that when the name of the `MainForm` changes, you must also manually modify the static `Main` method as follows:

```
[STAThread]
static void Main()
{
    Application.Run(new MainForm()); // change the application name
}
```

Drag a MainMenu from the toolbox onto the MainForm. Type the word **&File** as the menu name and add three menu items—**&New**, **&Open**, and **&Exit**.

Drag an `OpenFileDialog` and a `SaveFileDialog` from the toolbox onto the `MainForm`. These will show up in the icon tray below the form.

Double-click the Open menu item in the main menu and type the following into the handler provided:

```
this.openFileDialog1.Filter="Bitmap files(*.BMP)|*.bmp";
this.openFileDialog1.ShowDialog();
```

Create a second menu called **Windows**. This will be used to keep track of the MDI child forms in the application. This is done automatically for you if you set the MDIList property of the menu to true.

Next, add a new Windows Form to the project, call it **ChildForm**. Set the `BackColor` to green.

Add a private `Image` variable called **myImage** to the child form and a public accessor property as follows:

```
private Image myImage;
public Image Image
{
    set{myImage =value;}
    get{return myImage;}
}
```

Now, double-click the OpenFileDialog in the icon tray. This action will create a `FileOk` handler for you. Type the following into the resulting handler:

```
ChildForm c=new ChildForm();
c.MdiParent=this;
c.Image=Image.FromFile(this.openFileDialog1.FileName);
c.Text=this.openFileDialog1.FileName);
c.Show();
```

This will open a file, create a child form, and load the image into the child form. The child form now needs to display the image. Select the ChildForm design page, click the Events button in the Property Browser, and double-click the Paint event. This creates a `PaintEventHandler` delegate for the `ChildForm` and opens the editor at the correct place in the file. Type the following into the handler:

```
e.Graphics.DrawImage(myImage,0,0,myImage.Width,myImage.Height);
```

This is a good place to stop and take stock of the project. Compile and run the code using the F5 key. You'll see an application that lets you load and display images in multiple windows. Figure 3.6.4 shows this basic application in action.

This portion of the program is available as FormPaint Step1 on the Sams Web site associated with this book.

Part 2: Scrolling a Window and Creating New Images

If you've run the fledgling `FormPaint` program and loaded up a few images, you'll have noticed that the windows will resize. But, when they become too small to display the picture, they simply chop it off without giving you a chance to see the sides with a scrollbar. We'll correct this quickly by adding some simple code to the `ChildForm`.

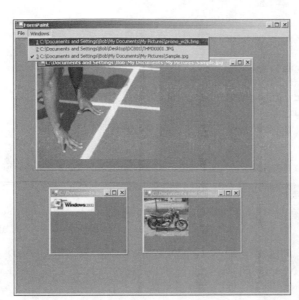

FIGURE 3.6.4
The basic MDI application.

First, in the Image property set accessor for the ChildForm, we'll add a command to set the AutoScrollMinSize property to the size of the image in myImage. The following code snippet shows the added functionality on line 6.

```
1: public Image Image
2: {
3:   set
4:   {
5:     myImage =value;
6:     this.AutoScrollMinSize=myImage.Size;
7:   }
8:   get{return myImage;}
9: }
```

Now, whenever the client rectangle size drops below the minimum size in either dimension, the corresponding scroll bar will appear.

A second change must be made to the OnPaint handler to position the scrollbars. Here, we need to offset the image by the value of the scrollbar position so that the image is painted correctly. The form also provides a property for the scrollbar positions that is shown in the following code snippet.

```
1: private void ChildForm_Paint(object sender,
➥System.Windows.Forms.PaintEventArgs e)
2: {
3:   e.Graphics.DrawImage(myImage,
4:     this.AutoScrollPosition.X,
5:     this.AutoScrollPosition.Y,
6:     myImage.Width,
7:     myImage.Height);
8: }
```

On lines 4 and 5, you can see that the X and Y values of the form's `AutoScrollPosition` property offset the origin of the image by the correct amount.

So far, the program can only load an image that exists on disk. We need to create an image, perhaps with a choice of sizes, and to allow that image to be saved to disk also.

Creating the image can be accomplished as follows. Using the MainForm design page, select and double-click the New menu entry in the File menu. This will create a handler that we'll fill in later.

Now, right-click the `FormPaint` project and choose Add, New Item. Choose a new Form and call it **NewImageDialog.cs**. Drag three radio buttons and two buttons from the toolbox onto the dialog. Then arrange them, as shown in Figure 3.6.5

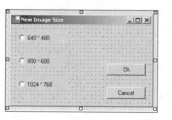

FIGURE 3.6.5

Button arrangement dialog.

The `DialogResult` properties of the OK and Cancel buttons must be set to `DialogResult.Ok` and `DialogResult.Cancel` respectively. To retrieve the setting from the radio buttons, we can add a simple property that returns a size. Hand-edit the `NewImageDialog.cs` code and add the following public property:

```
public Size ImageSize
{
  get
  {
    if(this.radioButton2.Checked)
      return new Size(800,600);
```

```
    if(this.radioButton3.Checked)
      return new Size(1024,768);
    return new Size(640,480);
  }
}
```

Now we can return to the handler we created earlier and fill it out to create a blank image. Find the handler in the MainForm.cs file and add the necessary code as follows:

```
 1: private void menuItem2_Click(object sender, System.EventArgs e)
 2: {
 3:   // To create a new file...
 4:   NewImageDialog dlg = new NewImageDialog();
 5:   if(dlg.ShowDialog()==DialogResult.OK)
 6:   {
 7:     ChildForm c=new ChildForm();
 8:     c.MdiParent=this;
 9:     c.Image=new Bitmap(dlg.ImageSize.Width,dlg.ImageSize.Height);
10:     Graphics g=Graphics.FromImage(c.Image);
11:     g.FillRectangle(new SolidBrush(Color.White),0,0,
         ➥c.Image.Width,c.Image.Height);
12:     c.Show();
13:   }
14: }
```

Adding the Save Functions

Saving the file or saving "as" a different file will be performed through the main File menu. Add a Save and Save As menu item, remembering to use the ampersand before the key-select characters—for example, **&Save** and **Save &As**. For esthetic reasons, you might also want to move these into a sensible place on the menu and place a separator between the file and exit functions.

When you've created these entries, go ahead and double-click each one in turn to create the handlers for them. The following code snippet shows the two save handlers:

```
 1: private void menuItem6_Click(object sender, System.EventArgs e)
 2: {
 3:   //Save the image file.
 4:   ChildForm child = (ChildForm)this.ActiveMdiChild;
 5:   child.Image.Save(child.Text);
 6: }
 7:
 8: private void menuItem7_Click(object sender, System.EventArgs e)
 9: {
10:   //Save the image file as a different filename
11:   ChildForm child = (ChildForm)this.ActiveMdiChild;
12:   this.saveFileDialog1.FileName=child.Text;
```

```
13:   if(this.saveFileDialog1.ShowDialog()==DialogResult.OK)
14:   {
15:     child.Image.Save(this.saveFileDialog1.FileName);
16:     child.Text=this.saveFileDialog1.FileName;
17:   }
18: }
```

Lines 1–6 are the simple save handler. The filename is already known, so a save is performed using the titlebar text of the `ChildForm`.

Lines 8–18 use this filename as a starting point but invoke the `SaveFileDialog` to allow the user to choose a new name.

This behavior is fine if you can guarantee that a `ChildWindow` is always open from which to get the text. If you use the handlers on an empty main form, though, an exception will occur because there is no active MDI child. This problem can be overcome in one of two ways. Either write an exception handling `try...catch` block into both handlers or, alternatively, never allow the handler to be called if there are no MDI children. The second method is best for the purposes of this demonstration because it allows us to use the menu pop-up events correctly.

You might remember from Chapter 3.1, "Introduction to Windows Forms," that the menu `Popup` event is fired when the user selects the top-level menu on the toolbar just before the menu is drawn. This gives us the chance to modify the menu behavior to suit the current circumstances. The following code snippet shows the `Popup` handler for the File menu item.

```
1: private void menuItem1_Popup(object sender, System.EventArgs e)
2: {
3:   if(this.MdiChildren.Length!=0)
4:   {
5:     menuItem6.Enabled=true;
6:     menuItem7.Enabled=true;
7:   }
8:   else
9:   {
10:     menuItem6.Enabled=false;
11:     menuItem7.Enabled=false;
12:   }
13: }
```

The handler checks to see if there are any MDI children in the main form (line 3). If there are, it enables both the save menus on lines 5 and 6. If there are none, it disables these menus on lines 10 and 11.

This part of the application is available as `FormPaint Step2` on the Sams Web site associated with this book.

Part 3: More User Interface

With the image loading, display, and saving in place, we can get on with the task of adding the rest of the user interface items that will be used to drive the program. We need a tool palette; in this case, a simple one will suffice to demonstrate principles, a status bar, some mouse handling, and a custom button class based on UserControl.

Creating a Custom User Control

A big advantage to user controls in .NET is their ease of reuse. A quick side-trip into a custom control project can result in a handy component that you'll use many times in various projects. These controls play nicely in the design environment and can be shipped as separate assemblies if you want.

To begin with, add a new C# control library project to the current solution. Remember to choose the Add to Current Solution radio button on the wizard dialog. Call the project **FormPaintControl**. You'll be presented with a wizard to choose the type of control to add. Select a new UserControl and name it **CustomImageButton.cs**.

Listing 3.6.5 shows the full source code of the CustomImageButton control.

LISTING 3.6.5 CustomImageButton.cs: The Custom Image Button Class

```
 1: using System;
 2: using System.Collections;
 3: using System.ComponentModel;
 4: using System.Drawing;
 5: using System.Drawing.Drawing2D;
 6: using System.Data;
 7: using System.Windows.Forms;
 8: using System.Drawing.Imaging;
 9:
10: namespace FormPaintControl
11: {
12:     /// <summary>
13:     /// Summary description for CustomImageButton.
14:     /// </summary>
15:     public class CustomImageButton : System.Windows.Forms.UserControl
16:     {
17:         private Image image;
18:         private Color transparentColor;
19:         private bool ownerDraw;
20:         private bool down;
21:
22:         [
23:         Category("Behavior"),
```

LISTING 3.6.5 Continued

```
24:          Description("Allows external paint delegates to draw he control")
25:          ]
26:          public bool OwnerDraw
27:          {
28:             get
29:             {
30:                return ownerDraw;
31:             }
32:             set
33:             {
34:                ownerDraw=value;
35:             }
36:          }
37:
38:          [
39:          Category("Appearance"),
40:          Description("The image displayed on the control")
41:          ]
42:          public Image Image
43:          {
44:             get
45:             {
46:                return image;
47:             }
48:             set
49:             {
50:                image=value;
51:             }
52:          }
53:
54:          [
55:          Category("Appearance"),
56:          Description("The transparent color used in the image")
57:          ]
58:          public Color TransparentColor
59:          {
60:             get
61:             {
62:                return transparentColor;
63:             }
64:             set
65:             {
66:                transparentColor=value;
67:             }
```

LISTING 3.6.5 Continued

```
68:        }
69:
70:        protected override void OnSizeChanged(EventArgs e)
71:        {
72:           if(DesignMode)
73:               Invalidate();
74:           base.OnSizeChanged(e);
75:        }
76:
77:        public void DrawFocusRect(Graphics g)
78:        {
79:           Pen p=new Pen(Color.Black,1);
80:           p.DashStyle=DashStyle.Dash;
81:           Rectangle rc=ClientRectangle;
82:           rc.Inflate(-1,-1);
83:           g.DrawRectangle(p,rc);
84:        }
85:
86:        protected override void OnLostFocus(EventArgs e)
87:        {
88:           Invalidate();
89:           base.OnLostFocus(e);
90:        }
91:
92:        protected override void OnPaint(PaintEventArgs e)
93:        {
94:           Rectangle rc=ClientRectangle;
95:           rc.Offset(4,4);
96:           e.Graphics.SetClip(ClientRectangle);
97:           if(!ownerDraw)
98:           {
99:               if(image==null || !(image is Bitmap))
100:              {
101:                 Pen p=new Pen(Color.Red,2);
102:                 e.Graphics.DrawRectangle(p,ClientRectangle);
103:                 e.Graphics.DrawLine(p,ClientRectangle.Location.X,
104:                     ClientRectangle.Location.Y,
105:                     ClientRectangle.Location.X+ClientRectangle.Width,
106:                     ClientRectangle.Location.Y+ClientRectangle.Height);
107:                 e.Graphics.DrawLine(p,
108:                     ClientRectangle.Location.X+ClientRectangle.Width,
109:                     ClientRectangle.Location.Y,
110:                     ClientRectangle.Location.X,
111:                     ClientRectangle.Location.Y+ClientRectangle.Height);
```

LISTING 3.6.5   Continued

```
112:              return;
113:            }
114:          Bitmap bm=(Bitmap)image;
115:          bm.MakeTransparent(transparentColor);
116:          if(down || Focused)
117:          {
118:              e.Graphics.DrawImage(bm,
119:                  rc.Location.X,
120:                  rc.Location.Y,
121:                  bm.Width,bm.Height);
122:              if(Focused)
123:                  DrawFocusRect(e.Graphics);
124:          }
125:          else
126:          {
127:              ControlPaint.DrawImageDisabled(e.Graphics,bm,
128:                  rc.Location.X,rc.Location.Y,BackColor);
129:              e.Graphics.DrawImage(bm,
130:                  ClientRectangle.Location.X,
131:                  ClientRectangle.Location.Y,
132:                  bm.Width,bm.Height);
133:          }
134:        }
135:        base.OnPaint(e);
136:      }
137:
138:      /// <summary>
139:      /// Required designer variable.
140:      /// </summary>
141:      private System.ComponentModel.Container components = null;
142:
143:      public CustomImageButton()
144:      {
145:          // This call is required by the Windows.Forms Form Designer.
146:          InitializeComponent();
147:
148:          // TODO: Add any initialization after the InitForm call
149:
150:      }
151:
152:      protected override void OnMouseEnter(EventArgs e)
153:      {
154:          base.OnMouseEnter(e);
155:          down=true;
156:          Invalidate();
```

LISTING 3.6.5   Continued

```
157:          }
158:
159:          protected override void OnMouseLeave(EventArgs e)
160:          {
161:              base.OnMouseLeave(e);
162:              down=false;
163:              Invalidate();
164:          }
165:
166:          [
167:          Browsable(true),
168:          DesignerSerializationVisibility(
                  ➥DesignerSerializationVisibility.Visible)
169:          ]
170:          public override string Text
171:          {
172:              get
173:              {
174:                  return base.Text;
175:              }
176:              set
177:              {
178:                  base.Text = value;
179:              }
180:          }
181:
182:          /// <summary>
183:          /// Clean up any resources being used.
184:          /// </summary>
185:          protected override void Dispose( bool disposing )
186:          {
187:              if( disposing )
188:              {
189:                  if( components != null )
190:                      components.Dispose();
191:              }
192:              base.Dispose( disposing );
193:          }
194:
195:          #region Component Designer generated code
196:          /// <summary>
197:          /// Required method for Designer support - do not modify
198:          /// the contents of this method with the code editor.
199:          /// </summary>
```

PRACTICAL
WINDOWS FORMS
APPLICATIONS

LISTING 3.6.5 Continued

```
200:        private void InitializeComponent()
201:        {
202:          //
203:          // CustomImageButton
204:          //
205:          this.Name = "CustomImageButton";
206:          this.Size = new System.Drawing.Size(64, 56);
207:
208:        }
209:      #endregion
210:
211:    }
212: }
```

Beginning with line 1, note the added use of namespaces in the control. The default is only to use the System namespace.

Line 10 defines the FormPaintControl namespace with line 15 beginning the control itself—CustomImageButton.

Lines 17 through 20 define private data members to store information used in the drawing of the control. There is an Image, a transparent color key, and two Boolean flags for an owner draw property and to decide whether the button should be rendered down or up.

Public accessor properties for the relevant members ensure that the control will integrate nicely with the design environment and give some user feedback. Notice the Category and Description attributes preceding the property definitions on lines 26, 42, and 58.

Line 70 defines the OnSizeChanged method. When this control is used in Design mode, it needs to paint itself whenever it's resized. It should also call the base class method to ensure that any other delegates added to the SizeChanged event will also be called.

Line 77 defines a new method that draws a dotted line around the control when it has the focus. This is called from the OnPaint method.

The method on line 86 ensures that the control is redrawn when focus is lost.

The OnPaint method, beginning on line 92, has to contend with normal drawing of the control and drawing of the control when it's used in the design environment. This means that in the initial instance, the control will be instantiated by the designer with an empty image property. So that exceptions do not occur, the control will draw a red rectangle with a red cross in it if there is no image with which to paint. This is accomplished on lines 102–122. Otherwise, normal drawing takes place on lines 118–123 if the button is down or focused. Lines 127–132 draw the button in its up position. Note the use of the `ControlPaint` method on lines 127 and 128 that draws a "disabled" image behind the main bitmap as a drop shadow. This method also calls the base `OnPaint` method to ensure correct painting when other paint handler delegates are added to the `Paint` event.

The standard control added all lines from 138–150, and our additions continue with the `MouseEnter` and `MouseLeave` handlers on lines 152 and 159, respectively. These make the button depress whenever the mouse floats over it.

On line 167, there is an attribute to allow the `Text` property to be seen in the property browser. The `UserControl` from which this class is derived hides this property, so we need to override it (lines 170–180) and make it visible in the browser. Notice that the implementation calls the base class explicitly. On line 169, the `DesignerSerializationVisibility` attribute is used to ensure that the text is stored in the `InitializeComponent` method.

The rest of the file is standard stuff added by the control wizard and includes a `Dispose` method and an `InitializeComponent` method.

Compile the control and then right-click the toolbox, select Customize Toolbox and you'll see the dialog shown in Figure 3.6.6.

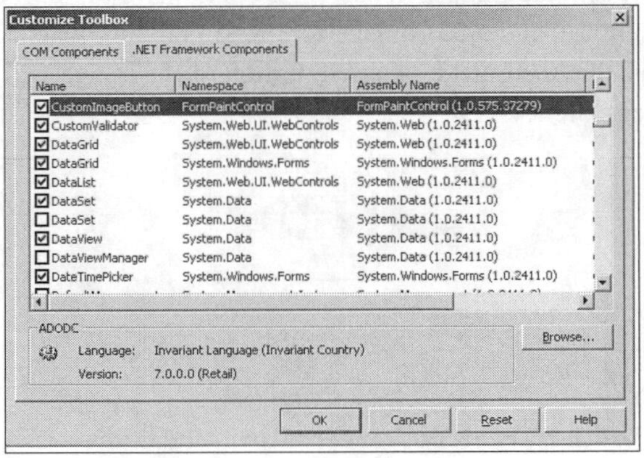

FIGURE 3.6.6
Adding the control to the toolbox.

To see the `CustomImageButton`, you must first find the compiled DLL that contains the control. This could be

`<your Projects>\FormPaint\FormPaintControl\Debug\Bin\FormPaintControl.dll`

Ensure that the check box is ticked and the control will appear in your toolbox.

> **NOTE**
>
> You can make this a permanent tool to use in your programs if you change to Release mode, compile the control, and then select the release version of the `FormPaintControl` DLL. You might also want to copy the release DLL to a place on your hard disk where it's unlikely to be erased.

Using the `CustomImageControl`

To the `MainForm`, add a panel and dock it to the right side of the form. This area will be used to host our simple tool palette. Drag a status bar from the toolbox onto the form, select the Panels collection in the property browser, and click the button in the combo-box that will appear. You'll see a dialog that will allow you to add one or more `StatusBarPanel` objects; for now, just add one. Remember to set the `StatusBar` objects `ShowPanels` property to true.

Drag four `CustomImageControl` objects onto the panel and arrange them vertically to make a place for selecting drawing tools. Initially, each will be displayed as a red rectangle with a cross in it.

Using the property browser, add images to each of the buttons' `Image` properties. We selected a paintbrush, rectangle, ellipse, and eraser image for our simple tool palette. Figure 3.6.7 shows these four images. Note that the outside, unused portion of the image will be color-keyed magenta to use as a transparency key.

FIGURE 3.6.7

The bitmap images used for the buttons.

When four images, `brush.bmp`, `rect.bmp`, `ellipse.bmp`, and `eraser.bmp` are added to their buttons, the `Paint` method will display them for us, even in the Designer.

The design should look similar to the one in Figure 3.6.8.

The `CustomImageControl` can hold text for us so we can use this to create a simple UI integration and feedback mechanism. We'll store information in the text to annotate the button with tooltips and status bar feedback. Later, we'll use the same feedback mechanism to enhance the menus.

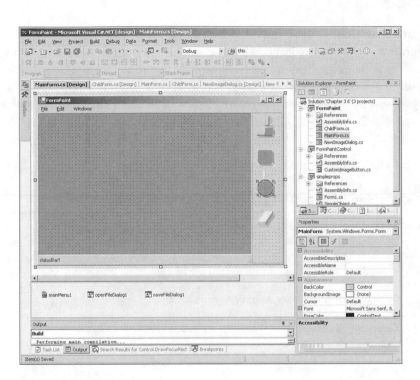

FIGURE 3.6.8

The MainForm final design layout.

In the Text property of the four buttons, the following text will provide more than just a button caption. The text will contain a caption, tooltip, and status bar text separated by the | vertical line (character 124). For an example, the following line shows the format.

Caption Text|Status Bar feedback|Tooltip text

For each text property in turn, add the relevant line using the property browser:

CustomImageButton1.Text   "|Apply color with a brush tool|Paintbrush"

CustomImageButton2.Text   "|Draw a rectangle|Rectangle"

CustomImageButton3.Text   "|Draw an ellipse|Ellipse"

CustomImageButton 4.Text   "|Erase an area|Eraser"

Note that none of the text entries have a caption portion, because a text caption is unnecessary.

Status and Tooltips

A tooltip gives added useful feedback to the user and our tool palette items have text that they can display when the mouse hovers over them, so the FormPaint program uses a simple method to display tooltip and status bar text. Taking advantage of the String classes' ability to split strings at given delimiters, we can create a simple class that will extract the tooltip, status bar, and caption text for us. Add a new C# class to the project and call it **CSTSplit** for caption–status–tooltip splitter.

The CSTSplit class is simple and is shown in Listing 3.6.6.

LISTING 3.6.6   CSTSplit.cs: The Caption–Status–Tooltip Splitter

```
 1: using System;
 2:
 3: namespace FormPaint
 4: {
 5:     /// <summary>
 6:     /// CSTSplit divides up a given string into
 7:     /// peices at a "|" delimiter to provide
 8:     /// Caption, Status, and Tooltip text.
 9:     /// </summary>
10:     public class CSTSplit
11:     {
12:         string[] splitStrings;
13:
14:         public CSTSplit(string toSplit)
15:         {
16:             splitStrings = toSplit.Split(new char[]{'|'});
17:         }
18:
19:         public string Caption
20:         {
21:             get
22:             {
23:                 if(splitStrings.Length>0)
24:                     return splitStrings[0];
25:                 return "";
26:             }
27:         }
28:
29:         public string Status
30:         {
31:             get
32:             {
33:                 if(splitStrings.Length>1)
```

LISTING 3.6.6 Continued

```
34:                 return splitStrings[1];
35:             return "";
36:         }
37:     }
38:
39:     public string Tooltip
40:     {
41:         get
42:         {
43:             if(splitStrings.Length>2)
44:                 return splitStrings[2];
45:             return "";
46:         }
47:     }
48:   }
49: }
```

The constructor on line 10 splits the string provided into an array of up to three strings divided at the vertical line delimiters.

The Caption, Status, and Tooltip properties (lines 19, 29, and 39, respectively) retrieve the correct string or provide a blank if no text for that portion of the string was included.

The initial use for this class will be to add tooltips to the four buttons in the tool palette. This is accomplished in the constructor of the MainForm, just after the InitializeComponent call. To display the tooltips, drag a ToolTip object from the toolbox onto the MainForm design page. The ToolTip will appear in the icon tray below the main window. Then add the following code to the MainForm constructor:

```
CSTSplit splitter=new CSTSplit(this.customImageButton1.Text);
this.toolTip1.SetToolTip(this.customImageButton1,splitter.Tooltip);
splitter=new CSTSplit(this.customImageButton2.Text);
this.toolTip1.SetToolTip(this.customImageButton2,splitter.Tooltip);
splitter=new CSTSplit(this.customImageButton3.Text);
this.toolTip1.SetToolTip(this.customImageButton3,splitter.Tooltip);
splitter=new CSTSplit(this.customImageButton4.Text);
this.toolTip1.SetToolTip(this.customImageButton4,splitter.Tooltip);
```

You can see that each CustomImageButton in turn is interrogated for its text, and the ToolTip property from the CSTSplit object returns the correct text that is handed to the ToolTip's ShowTip method.

Now, when the mouse rests on the control for half a second or more, a tooltip will be displayed containing the correct text.

3.6

PRACTICAL WINDOWS FORMS APPLICATIONS

Each of these controls contain text for the status bar also. To make this text show itself, select the first `CustomImageButton` control in the designer and type the method name **ShowStatus** into the `MouseEnter` event in the property browser. A handler will be created that should be filled out as follows.

```
private void ShowStatus(object sender, System.EventArgs e)
{
    Control c=(Control)sender;
    CSTSplit splitter=new CSTSplit(c.Text);
    this.statusBarPanel1.Text=splitter.Status;
}
```

Now, compiling and running the program will show that the tooltips and status bar messages are functioning correctly.

This version of the code is saved as **FormPaint Step3**.

Part 4: Tool Properties and Application

The program is now in a state where we can begin to do real work. We need to be able to select individual properties for the tools and to apply them to the bitmap image.

The `Paintbrush` object requires several properties, such as brush shape, color, and size. The ellipse and rectangle tool only need to define line color, fill color, and line thickness. The eraser will have a size and shape, like the paintbrush, but will always erase to white.

So that we can use the `PropertyGrid` to select these properties, we'll create a class for each of these tools that will be used to retain the user selections.

Defining the Tool Properties

The three tool description objects are shown in Listings 3.6.7, 3.6.8 and 3.6.9.

LISTING **3.6.7**   `PaintBrushProperties.cs`: The Paintbrush Tool Properties

```
 1: using System;
 2: using System.ComponentModel;
 3: using System.Drawing;
 4: using System.Globalization;
 5:
 6: namespace FormPaint
 7: {
 8:
 9:     public enum Shape
10:     {
11:         Round,
12:         Square,
```

LISTING 3.6.7   Continued

```
13:        Triangle
14:    };
15:
16:
17:    public class PaintBrushProperties
18:    {
19:        private Shape shape;
20:        private int size;
21:        private Color color;
22:        private int transparency;
23:
24:        public object Clone()
25:        {
26:            return new PaintBrushProperties(shape,size,color,transparency);
27:        }
28:
29:        protected PaintBrushProperties(Shape _shape, int _size,
30:                                       Color _color, int _transparency)
31:        {
32:            shape=_shape;
33:            size=_size;
34:            color=_color;
35:            transparency=_transparency;
36:        }
37:
38:        [
39:        Category("Brush"),
40:        Description("The brush shape")
41:        ]
42:        public Shape Shape
43:        {
44:            get{ return shape;}
45:            set{ shape = value; }
46:        }
47:
48:        [
49:        Category("Brush"),
50:        Description("The brush color")
51:        ]
52:        public Color Color
53:        {
54:            get{return color;}
55:            set{color = value;}
56:        }
```

LISTING 3.6.7   Continued

```
57:
58:        [
59:        Category("Brush"),
60:        Description("The size of the brush in pixels")
61:        ]
62:        public int Size
63:        {
64:           get{return size;}
65:           set{size = value;}
66:        }
67:
68:        [
69:        Category("Brush"),
70:        Description("Percentage of transparency for the brush")
71:        ]
72:        public int Transparency
73:        {
74:           get{return transparency;}
75:           set{transparency = value;}
76:        }
77:
78:        public PaintBrushProperties()
79:        {
80:           color=Color.Black;
81:           size=5;
82:           shape=Shape.Round;
83:           transparency = 0;
84:        }
85:    }
86: }
```

NOTE

Notice the Shape enumeration at the beginning of this file.

LISTING 3.6.8   ShapeProperties.cs: The Shape Properties Class

```
1: using System.Drawing;
2:
3: namespace FormPaint
4: {
5:    public class ShapeProperties
```

LISTING 3.6.8 Continued

```
6:    {
7:        private Color fillColor;
8:        private Color lineColor;
9:        private bool line;
10:       private bool fill;
11:       private int lineWidth;
12:
13:       public object Clone()
14:       {
15:           return new ShapeProperties(fillColor,lineColor,
16:                                   line,fill,lineWidth);
17:       }
18:
19:       protected ShapeProperties(Color _fillColor, Color _lineColor,
20:                           bool _line, bool _fill, int _lineWidth)
21:       {
22:           fillColor = _fillColor;
23:           lineColor = _lineColor;
24:           fill = _fill;
25:           line = _line;
26:           lineWidth = _lineWidth;
27:       }
28:
29:
30:       [
31:       Category("Geometric Shape"),
32:       Description("The color to fill the shape with")
33:       ]
34:       public Color FillColor
35:       {
36:           get{return fillColor;}
37:           set{fillColor=value;}
38:       }
39:
40:       [
41:       Category("Geometric Shape"),
42:       Description("The color to outline the shape with")
43:       ]
44:       public Color LineColor
45:       {
46:           get{return lineColor;}
47:           set{lineColor=value;}
48:       }
49:
```

LISTING 3.6.8   Continued

```
50:        [
51:        Category("Geometric Shape"),
52:        Description("The width of the line")
53:        ]
54:        public int LineWidth
55:        {
56:           get{return lineWidth;}
57:           set{lineWidth=value;}
58:        }
59:
60:        [
61:        Category("Geometric Shape"),
62:        Description("Draw the outline")
63:        ]
64:        public bool Line
65:        {
66:           get{return line;}
67:           set{line = value;}
68:        }
69:
70:        [
71:        Category("Geometric Shape"),
72:        Description("Fill the shape")
73:        ]
74:        public bool Fill
75:        {
76:           get{return fill;}
77:           set{fill = value;}
78:        }
79:
80:        public ShapeProperties()
81:        {
82:        }
83:    }
84: }
```

LISTING 3.6.9   EraserProperties.cs: The Eraser Properties Class

```
1: using System;
2: using System.ComponentModel;
3:
4: namespace FormPaint
5: {
6:    public class EraserProperties
```

LISTING 3.6.9 Continued

```
 7:    {
 8:        private Shape shape;
 9:        private int size;
10:
11:        public object Clone()
12:        {
13:            return new EraserProperties(shape,size);
14:        }
15:
16:        protected EraserProperties(Shape _shape, int _size)
17:        {
18:            shape=_shape;
19:            size=_size;
20:        }
21:
22:        [
23:        Category("Eraser"),
24:        Description("The Eraser shape")
25:        ]
26:        public Shape Shape
27:        {
28:            get{ return shape;}
29:            set{ shape = value; }
30:        }
31:
32:        [
33:        Category("Eraser"),
34:        Description("The size of the Eraser in pixels")
35:        ]
36:        public int Size
37:        {
38:            get{return size;}
39:            set{size = value;}
40:        }
41:
42:        public EraserProperties()
43:        {
44:            shape=Shape.Square;
45:            size=10;
46:        }
47:    }
48: }
```

Notice that all these objects have a `Clone()` method. This is used when the properties are edited in a dialog box, which we'll define next, and the user has the option to click the Cancel button. If the dialog is cancelled, the clone of the object is discarded.

Editing the Tool Properties

The editing for all tool properties is accomplished with the same dialog box. This simple form hosts a property grid that deals with all the editing of the properties within the classes.

This dialog, `ToolProperties`, is created with the IDE as follows.

Drag two buttons from the toolbar to the dialog, label them **Ok** and **Cancel**, and then set their `DialogResult` properties to the corresponding value.

Drag and position a `PropertyGrid` object onto the design surface. The final result should look similar to the image in Figure 3.6.9.

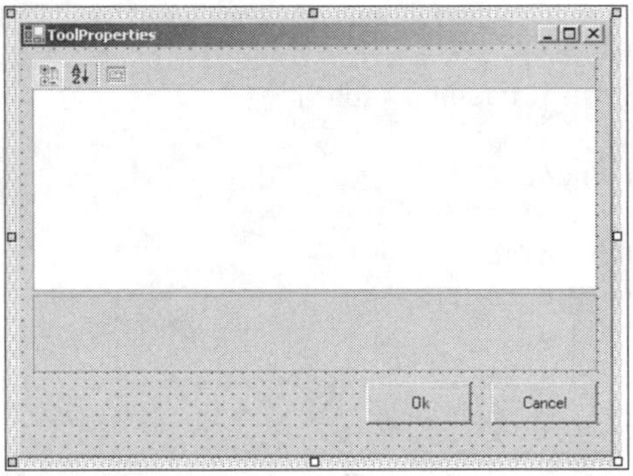

Figure 3.6.9
The ToolProperties dialog.

This dialog needs some added behavior, so we'll add a property to set and retrieve the object that the property grid edits. The following code snippet shows this simple accessor:

```
public object Object
{
    get{return this.propertyGrid1.SelectedObject;}
    set{this.propertyGrid1.SelectedObject=value;}
}
```

After this accessor is in place, we can add the functionality for editing and using the properties.

The `MainForm` must be modified to hold the properties and the tool currently in use. The code snippets that follow show these additions.

The Tool structure is added to the FormPaint namespace and is used to define which tool is in use:

```
public enum Tool
{
    Paintbrush,
    Rectangle,
    Ellipse,
    Eraser
}
```

The following private members are added to the MainForm class:

```
private Tool currentTool;
private PaintBrushProperties paintbrushProperties;
private ShapeProperties shapeProperties;
private EraserProperties eraserProperties;
```

The following additions are made to the MainForm constructor:

```
paintbrushProperties = new PaintBrushProperties();
shapeProperties = new ShapeProperties();
eraserProperties = new EraserProperties();
```

Adding Handlers for the Tool Properties

To use a tool, the user will single click it. To edit the properties for a tool, the user will double-click. To do this, add a click handler to each of the four tool buttons on the main form. The following code snippet shows how to fill these out:

```
private void ClickPaintbrush(object sender, System.EventArgs e)
{
    currentTool=Tool.Paintbrush;
}

private void ClickRectangle(object sender, System.EventArgs e)
{
    currentTool=Tool.Rectangle;
}

private void ClickEllipse(object sender, System.EventArgs e)
{
    currentTool=Tool.Ellipse;
}

private void ClickEraser(object sender, System.EventArgs e)
{
    currentTool=Tool.Eraser;
}
```

3.6

PRACTICAL WINDOWS FORMS APPLICATIONS

You can see that these handlers simply change the values of the `currentTool` member in the `MainForm`.

All four buttons now need to be tied to the same `DoubleClick` handler. Begin by creating a handler, called **OnToolProperties**, for one button and filling it out as follows:

```
private void OnToolProperties(object sender, System.EventArgs e)
{
    ToolProperties dlg=new ToolProperties();
    switch(currentTool)
    {
        case Tool.Paintbrush:
            dlg.Object=paintbrushProperties.Clone();
            break;
        case Tool.Rectangle:
            dlg.Object=shapeProperties.Clone();
            break;
        case Tool.Ellipse:
            dlg.Object=shapeProperties.Clone();
            break;
        case Tool.Eraser:
            dlg.Object=eraserProperties.Clone();
            break;
    }
    if(dlg.ShowDialog()==DialogResult.OK)
    {
        switch(currentTool)
        {
            case Tool.Paintbrush:
                paintbrushProperties=(PaintBrushProperties)dlg.Object;
                break;
            case Tool.Rectangle:
                shapeProperties=(ShapeProperties)dlg.Object;
                break;
            case Tool.Ellipse:
                shapeProperties=(ShapeProperties)dlg.Object;
                break;
            case Tool.Eraser:
                eraserProperties=(EraserProperties)dlg.Object;
                break;
        }
    }
}
```

This handler decides which of the property classes to use, hands the correct class to the editor, invokes the editor and then discards or replaces the edited property, depending on the `DialogReturn` value.

To allow the `ChildForm` to access the `MainForm` variables, such as the current drawing tool or the brush and shape properties, we have added some accessor properties. In addition, there is an accessor that allows the `ChildForm` to place text in the `MainForm`'s status bar. This is useful for user feedback. The snippet that follows contains the final additions to the class:

```
public Tool CurrentTool
{
    get{return currentTool;}
}

public ShapeProperties ShapeProperties
{
    get{return shapeProperties;}
}

public EraserProperties EraserProperties
{
    get{return eraserProperties;}
}

public PaintBrushProperties PaintBrushProperties
{
    get{return paintbrushProperties;}
}

public string StatusText
{
    set{this.statusBarPanel1.Text=value;}
}
```

Running the application now will allow you to test the tool selection and property editing.

Putting Paint on Paper

Now we can finally put paint on our bitmaps. This is all done by handlers in the `ChildForm` class.

This class performs two basic operations. The first is to place a shaped blob of color wherever the mouse is when the mouse button is pressed. The other is to allow the user to place a geometric shape and size it by dragging.

Listing 3.6.10 shows the full source of the `ChildForm` class interspersed with analysis.

LISTING 3.6.10 The `ChildForm` Class

```
1: using System;
2: using System.Drawing;
3: using System.Drawing.Drawing2D;
4: using System.Collections;
```

LISTING 3.6.10   Continued

```
 5: using System.ComponentModel;
 6: using System.Windows.Forms;
 7:
 8: namespace FormPaint
 9: {
10:    /// <summary>
11:    /// Summary description for ChildForm.
12:    /// </summary>
13:    public class ChildForm : System.Windows.Forms.Form
14:    {
15:      private Image myImage;
16:      private Bitmap tempBM;
17:
18:      private Pen pen;
19:      private SolidBrush brush;
20:      private GraphicsPath path;
21:      private Point firstPoint;
22:      private Point lastPoint;
23:      private Size blitBounds;
24:      private Point blitPos;
25:
26:      private bool Drawing;
27:      private bool dirty;
28:      private bool fill;
29:      private bool stroke;
30:
31:      private Graphics myGraphics;
32:      private Graphics imageGraphics;
33:
34:
35:      public Image Image
36:      {
37:        set
38:        {
39:          myImage =value;
40:          this.AutoScrollMinSize=myImage.Size;
41:          tempBM=new Bitmap(myImage.Size.Width,myImage.Size.Height);
42:        }
43:        get{return myImage;}
44:      }
```

The simple declaration of variables on lines 15–32 is followed by the Image accessor function that assigns an image to the child form and resets the AutoScroll limits to fit the picture. This accessor also allows other methods to get the image contained in the form.

LISTING 3.6.10 Continued

```
45:
46:      public bool Dirty
47:      {
48:        get{return dirty;}
49:        set{dirty=value;}
50:      }
51:
52:      /// <summary>
53:      /// Required designer variable.
54:      /// </summary>
55:      private System.ComponentModel.Container components = null;
56:
57:
58:      public ChildForm()
59:      {
60:        //
61:        // Required for Windows Form Designer support
62:        //
63:        InitializeComponent();
64:
65:        //
66:        // TODO: Add any constructor code after InitializeComponent call
67:        //
68:        Drawing = false;
69:        Dirty=false;
70:        Text="Untitled.bmp";
71:      }
72:
```

The constructor on lines 58–71 calls the all-important InitializeComponent, sets up the initial values for the flags used to determine if the drawing has been changed or if a drawing action is taking place, and sets the text of the form to untitled.bmp in case this is a new image—not one loaded from disk.

```
73:      /// <summary>
74:      /// Clean up any resources being used.
75:      /// </summary>
76:      protected override void Dispose( bool disposing )
77:      {
78:        if( disposing )
79:        {
80:          tempBM.Dispose();
81:          if(components != null)
82:          {
83:            components.Dispose();
```

LISTING 3.6.10   Continued

```
 84:        }
 85:      }
 86:      base.Dispose( disposing );
 87:    }
 88:
 89:    #region Windows Form Designer generated code
 90:    /// <summary>
 91:    /// Required method for Designer support - do not modify
 92:    /// the contents of this method with the code editor.
 93:    /// </summary>
 94:    private void InitializeComponent()
 95:    {
 96:      //
 97:      // ChildForm
 98:      //
 99:      this.AutoScaleBaseSize = new System.Drawing.Size(5, 13);
100:      this.BackColor = System.Drawing.Color.Green;
101:      this.ClientSize = new System.Drawing.Size(808, 565);
102:      this.Name = "ChildForm";
103:      this.Text = "ChildForm";
104:      this.MouseDown +=
    ➥new System.Windows.Forms.MouseEventHandler(this.OnMouseDown);
105:      this.Closing +=
    ➥new System.ComponentModel.CancelEventHandler(this.ChildForm_Closing);
106:      this.MouseUp +=
    ➥new System.Windows.Forms.MouseEventHandler(this.OnMouseUp);
107:      this.Paint +=
    ➥new System.Windows.Forms.PaintEventHandler(this.ChildForm_Paint);
108:      this.MouseMove +=
    ➥new System.Windows.Forms.MouseEventHandler(this.OnMouseMove);
109:
110:    }
111:    #endregion
```

The `Dispose` method and the `InitializeComponent` are added by the IDE. The only addition to `Dispose` is to clean up the intermediate bitmap. The handlers are added to the `ChildForm` on lines 104–108. On lines 113–116 following the `ToRadians` routine, simply convert from degrees to radians for use by the math routines.

```
112:
113:    private double ToRadians(double angle)
114:    {
115:      return angle/180*Math.PI;
116:    }
117:
```

LISTING 3.6.10   Continued

```
118:     private void CreateBrushPath(Shape s)
119:     {
120:
121:       path=new GraphicsPath();
122:
123:       MainForm form = (MainForm)this.ParentForm;
124:       int Toolsize=3;
125:       switch(form.CurrentTool)
126:       {
127:         case Tool.Paintbrush:
128:           Toolsize = form.PaintBrushProperties.Size;
129:           break;
130:         case Tool.Eraser:
131:           Toolsize = form.EraserProperties.Size;
132:           break;
133:       }
134:
135:       if(Toolsize<3)
136:         Toolsize=3;
137:       if(Toolsize>100)
138:         Toolsize=100;
139:
140:       switch(s)
141:       {
142:         case Shape.Round:
143:           path.AddEllipse(-Toolsize/2,-Toolsize/2,
144:             Toolsize,Toolsize);
145:           break;
146:         case Shape.Square:
147:           path.AddRectangle(new Rectangle(-Toolsize/2,-Toolsize/2,
148:             Toolsize,Toolsize));
149:           break;
150:         case Shape.Triangle:
151:           Point[] points=new Point[3];
152:           points[0]=new Point((int)(Math.Cos(ToRadians(90))*Toolsize),
153:             (int)(Math.Sin(ToRadians(90))*Toolsize));
154:           points[1]=new Point((int)(Math.Cos(ToRadians(210))*Toolsize),
155:             (int)(Math.Sin(ToRadians(210))*Toolsize));
156:           points[2]=new Point((int)(Math.Cos(ToRadians(330))*Toolsize),
157:             (int)(Math.Sin(ToRadians(330))*Toolsize));
158:           path.AddPolygon(points);
159:           break;
160:       }
```

3.6

**PRACTICAL
WINDOWS FORMS
APPLICATIONS**

LISTING 3.6.10   Continued

```
161:        }
162:
```

The `CreateBrushPath` method generates a path object that is used to fill a shaped area with color. In this simple demonstration, the color can be applied as a square, round, or triangular shape. The `switch` statement and its cases on lines 140–161 manage the creation of this path that is stored for use every time the mouse moves when the mouse button is pressed. Following that, on lines 163–171, the very simple paint routine does nothing more than copy the background image to the main screen.

```
163:      private void ChildForm_Paint(object sender,
164:          System.Windows.Forms.PaintEventArgs e)
165:      {
166:        e.Graphics.DrawImage(myImage,
167:          this.AutoScrollPosition.X,
168:          this.AutoScrollPosition.Y,
169:          myImage.Width,
170:          myImage.Height);
171:      }
172:
173:      private void OnMouseDown(object sender,
174:        System.Windows.Forms.MouseEventArgs e)
175:      {
176:        this.Dirty=true;
177:
178:        if(this.MdiParent.ActiveMdiChild==this)
179:        {
180:          Color brushColor;
181:          myGraphics = this.CreateGraphics();
182:          imageGraphics = Graphics.FromImage(this.Image);
183:
184:          myGraphics.SetClip(new Rectangle(0,0,this.Image.Width,
185:                          this.Image.Height));
186:
187:          MainForm form = (MainForm)this.MdiParent;
188:          switch(form.CurrentTool)
189:          {
190:            case Tool.Paintbrush:
191:              brushColor=Color.FromArgb(
192:                255-(int)(255.0/
193:                100*form.PaintBrushProperties.Transparency),
194:                form.PaintBrushProperties.Color);
195:              brush = new SolidBrush(brushColor);
196:              CreateBrushPath(form.PaintBrushProperties.Shape);
```

LISTING 3.6.10 Continued

```
197:                break;
198:            case Tool.Eraser:
199:                brush = new SolidBrush(Color.White);
200:                CreateBrushPath(form.EraserProperties.Shape);
201:                break;
202:            case Tool.Rectangle:
203:                goto case Tool.Ellipse;
204:            case Tool.Ellipse:
205:                fill = form.ShapeProperties.Fill;
206:                stroke = form.ShapeProperties.Line;
207:                firstPoint=new Point(e.X,e.Y);
208:                lastPoint = firstPoint;
209:                pen = new Pen(form.ShapeProperties.LineColor,
210:                    form.ShapeProperties.LineWidth);
211:                brush = new SolidBrush(form.ShapeProperties.FillColor);
212:                break;
213:            }
214:        }
215:
216:    Drawing = true;
217:    OnMouseMove(sender,e);
218:
219:    }
```

The OnMouseDown handler is the first action in the drawing process. It handles two main cases. If the mouse button is pressed and the paint or eraser tool is selected, it makes a new paint-brush path of the correct size and shape then sets the brush colors and transparency. In the case of a shape tool, it stores the first point in the shape, usually the top-left corner point, and then defines the pen color and width followed by the brush color. Finally, this method calls the mouse move handler once to ensure that the first paint is applied to the paper.

Following, on lines 221–257, the mouse up handler only deals with the final painting of the desired shape—either a rectangle or ellipse—on the canvas. The paintbrush or eraser color is applied on every mouse move. This drawing is performed not on the screen but on the image being held in memory by the form. This image is never scrolled, so the positions of the mouse and scrollbars must be compensated for on lines 229–232.

```
220:
221:    private void OnMouseUp(object sender,
222:        System.Windows.Forms.MouseEventArgs e)
223:    {
224:
225:        if(this.MdiParent.ActiveMdiChild==this)
```

LISTING 3.6.10   Continued

```
226:        {
227:          Point topLeft;
228:          Size bounds;
229:          topLeft=new Point(Math.Min(this.firstPoint.X,e.X),
230:            Math.Min(this.firstPoint.Y,e.Y));
231:          bounds=new Size(Math.Abs(e.X-firstPoint.X),
232:            Math.Abs(e.Y-firstPoint.Y));
233:          topLeft.Offset(-AutoScrollPosition.X,-AutoScrollPosition.Y);
234:          MainForm form = (MainForm)this.MdiParent;
235:          switch(form.CurrentTool)
236:          {
237:            case Tool.Rectangle:
238:              if(fill)
239:                imageGraphics.FillRectangle(brush,topLeft.X,
240:                  topLeft.Y,bounds.Width,bounds.Height);
241:              if(stroke)
242:                imageGraphics.DrawRectangle(pen,topLeft.X,
243:                  topLeft.Y,bounds.Width,bounds.Height);
244:              break;
245:            case Tool.Ellipse:
246:              if(fill)
247:                imageGraphics.FillEllipse(brush,topLeft.X,
248:                  topLeft.Y,bounds.Width,bounds.Height);
249:              if(stroke)
250:                imageGraphics.DrawEllipse(pen,topLeft.X,
251:                  topLeft.Y,bounds.Width,bounds.Height);
252:              break;
253:          }
254:        }
255:        Drawing=false;
256:        Invalidate();
257:      }
258:
259:      private void OnMouseMove(object sender,
260:        System.Windows.Forms.MouseEventArgs e)
261:      {
262:        if(!Drawing)
263:          return;
264:        if(this.MdiParent.ActiveMdiChild==this)
265:        {
266:          Graphics gTemp=Graphics.FromImage(tempBM);
267:          MainForm form = (MainForm)this.MdiParent;
268:          if(form.CurrentTool==Tool.Ellipse ||
269:            form.CurrentTool==Tool.Rectangle)
```

LISTING 3.6.10 Continued

```
270:          {
271:            blitPos= new Point(
272:              Math.Min(Math.Min(e.X,firstPoint.X),lastPoint.X),
273:              Math.Min(Math.Min(e.Y,firstPoint.Y),lastPoint.Y));
274:            blitBounds = new Size(Math.Max(e.X,
275:              Math.Max(firstPoint.X,lastPoint.X))-blitPos.X,
276:              Math.Max(e.Y,Math.Max(firstPoint.Y,lastPoint.Y))-
277:              blitPos.Y);
278:            blitPos.Offset(-(int)(1+pen.Width/2),-(int)(1+pen.Width/2));
279:            blitBounds.Width+=(int)(2+pen.Width);
280:            blitBounds.Height+=(int)(2+pen.Width);
281:            form.StatusText=blitPos.ToString()+" "+blitBounds.ToString();
282:          }
283:          switch(form.CurrentTool)
284:          {
285:            case Tool.Paintbrush:
286:              GraphicsContainer ctr=myGraphics.BeginContainer();
287:              myGraphics.Transform.Reset();
288:              myGraphics.TranslateTransform(e.X,e.Y);
289:              myGraphics.FillPath(this.brush,this.path);
290:              myGraphics.EndContainer(ctr);
291:              ctr=imageGraphics.BeginContainer();
292:              imageGraphics.Transform.Reset();
293:              imageGraphics.TranslateTransform(e.X-AutoScrollPosition.X,
294:                            e.Y-AutoScrollPosition.Y);
295:              imageGraphics.FillPath(this.brush,this.path);
296:              imageGraphics.EndContainer(ctr);
297:
298:              break;
299:            case Tool.Eraser:
300:              goto case Tool.Paintbrush;
301:            case Tool.Rectangle:
302:              gTemp.DrawImage(myImage,
303:                      new Rectangle(blitPos,blitBounds),
304:                      blitPos.X-AutoScrollPosition.X,
305:                      blitPos.Y-AutoScrollPosition.Y,
306:                      blitBounds.Width,blitBounds.Height,
307:                      GraphicsUnit.Pixel);
308:              if(fill)
309:                gTemp.FillRectangle(brush,
310:                  Math.Min(this.firstPoint.X,e.X),
311:                  Math.Min(this.firstPoint.Y,e.Y),
312:                  Math.Abs(e.X-firstPoint.X),
313:                  Math.Abs(e.Y-firstPoint.Y));
```

LISTING 3.6.10 Continued

```
314:            if(stroke)
315:              gTemp.DrawRectangle(pen,
316:                Math.Min(this.firstPoint.X,e.X),
317:                Math.Min(this.firstPoint.Y,e.Y),
318:                Math.Abs(e.X-firstPoint.X),
319:                Math.Abs(e.Y-firstPoint.Y));
320:            myGraphics.DrawImage(tempBM,
321:                    new Rectangle(blitPos,blitBounds),
322:                    blitPos.X,blitPos.Y,
323:                     blitBounds.Width,
324:                    blitBounds.Height,
325:                    GraphicsUnit.Pixel);
326:          break;
327:        case Tool.Ellipse:
328:          gTemp.DrawImage(myImage,
329:                  new Rectangle(blitPos,blitBounds),
330:                  blitPos.X-AutoScrollPosition.X,
331:                  blitPos.Y-AutoScrollPosition.Y,
332:                  blitBounds.Width,
333:                  blitBounds.Height,
334:                  GraphicsUnit.Pixel);
335:          if(fill)
336:            gTemp.FillEllipse(brush,
337:              Math.Min(this.firstPoint.X,e.X),
338:              Math.Min(this.firstPoint.Y,e.Y),
339:              Math.Abs(e.X-firstPoint.X),
340:              Math.Abs(e.Y-firstPoint.Y));
341:          if(stroke)
342:            gTemp.DrawEllipse(pen,
343:              Math.Min(this.firstPoint.X,e.X),
344:              Math.Min(this.firstPoint.Y,e.Y),
345:              Math.Abs(e.X-firstPoint.X),
346:              Math.Abs(e.Y-firstPoint.Y));
347:          myGraphics.DrawImage(tempBM,
348:                  new Rectangle(blitPos,blitBounds),
349:                  blitPos.X,blitPos.Y,
350:                  blitBounds.Width,
351:                  blitBounds.Height,
352:                  GraphicsUnit.Pixel);
353:          break;
354:        }
355:    lastPoint.X=e.X;
356:    lastPoint.Y=e.Y;
```

LISTING 3.6.10 Continued

```
357:        }
358:    }
```

The `OnMouseMove` method on lines 259–358 is the work-horse routine in the program. It works in two modes, differentiating between paintbrush or eraser operations and shape drawing operations. In the former mode, the paint is applied to the bitmap using the `GraphicsPath` created in the `OnMouseDown` event. The color is placed in both the screen memory and on the internal image. This means that a paint operation is instant and affects the image immediately. This takes place on lines 285–300 with line 289 performing the paint onscreen and line 295 placing color on the background image.

The operations that take place in shape drawing are more complex. As a shape is drawn, the user might want to "rubberband" the shape around to get the size correct. This means that paint cannot be placed directly onto the background image. A double buffering technique is used where an intermediate image is used to composite an area from the background with the graphical shape. This image is then copied to the screen, and the process repeated until the mouse button is released. This technique removes any flicker caused by refreshing and repainting the shape directly on the screen.

Line 269 decides if a `Rectangle` or `Ellipse` operation is underway. If so, the maximum size of the affected screen area, taking into account the start position, the current position, and the previous position of the mouse on lines 271 and 274. The area is increased by half a line width all around to compensate for the thickness of the current pen on lines 278–280 and then the double-buffered draw for rectangles happens on lines 301–326 and for ellipses on lines 327–353.

Also note line 281, which updates the status bar with the shape position and size.

```
359:
360:    private void ChildForm_Closing(object sender,
361:      System.ComponentModel.CancelEventArgs e)
362:    {
363:      if(Dirty)
364:      {
365:        DialogResult result=MessageBox.Show(this,
366:          "This file has changed, do you wish to save",
367:          "Save file",
368:          MessageBoxButtons.YesNoCancel,
369:          MessageBoxIcon.Question);
370:        switch(result)
371:        {
372:          case DialogResult.Cancel:
373:            e.Cancel=true;
374:            break;
```

3.6

PRACTICAL
WINDOWS FORMS
APPLICATIONS

LISTING 3.6.10 Continued

```
375:            case DialogResult.No:
376:              break;
377:            case DialogResult.Yes:
378:              this.Image.Save(this.Text);
379:              break;
380:          }
381:        }
382:      }
383:
384:    protected override void OnPaintBackground(PaintEventArgs e)
385:    {
386:      Region r=new Region(new Rectangle(0,0,Image.Width,Image.Height));
387:      Region w=new Region(new Rectangle(AutoScrollPosition.X,
388:        AutoScrollPosition.Y,
389:        ClientRectangle.Width,
390:        ClientRectangle.Height));
391:      r.Complement(w);
392:      e.Graphics.FillRegion(new SolidBrush(this.BackColor),r);
393:    }
394:
395:    protected override void OnSizeChanged(EventArgs e)
396:    {
397:      Invalidate();
398:      base.OnSizeChanged(e);
399:    }
400:  }
401: }
```

Finally, the last few methods deal with saving the file if it has been altered (lines 360–381).
This handler is called before the form closes to see if it is allowed to continue. The message
box used on lines 365–369 determines if the user wants to save or discard the image or cancel
the close altogether. In the case of a cancel, the CancelEventArgs provided through the delegate call must be updated. This happens on line 373.

The OnPaintBackground override is provided to eliminate flicker. With a green background
and the default settings, the whole bitmap is over-painted with green before the image is
redrawn. This caused a nasty flicker unless the steps taken here are used. This method calcu-
lates the region of screen outside of the image by using the complement of this area and the
area covered by the image (lines 386–391) and only repaints the piece required.

The OnSizeChanged override of the base class method in lines 395–399 ensures that the background is correctly repainted by just invalidating the window.

The image in Figure 3.6.10 shows `FormPaint` working, albeit with some abysmal artistic talent.

FIGURE 3.6.10
The working FormPaint *application.*

Summary

In this section's final chapter, you've seen the property grid, how to create a working Windows Forms application with a step-by-step walkthrough, and how to enhance the user experience by customizing controls.

We hope that this part of the book will enable you to get a running start at the Windows Forms development system, and that you begin to produce powerful and productive applications.

In the next section of this book, "Web Technologies," we'll be examining the details of assemblies and how to sign and version your code to put a stop to DLL hell once and for all.

Web Technologies

IN THIS PART

ASP.NET

IN THIS CHAPTER

The New Web

During the last couple of years, a strong trend in moving traditional desktop applications to Web-based applications has been a hot topic. The ability to create and deploy Web-based applications that afforded the user the same rich experience found in desktop applications has never been a simple task. As new technologies begin to emerge, such as advanced scripting support and DHTML, the ability to create a powerful Web-based UI is starting to take hold. Application users expect not only a functional application, but the application itself must also be aesthetically pleasing.

The main reason to switch to Web-based applications is the ease of deployment. Consider a company with 10,000 employees nationwide. Do you want to install the newest software on 10,000+ computers? NO! By moving applications to an intranet/extranet development and deployment model, there is no need to install client code on an end-users computer. Changes in the application are immediately available to all end users with timely delays associated with traditional application rollout.

The largest drawback to typical Web development was performance. Because ASP pages were not compiled code, the Web server had to interpret the ASP code. With the advent of ASP.NET, ASP.NET pages are compiled .NET components and, as such, execute at native speed. ASP.NET allows developers to use any .NET targeted language, such as C#, VB.NET, Managed C++ and even COBOL. (Yes, I've seen an ASP.NET page written in COBOL.)

ASP.NET Essentials

For ASP.NET pages to execute, IIS needs to be properly configured with FrontPage extensions. During the .NET SDK install or the Visual Studio .NET install, the required version of FrontPage extensions should have been installed. To verify, open the Internet Information Services Manager, right-click the Web site, most likely the default Web site, and select Check Server Extensions from the All Task menu. The All Task menu option appears when you right-click the local server. This will bring up a context pop-up menu. Figure 4.1.1 shows the context menu for the local server with the All Tasks menu item expanded.

With IIS properly configured for FrontPage extensions, the next step is to create Hello ASP.NET!

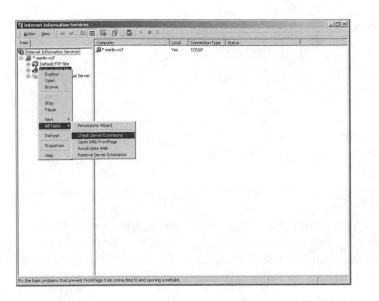

FIGURE 4.1.1
IIS Configuration Manager.

Hello ASP.NET

Typically, I tend to stay away from any particular IDE because such conversations can lead to an all out religious war. However, when it comes to building ASP.NET applications, Visual Studio .NET (VS.NET) fits the bill rather well. With the release of VS.NET, all development can take place in a single, familiar IDE. Application development in VB.NET, C#, MC++, FoxPro, and of course ASP.NET is now hosted in a single fully-integrated IDE. As such, Intellisense is now available to the ASP.NET developer. I don't know about you, but I'm starting to really rely on Intellisense.

To create the Hello ASP.NET sample, launch VS.NET and start a new Web Application. Figure 4.1.2 shows the New Project dialog with the ASP.NET Web Application icon selected. The dialog with provide the default project name "WebApplication." For now, just leave the project named as is. When generated, the name of the project should be WebApplication1.

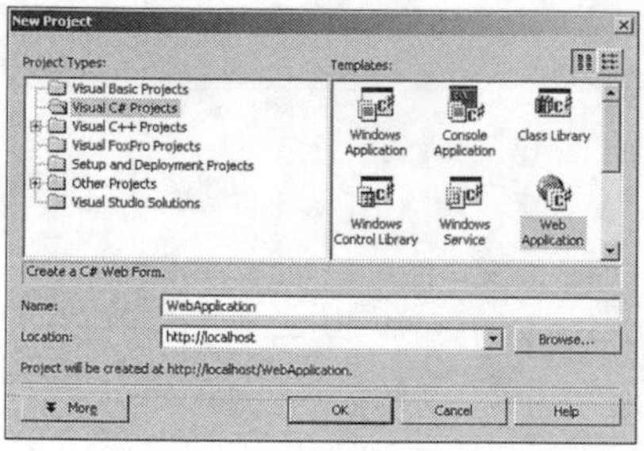

FIGURE 4.1.2
VS.NET New Project dialog box.

After VS.NET has created the new Web project, you should open the IIS manager and view the structure and files created by VS.NET. Figure 4.1.3 shows the IIS Manager explorer. The WebApplication1 created by VS.NET is expanded to show the extent of the generated framework provided by the VS.NET project for a new Web Application.

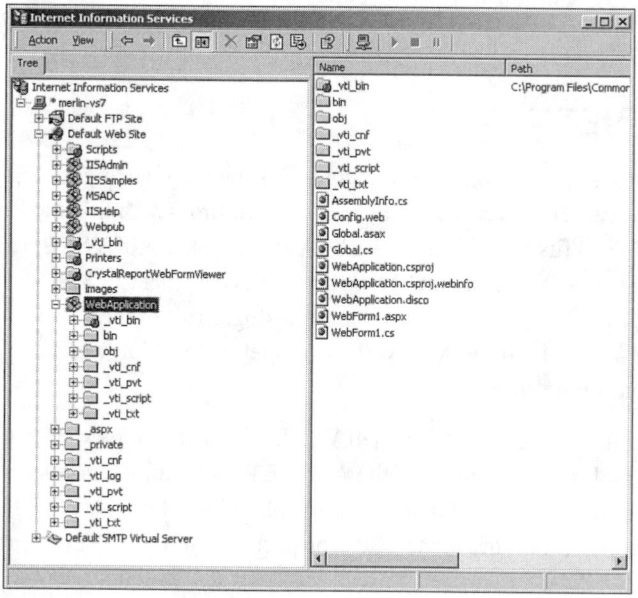

FIGURE 4.1.3
IIS Manager.

Contained within the WebApplication1 folder, exists VS.NET project files, `*.csproj`, along with the ASPX page, and the C# code for the ASP.NET page. ASPX pages consist of two parts, the HTML and the source page—in our case, the `.cs` file. This separation of UI and business logic is essential to all application development and the ASP.NET team certainly did not overlook this detail.

Of the files created for the ASP.NET application, the main ones of interest at this point are

- `WebForm1.aspx` The ASP page to be requested by the client browser.
- `WebForm1.asxp.cs` The C# code used to implement any business logic for the `aspx` page.
- `Web.config` An XML configuration file. ASP.NET allows for easy administration through this simple XML-based file.

When browsing the Solution Explorer in VS.NET, you'll notice that the `WebForm1.aspx.cs` file does not appear. To view the "code behind" page for `WebForm1.aspx`, you need to select the View Code option from the context menu. When right-clicking the `WebForm1.aspx` file within the Solution Explorer window, you should see something similar to Figure 4.1.4.

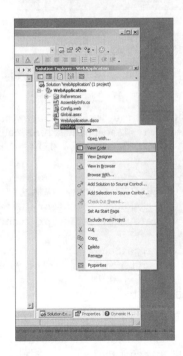

FIGURE 4.1.4

The solution explorer.

To get things going, drag a label control onto the `WebForm1.aspx` design surface and set the properties shown in Figure 4.1.5.

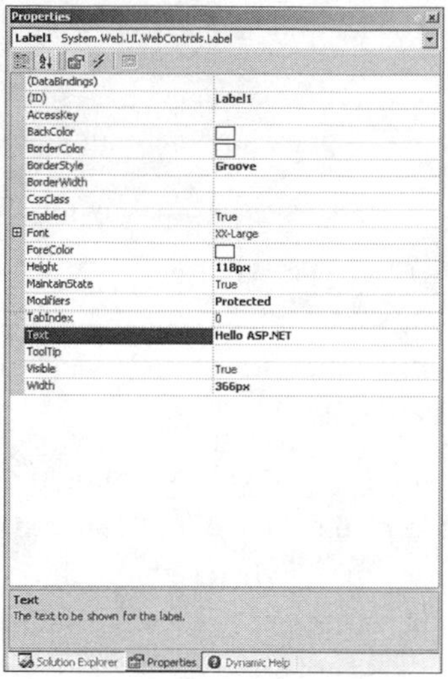

FIGURE 4.1.5
Label Properties.

To view the HTML code for the `WebForm1.aspx` page, select View HTML Source from the context menu.

```
 1: <%@ Page language="c#" Codebehind="WebForm1.aspx.cs"
➥AutoEventWireup="false" Inherits="WebApplication2.WebForm1" %>
 2: <!DOCTYPE HTML PUBLIC "-//W3C//DTD HTML 4.0 Transitional//EN" >
 3: <HTML>
 4:     <HEAD>
 5:             <meta name="GENERATOR" Content="Microsoft Visual Studio 7.0">
 6:             <meta name="CODE_LANGUAGE" Content="C#">
 7:             <meta name="vs_defaultClientScript" content="JavaScript
(ECMAScript)">
 8:             <meta name="vs_targetSchema"
➥content="http://schemas.microsoft.com/intellisense/ie5">
 9:     </HEAD>
10:     <body MS_POSITIONING="GridLayout">
11:             <form id="Form1" method="post" runat="server">
12:                     <asp:Label id="Label1"
➥style="Z-INDEX: 101; LEFT: 33px; POSITION: absolute; TOP: 108px"
➥runat="server">Hello ASP.NET</asp:Label>
13:             </form>
14:     </body>
15: </HTML>
```

With the label properties set, build and execute the Web Application project; this can be done by pressing F5. The first time the `aspx` page is requested from IIS, it will be compiled and an assembly, WebApplication1.dll in this case, will be created and placed in the bin directory. On subsequent requests, IIS will check to ensure that the dll is up to date and either use the compiled assembly or compile again if the source has changed.

The single largest benefit of ASP.NET and VS.NET is the ability to debug! an ASPX Web Application using the VS.NET debugger. View the code for WebForm1.aspx and locate the following code segment:

```
1: private void Page_Init(object sender, EventArgs e)
2: {
3:     //
4:     // CODEGEN: This call is required by the ASP.NET Web Form Designer.
5:     //
6:     InitializeComponent();
7: }
```

Place a break point on the InitializeComponent statement. A break point can be placed by using the F9 key. With the break point in place, as depicted in Figure 4.1.6, press F5 to launch the Web Application project and you should see IE start up. Control will then transfer to the VS.NET Debugger when the Page_Init method is invoked and the break point on line 6 is reached.

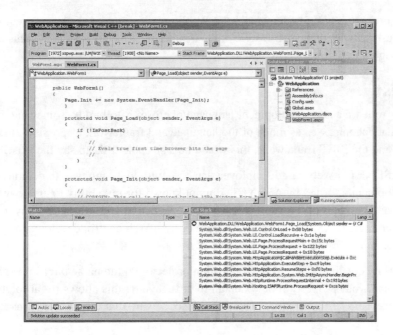

4.1

ASP.NET

FIGURE 4.1.6
Debugging ASP.NET.

Developers who are already familiar with previous versions of Microsoft Visual Studio will be right at home when developing ASP.NET applications. Before .NET and VS.NET, the process of debugging an ASP-based application was similar to sliding down a sharp razor into a vat of alcohol.

Adding Some Meat

The goal of ASP.NET is rapid Web-based application development, so Microsoft has created 45 controls for ASP.NET applications. ASP.NET controls run server-side and automatically down level to the requesting client. Most Web sites today have code to support IE and Netscape, thus requiring the Web Developer to maintain two sets of code that accomplish the same thing. With the advent of server-side controls, this burden is soon to go away.

ASP.NET supports standard HTML controls as well as ASP.NET controls. In fact, the controls can co-exist within the same page and even nested within each other.

One of the main purposes of any application is to gather data and to present data in a meaningful fashion. Consider an internal Web Application that is used to gather information about a new hire. This information will then be submitted to HR for processing and stored in the company database.

To begin the process, a basic understanding of WebForms is required. Just as current ASP applications use a Request/Response style of data gathering, so does ASP.NET. This action happens through a traditional Form Post.

Ideas Test

The best way to learn a new development language/platform is to build a somewhat useful application that encompasses as much of the language and framework as possible. In the case of ASP.NET and the .NET framework, this would be a sizeable task, to say the least.

To explore ASP.NET, a Web-based Employee database will go a long way to demonstrate the ease of development afforded by ASP.NET. I'm not known for my ability to create wonderful page layouts and graphics design, so I'll leave the aesthetics to you. Along the way, topics that will be covered include ASP controls, ADO.NET, custom Web control development, client-side file uploading, and anything else that might be of use.

To begin, start by creating a new Web Application project with the name `DataForm`. Next, the `DOCUMENT.pageLayout` property should default to `GridLayout`; this allows for absolute positioning of controls in terms of (x,y) coordinates. Also, be sure that the `targetSchema` is set to Internet Explorer 5.

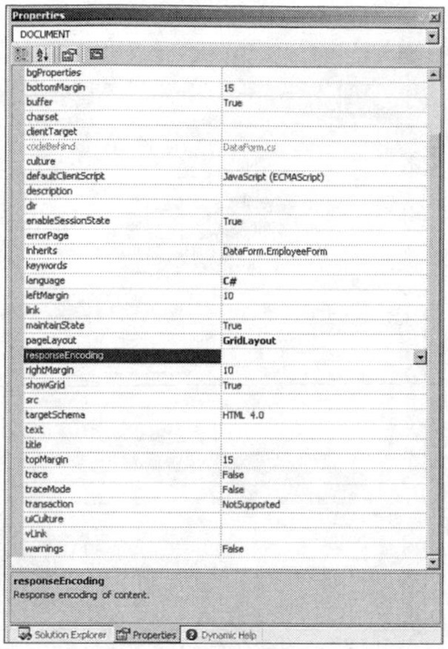

FIGURE 4.1.7
The document Properties.

Next, create the layout as show in Figure 4.1.8 and use the variable names listed in Table 4.1.1.

TABLE 4.1.1   Variables for the `DataForm.aspx` Page

Control Type	Variable Name	Text
asp:label	FirstNameLabel	First Name
asp:label	LastNameLabel	Last Name
asp:label	SSNLabel	SSN
asp:label	DepartmentLabel	Department
asp:label	JobTitleTable	Job Title
asp:label	SalaryLabel	Salary
asp:textbox	FirstName	
asp:textbox	LastName	
asp:textbox	SSN	
asp:textbox	Dept	
asp:textbox	JobTitle	
asp:textbox	Salary	
asp:button	AddEmployee	Add New Employee

The basic form should look similar to Figure 4.1.8.

FIGURE 4.1.8
The DataForm layout.

With the form layout in place, it's a good time to view the generated HTML code for the aspx page and the C# source file.

LISTING 4.1.1   Code for DataForm.aspx

```
1: <%@ Page language="c#" Codebehind="DataForm.aspx.cs"
AutoEventWireup="false" Inherits="DataForm.DataFormBehind" %>
2: <!DOCTYPE HTML PUBLIC "-//W3C//DTD HTML 4.0 Transitional//EN" >
3: <HTML>
4:     <HEAD>
5:         <meta name="GENERATOR" Content="Microsoft Visual Studio 7.0">
6:         <meta name="CODE_LANGUAGE" Content="C#">
7:         <meta name="vs_defaultClientScript" content="JavaScript
 (ECMAScript)">
8:         <meta name="vs_targetSchema" content=
"http://schemas.microsoft.com/intellisense/ie5">
9:     </HEAD>
10:     <body MS_POSITIONING="GridLayout">
11:         <form id="Form1" method="post" runat="server">
12:             <asp:Label id="FirstNameLabel"
style="Z-INDEX: 100; LEFT: 47px; POSITION: absolute;
 TOP: 78px"
runat="server" Width="80px" Height="20px">First Name</asp:Label>
13:             <asp:Label id="LastNameLabel"
style="Z-INDEX: 101; LEFT: 48px; POSITION: absolute; TOP: 112px"
runat="server" Width="80px" Height="20px">LastName</asp:Label>
```

LISTING 4.1.1   Continued

```
14:              <asp:Label id="SSNLabel"
style="Z-INDEX: 102; LEFT: 48px; POSITION: absolute; TOP: 144px"
runat="server" Width="80px" Height="20px">SSN</asp:Label>
15:              <asp:Label id="DepartmentLabel" style="Z-INDEX: 103;
 LEFT: 48px; POSITION: absolute; TOP: 176px" runat="server" Width="80px"
Height="20px">Department</asp:Label>
16:              <asp:Label id="JobTitleLabel" style="Z-INDEX: 104;
 LEFT: 48px; POSITION: absolute; TOP: 208px" runat="server" Width="80px"
Height="20px">Job Title</asp:Label>
17:              <asp:Label id="SalaryLabel" style="Z-INDEX: 105;
 LEFT: 48px; POSITION: absolute; TOP: 240px" runat=
"server" Width="80px" Height="20px">Salary</asp:Label>
18:              <asp:TextBox id="Salary" style="Z-INDEX: 111;
 LEFT: 136px; POSITION: absolute; TOP: 240px" runat="server" Width="150px"
Height="20px"></asp:TextBox>
19:              <asp:TextBox id="JobTitle" style="Z-INDEX: 110;
 LEFT: 136px; POSITION: absolute; TOP: 208px"
 runat="server" Width="150px" Height="20px"></asp:TextBox>
20:              <asp:TextBox id="Dept" style="Z-INDEX: 109;
 LEFT: 136px; POSITION: absolute; TOP: 176px"
 runat="server" Width="150px" Height="20px"></asp:TextBox>
21:              <asp:TextBox id="SSN" style="Z-INDEX: 108;
 LEFT: 136px; POSITION: absolute; TOP: 144px"
 runat="server" Width="150px" Height="20px"></asp:TextBox>
22:              <asp:TextBox id="LastName" style="Z-INDEX: 107;
 LEFT: 136px; POSITION: absolute; TOP: 112px"
 runat="server" Width="150px" Height="20px"></asp:TextBox>
23:              <asp:TextBox id="FirstName" style="Z-INDEX: 106;
 LEFT: 136px; POSITION: absolute; TOP: 80px"
 runat="server" Width="150px" Height="20px"></asp:TextBox>
24:              <asp:Button id="AddEmployee" style="Z-INDEX: 112;
 LEFT: 136px; POSITION: absolute; TOP: 272px"
 runat="server" Width="128px" Height="24px" Text="Add Employee"></asp:Button>
25:
26:                      <!--Place holder for asp:Repeater control -->
27:          </form>
28:      </body>
29: </HTML>
```

Just as the Windows Forms designer produces some of the most atrocious code known to man, so does the WebForms designer. In fact, I went through and trimmed and cleaned the code for DataForm.aspx so it could actually be read. The HTML for the DataForm.aspx is basically

XHTML. Notice on line 26 that I've inserted a comment declaring that an asp:repeater control will be added later. The asp:repeater control will be used to display the employees as they are added.

A WebForm is derived from System.Web.UI.Page, and the DataForm aspx page is then derived from the DataForm.DataFormBehind class as listed in the Inherits attribute for the page. The DataFormBehind class is the CodeBehind page and is renamed from the default WebForm1 class. It is important to note that ASP .NET seems to have problems when dealing with a class name that shares the same name as the namespace in which it lives. This is the reason the class name for the code behind page is different from the filename. VS.NET generates the most generic name possible rather than prompting you for the proper name. This is certainly one of my pet peeves! You'll often waste time renaming generated classes and forms and all references to them.

Along with the declaration of variables within the actual apsx page, the DataForm.aspx.cs file will also contain the variable declarations. This allows for access to the controls properties and methods during page loading and other events handled by the DataFormBehind class. If you're wondering how this happens, ASP.NET does code generation the first time the page is accessed, during which time the necessary glue-code is generated to link the aspx controls to the variables declared within the CodeBehind page. The DataFormBehind class in Listing 4.1.2 is used during this process as well and contains the page logic for such actions as databinding, layout, validation, and other business logic as required by the application.

LISTING 4.1.2 The DataFormBehind Class

```
 1: using System;
 2: using System.Collections;
 3: using System.ComponentModel;
 4: using System.Data;
 5: using System.Drawing;
 6: using System.Web;
 7: using System.Web.SessionState;
 8: using System.Web.UI;
 9: using System.Web.UI.WebControls;
10: using System.Web.UI.HtmlControls;
11:
12: namespace DataForm
13: {
14:     /// <summary>
15:     /// Summary description for DataForm.
16:     /// </summary>
17:     public class DataFormBehind : System.Web.UI.Page
18:     {
19:         protected System.Web.UI.WebControls.Label FirstNameLabel;
```

LISTING 4.1.2   Continued

```
20:          protected System.Web.UI.WebControls.Label LastNameLabel;
21:          protected System.Web.UI.WebControls.Label SSNLabel;
22:          protected System.Web.UI.WebControls.Label DepartmentLabel;
23:          protected System.Web.UI.WebControls.Label JobTitleLabel;
24:          protected System.Web.UI.WebControls.Label SalaryLabel;
25:          protected System.Web.UI.WebControls.Button AddEmployee;
26:          protected System.Web.UI.WebControls.TextBox FirstName;
27:          protected System.Web.UI.WebControls.TextBox LastName;
28:          protected System.Web.UI.WebControls.TextBox SSN;
29:          protected System.Web.UI.WebControls.TextBox Dept;
30:          protected System.Web.UI.WebControls.TextBox JobTitle;
31:          protected System.Web.UI.WebControls.TextBox Salary;
32:
33:          protected System.Web.UI.WebControls.Repeater EmployeeRepeater;
34:
35:             public DataFormBehind()
36:             {
37:                 Page.Init += new System.EventHandler(Page_Init);
38:             }
39:
40:          private void Page_Load(object sender, System.EventArgs e)
41:          {
42:              if( !this.IsPostBack ) {
43:                  //Create an ArrayList to hold Employees
44:                  ArrayList employees = new ArrayList( );
45:                  this.Session[ "Employees" ] = employees;
46:              } else {
47:
48:                  //Since only one button exists on the form
49:                  //it must have been clicked so add the
50:                  //new employee and update the databinding
51:                  //for the EmployeeRepeater control
52:                  Employee emp   = new Employee( );
53:                  emp.FirstName  = FirstName.Text;
54:                  emp.LastName   = LastName.Text;
55:                  emp.SSN        = SSN.Text;
56:                  emp.Dept       = Dept.Text;
57:                  emp.JobTitle   = JobTitle.Text;
58:                  emp.Salary     = Double.Parse( Salary.Text );
59:
60:                  ((ArrayList)this.Session["employees"]).Add( emp );
61:                  EmployeeRepeater.DataSource =
➥ (ArrayList)this.Session["employees"];
62:                  EmployeeRepeater.DataBind( );
```

LISTING 4.1.2   Continued

```
63:
64:                 }
65:         }
66:
67:         private void Page_Init(object sender, EventArgs e)
68:         {
69:                 //
70:                 // CODEGEN: This call is required by the ASP.NET
➥ Web Form Designer.
71:                 //
72:                 InitializeComponent();
73:         }
74:
75:         #region Web Form Designer generated code
76:         /// <summary>
77:         /// Required method for Designer support - do not modify
78:         /// the contents of this method with the code editor.
79:         /// </summary>
80:         private void InitializeComponent()
81:         {
82:                 this.Load += new System.EventHandler(this.Page_Load);
83:
84:         }
85:         #endregion
86:     }
87: }
```

I've made some additions to the `DataFormBehind` class that you will also need to make. The first is the declaration of the `EmployeeRepeater` variable. A `Repeater` allows for template expansion of HTML code during page processing. In the case of this example, rows will be added to an HTML table for each employee. The `Repeater` class makes use of reflection to glean information about the object(s) it is enumerating over to access the public properties of that object. Update the `DataForm.cs` source to reflect the added code presented in Listing 4.1.2.

Next, there needs to exist a class that represents an employee. For now, when a new employee is added, the employee will be stored in an array list. This array list will then be used as the data source for the Repeater control. A very basic class will be constructed for the purpose of maintaining the employee information. Listing 4.1.3 contains the `Employee` class.

LISTING 4.1.3   The `Employee` Class

```
1: namespace DataForm
2: {
3:     using System;
```

LISTING 4.1.3 Continued

```
 4:
 5:    /// <summary>
 6:    ///     Summary description for Employee.
 7:    ///     NOTE:  Since the employee class will be used in conjunction
➡ with DataBinding, public properties
 8:    ///     are required.  DataBinding makes use
 of the System.Reflection API
➡to access the get/set Properties.
 9:    /// </summary>
10:    public class Employee
11:    {
12:        private string    _FirstName;
13:        private string    _LastName;
14:        private string    _SSN;
15:        private string    _Dept;
16:        private string    _JobTitle;
17:        private double    _Salary;
18:
19:
20:        public string FirstName {
21:            get { return _FirstName; }
22:            set { _FirstName = value; }
23:        }
24:        public string LastName {
25:            get { return _LastName; }
26:            set { _LastName = value; }
27:        }
28:        public string SSN {
29:            get { return _SSN; }
30:            set { _SSN = value; }
31:        }
32:        public string Dept {
33:            get { return _Dept; }
34:            set { _Dept = value; }
35:        }
36:        public string JobTitle {
37:            get { return _JobTitle; }
38:            set{ _JobTitle = value; }
39:        }
40:        public double Salary {
41:            get { return _Salary; }
42:            set { _Salary = value; }
43:        }
44:    }
45: }
46:
```

4.1

ASP.NET

Although this class doesn't really accomplish anything of value, it will serve the purpose of illustrating how the Repeater control works. It is also worth noting that any asp control that uses data binding does so through the properties of the bound object. Bound controls seem to ignore public fields and only seem to look for public properties.

To make use of the Repeater control, add the code in Listing 4.1.4 to the DataForm.aspx file where I had originally inserted the comment referring to the repeater control.

LISTING 4.1.4   The EmployeeRepeater Template Code

```
 1: <asp:Repeater id="EmployeeRepeater" runat="server">
 2:     <HeaderTemplate>
 3:         <table
➥style="BORDER-RIGHT: gray thin ridge; BORDER-TOP: gray thin ridge;
➥ LEFT: 300px; BORDER-LEFT: gray thin ridge;
➥BORDER-BOTTOM: gray thin ridge; POSITION: absolute; TOP: 80px">
 4:             <tr style="BORDER-RIGHT: aqua thin groove;
➥BORDER-TOP: aqua thin groove; BORDER-LEFT: aqua thin groove;
➥COLOR: purple; BORDER-BOTTOM: aqua thin groove;
➥BACKGROUND-COLOR: lightgrey">
 5:                     <td>Name</td>
 6:                     <td>Department</td>
 7:                     <td>Job Title</td>
 8:             </tr>
 9:     </HeaderTemplate>
10:     <ItemTemplate>
11:         <tr>
12:             <td>
13:                 <%# DataBinder.Eval( Container.DataItem, "LastName" ) %>,
14:                 <%# DataBinder.Eval( Container.DataItem, "FirstName" ) %>
15:             </td>
16:             <td>
17:                 <%# DataBinder.Eval( Container.DataItem, "Dept" ) %>
18:             </td>
19:             <td>
20:                 <%# DataBinder.Eval( Container.DataItem, "JobTitle" ) %>
21:             </td>
22:         </tr>
23:     </ItemTemplate>
24:     <FooterTemplate>
25:         </tbody> </table>
26:     </FooterTemplate>
27: </asp:Repeater>
```

With the addition of the `asp:repeater` template code in place, a new row will be added to the table each time a new employee is added. C++ developers are already familiar with the idea of templates and their use during development. Templates allow for a generic framework that can be expanded as needed. You should become comfortable with the `asp:repeater` because it will save you countless hours of development time. The final product should look similar to Figure 4.1.9.

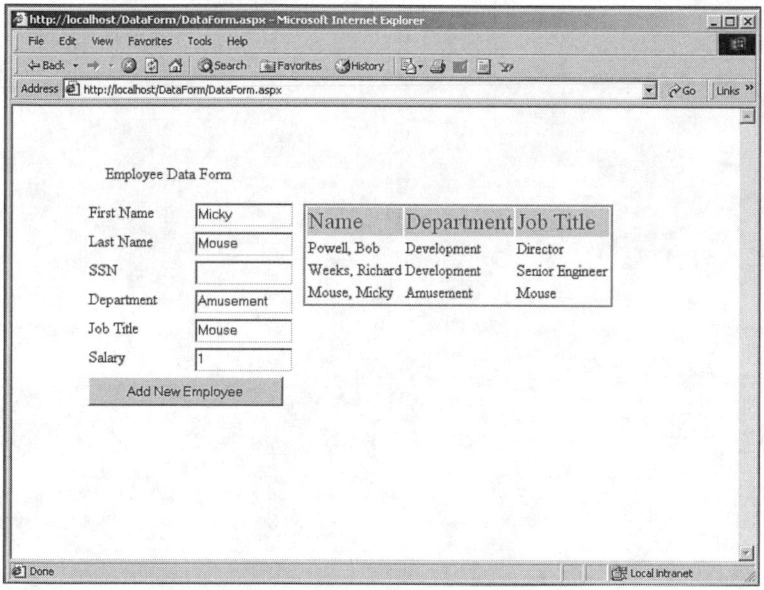

FIGURE 4.1.9
The basic ideas page.

The basic premise of the application has now been established. An initial feel for ASP.NET development should leave you with a warm fuzzy feeling inside and ready to tackle a much larger Web Application.

Summary

In this chapter, the basics of Web development using ASP.NET were thoroughly covered. In the chapters to follow, a deeper look at the various aspects of ASP.NET will be covered. Each topic building in conjunction to produce the final Employee Browser application. I encourage you to take time and further explore each topic on your own before moving onto the next section. This will help develop a further understanding of ASP.NET and allow for your own discovery.

.NET Data Access

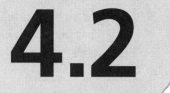

CHAPTER

4.2

IN THIS CHAPTER

When learning a new language/platform/framework, a good approach is to develop an application that makes use of as many features as possible. When designing an application, the general process includes creating a specification document along with use cases. Well, I think a short punch list will suffice for this example. The employee database should support the following features:

1. Search
   a. By Department
   b. By Name
   c. Name within a Department
2. Edit
3. Add
4. Upload Picture

The requirements will allow for a fairly decent tour of ASP.NET, attributes, reflection, pagelets, and ASP Controls. This is, of course, the overall goal, to dig into ASP and .NET as much as possible within the context of an example application that somehow relates to the real world.

DataLayer

Because the goal is to poke around APS.NET, the data model is short and simple. Two tables will be constructed—Department and Employee. The table layouts appear in Figure 4.2.1.

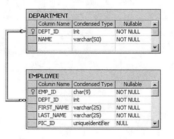

FIGURE 4.2.1
The Stingray database tables.

Custom attributes were briefly discussed earlier, but now is a good time to make full use of them. The data layer will define two attributes, a `DBTableAttribute` and a `DBFieldAttribute`. These attributes will contain the necessary information to invoke stored procedures in a fairly generic manner. The Reflection API can be used to locate attributes and properties of an object. Thus, our custom attributes can be located and the necessary information acquired.

A class will model every entity in the database. These classes will derive from a common abstract base class—DBEntity. DBEntity defines two properties—IsDirty and IsNew—along with the abstract method FromDataRow. The IsDirty property will be used to determine if the DBEntity needs to be updated in the database. The IsNew property is used to determine whether to use an update or insert. The abstract method FromDataRow is used to construct the DBEntity from a DataRow element from a DataSet object. Listing 4.2.1 contains the DBEntity class.

LISTING 4.2.1   The DBEntity Abstract Base Class

```
 1: ///<summary>
 2: /// DBEntity defines a basic database entity and serves as the
 3: /// base class of all entities with a database
 4: ///</summary>
 5:
 6:
 7: namespace Stingray.Data
 8: {
 9:     using System;
10:     using System.Data;
11:
12:
13:
14:     /// <summary>
15:     /// The DBEntity abstract base class
16:     /// </summary>
17:     public abstract class DBEntity        {
18:
19:         private bool m_bIsDirty = false;
20:         private bool m_bIsNew = true;
21:
22:             public virtual bool IsDirty {
23:                 get { return m_bIsDirty; }
24:                 set { m_bIsDirty = value;}
25:             }
26:
27:             public virtual bool IsNew {
28:                 get { return m_bIsNew; }
29:                 set { m_bIsNew = value; }
30:             }
31:
32:             public abstract bool FromDataRow( System.Data.DataRow data );
33:     }
34:
35: }
```

DBEntity provides common implementation for the IsNew and IsDirty properties. For the purposes of this example, these default implementations will suffice.

The next order of business is to create the custom attribute classes DBTableAttribute and DBFieldAttribute. DBTableAttribute will contain the table name, the insert stored procedure name, and the update stored procedure name. DBFieldAttribute defines the parameter name, data type, and length for the data if necessary. These attributes will be applied to each object that represents an entity within the database. Making use of the Reflection API, these attributes will be used to handle tasks, such as inserting and updating these entities. Listing 4.2.2 provides the implementation of both DBTableAttribute and DBFieldAttribute classes.

LISTING 4.2.2   Custom Attribute Classes

```
1: namespace Stingray.Data
2: {
3:      using System;
4:      using System.Data;
5:      using System.Data.SqlClient;
6:      using System.Data.SqlTypes;
7:
8:
9:
10:     ///<summary>
11:     ///The class DBTableAttribute defines the table within which
12:     ///a particular enity resides.  In addition, this attribute
13:     ///also contains properties for the SQL Insert and Update stored
14:     ///procedures used by the enity
15:     ///</summary>
16:     [System.AttributeUsage(AttributeTargets.Class)]
17:     public class DBTableAttribute : System.Attribute {
18:
19:         /*****[Fields ]*****/
20:
21:         private string    m_TableName;
22:         private string    m_SPInsertCommand;
23:         private string    m_SPUpdateCommand;
24:
25:
26:         /*****[Properties ]*****/
27:
28:         public string TableName {
29:             get { return m_TableName; }
30:             set { m_TableName = value; }
31:         }
32:
```

LISTING 4.2.2 Continued

```
33:          public string InsertCommand {
34:              get { return m_SPInsertCommand; }
35:              set { m_SPInsertCommand = value; }
36:          }
37:
38:          public string UpdateCommand {
39:              get { return m_SPUpdateCommand; }
40:              set { m_SPUpdateCommand = value; }
41:          }
42:
43:          /*****[Constructor(s)]*****/
44:          public DBTableAttribute( string TableName ) {
45:              m_TableName = TableName;
46:          }
47:      }
48:
49:
50:
51:      ///<summary>
52:      ///The DBFieldAttribute is used to map class properties
53:      ///onto SQL Stored procedure parameters.
54:      ///</summary>
55:      [System.AttributeUsage(AttributeTargets.Property)]
56:      public class DBFieldAttribute : System.Attribute {
57:
58:          /*****[Fields]*****/
59:
60:          private string        m_ParamName;
61:          private SqlDbType      m_DataType;
62:          private int        m_Length = 0;
63:
64:
65:          /*****[Properties]*****/
66:          public string ParameterName {
67:              get { return m_ParamName; }
68:              set { m_ParamName = value; }
69:          }
70:
71:          public SqlDbType DataType {
72:              get { return m_DataType; }
73:              set { m_DataType = value; }
74:          }
75:
76:          public int Length {
```

4.2

.NET DATA
ACCESS

LISTING 4.2.2   Continued

```
77:             get { return m_Length; }
78:             set { m_Length = value; }
79:         }
80:
81:         /*****[Constructor(s)]*****/
82:         public DBFieldAttribute( string ParameterName ) {
83:             m_ParamName = ParameterName;
84:         }
85:     }
86:
87: }
```

The first thing to notice about each attribute is the attribute to which it is applied. The DBTableAttribute is attributed with the AttributeUsage attribute. Because the DBTableAttribute should only be used on a class, the AttributeTargets enum is used to indicate that. The AttributeUsage allows control over how attributes are used and applied. The AttributeTargets enum contains the following defined values:

```
public enum AttributeTargets {
    All,
    Assembly,
    Class,

    Constructor,
Delegate,
Enum,
Event,
Field,
Interface,
Method,
Module,
Parameter,
Property,
ReturnValue,
Struct
}
```

As far as the implementation of an attribute, there really is not much to it. The System.Attribute serves as the base class from which a user-defined attribute class can be derived. As with any user-defined class, the details of its usage and its implementation will depend on the purpose the new attribute should serve.

With DBEntity, DBTableAttribute, and DBFieldAttribute in place, the generic DBAccess class can be constructed. DBAccess will make use of the Reflection API to insert or update any

DBEntity-derived class. DBAccess contains three static methods. The AcquireConnection is hard-coded to return a connection to the localhost database, along with necessary login information. Because this object is used on a constant basis, it could actually get the connection string from some configuration file and then be cached for later access. However, sometimes simple is better.

The DBAccess class also provides a public Save method. As its name suggests, this method is used to save any DBEntity-derived class. Listing 4.2.3 contains the source listing for the DBEntity class.

LISTING 4.2.3 DBAccess

```
1: namespace Stingray.Data
2: {
3:     using System;
4:     using System.Reflection;
5:     using System.Data;
6:     using System.Data.SqlClient;
7:
8:
9:     public class DBAccess
10:     {
11:
12:         /// <summary>
13:         /// Get an active connection to the stingray database
14:         /// </summary>
15:         public static SqlConnection AcquireConnection( ) {
16:             SqlConnection dbCon =
17:                     new SqlConnection(
18:                         "user id=sa;password=;initial catalog=Stingray;
    ➥data source=.;Connect Timeout=30"
19:                                                 );
20:             try {
21:                 dbCon.Open( );
22:             } catch( Exception ) {
23:                 dbCon.Dispose( );
24:                 dbCon = null;
25:             }
26:
27:             return dbCon;
28:         }
29:
30:
31:         /// <summary>
32:         /// Save a DBEntity into the Stingray Database
```

LISTING 4.2.3   Continued

```
33:        /// </summary>
34:        /// <param name="ActiveConnection">
➥Active Database Connection</param>
35:        /// <param name="entity"> The Entity to be saved</param>
36:        public static bool Save( SqlConnection ActiveConnection,
➥ DBEntity entity ) {
37:
38:            //Is there anyting to save?
39:            if( !entity.IsDirty )
40:                return true;
41:
42:            object[] Attributes = entity.GetType( ).GetCustomAttributes(
43:                            typeof(Stingray.Data.DBTableAttribute),
44:                                    false
45:                                                            );
46:
47:            if(Attributes.Length != 1 )
48:                return false;
49:
50:            System.Data.SqlClient.SqlCommand SqlCmd = new SqlCommand( );
51:            SqlCmd.Connection = ActiveConnection;
52:            SqlCmd.CommandType = System.Data.CommandType.StoredProcedure;
53:
54:            ///
55:            ///Do we insert or Update?
56:            ///
57:            DBTableAttribute TableAttribute =
➥(DBTableAttribute)Attributes[0];
58:
59:            if( entity.IsNew ) {
60:                SqlCmd.CommandText = TableAttribute.InsertCommand;
61:            } else {
62:                SqlCmd.CommandText = TableAttribute.UpdateCommand;
63:            }
64:
65:            AddCmdParam( SqlCmd, entity );
66:
67:            try {
68:
69:                SqlCmd.ExecuteNonQuery( );
70:                return true;
71:
```

LISTING 4.2.3 Continued

```
72:                } catch( Exception ) {
73:                    //Do something for Heavens sake!!
74:                }
75:
76:            //Should not make it to here unless it go BOOM!
77:            return false;
78:        }
79:
80:        /// <summary>
81:        /// Create the SQLParameter(s) for the DBEnity object
82:        /// </summary>
83:        /// <param name="cmd"> The SqlCommand object to
➥ add the Prameters to</param>
84:        /// <param name="entity">The DBEnity to scrape </param>
85:        protected static void AddCmdParam( SqlCommand SqlCmd,
➥DBEntity entity ) {
86:
87:            ///
88:            ///Get the Public properties and create the SQL Parameters
89:            ///
90:            Type T = entity.GetType( );
91:            PropertyInfo[] Properties =
92:                    T.GetProperties(
93:                        BindingFlags.DeclaredOnly | BindingFlags.Instance
➥ | BindingFlags.Public
94:                                    );
95:
96:            foreach( PropertyInfo pi in Properties) {
97:                object[] Attributes =
98:                        pi.GetCustomAttributes(
99:                            typeof(Stingray.Data.DBFieldAttribute),
➥false
100:                                    );
101:                if(Attributes.Length == 1) {
102:                    DBFieldAttribute Field =
➥(DBFieldAttribute)Attributes[0];
103:                    MethodInfo mi = pi.GetGetMethod( false );
104:
105:                    object result = mi.Invoke( entity, null );
106:
107:                    SqlCmd.Parameters.Add( Field.ParameterName,
➥ Field.DataType  );
```

4.2

.NET DATA
ACCESS

LISTING 4.2.3   Continued

```
108:                        SqlCmd.Parameters[ Field.ParameterName ].Value =
➥result;
109:
110:                        if( Field.Length > 0 )
111:                            SqlCmd.Parameters[ Field.ParameterName ].Size =
➥Field.Length;
112:                    }
113:
114:                }
115:
116:            }
117:        }
118: }
```

DBAccess deserves some explanation as to what it is doing. It begins by looking for the custom attribute DBTableAttribute. If found, the process of accessing the necessary properties for serialization begins. The method AddCmdParam grabs the current instance properties and looks for the custom DBFieldAttribute. Remember that the DBFieldAttribute contains properties for the parameter name, data type, and length of the parameter if applicable.

The reason for designing the data layer in such a way is merely to experiment with custom attributes and the Reflection API. I'm not suggesting this as a model for all future database development, but I'm sure you'll find a use for this type of implementation.

Employee and Department Class

With the basic database framework in place, the next step is to create the Employee and Department classes and their respective stored procedures. To keep focused, the stored procedures will not implement any type of error checking or result codes. Instead, SQLServer® constraints will be used to ensure that there are no primary or foreign key conflicts.

Stored Procedures

The Employee Browser will make use of only four simple stored procedures. SQL Server® Enterprise Manager allows for viewing and creating user stored procedures from the management console. Figure 4.2.2 shows the stored procedure editor contained within SQL Server.

FIGURE 4.2.2

SQL Server stored procedure editor.

Using the editor, the following stored procedures need to be created:

```
CREATE PROCEDURE sp_InsertDept
    @DEPT_ID int,
    @NAME varchar(50)
AS
    INSERT INTO DEPARTMENT VALUES(@DEPT_ID,@NAME)
GO


CREATE PROCEDURE sp_UpdateDept
    @DEPT_ID int,
    @NAME varchar(50)
AS

    UPDATE DEPARTMENT SET NAME = @NAME WHERE DEPT_ID = @DEPT_ID

Go

CREATE PROCEDURE sp_InsertEmployee
    @EMP_ID char(9),
    @DEPT_ID int,
    @FIRST_NAME varchar(25),
    @LAST_NAME varchar(25),
    @PIC_ID uniqueidentifier
AS
    INSERT INTO EMPLOYEES
```

```
VALUES(@EMP_ID,@DEPT_ID,@FIRST_NAME,@LAST_NAME,@PIC_ID)
GO

CREATE PROCEDURE sp_UpdateEmployee
    @EMP_ID char(9),
    @DEPT_ID int,
    @FIRST_NAME varchar(25),
    @LAST_NAME varchar(25),
    @PIC_ID uniqueidentifier
AS
    UPDATE EMPLOYEE SET DEPT_ID = @DEPT_ID,
                    FIRST_NAME= @FIRST_NAME,
                     LAST_NAME = @LAST_NAME,
                  PIC_ID = @PIC_ID
    WHERE EMP_ID = @EMP_ID
GO
```

These are about as easy as they come; no real work is taking place other than straightforward TSQL statements. If you need further information about TSQL, use the help within SQL Server to locate TSQL. The online help is very comprehensive and should address any questions you might have.

Class Implementation

The Employee and Department classes are nothing more than mapping models for the database information. As such, the only implementation code they provide is the properties that will be used when inserting or updating a particular record. Each class inherits from the abstract base class DBEntity and makes use of the custom attributes developed previously.

Because the Department class is the smallest, it serves as a good starting point and its source appears in Listing 4.2.4.

LISTING 4.2.4 The Department Class

```
 1: namespace Stingray.Data
 2: {
 3:     using System;
 4:     using System.Data;
 5:     using System.Data.SqlClient;
 6:
 7:     /// <summary>
 8:     ///  Simple class for a Department
 9:     /// </summary>
10:     [
11:         Stingray.Data.DBTableAttribute(
12:                             "DEPARTMENT",
```

LISTING 4.2.4 Continued

```
13:                                    InsertCommand="sp_InsertDept",
14:                                    UpdateCommand="sp_UpdateDept"
15:                                        )
16:     ]
17:     public class Department : Stingray.Data.DBEntity {
18:
19:
20:     /*****[Department Implementation]*****/
21:         private int         m_Id;
22:         private string      m_Name;
23:
24:         /// <summary>
25:         /// Department Id Property
26:         /// </summary>
27:         [Stingray.Data.DBFieldAttribute("@DEPT_ID",
➥DataType=SqlDbType.Int)]
28:         public int Id {
29:             get { return m_Id; }
30:             set {
31:                 if( m_Id != (int)value) {
32:                     m_Id = value;
33:                     IsDirty = true;
34:                 }
35:             }
36:         }
37:
38:         /// <summary>
39:         /// Department Name property
40:         /// </summary>
41:         [Stingray.Data.DBFieldAttribute("@NAME",
➥DataType=SqlDbType.VarChar)]
42:         public string Name {
43:             get { return m_Name; }
44:             set {
45:                 if( m_Name != (string)value) {
46:                     m_Name = value;
47:                     IsDirty = true;
48:                 }
49:             }
50:         }
51:
52:         /// <summary>
53:         ///
54:         /// </summary>
55:         /// <param name="data"> </param>
```

LISTING 4.2.4 Continued

```
56:        public override bool FromDataRow( DataRow data ) {
57:            this.m_Id = (int)data["DEPT_ID"];
58:            this.m_Name = (string)data["NAME"];
59:            return true;
60:        }
61:
62:    }
63: }
```

The Department class represents a very simple mapping of data from the DEPARTMENT table into a class structure. The custom attributes are used by the DBAccess class to insert or update a DEPARTMENT record as needed. The same implementation style is used to create the Employee class in Listing 4.2.5.

LISTING 4.2.5 The Employee Class

```
 1: namespace Stingray.Data
 2: {
 3:
 4:     using System;
 5:     using System.Data;
 6:     using System.Data.SqlClient;
 7:
 8:     /// <summary>
 9:     ///    The Employee Class
10:     /// </summary>
11:     ///
12:     [
13:       Stingray.Data.DBTableAttribute(
14:                "EMPLOYEE",
15:                 InsertCommand="sp_InsertEmployee",
16:            UpdateCommand="sp_UpdateEmployee")
17:     ]
18:     public class Employee : DBEntity
19:     {
20:
21:         /*****[Data Members]*****/
22:         private string    m_EmpId;      //SSN
23:         private int       m_DeptId;
24:         private string    m_FirstName;
25:         private string    m_LastName;
26:         private Guid      m_PicId;
27:
```

LISTING 4.2.5 Continued

```
28:          /*****[Properties]*****/
29:          [
30:            Stingray.Data.DBFieldAttribute("@EMP_ID",
➥DataType=SqlDbType.Char,Length=9)
31:          ]
32:          public string Id {
33:              get { return m_EmpId; }
34:              set {
35:                  if(m_EmpId != (string)value) {
36:                      m_EmpId = (string)value;
37:                      IsDirty = true;
38:                  }
39:              }
40:          }
41:
42:
43:          [
44:            Stingray.Data.DBFieldAttribute("@DEPT_ID",
➥DataType=SqlDbType.Int)
45:          ]
46:          public int DeptId {
47:              get { return m_DeptId; }
48:              set {
49:                  if( m_DeptId != (int)value ) {
50:                      m_DeptId = (int)value;
51:                      IsDirty = true;
52:                  }
53:              }
54:          }
55:
56:          [
57:        Stingray.Data.DBFieldAttribute("@FIRST_NAME",
➥DataType=SqlDbType.VarChar)
58:          ]
59:          public string FirstName {
60:              get { return m_FirstName; }
61:              set {
62:                  if(m_FirstName != (string)value) {
63:                      m_FirstName = (string)value;
64:                      IsDirty = true;
65:                  }
66:              }
67:          }
68:
69:
```

4.2

.NET DATA
ACCESS

LISTING 4.2.5   Continued

```
70:           [
71:               Stingray.Data.DBFieldAttribute("@LAST_NAME",
➡DataType=SqlDbType.VarChar)
72:           ]
73:       public string LastName {
74:           get { return m_LastName; }
75:           set {
76:               if( m_LastName != (string)value) {
77:                   m_LastName = (string)value;
78:                   IsDirty = true;
79:               }
80:           }
81:       }
82:
83:           [
84:               Stingray.Data.DBFieldAttribute("@PIC_ID",
➡DataType=SqlDbType.UniqueIdentifier)
85:       ]
86:       public Guid PictureId {
87:           get { return m_PicId; }
88:           set {
89:               if( m_PicId != (Guid)value) {
90:                   m_PicId = new Guid( ((Guid)value).ToString( ) );
91:                   IsDirty = true;
92:               }
93:           }
94:       }
95:
96:       /// <summary>
97:       /// Create from a row of data
98:       /// </summary>
99:       /// <param name="data"> </param>
100:      public override bool FromDataRow( DataRow data ) {
101:          this.Id = (string)data["EMP_ID"];
102:          this.DeptId = (int)data["DEPT_ID"];
103:          this.FirstName = (string)data["FIRST_NAME"];
104:          this.LastName = (string)data["LAST_NAME"];
105:          if( data["PIC_ID"].ToString() != "")
106:              this.m_PicId = new Guid( data["PIC_ID"].ToString( ) );
107:
108:              this.IsNew = false;
109:              return true;
110:      }
111:
112:
```

LISTING 4.2.5 Continued

```
113:        /*****[Constructor(s)]*****/
114:        public Employee() {
115:            //What to do??
116:            IsNew = true;
117:            IsDirty = false;
118:        }
119:
120:    }
121: }
```

Testing

Now that the basic entities are in place, a small test program can be devised to ensure that the code is working as expected. The test program in Listing 4.2.6 also serves as a code example of how to use the classes constructed so far.

LISTING 4.2.6 Test Example

```
1: namespace TestBed
2: {
3:     using System;
4:     using System.Data;
5:     using System.Data.SqlClient;
6:     using Stingray.Data;
7:     using System.Reflection;
8:
9:
10:
11:     public class DBTest
12:     {
13:
14:         public static int Main(string[] args)
15:         {
16:
17:         SqlConnection dbCon =
18:                 new SqlConnection(
19:                     "user id=sa;password=;initial catalog=Stingray;
➥data source=.;Connect Timeout=30"
20:                                 );
21:
22:             Department[] Departments = new Department[5];
23:             string[] names = { "Development","Tech Support",
➥"Sales","Consulting","Marketing" };
24:
```

LISTING 4.2.6   Continued

```
25:                    for(int i = 0; i < 5; i++) {
26:                        Departments[i] = new Department( );
27:                        Departments[i].IsNew = true;
28:                        Departments[i].Id = (i+1);
29:                        Departments[i].Name = names[i];
30:                    }
31:
32:                    dbCon.Open( );
33:
34:                    //Save the Departments
35:                    foreach( Department dept in Departments ) {
36:                        DBAccess.Save( dbCon, dept );
37:                    }
38:
39:                    //Do a select and display the results
40:                    System.Data.SqlClient.SqlDataAdapter dsCmd =
➡ new SqlDataAdapter("SELECT * FROM DEPARTMENT", dbCon );
41:                    System.Data.DataSet dataSet = new System.Data.DataSet(   );
42:                    dsCmd.Fill( dataSet,"DEPARTMENT" );
43:
44:                    //display the records
45:                    foreach( System.Data.DataRow row in
➡dataSet.Tables["DEPARTMENT"].Rows )
46:                        Console.WriteLine("{0} : {1}",
47:
➡row[dataSet.Tables["DEPARTMENT"].Columns["DEPT_ID"]],
48:                            row[dataSet.Tables["DEPARTMENT"].Columns["NAME"]]);
49:
50:
51:                    return 0;
52:                }
53:
54:            }
55: }
56:
```

If all goes well, the test bed example should populate the DEPARTMENT table and display the select results. Also, using SQL Server Query Analyzer, a select statement can be executed to return all rows with the DEPARTMENT table, as shown in Figure 4.2.3.

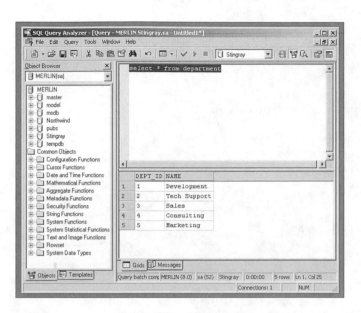

FIGURE 4.2.3
New records in the DEPARTMENT table.

Simple Search Support

One of the requirements for the Employee database is the ability to search for a particular employee. The search should allow for searching by name, name and department, or to list all employees in a given department. Instead of using a custom attribute, a search class will be created that returns results as a System.Data.DataSet class.

The Search class will only provide static methods in the same vein as the DBAccess class. One reason for doing so is that neither class requires any state information so the added overhead of object allocation can be avoided. Our Search class will provide two methods: Find with one overload and Retrieve. The Find method will be used to locate an individual employee, but the method makes use of the SQL LIKE predicate. As such, any wild card matches will be returned. The overload Find method allows for a department ID to be specified and uses the same LIKE predicate for the name matching. The final method, Retrieve, takes a department Id and returns all employees from that department. Listing 4.2.7 contains the source for the Search class.

LISTING 4.2.7   The Search Class

```
1: namespace Stingray.Data
2: {
3:     using System;
4:     using System.Data;
5:     using System.Data.SqlClient;
6:
7:     /// <summary>
8:     ///  Basic search class
9:     /// </summary>
10:     public class Search
11:     {
12:
13:         /// <summary>
14:         /// Try and locate an employee
15:         /// </summary>
16:         /// <param name="ActiveConnection"> </param>
17:         /// <param name="FirstName"> </param>
18:         /// <param name="LastName"> </param>
19:         public static DataSet Find( SqlConnection ActiveConnection,
20:                                     string FirstName,
21:                                     string LastName ) {
22:             string SelectStmt =
23:             string.Format(
24:                 "SELECT * FROM EMPLOYEE WHERE FIRST_NAME LIKE
➥'{0}%' and LAST_NAME LIKE '{1}%'",
25:                 FirstName,LastName);
26:
27:             return Execute( ActiveConnection, SelectStmt, "EMPLOYEE" );
28:
29:         }
30:
31:         /// <summary>
32:         /// Try and locate an employee within a department
33:         /// </summary>
34:         /// <param name="ActiveConnection"> </param>
35:         /// <param name="DepartmentId"> </param>
36:         /// <param name="FirstName"> </param>
37:         /// <param name="LastName"> </param>
38:         public static DataSet Find( SqlConnection ActiveConnection,
39:                                     int DepartmentId,
40:                                     string FirstName,
41:                                 string LastName ) {
42:
```

LISTING 4.2.7   Continued

```
43:                  object[] args = { FirstName, LastName, DepartmentId };
44:
45:                  string SelectStmt =
46:                      string.Format(
47:                          "SELECT * FROM EMPLOYEE WHERE FIRST_NAME LIKE '{0}%'
➥ and LAST_NAME LIKE '{1}%' and DEPT_ID = {2}",
48:                          args);
49:
50:              return Execute( ActiveConnection, SelectStmt, "EMPLOYEE" );
51:          }
52:
53:          /// <summary>
54:          /// Retrieve a list of employees for a given department
55:          /// </summary>
56:          /// <param name="ActiveConnection"> </param>
57:          /// <param name="DepartmentId"> </param>
58:          public static DataSet Retrieve( SqlConnection ActiveConnection,
59:                                      int DepartmentId ) {
60:              string SelectStmt =
61:                  string.Format(
62:                   "SELECT * FROM EMPLOYEE WHERE DEPT_ID = {0}",
63:                   DepartmentId );
64:
65:              return Execute( ActiveConnection, SelectStmt, "EMPLOYEE" );
66:          }
67:
68:          /// <summary>
69:          /// Nice and tidy.  Do the grunt work in one place
70:          /// </summary>
71:          /// <param name="ActiveConnection"> </param>
72:          /// <param name="Stmt"> </param>
73:          /// <param name="TableName"> </param>
74:          private static DataSet Execute( SqlConnection ActiveConnection,
75:                                      string SelectStmt,
76:                                      string TableName ) {
77:
78:              SqlDataAdapter dataAdapter = new SqlDataAdapter
➥ ( SelectStmt, ActiveConnection );
79:              DataSet dsResult = new DataSet( TableName );
80:
81:              try {
82:                  dataAdapter.Fill( dsResult, TableName );
```

LISTING 4.2.7   Continued

```
83:                    } catch( Exception ) {
84:                        //Do some magic here
85:                    }
86:
87:                    return dsResult;
88:            }
89:        }
90: }
```

The implementation for Search is fairly straightforward and does not really involve any heavy-duty database sorcery. Each method requires an SqlConnection object, which is assumed to be connected to the database. The return type from each method is a DataSet object. In .NET, a DataSet object is very much a generic data container and can be used in data classes such as the SqlAdapter class. It is important not to draw a parallel between a DataSet and a RecordSet. In fact, a DataSet can be used to hold multiple tables where as a RecordSet contains records from a single result set.

As with the previous database classes, a small test application will give a better understanding of how to make use of the Search class (see Listing 4.2.8).

LISTING 4.2.8   Test 2

```
 1: namespace TestBed
 2: {
 3:     using System;
 4:     using System.Data;
 5:     using System.Data.SqlClient;
 6:     using Stingray.Data;
 7:
 8:     public class TestBed2
 9:     {
10:         public static void Main( )
11:         {
12:             SqlConnection dbCon =
13:                     new SqlConnection(
14:                         "user id=sa;password=;initial catalog=Stingray;
➥data source=.;Connect Timeout=30"
15:                                         );
16:
17:             dbCon.Open( );
18:
```

LISTING 4.2.8 Continued

```
19:              //Find me
20:              DataSet dsResult = Search.Find( dbCon, "Richard", "Weeks" );
21:              if( dsResult != null && dsResult.Tables["EMPLOYEE"] != null) {
22:                  foreach( DataColumn c in
➥dsResult.Tables["EMPLOYEE"].Columns) {
23:                      Console.WriteLine(
➥dsResult.Tables["EMPLOYEE"].Rows[0][c] );
24:                  }
25:              }
26:
27:              //Get Development
28:              dsResult = Search.Retrieve( dbCon, 1 );
29:              if( dsResult != null) {
30:                  foreach( DataRow row in
➥dsResult.Tables["EMPLOYEE"].Rows) {
31:                      Console.WriteLine("*****************
➥****************");
32:                      foreach( DataColumn col in
➥dsResult.Tables["EMPLOYEE"].Columns ) {
33:                          Console.WriteLine( row[col] );
34:                      }
35:                  }
36:              }
37:          }
38:
39:      }
40: }
41:
```

With the implementation and testing of the Search class, the data layer is complete. Figure 4.2.13 illustrates the development effort to this point with a pseudo UML-style diagram.

The next step in developing the Employee database is to create ASP.NET pagelets and aspx pages for displaying and editing employee information along with a search page.

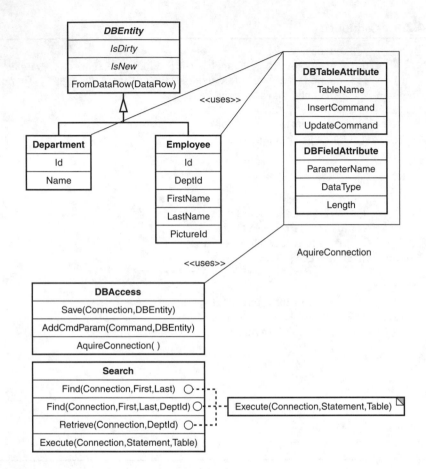

FIGURE 4.2.4
Current object model.

Summary

As with most applications, the ability to work with a database is a common requirement. The .NET framework provides a rich set of database APIs for you to employ within your applications. Through the use of the Reflection API, generic data access and entity serialization to and from SQL Server can be realized with a minimal amount of effort. The following chapters will make use of this simple data layer to develop the Employee Browser application.

WebForms

IN THIS CHAPTER

Introduction to ASP.NET WebForms

With the addition of WebForms, ASP.NET provides for a truly developer-oriented environment. The ability to separate code from HTML layout allows for greater flexibility and reusability on the part of Web developers. ASP.NET allows for the creation of `UserControls`, also known as `pageletes`. These `UserControls` are analogous to Windows custom controls. Web developers can now create these custom controls and easily reuse them throughout various Web applications. This chapter will explore several different methods of creating UserControls and the supporting code along with the ASPX pages, which host these controls.

UserControls

ASP.NET allows for the creation of `UserControls` that can be embedded within other `UserControls` or aspx pages. Think of a `UserControl` as a small reusable component consisting of markup, both ASP.NET and HTML, along with supporting source code. Within a typical Web site, there are many aspects that are often repeated, such as a product view, search controls, and even the banner on the top the page. Such entities make ideal candidates for building `UserControls`.

HeaderControl

As a quick entry into developing `UserControls`, a custom header control with two properties should suffice to get the blood rushing. The header control will be developed to allow for interaction with the ASP controls on the page. Later, a different approach will be taken, showing that there is more than one way to accomplish a task.

The header control, shown in Figure 4.3.1, will be developed using the following ASP `WebControls`:

- `asp:table`   Similar to the HTML table tag
- `asp:image`   Similar to the HTML `img` tag
- `asp:label`   Generates an HTML span

One of the benefits of using `asp:*` controls is their ability to generate HTML for the requesting client's ability. Down-leveling is a built-in feature and will no doubt save you time and effort.

The header control consists of two files—`HeaderControl.aspx` and `HeaderControl.ascx.cs`. A file with the extension of `.aspx` denotes a `UserControl` derived entity. This is one of the advantages offered by ASP.NET—the ability to have actual program code behind a Web page or `UserControl` to handle tasks that require more than just simple script.

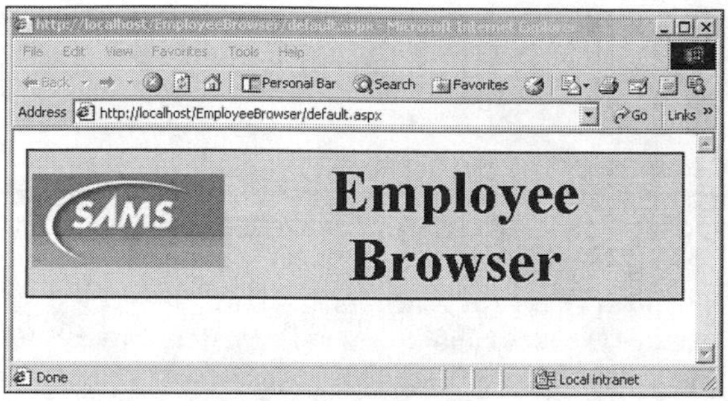

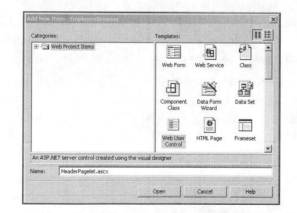

FIGURE 4.3.1
The header control.

To build the header control, and in fact the entire Web project about to be designed, create a new `ASP.NET Web Application` in VS7. The project should be named `EmployeeBrowser`. One of my pet peeves about Visual Studio, or any development environment for that matter, is the default choices made by the editor. I promptly delete any source files it generates, because the main page needs to be `default.aspx` and not `WebForm1.aspx`.

The header control is merely a small table with two cells—an image control and a label. The code for creating the control is rather small. First, create a folder within the `EmployeeBrowser` solution named `Pagelets`; this will allow for some organization of the code within the project. Right-click the folder and select Add, Add Web User Control from the context menu. This will bring up the Add New Item dialog, as shown in Figure 4.3.2.

FIGURE 4.3.2
New Item dialog.

Assign the name **HeaderPagelet** to the new UserControl. Open the HeaderPagelet.ascx file for HTML editing and enter the code in Listing 4.3.1.

LISTING 4.3.1 ASPX source for the HeaderPagelet

```
 1: <%@ Control Language="c#" AutoEventWireup="false"
➥Codebehind="HeaderPagelet.ascx.cs"
➥Inherits="EmployeeBrowser.Pagelets.HeaderPagelet"%>
 2: <asp:Table id="HeaderTable" runat="server" Width="100%" Height="25%"
➥ BorderColor="Purple" BackColor="LightGray" BorderStyle="Groove"
➥ BorderWidth="2px" HorizontalAlign="Center">
 3:     <asp:TableRow>
 4:         <asp:TableCell width="1" VerticalAlign="Middle"
➥HorizontalAlign="Center">
 5:             <!-- The Image for the control -->
 6:             <asp:Image runat="server" id="HeaderImage" />
 7:         </asp:TableCell>
 8:         <asp:TableCell VerticalAlign="Middle" HorizontalAlign="Center">
 9:             <asp:Label runat="server" id="HeaderLabel" runat="server"
➥Font-Size="XX-Large" Font-Bold="True" Font-Names="Times New Roman"
➥Width="317px" Height="55px" ForeColor="Black" />
10:         </asp:TableCell>
11:     </asp:TableRow>
12: </asp:Table>
```

Before diving into the C# code behind this ascx page, a minute to detail the markup listed is necessary. In this case, I've created all UserControl derived classes in the EmployeeBrowser.Pagelets namespace. Remember that namespaces are a useful way of organizing your source tree. By keeping all pagelets within a particular namespace, other developers using your code can quickly associate the namespace with the items contained with it.

Line 1 of Listing 4.3.1, declares this is a control and specifies the C# language, the CodeBehind page, and that this control inherits from EmployeeBrowser.Pagelets.HeaderPagelet. ASP.NET uses the CodeBehind page to generate code to handle the binding of asp elements and the variables contained with the source page.

The asp:table, asp:image, and asp:label tags make use of the runat="Server" property. This allows for server-side processing of the controls and data binding between the control and code. Only the asp:image and asp:label tags use the id=*X*, where *X* is the variable name defined within the CodeBehind source. Listing 4.3.2 contains the CodeBehind source for the HeaderControl.

LISTING 4.3.2 HeaderControl.ascx.cs

```
1: namespace EmployeeBrowser.Pagelets
2: {
3:     using System;
4:     using System.Data;
5:     using System.Drawing;
6:     using System.Web;
7:     using System.Web.UI.WebControls;
8:     using System.Web.UI.HtmlControls;
9:
10:    /// <summary>
11:    ///     Summary description for HeaderPagelet.
12:    /// </summary>
13:    public abstract class HeaderPagelet : System.Web.UI.UserControl
14:    {
15:        protected System.Web.UI.WebControls.Table HeaderTable;
16:        protected System.Web.UI.WebControls.Image HeaderImage;
17:        protected System.Web.UI.WebControls.Label HeaderLabel;
18:
19:        public string ImageUrl
20:        {
21:            set
22:            {
23:                HeaderImage.ImageUrl = value;
24:            }
25:        }
26:
27:        public string Text
28:        {
29:            set
30:            {
31:                HeaderLabel.Text = value;
32:            }
33:        }
34:
35:
36:        /// <summary>
37:        public HeaderPagelet()
38:        {
39:            this.Init += new System.EventHandler(Page_Init);
40:        }
41:
42:        private void Page_Load(object sender, System.EventArgs e)
43:        {
44:            // Put user code to initialize the page here
```

LISTING 4.3.2 Continued

```
45:          }
46:
47:          private void Page_Init(object sender, EventArgs e)
48:          {
49:              //
50:              // CODEGEN: This call is required by the ASP.NET Web Form
➥Designer.
51:              //
52:              InitializeComponent();
53:          }
54:
55:          #region Web Form Designer generated code
56:          ///    Required method for Designer support - do not modify
57:          ///     the contents of this method with the code editor.
58:          /// </summary>
59:          private void InitializeComponent()
60:          {
61:              this.Load += new System.EventHandler(this.Page_Load);
62:
63:          }
64:          #endregion
65:      }
66: }
```

The HeaderControl code is short and sweet. Two properties are defined—Text and ImageUrl. These properties can be manipulated within another ascx control or aspx page. In effect, our HeaderControl will appear just as if it were a part of ASP.NET. Notice that the ImageCtrl and HeaderText variables match their corresponding markup counterparts within HeaderPagelet.ascx. Again, this is necessary because ASP.NET will generate binding code the first time the page is accessed.

Any UserControl derived class can respond to ASP.NET events just as aspx pages can. When the EmployeeViewPagelet is developed, we'll see this in action.

To test the HeaderControl, add a new Web Form to the project with the name default.aspx. IIS looks for a starting page; in the case of ASP.NET, default.aspx fits the bill. Of course, you'll need to change the name of the class from default to MainPage because default is a C# keyword. Listing 4.3.3 contains the HTML code for the default.aspx file.

LISTING 4.3.3 default.aspx

```
1: <%@ Register   TagPrefix="EmployeeBrowser"
2:                TagName="HeaderControl"
```

LISTING 4.3.3 Continued

```
 3:                      Src="Pagelets/HeaderPagelet.ascx" %>
 4:
 5: <%@ Page language="c#" Codebehind="default.aspx.cs"
 6:                       AutoEventWireup="false"
 7:                       Inherits="EmployeeBrowser.MainPage" %>
 8:
 9: <!DOCTYPE HTML PUBLIC "-//W3C//DTD HTML 4.0 Transitional//EN" >
10: <HTML>
11:     <HEAD>
12:         <meta name="GENERATOR" Content="Microsoft Visual Studio 7.0">
13:         <meta name="CODE_LANGUAGE" Content="C#">
14:         <meta name="vs_defaultClientScript" content="JavaScript
➥(ECMAScript)">
15:         <meta name="vs_targetSchema"
➥content="http://schemas.microsoft.com/intellisense/ie5">
16:     </HEAD>
17:     <body MS_POSITIONING="GridLayout">
18:         <form id="Form1" method="post" runat="server">
19:             <!--
20:                 Show off the newly created header control
21:             -->
22:             <EmployeeBrowser:HeaderControl runat="server"
23:                                         ImageUrl="~/images/logo.jpg"
24:                                         Text="Employee Browser" />
25:         </form>
26:     </body>
27: </HTML>
```

Line 1 introduces the concept of registering a tag. The HeaderControl can be given any TagPrefix and TagName you wish. My only suggestion would be to keep it meaningful. Finally, line 22 is the declaration of the HeaderControl. Notice that the TagPrefix:TagName combination is used to identify an instance of the header control. Doesn't this syntax look familiar—somewhat similar to asp:label or asp:image? Yes, asp is the TagPrefix and label or image is the TagName.

EmployeeViewPagelet: A Different Approach

Instead of directly manipulating ASP controls with the CodeBehind source, the EmployeeViewPagelet will make use of server-side processing to set the various properties of the elements contained within it. Figure 4.3.3 shows what the finished EmployeeViewPagelet will look like.

FIGURE 4.3.3

`EmployeeViewPagelet` *control.*

The `EmployeeViewPagelet` control will be used to display an Employee's ID, name, photo, and an Edit button that will be tied to an Edit page. The HTML and ASP.NET markup is fairly simple, but there is a subtle difference between this control's implementation and that of the `HeaderControl`. Listing 4.3.4 shows the HTML for the `EmployeeViewPagelet`.

LISTING 4.3.4   EmployeeViewPagelet.ascx

```
 1: <%@ Control Language="c#"
 2:             AutoEventWireup="false"
 3:             Codebehind="EmployeeViewPagelet.ascx.cs"
 4:             Inherits="EmployeeBrowser.Pagelets.EmployeeViewPagelet"%>
 5:
 6: <asp:Table id="EmpViewTable"
 7:             runat="server"
 8:             BackColor="LightGray"
 9:             BorderColor="Purple"
10:             BorderStyle="Ridge"
11:             BorderWidth="2px"
12:             Height="100px"
13:             Width="25%">
14:
15:   <asp:TableRow>
16:     <asp:TableCell BorderStyle="Ridge"
17:                    BorderWidth="2px"
18:                    VerticalAlign="Middle"
19:                    BackColor="Black"
20:                    HorizontalAlign="Center"
21:                    BorderColor="Gray"
22:                    ID="EmpPicCell">
23:
24:       <asp:Image runat="server"
25:                  ImageUrl='<%# "~/images/employees/" +
➥ DataBinder.Eval( this, "ImageName" ) %>' ID="Image1"/>
26:
27:         </asp:TableCell>
28:           <asp:TableCell BorderStyle="Solid"
```

LISTING 4.3.4 Continued

```
29:                         BorderWidth="2px"
30:                         BorderColor="Red"
31:                         ID="EmpDataCell">
32:
33:          <asp:Table id="EmpDataTbl"
34:                       runat="server"
35:                       width="100%">
36:
37:            <asp:TableRow>
38:              <asp:TableCell VerticalAlign="Middle"
39:                             HorizontalAligh="Center"
40:                             style="FONT-WEIGHT: bold;
➥FONT-SIZE: medium; COLOR: purple"
41:                             BorderSytle="Ridge" BorderWidth="2px"
➥Text="Employee ID" />
42:
43:              <asp:TableCell VerticalAlign="Middle"
44:                             HorizontalAligh="Center"
45:                             style="FONT-WEIGHT: bold;
➥FONT-SIZE: medium; COLOR: purple"
46:                             BorderSytle="Ridge" BorderWidth="2px">
47:                <%# DataBinder.Eval( this, "EmployeeId" ) %>
48:              </asp:TableCell>
49:            </asp:TableRow>
50:
51:            <asp:TableRow>
52:              <asp:TableCell VerticalAlign="Middle"
53:                             HorizontalAligh="Center"
54:                             style="FONT-WEIGHT: bold;
➥FONT-SIZE: medium; COLOR: purple"
55:                             BorderSytle="Ridge" BorderWidth="2px"
➥Text="Employee Name" />
56:
57:              <asp:TableCell VerticalAlign="Middle"
58:                             HorizontalAligh="Center"
59:                             style="FONT-WEIGHT: bold;
➥FONT-SIZE: medium; COLOR: purple"
60:                             BorderSytle="Ridge" BorderWidth="2px">
61:                <%# DataBinder.Eval( this, "FullName" ) %>
62:              </asp:TableCell>
63:
64:            </asp:TableRow>
65:            <asp:TableRow>
66:              <asp:TableCell />
```

LISTING 4.3.4   Continued

```
67:                  <asp:TableCell HorizontalAlign="Right">
68:                    <asp:Button id="btnEdit"
69:                                runat="server"
70:                                onclick="OnEdit_Click"
71:                                Text="Edit"
72:                                CommandArgument=
➡'<%# DataBinder.Eval( this, "EmployeeId" ) %>' />
73:                  </asp:TableCell>
74:               </asp:TableRow>
75:            </asp:Table>
76:          </asp:TableCell>
77:       </asp:TableRow>
78: </asp:Table>
```

The only lines of real interest here are lines 25, 47, 61 and 72. Notice `<%# DataBinder.Eval( this, "EmployeeId" %>` on line 47. This directive is similar to a script block that is denoted with `<% script %>`. However, this little block causes data-binding between a property `EmployeeId` as defined within the `EmployeeView.ascx.cs`. Rather than having to manipulate every aspect of a control, this type of data-binding can be used. The `EmployeeView` class defines several properties that can be bound to asp elements. During the loading of the page containing the `EmployeeViewPagelet` control, all data binding directives will be evaluated. This technique allows for easier development because it is not necessary to do all of the grunt work yourself.

One of the most interesting aspects of Listing 4.3.4 is found on line 72:

```
72: <asp:Button onclick="OnEdit_Click" runat="Server"
➡Text="Edit"
➡commandargument="<%# DataBinder.Eval( this, "EmployeeId" ) %>"
```

Here, an `asp:Button` is declared and the `onclick` event is tied to `OnEdit_Click` method. Whenever a server-side control is activated, a PostBack event is sent to the server along with state information that is carried in hidden fields on the form. An `asp:Button` has a property known as `commandargument` that can be used to supply additional information, such as the context of how the button is being used. In this case, `EmployeeId` is being used as the `commandargument`. This will make sense in just a minute. Listing 4.3.5 contains the code for the `EmployeeViewPagelet` in the form of a `CodeBehind` page named `EmployeeView.cs`.

LISTING 4.3.5   `EmployeeViewPagelet.ascx.cs`

```
1: namespace EmployeeBrowser.Pagelets
2: {
3:     using System;
```

LISTING 4.3.5 Continued

```
4:      using System.Data;
5:      using System.Drawing;
6:      using System.Web;
7:      using System.Web.UI.WebControls;
8:      using System.Web.UI.HtmlControls;
9:
10:     /// <summary>
11:     ///     Summary description for EmployeeViewPagelet.
12:     /// </summary>
13:     public abstract class EmployeeViewPagelet : System.Web.UI.UserControl
14:     {
15:         protected System.Web.UI.WebControls.Button    btnEdit;
16:
17:         private string        employeeId;
18:         private string    firstName;
19:         private string        lastName;
20:         protected System.Web.UI.WebControls.Table EmpViewTable;
21:         private Guid      pictureId;
22:
23:
24:         public string EmployeeId
25:         {
26:             get
27:             {
28:                 return employeeId;
29:             }
30:             set
31:             {
32:                 employeeId = value;
33:             }
34:         }
35:
36:         public string FirstName
37:         {
38:             get
39:             {
40:                 return firstName;
41:             }
42:             set
43:             {
44:                 firstName = value;
45:             }
46:         }
47:
48:         public string LastName
```

LISTING 4.3.5   Continued

```
49:          {
50:              get
51:              {
52:                  return lastName;
53:              }
54:              set
55:              {
56:                  lastName = value;
57:              }
58:          }
59:
60:      public string FullName
61:          {
62:              get
63:              {
64:                  return string.Format("{0}, {1}", lastName, firstName );
65:              }
66:          }
67:
68:       public Guid PictureId
69:          {
70:              get
71:              {
72:                  return pictureId;
73:              }
74:              set
75:              {
76:                  pictureId = new Guid( value.ToString( ) );
77:              }
78:          }
79:
80:      public string ImageName
81:          {
82:              get
83:              {
84:                  return string.Format("{0}.jpg", pictureId.ToString( ) );
85:              }
86:          }
87:
88:          /// <summary>
89:          public EmployeeViewPagelet()
90:          {
91:              this.Init += new System.EventHandler(Page_Init);
92:          }
93:
```

LISTING 4.3.5 Continued

```
94:         private void Page_Load(object sender, System.EventArgs e)
95:         {
96:          // Put user code to initialize the page here
97:         }
98:
99:         private void Page_Init(object sender, EventArgs e)
100:        {
101:            //
102:            // CODEGEN: This call is required by the ASP.NET
➡ Web Form Designer.
103:            //
104:              InitializeComponent();
105:          }
106:
107:          /// <summary>
108:          /// Click Event handler for Edit Button.  THis method
➡redirects to an editing page passing
109:          /// the EmployeeId as an URL argument to the page
110:          /// </summary>
111:          /// <param name="sender"></param>
112:          /// <param name="e"></param>
113:          protected void OnEdit_Click( object sender, EventArgs e )
114:          {
115:              Response.Redirect(
116:                      string.Format( "~/EmployeeEdit.aspx?EmpId={0}",
117:                                  btnEdit.CommandArgument )
118:                                );
119:          }
120:
121:          #region Web Form Designer generated code
122:          /// Required method for Designer support - do not modify
123:          /// the contents of this method with the code editor.
124:          /// </summary>
125:          private void InitializeComponent()
126:          {
127:              this.Load += new System.EventHandler(this.Page_Load);
128:
129:          }
130:          #endregion
131:      }
132: }
```

The EmployeeViewPagelet class is really just a collection of various properties and the event handler for the click event of the asp:Button. When the click event is raised, the EmployeeId is obtained from the `CommandArgument` property. Next, the `Response.Redirect` method is used to transfer to an Edit page and the `EmployeeId` is passed in typical HTTP GET fashion.

So far, two controls have been created. Each control uses a different aspect of ASP.NET to implement the required functionality.

ASPX Pages

Now that there exists two `UserControls`, it is time to create some aspx pages to host those controls. The first page to implement is the `EmployeeEdit` page. This allows the `EmployeeViewPaglet` control to navigate to an edit page. The edit page should allow for changes to the name, department, and to upload a photograph. ASP.NET makes client-side file transfer a snap.

EmployeeEdit

One of the requirements for the `EmployeeBrowser` site was the ability to edit employee information and the associated photograph. Rather than build another `UserControl`, this functionality will be implemented within the context of an aspx page. The only reason for doing so is to poke around ASP.NET. The `EmployeeEdit` page would be a good candidate for a `UserControl`; I'll leave that to you.

There's no real magic to the layout, so the markup will be omitted from the text. Only new or interesting markup will be shown. The full code is contained on the CD-ROM included with this book, and you should refer to it if needed. Figure 4.3.4 shows the `EmployeeEdit` page with a record ready to edit.

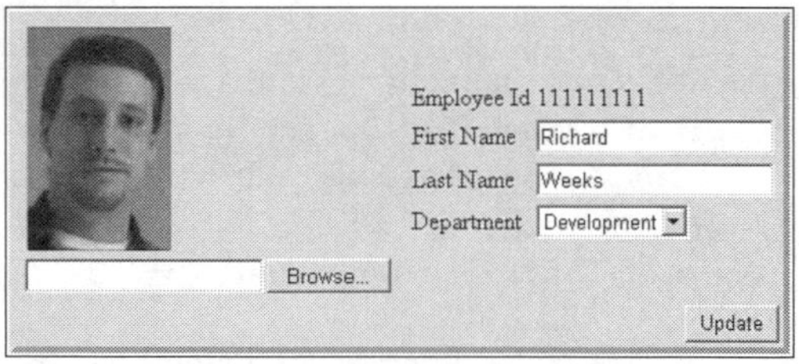

FIGURE 4.3.4
`EmployeeEdit` *page.*

The first control to look at is the drop-down list used to hold the names of the various departments. In standard HTML, it was necessary to hard-code the values for list boxes or drop-down menus. You could use script woven in to produce some type of data dependant list, but this fails in comparison to ASP.NET and databinding. Listing 4.3.6 shows the declaration for an `asp:dropdownlist` which will be bound to a variable within the `EmployeeEdit.cs` source code.

LISTING 4.3.6 dropdownlist Snipit from EmployeEdit.aspx

```
1: <tr>
2:    <td>Department</td>
3:    <td>
4:        <asp:dropdownlist runat="Server" id="Departments" />
5:    </td>
6: </tr>
```

Listing 4.3.6 comes from the EmployeeEdit.aspx page. Although there seems to be nothing worth noting, don't overlook the fact that the dropdownlist does not define any listitems. Instead of declaring the listitems within the aspx page, each ASP.NET WebControl supports databinding similar to the Windows Forms controls. In the code supporting the EmployeeEdit aspx page, there will exist the code to set up the databinding for the control. As with any data-binding source, the container must implement GetEnumerator() or the IEnumerable interface. The departments will be held within an array list, so the general code looks something like the following:

```
ArrayList Depts = new ArrayList( );
FillDepts( Depts );
Departments.DataSource = Depts;
Departments.DataBind( );
```

Setting a databound control really doesn't require a lot of effort on the developer's part. Of course, like any WebControl, pragmatic access is always an option. If the default databinding doesn't fit the bill, there is the ability to write C# code and take full control.

The next control of interest is the input control that has its type set to file. This allows for the user to browse for a new photograph and upload it to the Web server.

```
<input type="file" id="EmpImageFile" name="EmpImageFile" runat="server">
```

Wait, this is not an asp:* type control, so how can it be accessed behind the scenes? It just so happens that ASP.NET supports binding of HTML controls just like WebControls. When the input tag is specified with type="file", the designer will create a variable of the following type:

```
System.Web.UI.HtmlControls.HtmlInputFile
```

This allows the code page to again access the HTML element. Listing 4.3.7 shows the C# code for EmployeeEdit.aspx.cs.

4.3

WEBFORMS

LISTING 4.3.7 EmployeeEdit.aspx.cs

```
1: using System;
2: using System.Collections;
```

LISTING 4.3.7   Continued

```
 3: using System.ComponentModel;
 4: using System.Data;
 5: using System.Data.SqlClient;
 6: using System.Drawing;
 7: using System.Web;
 8: using System.Web.SessionState;
 9: using System.Web.UI;
10: using System.Web.UI.WebControls;
11: using System.Web.UI.HtmlControls;
12:
13: using Stingray.Data;
14:
15: namespace EmployeeBrowser
16: {
17:     /// <summary>
18:     /// Summary description for EmployeeEdit.
19:     /// </summary>
20:     public class EmployeeEdit : System.Web.UI.Page
21:     {
22:         protected System.Web.UI.WebControls.Image EmployeeImage;
23:         protected System.Web.UI.WebControls.Label EmployeeId;
24:         protected System.Web.UI.WebControls.TextBox FirstName;
25:         protected System.Web.UI.WebControls.TextBox LastName;
26:         protected System.Web.UI.WebControls.DropDownList Departments;
27:         protected System.Web.UI.WebControls.Button btnUpdate;
28:         protected System.Web.UI.HtmlControls.HtmlInputFile EmpImageFile;
29:
30:         public EmployeeEdit()
31:         {
32:             Page.Init += new System.EventHandler(Page_Init);
33:         }
34:
35:         private void Page_Load(object sender, System.EventArgs e)
36:         {
37:             // Put user code to initialize the page here
38:
39:             //Enable Data binding
40:             DataBind( );
41:
42:             if( !IsPostBack )
43:                 PopulateForm( );
44:             else
45:                 UpdateEmployee( );
46:         }
47:
```

LISTING 4.3.7 Continued

```
48:          private void PopulateForm( )
49:          {
50:
51:              string EmpId = this.Request.QueryString["EmpId"].ToString( );
52:              SqlConnection dbCon = DBAccess.AcquireConnection( );
53:              SqlDataAdapter cmd = new SqlDataAdapter(string.Format(
➡"SELECT * FROM EMPLOYEE WHERE EMP_ID = {0}", EmpId),dbCon);
54:              DataSet dsResult = new DataSet( );
55:              Employee emp = new Employee( );
56:
57:              cmd.Fill( dsResult, "EMPLOYEE" );
58:              if( dsResult.Tables["EMPLOYEE"] != null)
59:                  emp.FromDataRow( dsResult.Tables["EMPLOYEE"].Rows[0] );
60:
61:              //Set the values for stuff
62:              this.EmployeeId.Text = emp.Id;
63:              this.FirstName.Text = emp.FirstName;
64:              this.LastName.Text  = emp.LastName;
65:              this.EmployeeImage.ImageUrl =
66:              string.Format("~/images/employees/{0}.jpg",
➡emp.PictureId.ToString( ));
67:
68:              //Populate the Department list
69:              cmd.SelectCommand.CommandText = "SELECT * FROM DEPARTMENT";
70:              cmd.Fill( dsResult, "DEPARTMENT" );
71:              Hashtable ht = new Hashtable( );
72:
73:              foreach( DataRow row in dsResult.Tables["DEPARTMENT"].Rows)
74:              {
75:                  int nValue = (int)row["DEPT_ID"];
76:                  string Name = (string)row["NAME"];
77:                  ht.Add( Name, nValue );
78:                  this.Departments.Items.Add( Name );
79:              }
80:
81:              this.Session["DEPT_MAPPING"] = ht;
82:              this.Session["CACHE:EMP"] = emp;            //save the employee
83:
84:          }
85:
86:          private void UpdateEmployee( )
87:          {
88:
89:              Employee emp = (Employee)Session["CACHE:EMP"];
90:
```

LISTING 4.3.7   Continued

```
91:                   emp.FirstName = this.FirstName.Text;
92:                   emp.LastName = this.LastName.Text;
93:
94:
95:               //get new department
96:               Hashtable ht = (Hashtable)Session["DEPT_MAPPING"];
97:               int DeptId = (int)ht[ this.Departments.SelectedItem.Text ];
98:               emp.DeptId = DeptId;
99:
100:
101:
102:              //Get the Photo
103:              if( this.EmpImageFile.PostedFile != null &&
104:                  this.EmpImageFile.PostedFile.FileName.Length > 0 )
105:              {
106:
107:                  //Remove the Old Photo
108:                  string strFileName =
109:                              string.Format(
110:          "C:/Inetpub/wwwroot/EmployeeBrowser/images/employees/{0}.jpg",
111:          emp.PictureId.ToString( )
112:                                  );
113:
114:                  System.IO.File.Delete( strFileName );
115:
116:                  emp.PictureId =  System.Guid.NewGuid( );
117:                  strFileName =
118:                       string.Format(
119:          "C:/Inetpub/wwwroot/EmployeeBrowser/images/employees/{0}.jpg",
120:          emp.PictureId.ToString( )
121:                                  );
122:
123:                      this.EmpImageFile.PostedFile.SaveAs( strFileName );
124:              }
125:
126:              //Update the Employee
127:              DBAccess.Save( DBAccess.AcquireConnection( ), emp );
128:
129:              string strUrl =
130:                      string.Format(
131:          "EmployeeListing.aspx?DeptId={0}&FirstName={1}&LastName={2}",
132:                      emp.DeptId,emp.FirstName,emp.LastName
133:                          );
134:
135:              Response.Redirect( strUrl );
```

LISTING 4.3.7 Continued

```
136:
137:            }
138:
139:            private void Page_Init(object sender, EventArgs e)
140:            {
141:                //
142:                // CODEGEN: This call is required by the ASP.NET
➥Web Form Designer.
143:                //
144:                InitializeComponent();
145:            }
146:
147:            #region Web Form Designer generated code
148:            /// <summary>
149:            /// Required method for Designer support - do not modify
150:            /// the contents of this method with the code editor.
151:            /// </summary>
152:            private void InitializeComponent()
153:            {
154:                this.Load += new System.EventHandler(this.Page_Load);
155:
156:            }
157:            #endregion
158:    }
159: }
```

The EmployeeEdit page was designed to accept a query string containing the Employee ID as EmpId; recall the EmployeeViewPagelet and the code contained within the OnEdit_Click method.

The following lines are from Listing 4.3.5:

```
113: protected void OnEdit_Click( object sender, EventArgs e )
114: {
115:     Response.Redirect(
116:         string.Format( "~/EmployeeEdit.aspx?EmpId={0}",
117:                        btnEdit.CommandArgument )
118:         );
119: }
```

When the Edit button raises a click event, the CommandArgument property contains the Employee ID. This Employee ID is used to create an HTTP GET request. Line 115 shows the syntax for passing parameters from one page to another.

The `PopulateForm` method, found in Listing 4.3.7, accesses the `QueryString` collection found in the `Request` object. I've omitted error checking and redirection to an error page, but you get the idea. The Employee ID contains all the state information necessary to populate the controls found within the page.

To hold on to information, such as state information or objects, there are two options—`Session` or `Cache`. The `EmployeeEdit` page makes use of the session to store any necessary data. A `Session` can survive IIS crashes and work process restarts, but the `Cache` does not. When deciding where information should be stored, you'll need to examine the uses of the data and the necessity of ensuring that the data exists.

The `Session` and `Cache` objects both contain a hash table that maps a key to the object you want to store. The `EmployeeEdit` page stores both a hash table and the employee within the `Session`.

When the Update button raises a click event, the page is reloaded with `IsPostBack` set to `true`. `Page_Load` tests for this condition and calls `UpdateEmployee` rather than `PopulateForm`.

EmployeeListing

The `EmployeeBrowser` Web application is starting to come together. With the basic `HeaderContol`, `EmployeeView` control, and the `EmployeeEdit` page complete, it's time to create a Listings page. The Listings page will host one or more `EmployeeView` controls and allow for paging back and forth through the various employees.

Figure 4.3.5 shows the basic listing control with 2 rows per screen. Also notice the Next >> button at the bottom of the form. When paging takes place, the `EmployeeListing.aspx` will determine if there are previous records, and display a << Prev button when appropriate, as shown in Figure 4.3.5. The same is true for the Next >> button. If there are additional records, it will be visible; if not, the Next >> button will be hidden.

As you can see, I didn't enforce any type of sizing constraint on the images. The simplest way, of course, is to specify the allowed image size and reject any image that does not fit the sizing criteria.

So how does the `EmployeeListing` page display the `EmployeeViewPagelets`? Easy. The secret is to make use of the `asp:repeater` control. Remember the repeater control we discussed? The `EmployeeListing` makes use of the repeater control to display the appropriate number of employees per page. Listing 4.3.8 shows the binding for the `EmployeeView` control.

FIGURE 4.3.5

EmployeeListing *with two rows.*

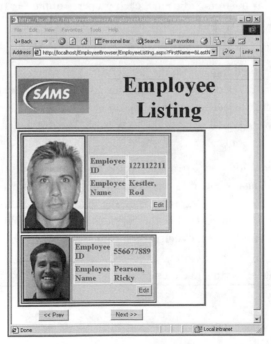

4.3

WEBFORMS

FIGURE 4.3.6

EmployeeListing *with two rows and the Prev button enabled.*

LISTING 4.3.8   Snippet from `EmployeeListing.aspx`

```
 1: <asp:repeater id="EmployeeRepeater" runat="server">
 2:   <ItemTemplate>
 3:     <tr>
 4:       <td>
 5:         <EmployeeBrowser:EmployeeViewControl runat="server"
 6:           EmployeeId='<%# DataBinder.Eval(
➡Container.DataItem, "Id" )  %>'
 7:           FirstName='<%# DataBinder.Eval(
➡Container.DataItem, "FirstName" )  %>'
 8:           LastName='<%# DataBinder.Eval(
➡Container.DataItem, "LastName" )  %>'
 9:           PictureId='<%# DataBinder.Eval(
➡Container.DataItem,"PictureId" ) %>'>
10:         </EmployeeBrowser:EmployeeViewControl>
11:       </td>
12:     </tr>
13:   </ItemTemplate>
14: </asp:repeater>
```

The `EmployeeListing` makes use of `WebControl` databinding to set the various properties of the `EmployeeViewPagelet` control. Notice that each property of the `EmployeeViewPagelet` control is assigned its value through the use of

```
DataBinder.Eval( Container.DataItem, X )
```

where X is the name of a field found with the datasource. The source code behind the page creates an `ArrayList` of `Employee` objects and binds that list to the repeater control, `EmployeeRepeater`. Using this technique, binding property values is a breeze! In fact, the snippet in Listing 4.3.8 is the only real meat of the aspx page. The rest is just HTML markup and the inclusion of the `HeaderControl`.

As with every aspx page so far, the `EmployeeListing` page implements the paging logic in a C# source file. After the data is bound to the repeater control, the current index is pushed on a stack and that stack is saved in the `Session`. When the *Next* or *Prev* buttons are pressed, the index is either calculated for the next set or the pervious index is popped of the stack. Listing 4.3.9 presents the source for the `EmployeeListing` page.

LISTING 4.3.9   `EmployeeListing.aspx.cs`

```
1: using System;
2: using System.Collections;
3: using System.ComponentModel;
4: using System.Data;
```

LISTING 4.3.9 Continued

```
 5: using System.Data.SqlClient;
 6: using System.Drawing;
 7: using System.Web;
 8: using System.Web.SessionState;
 9: using System.Web.UI;
10: using System.Web.UI.WebControls;
11: using System.Web.UI.HtmlControls;
12:
13: using Stingray.Data;
14:
15: namespace EmployeeBrowser
16: {
17:
18:     class ViewerState
19:     {
20:         public static string VIEW_STATE_SESSION_KEY =
➥"EMPLOYEE_VIEWER_STATE";
21:         public DataSet      m_EmployeeCache;
22:         public int          m_RowCount = 0;
23:         public int          m_MaxPerPage = 5;
24:         public int          m_CurrentIndex = 0;
25:         public Stack        m_IdxStack = new Stack( );
26:     }
27:
28:     /// <summary>
29:     /// Summary description for EmployeeListing.
30:     /// </summary>
31:     public class EmployeeListing : System.Web.UI.Page
32:     {
33:         protected System.Web.UI.WebControls.Button    btnNext;
34:         protected System.Web.UI.WebControls.Button    btnPrev;
35:         protected System.Web.UI.WebControls.Repeater  EmployeeRepeater;
36:         private ArrayList                             m_EmployeeList;
37:         private ViewerState                           m_ViewerState;
38:
39:
40:
41:         public EmployeeListing()
42:         {
43:             Page.Init += new System.EventHandler(Page_Init);
44:         }
45:
46:         private void Page_Load(object sender, System.EventArgs e)
47:         {
```

LISTING 4.3.9   Continued

```
48:              if (!IsPostBack)
49:              {
50:
51:                  int     DeptId = 0;
52:                  string  FirstName;
53:                  string  LastName;
54:
55:
56:                  m_ViewerState = new ViewerState( );
57:                  this.Session.Add(ViewerState.VIEW_STATE_SESSION_KEY
➥,m_ViewerState);
58:
59:                  GetParams( out FirstName, out LastName, ref DeptId,
➥ ref m_ViewerState.m_MaxPerPage );
60:
61:                  LoadDataSet( FirstName, LastName, DeptId );
62:
63:
64:                  //save current index
65:                  m_ViewerState.m_IdxStack.Push( 0 );
66:                  int Index = this.CalcNextIndex( );
67:                  m_ViewerState.m_CurrentIndex = Index;
68:                  this.DisplayData( 0, m_ViewerState.m_CurrentIndex );
69:                  UpdateNavigationButtons( );
70:
71:              } else {
72:
73:                  m_ViewerState = (ViewerState)this.Session[
➥ViewerState.VIEW_STATE_SESSION_KEY];
74:              }
75:
76:          }
77:
78:          private void Page_Init(object sender, EventArgs e)
79:          {
80:              //
81:              // CODEGEN: This call is required by the ASP.NET Web
➥Form Designer.
82:              //
83:              InitializeComponent();
84:          }
85:
86:          protected void GetParams(out string FirstName,
➥out string LastName, ref int DeptId, ref int MaxPerPage )
```

LISTING 4.3.9   Continued

```
 87:              {
 88:                  DeptId     = this.Request.QueryString["DeptId"] == null ?
 89:                              -1 : Int32.Parse(this.Request.QueryString[
➥"DeptId"].ToString( ));
 90:
 91:                  FirstName  = this.Request.QueryString["FirstName"] == null ?
 92:                              "" : this.Request.QueryString["
➥FirstName"].ToString();
 93:
 94:                  LastName   = this.Request.QueryString["LastName"] == null ?
 95:                              "" : this.Request.QueryString["
➥LastName"].ToString();
 96:
 97:                  MaxPerPage = this.Request.QueryString["MaxPerPage"] == null ?
 98:                              5 : Int32.Parse(this.Request.QueryString["
➥MaxPerPage"].ToString( ));
 99:              }
100:
101:          protected void LoadDataSet(string FName, string LName, int DeptId
)
102:              {
103:
104:              if( DeptId != -1 )
105:              {
106:                  m_ViewerState.m_EmployeeCache = Search.Find(
➥DBAccess.AcquireConnection( ), DeptId, FName, LName);
107:              } else {
108:                  m_ViewerState.m_EmployeeCache = Search.Find(
➥DBAccess.AcquireConnection( ), FName, LName);
109:              }
110:
111:              m_ViewerState.m_RowCount = m_ViewerState.
➥m_EmployeeCache.Tables["EMPLOYEE"].Rows.Count;
112:              }
113:
114:
115:          protected void DisplayData( int StartIndex, int StopIndex )
116:              {
117:
118:              m_EmployeeList = new ArrayList( );
119:
120:              for(int i = StartIndex; i < StopIndex; i++)
121:              {
122:                  Employee e = new Employee( );
```

LISTING 4.3.9   Continued

```
123:                  e.FromDataRow( m_ViewerState.m_EmployeeCache.
➥Tables["EMPLOYEE"].Rows[i] );
124:                  m_EmployeeList.Add( e );
125:              }
126:
127:          //Bind the data
128:          EmployeeRepeater.DataSource= m_EmployeeList;
129:          EmployeeRepeater.DataBind( );
130:
131:
132:      }
133:
134:      protected void OnNext_Click( object sender, EventArgs e )
135:      {
136:          //save current index
137:          int nLast =  m_ViewerState.m_CurrentIndex;
138:          m_ViewerState.m_IdxStack.Push( nLast);
139:          m_ViewerState.m_CurrentIndex = CalcNextIndex( );
140:          DisplayData( nLast, m_ViewerState.m_CurrentIndex );
141:          UpdateNavigationButtons( );
142:
143:      }
144:
145:      protected void OnPrev_Click( object sender, EventArgs e )
146:      {
147:          int nStop  = (int)m_ViewerState.m_IdxStack.Pop( );
148:          int nStart = (int)m_ViewerState.m_IdxStack.Peek( );
149:          DisplayData( nStart, nStop );
150:          m_ViewerState.m_CurrentIndex = nStop;
151:          UpdateNavigationButtons( );
152:      }
153:
154:      protected int CalcNextIndex( )
155:      {
156:          return (m_ViewerState.m_CurrentIndex +
➥m_ViewerState.m_MaxPerPage) > m_ViewerState.m_RowCount
157:                  ? m_ViewerState.m_RowCount :
➥(m_ViewerState.m_CurrentIndex + m_ViewerState.m_MaxPerPage);
158:
159:      }
160:
161:      protected void UpdateNavigationButtons( )
162:      {
163:          this.btnNext.Visible = m_ViewerState.m_CurrentIndex
➥< m_ViewerState.m_RowCount;
```

LISTING 4.3.9   Continued

```
164:              this.btnPrev.Visible =
➥(int)m_ViewerState.m_IdxStack.Peek( ) != 0;
165:          }
166:
167:
168:
169:          #region Web Form Designer generated code
170:          /// <summary>
171:          /// Required method for Designer support - do not modify
172:          /// the contents of this method with the code editor.
173:          /// </summary>
174:          private void InitializeComponent()
175:          {
176:              this.Load += new System.EventHandler(this.Page_Load);
177:          }
178:          #endregion
179:      }
180: }
```

To see how data binding is set up, look at the DisplayData method on line 115. An ArrayList is constructed and Employee objects are added based on the StartIndex and StopIndex arguments to the method. After the ArrayList has been filled as specified, the EmployeeRepeater control is bound to the ArrayList. These bindings are evaluated using the <%# DataBinder.Eval(Container.DataItem, X) %> embedded binding statements.

To maintain view state information, a small ViewerState class is created. The ViewerState maintains a DataSet corresponding to the parameters passed into the page. The ViewerState also maintains the current index and a stack object that holds the previous indexes. This stack is used to facilitate paging to previous pages. The remainder of the code for EmployeeListing consists of data loading, index calculation, and the onclick handlers for the bntNext and btnPrev WebControl buttons.

The Search Page: Where It All Begins

With the internals of the EmployeeBrowser Web application in place, an entry point into the application is needed. A simple search page will fit the bill and allow the user to select the department, first/last name, and the number of listings per page. These choices will then be passed as parameters to the EmployeeListing aspx page for processing.

The Search page shown in Figure 4.3.7 will be used to kick off the EmployeeBrowser Web application.

4.3

WEBFORMS

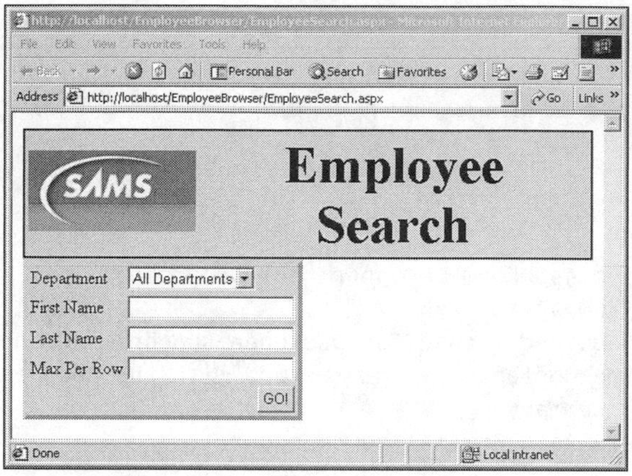

FIGURE 4.3.7
Search page.

This is the smallest of all the examples shown so far. Basically, all that is needed is to allow the user to select a department, a first/last name, and the number of listings per page. Again, rather than creating a UserControl-derived pagelet, a small aspx page will be used to gather the input and create the request URL for the EmployeeListing page. Listing 4.3.10 contains the HTML source for the EmployeeSearch.aspx page.

LISTING 4.3.10 EmployeeSearch.aspx

```
 1: <%@ Register TagPrefix="EmployeeBrowser" TagName="HeaderControl"
➥Src="~/Pagelets/HeaderPagelet.ascx" %>
 2: <%@ Page language="c#" Codebehind="EmployeeSearch.aspx.cs"
➥AutoEventWireup="false" Inherits="EmployeeBrowser.EmployeeSearch" %>
 3: <!DOCTYPE HTML PUBLIC "-//W3C//DTD HTML 4.0 Transitional//EN" >
 4: <HTML>
 5:     <HEAD>
 6:         <meta name="GENERATOR" Content="Microsoft Visual Studio 7.0">
 7:         <meta name="CODE_LANGUAGE" Content="C#">
 8:         <meta name="vs_defaultClientScript"
➥content="JavaScript (ECMAScript)">
 9:         <meta name="vs_targetSchema"
➥content="http://schemas.microsoft.com/intellisense/ie5">
10:     </HEAD>
11:     <body MS_POSITIONING="GridLayout">
12:         <form id="EmployeeSearch" method="post" runat="server">
13:
14:     <!--
15:             Insert the custom header control
16:         -->
```

LISTING 4.3.10   Continued

```
17:           <EmployeeBrowser:HeaderControl runat="server"
➥Text="Employee Search" ImageUrl="~/images/logo.jpg"
➥ID="Headercontrol1" NAME="Headercontrol1" />
18:
19:     <!--
20:             Begin the Search Page Layout
21:         -->
22:         <table style="BORDER-TOP-STYLE: outset;
➥BORDER-RIGHT-STYLE: outset; BORDER-LEFT-STYLE: outset;
➥BACKGROUND-COLOR: lightgrey; BORDER-BOTTOM-STYLE: outset">
23:           <tbody>
24:            <tr>
25:             <td>Department</td>
26:              <td>
27:               <asp:dropdownlist id="Departments" runat="server" />
28:              </td>
29:            </tr>
30:
31:            <tr>
32:             <td>First Name</td>
33:              <td>
34:               <asp:textbox runat="server" id="FirstName" />
35:              </td>
36:            </tr>
37:
38:            <tr>
39:             <td>Last Name</td>
40:              <td>
41:               <asp:textbox runat="server" id="LastName" />
42:              </td>
43:            </tr>
44:
45:            <tr>
46:             <td>Max Per Row</td>
47:              <td>
48:               <asp:textbox runat="server" id="MaxPerRow" />
49:              </td>
50:            </tr>
51:
52:            <tr>
53:             <td> <!-- Left Blank to push button to second column --></td>
54:             <td align="right">
55:               <asp:button id="btnGO" onclick="OnSearch_Click" text="GO!"
➥runat="server" />
```

4.3

WEBFORMS

LISTING 4.3.10   Continued

```
56:              </td>
57:              </tr>
58:
59:           </tbody>
60:         </table>
61:         </form>
62:      </body>
63: </HTML>
```

As you can see, the markup is fairly simple. Notice the mixture of standard HTML and ASP.NET. This freedom allows the developer to use the best tool for the job. There is not always a need to require server-side controls, so standard HTML elements fit the bill. The advantage of ASP.NET server-side controls is the ability of the controls to down-level to the client browser.

The code for EmployeeSearch.cs (see Listing 4.3.11) employs many of the techniques of the previous pages developed so far. The Session object is used to hold some mapping information, the asp:dropdownbox makes use of data-binding, and when a PostBack is processed, the element data is retrieved to form the HTTP GET request to the EmployeeListing.aspx page.

LISTING 4.3.11   EmployeeSearch.cs

```
 1: using System;
 2: using System.Collections;
 3: using System.ComponentModel;
 4: using System.Data;
 5: using System.Data.SqlClient;
 6: using System.Drawing;
 7: using System.Web;
 8: using System.Web.SessionState;
 9: using System.Web.UI;
10: using System.Web.UI.WebControls;
11: using System.Web.UI.HtmlControls;
12:
13: using Stingray.Data;
14:
15: namespace EmployeeBrowser
16: {
17:     /// <summary>
18:     /// Summary description for EmployeeSearch.
19:     /// </summary>
```

LISTING 4.3.11   Continued

```
20:      public class EmployeeSearch : System.Web.UI.Page
21:      {
22:          protected System.Web.UI.WebControls.DropDownList Departments;
23:          protected System.Web.UI.WebControls.TextBox FirstName;
24:          protected System.Web.UI.WebControls.TextBox LastName;
25:          protected System.Web.UI.WebControls.TextBox MaxPerRow;
26:          protected System.Web.UI.WebControls.Button btnGO;
27:
28:          protected ArrayList      DepartmentList;
29:          protected Hashtable      htDeptMapping;
30:
31:
32:          public EmployeeSearch()
33:          {
34:              Page.Init += new System.EventHandler(Page_Init);
35:          }
36:
37:          private void Page_Load(object sender, System.EventArgs e)
38:          {
39:            if( !this.IsPostBack )
40:            {
41:                htDeptMapping = new Hashtable( );
42:                LoadData( );
43:
44:                this.Session.Add( "SEARCH_HT_MAPPING", htDeptMapping );
45:                Departments.DataSource = DepartmentList;
46:                Departments.DataBind( );
47:            }
48:            else
49:            {
50:                htDeptMapping = (Hashtable)this.Session["
➥SEARCH_HT_MAPPING"];
51:            }
52:
53:          }
54:
55:          private void Page_Init(object sender, EventArgs e)
56:          {
57:              //
58:              // CODEGEN: This call is required by the ASP.NET
➥Web Form Designer.
59:              //
60:              InitializeComponent();
61:          }
```

LISTING 4.3.11   Continued

```
62:
63:         protected void OnSearch_Click( object sender, EventArgs e )
64:         {
65:
66:             //Get the Selected params
67:             if(this.htDeptMapping == null)
68:             {
69:                 Response.Redirect( "EmployeeListing.aspx?MaxPerPage=5" );
70:             }
71:             else
72:             {
73:
74:                 int    DeptId    = (int)this.htDeptMapping[Departments.
➥SelectedItem.Text];
75:                 string FirstName = this.FirstName.Text;
76:                 string LastName  = this.LastName.Text;
77:
78:                 int iMaxPerRow   = 5;
79:
80:                 if( MaxPerRow.Text != "" )
81:                 {
82:                     iMaxPerRow = Int32.Parse(this.MaxPerRow.Text);
83:                 }
84:
85:
86:                 //build the request URL
87:                 string request;
88:
89:                 if( DeptId != 0)
90:                 {
91:                     object[] args = { DeptId, FirstName, LastName,
➥ iMaxPerRow };
92:                     request = string.Format("DeptId={0}&FirstName={1}&
➥LastName={2}&MaxPerPage={3}", args);
93:                 } else {
94:                     object[] args = { FirstName, LastName, iMaxPerRow };
95:                     request = string.Format("FirstName={0}&LastName={1}
➥&MaxPerPage={2}", args);
96:                 }
97:
98:                 Response.Redirect( string.Format("EmployeeListing.aspx?
➥{0}", request) );
99:             }
100:        }
101:
```

LISTING 4.3.11 Continued

```
102:        protected void LoadData( )
103:        {
104:
105:            SqlConnection dbCon = DBAccess.AcquireConnection( );
106:            SqlDataAdapter cmd = new SqlDataAdapter(
➥"SELECT * FROM DEPARTMENT", dbCon );
107:            DataSet dsResult = new DataSet( );
108:            cmd.Fill( dsResult, "DEPARTMENT" );
109:
110:            DepartmentList = new ArrayList( );
111:            DepartmentList.Add( "All Departments" );
112:            htDeptMapping.Add( "All Departments", 0 );
113:
114:            foreach( DataRow row in dsResult.Tables["DEPARTMENT"].Rows )
115:            {
116:                Department d = new Department( );
117:                d.FromDataRow( row );
118:                DepartmentList.Add( d.Name );
119:                htDeptMapping.Add( d.Name, d.Id );
120:            }
121:
122:            dbCon.Close( );
123:            dbCon.Dispose( );
124:            dsResult.Dispose( );
125:        }
126:
127:
128:        #region Web Form Designer generated code
129:        /// <summary>
130:        /// Required method for Designer support - do not modify
131:        /// the contents of this method with the code editor.
132:        /// </summary>
133:        private void InitializeComponent()
134:        {
135:            this.Load += new System.EventHandler(this.Page_Load);
136:
137:        }
138:        #endregion
139:    }
140: }
```

With the completion of the EmployeeSearch page, the EmployeeBrowser application is ready. Of course, some layout and design work would go a long way towards improving the overall appearance of the page but, because the focus is on the code, I'll leave the rest to you.

Summary

ASP.NET WebForms brings traditional Web development a breath of fresh air. WebForms allows for dynamic Web Applications and the powerful expressive code to power today's demanding applications. With over 45 ASP controls shipping with Visual Studio .NET, it's possible to build Web Applications with all the functionality end users have come to expect from a traditional desktop application.

The ability to create truly reusable controls will allow for increased developer productivity and richer experiences for the end user. ASP.NET finally brings Web-based application development to the forefront of application development.

WebServices

IN THIS CHAPTER

Accessing data with distributed applications has produced various technologies over the years. From general Remote Procedure Calls (RPC) mechanisms, such as XML-RPC, to full-blown distributed objects, such as CORBA and DCOM. The WebServices paradigm is based on the simple premise of extending the basic XML-RPC mechanism to allow for procedure calls over the Internet using open transport protocols such as HTTP over TCP/IP connections.

.NET supports WebServices invocations through HTTP POST, HTTP GET, and Simple Object Access Protocol (SOAP). Before the introduction of WebServices support in .NET, developing a WebService host, proxy, and client was a non-trivial task. Microsoft even released a SOAP Toolkit for Visual Studio 6 that allowed a developer to expose a COM object over the Internet. This Toolkit falls short of the support offered by .NET and C#. Developing a `WebService` requires little more than defining a public set of methods to expose to clients, along with the proper return types and applying simple `WebMethodAttributes` to those methods.

In the course of this chapter, a small `EchoService` will serve as the starting point to familiarize you with the concept of `WebServices` and eventually a WebService interface will be added to the `EmployeeBrowser` ASP `WebApplication`.

Echo Service

Building client/server applications generally seems to resemble the chicken and egg problem. You need a server to test the client and a client to test the server. An echo server will bounce back any information it receives to the client who sent the data. Echo servers allow for a client application to test its connection and ensure that the data being sent is correct. Implementing an `EchoService` using .NET `WebServices` will serve as a good starting point.

VS.NET supports creation of WebServices directly from the IDE. VS.NET will connect to the specified IIS server using FrontPage extensions to open a Web folder, just as with the `WebApplication` developed in the previous chapters. Figure 4.4.1 shows the new project dialog for creating a `WebService`.

WebServices, as created by VS.NET, consists of two files—an `asmx` file and a C# source file. However, only the `asmx` file is necessary because all the C# code can reside within the `asmx` file. However, this is not the approach that will be taken when developing the examples presented in this chapter. Listing 4.4.1 shows the C# code for the `EchoService` `WebService`. In addition, I've changed the name of the default class from `Service1` to `EchoServer` for clarity.

FIGURE 4.4.1
WebService VS.NET project.

LISTING 4.4.1   The `EchoService.asmx.cs` Source

```
 1: using System;
 2: using System.Collections;
 3: using System.ComponentModel;
 4: using System.Data;
 5: using System.Diagnostics;
 6: using System.Web;
 7: using System.Web.Services;
 8:
 9: namespace EchoService
10: {
11:     /// <summary>
12:     /// Summary description for EchoServer.
13:     /// </summary>
14:     public class EchoServer : System.Web.Services.WebService
15:     {
```

LISTING 4.4.1 Continued

```
16:        public EchoServer()
17:        {
18:            //CODEGEN: This call is required by the
➥ ASP.NET Web Services Designer
19:            InitializeComponent();
20:        }
21:
22:        #region Component Designer generated code
23:        /// <summary>
24:        /// Required method for Designer support - do not modify
25:        /// the contents of this method with the code editor.
26:        /// </summary>
27:        private void InitializeComponent()
28:        {
29:        }
30:        #endregion
31:
32:        /// <summary>
33:        /// Clean up any resources being used.
34:        /// </summary>
35:        protected override void Dispose( bool disposing )
36:        {
37:        }
38:
39:
40:        [WebMethod]
41:        public string Echo( string Message ) {
42:            return Message;
43:        }
44:
45:        // WEB SERVICE EXAMPLE
46:        // The HelloWorld() example service returns the string Hello World
47:        // To build, uncomment the following lines then save and
➥build the project
48:        // To test this web service, press F5
49:
50: //      [WebMethod]
51: //       public string HelloWorld()
52: //      {
53: //          return "Hello World";
54: //      }
55:    }
56: }
```

The `EchoService.asmx.cs` in Listing 4.4.1 lays out a basic WebService. The `EchoServer` class inherits from `System.Web.Services.WebService` base class. The `WebService` base class does not require the derived class to override or implement any methods; instead, the `WebService` base class merely provides the implementation necessary to support the method invocations.

The `EchoServer` class itself provides only a single method that is exposed to clients—Echo. Notice the attribute used on the method. This `[WebMethod]` attribute is used by the runtime to locate methods that the class exposes to clients. In the same way that the `DBAccess` class implemented for the `EmployeeBrowser` example, the runtime makes use of the Reflection API to locate a `WebMethod` and invoke it with the proper parameters.

For IIS to host the WebService, there needs to exist an `asmx` file in the virtual Web directory containing the `EchoService` WebService. This `asmx` file is used to wire-up the WebService code to the `.dll` and class providing the actual WebService. This basic wiring of the `asmx` file to the necessary C# code is shown in Listing 4.4.2.

Listing 4.4.2   EchoService.asmx

```
1: <%@ WebService Language="c#"
2:                Codebehind="EchoService.asmx.cs"
3:                Class="EchoService.EchoService" %>
4:
```

As you can see, there really isn't too much to the `asmx` file. As with `aspx` pages, there is a language directive, a Codebehind directive, that specifies the source file and a class directive that gives the qualified name of the class providing the WebService implementation.

Because the `EchoService` has been implemented as a C# source file and not inline script, the `EchoService.asmx.cs` file needs to be compiled and the resulting `.dll` copied to the `bin` directory of the current virtual directory hosting the `EchoService`. VS.NET will automatically perform this process during the build process. Testing the service merely requires accessing the `asmx` file with the Internet Explorer Web browser, as show in Figure 4.4.2.

The WebServices system creates a basic HTML form from which the WebService can be tested. Locate the input box, enter some text, and click the Invoke button. This will cause the Echo method to be invoked and the return XML will be displayed in the browser (see Figure 4.4.3).

4.4

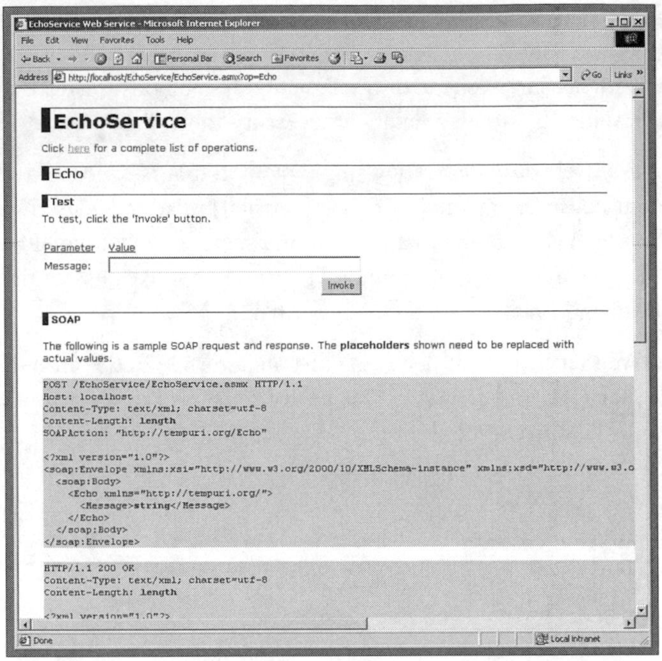

FIGURE 4.4.2
EchoService.asmx *within Internet Explorer.*

FIGURE 4.4.3
Result of Echo with "Hello World."

Building a Proxy Class

To invoke the WebService from C# code, a proxy class needs to exist. A proxy represents a gateway to the actual server code. In turn, the server has a stub to which the proxy connects. Figure 4.4.4 is a simple illustration of this.

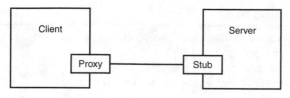

FIGURE 4.4.4

The proxy-stub relationship.

To create a proxy, you need to determine the particular protocol you want to use. The choices are HTTP POST, HTTP GET, or SOAP. Based on that decision, the proxy can then be derived from the property base class from `System.Web.Services.Protocols.X`, where *X* represents the corresponding protocol.

Listings 4.4.3 through 4.4.5 show the implementation for SOAP, HTTP POST, and HTTP GET, respectively. The basic structure for each implementation is the same. The differences to note include the `base classes` and the attributes applied to the `Echo` method and the parameter. Using the proxy object is no different than using any other object. Instantiate an instance and invoke the method with the proper parameter specified.

LISTING 4.4.3   Basic `EchoService` Proxy Class: SOAP

```
 1: //------------------------------------------------------------------
 2: // <autogenerated>
 3: //      This code was generated by a tool.
 4: //      Runtime Version: 1.0.2914.11
 5: //
 6: //      Changes to this file may cause incorrect behavior and will
➥be lost if
 7: //      the code is regenerated.
 8: // </autogenerated>
 9: //------------------------------------------------------------------
10:
11: //
12: // This source code was auto-generated by wsdl, Version=1.0.2914.11.
13: //
14: using System.Diagnostics;
15: using System.Xml.Serialization;
16: using System;
17: using System.Web.Services.Protocols;
18: using System.Web.Services;
19:
20:
```

LISTING 4.4.3   Continued

```
21: [System.Web.Services.WebServiceBindingAttribute(Name="EchoServerSoap",
➥Namespace="http://tempuri.org/")]
22: public class EchoServer :
➥System.Web.Services.Protocols.SoapHttpClientProtocol {
23:
24:     [System.Diagnostics.DebuggerStepThroughAttribute()]
25:     public EchoServer() {
26:         this.Url = "http://localhost/EchoService/EchoService.asmx";
27:     }
28:
29:     [System.Diagnostics.DebuggerStepThroughAttribute()]
30:     [System.Web.Services.Protocols.SoapDocumentMethodAttribute(
➥"http://tempuri.org/Echo",
➥Use=System.Web.Services.Description.SoapBindingUse.Literal,
ParameterStyle=System.Web.Services.Protocols.SoapParameterStyle.Wrapped)]
31:     public string Echo(string Message) {
32:         object[] results = this.Invoke("Echo", new object[] {
33:                     Message});
34:         return ((string)(results[0]));
35:     }
36:
37:     [System.Diagnostics.DebuggerStepThroughAttribute()]
38:     public System.IAsyncResult BeginEcho(string Message,
➥ System.AsyncCallback callback, object asyncState) {
39:         return this.BeginInvoke("Echo", new object[] {
40:                     Message}, callback, asyncState);
41:     }
42:
43:     [System.Diagnostics.DebuggerStepThroughAttribute()]
44:     public string EndEcho(System.IAsyncResult asyncResult) {
45:         object[] results = this.EndInvoke(asyncResult);
46:         return ((string)(results[0]));
47:     }
48: }
```

LISTING 4.4.4   Basic EchoService Proxy Class: HTTP POST

```
1: //-----------------------------------------------------------------
2: // <autogenerated>
3: //     This code was generated by a tool.
4: //     Runtime Version: 1.0.2914.11
5: //
6: //     Changes to this file may cause incorrect behavior and will be
➥lost if
```

LISTING 4.4.4 Continued

```
 7: //      the code is regenerated.
 8: // </autogenerated>
 9: //----------------------------------------------------------
10:
11: //
12: // This source code was auto-generated by wsdl, Version=1.0.2914.11.
13: //
14: using System.Diagnostics;
15: using System.Xml.Serialization;
16: using System;
17: using System.Web.Services.Protocols;
18: using System.Web.Services;
19:
20:
21: public class EchoServer :
➥System.Web.Services.Protocols.HttpPostClientProtocol {
22:
23:     [System.Diagnostics.DebuggerStepThroughAttribute()]
24:     public EchoServer() {
25:         this.Url = "http://localhost/EchoService/EchoService.asmx";
26:     }
27:
28:     [System.Diagnostics.DebuggerStepThroughAttribute()]
29:    [System.Web.Services.Protocols.HttpMethodAttribute(
➥typeof(System.Web.Services.Protocols.XmlReturnReader),
➥typeof(System.Web.Services.Protocols.HtmlFormParameterWriter))]
30:     [return: System.Xml.Serialization.XmlRootAttribute("string",
➥Namespace="http://tempuri.org/", IsNullable=true)]
31:     public string Echo(string Message) {
32:         return ((string)(this.Invoke("Echo", (this.Url + "/Echo"),
➥ new object[] {
33:                     Message})));
34:     }
35:
36:     [System.Diagnostics.DebuggerStepThroughAttribute()]
37:     public System.IAsyncResult BeginEcho(string Message,
➥System.AsyncCallback callback, object asyncState) {
38:         return this.BeginInvoke("Echo", (this.Url + "/Echo"),
➥new object[] {
39:                     Message}, callback, asyncState);
40:     }
41:
42:     [System.Diagnostics.DebuggerStepThroughAttribute()]
43:     public string EndEcho(System.IAsyncResult asyncResult) {
```

LISTING 4.4.4   Continued

```
44:           return ((string)(this.EndInvoke(asyncResult)));
45:       }
46: }
```

LISTING 4.4.5   Basic EchoService Proxy Class: HTTP GET

```
1: //---------------------------------------------------------------------
2: // <autogenerated>
3: //      This code was generated by a tool.
4: //      Runtime Version: 1.0.2914.11
5: //
6: //      Changes to this file may cause incorrect behavior and will be
➥lost if
7: //      the code is regenerated.
8: // </autogenerated>
9: //---------------------------------------------------------------------
10:
11: //
12: // This source code was auto-generated by wsdl, Version=1.0.2914.11.
13: //
14: using System.Diagnostics;
15: using System.Xml.Serialization;
16: using System;
17: using System.Web.Services.Protocols;
18: using System.Web.Services;
19:
20:
21: public class EchoServer :
➥System.Web.Services.Protocols.HttpGetClientProtocol {
22:
23:     [System.Diagnostics.DebuggerStepThroughAttribute()]
24:     public EchoServer() {
25:         this.Url = "http://localhost/EchoService/EchoService.asmx";
26:     }
27:
28:     [System.Diagnostics.DebuggerStepThroughAttribute()]
29:     [System.Web.Services.Protocols.HttpMethodAttribute(
➥typeof(System.Web.Services.Protocols.XmlReturnReader),
➥typeof(System.Web.Services.Protocols.UrlParameterWriter))]
30:     [return: System.Xml.Serialization.XmlRootAttribute("string",
➥Namespace="http://tempuri.org/", IsNullable=true)]
31:     public string Echo(string Message) {
32:         return ((string)(this.Invoke("Echo", (this.Url + "/Echo"),
➥new object[] {
```

LISTING 4.4.5 Basic `EchoService` Proxy Class: HTTP GET

```
33:                    Message})));
34:     }
35:
36:     [System.Diagnostics.DebuggerStepThroughAttribute()]
37:     public System.IAsyncResult BeginEcho(string Message,
➡System.AsyncCallback callback, object asyncState) {
38:         return this.BeginInvoke("Echo", (this.Url + "/Echo"),
➡new object[] {
39:                    Message}, callback, asyncState);
40:     }
41:
42:     [System.Diagnostics.DebuggerStepThroughAttribute()]
43:     public string EndEcho(System.IAsyncResult asyncResult) {
44:         return ((string)(this.EndInvoke(asyncResult)));
45:     }
46: }
```

The good news is that you don't have to type this code by hand. Shipped along with the .NET SDK is a tool named `WSDL.exe` whose purpose is to generate client code for WebServices. Running `WSDL.exe` with no parameters will display the command lines and their meanings. The basic form for WSDL looks like the following:

```
WSDL <url or wsdl document> <language> <protocol>
```

WebServices can be invoked synchronously or asynchronously. The common case is to use the synchronous method invocation. Asynchronous method invocation is useful in cases where the method call requires an extended time period for processing, the idea being that the client can continue to work while waiting for the async-response to return. This allows for other work to be performed without tying up the client application.

The various bindings—SOAP, HTTP GET, and HTTP POST—present an opportunity to develop a client application that utilizes a factory to create and return the requested binding. A WebService is capable of exposing several objects, and each of those objects can be viewed in terms of a public interface. This being the case, an interface that defines the public methods of a WebService can then be defined, and then each proxy implements this interface.

With respect to the EchoService, the interface for the WebService itself can be expressed as follows:

```
public interface IEchoService
{
    string Echo( string Message );
}
```

4.4

WEBSERVICES

This interface is conceptual only; in actual fact, the EchoService does not have an interface that can be referenced.

ProxyFactory

The Factory pattern helps to isolate clients from the underlying type that a factory creates. The Factory returns a well-known type—in this case, the IEchoService interface. Each proxy, as shown in Listings 4.4.3, 4.4.4, and 4.4.5, needs to implement the IEchoService interface. Actually, the listed proxies already do and only need the IEchoService interface added to the class declaration.

The ProxyFactory class will take an enum as a parameter to determine the underlying object to create and return. Listing 4.4.6 shows the ProxyFactory implementation.

LISTING 4.4.6   ProxyFactory.cs

```
 1: namespace ProxyFactory
 2: {
 3:     using System;
 4:
 5:
 6:     ///<summary>
 7:     /// Generalize the WebService as an
➥interface to be implemented by each proxy
 8:     ///</summary>
 9:     public interface IEchoService
10:     {
11:         string Echo( string Message );
12:     }
13:
14:
15:     ///<summary>
16:     ///Enumerate the Various Bindings
17:     ///</summary>
18:     public enum ProxyProtocol
19:     {
20:         SOAP,
21:         HttpGet,
22:         HttpPost
23:     }
24:
25:
26:     ///<summary>
27:     ///The Factory pattern can be used to construct
➥a proxy for the requested binding.
```

Listing 4.4.6   Continued

```
28:     ///The Factory will then return a well known
→interface to the web service
29:     ///</summary>
30:     public class ProxyFactory
31:     {
32:         public static IEchoService ConstructProxy( ProxyProtocol protocol )
33:         {
34:
35:             switch( protocol )
36:             {
37:                 case ProxyProtocol.SOAP:
38:                     return (IEchoService)new EchoServiceSoapProxy();
39:
40:
41:                 case ProxyProtocol.HttpGet:
42:                     return (IEchoService)new EchoServiceHttpGetProxy();
43:
44:
45:                 case ProxyProtocol.HttpPost:
46:                     return (IEchoService)new EchoServiceHttpPostProxy();
47:
48:
49:                 default:
50:                     throw new System.Exception( "Invalid Argument" );
51:
52:             }
53:         }
54:     }
55: }
56:
```

The `ProxyFactory` class encapsulates the creation of the requested proxy based on the binding passed into to the `ConstructProxy` method. Because the `IEchoService` interface has been implemented by each of the underlying proxy implementations, the `ProxyFactory` needs only to construct the proper proxy class and return the `IEchoService` interface.

Windows Forms Client

To put the `WebService` to the test, the following WinForms client provides a UI interface to the `EchoService`. Using VS.NET, create a C# Windows Forms application and construct the form shown in Figure 4.4.5.

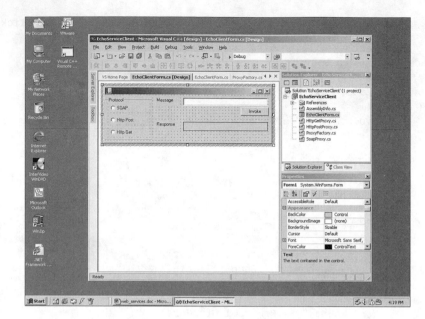

FIGURE 4.4.5
WinForms client.

Because the forms designer generates most of the code, only the relevant sections need to be reviewed rather than the complete code listing. Add the following protected variable:

```
private ProxyProtocol    SelectedProtocol=ProxyProtocol.SOAP;
```

This will allow the application to track the requested protocol for the WebService method invocation. Be sure to include the using ProxyFactory in the namespace declarations.

Next, I've hooked up each radio button to the same Click handler, which contains the following code:

```
protected void OnOpt_Click( object sender, EventArgs e )
{
    if( sender == optSOAP)
        this.SelectedProtocol = ProxyProtocol.SOAP;
    else if( sender == optHttpPost )
        this.SelectedProtocol = ProxyProtocol.HttpPost;
    else
        this.SelectedProtocol = ProxyProtocol.HttpGet;
}
```

This code serves to update the SelectedProtocol variable based on the currently selected radio button. Refer to the WinForms chapters for assigning delete handlers for controls.

Lastly, the invocation of the WebService happens when the Invoke button raises a `Click` event.

```
protected void btnInvoke_Click (object sender, System.EventArgs e)
{
    //Get an IEchoService interface
    IEchoService echo
        = ProxyFactory.ConstructProxy( this.SelectedProtocol );

    this.lblResponse.Text = echo.Echo( this.txtMessage.Text );
    this.txtMessage.Text = "";
}
```

With the event handler code in place, the Windows Forms client is ready to go. Figure 4.4.6 shows the client application ready to invoke the Echo WebService. In Figure 4.4.7, the result of the WebService invocation is displayed in the appropriate label showing the text echoed back from the EchoService.

FIGURE 4.4.6
Before clicking the WebService *Invoke button.*

FIGURE 4.4.7
After clicking the WebService *Invoke button.*

Now that the common case of using the synchronous method invocation has been discussed, the next step is to understand the asynchronous method invocation.

Asynchronous WebService invocation requires a delegate with the following method signature:

```
<access modifier> void <name>( System.IAsyncResult )
```

Fortunately, or unfortunately, there is no dark secret to how this mechanism works. The basic process for the call is the same as the synchronous version, only now a thread is created to handle the process of sending and receiving the request. After the request has been completed, an event is fired and the attached delegate is called.

Look at the various generated `WebService` proxies in Listings 4.4.3, 4.4.4, and 4.4.5; each proxy defines the following method:

```
public System.IAsyncResult BeginEcho(string message,
                            System.AsyncCallback callback,
                            object asyncState)
```

Just as the `Echo` method takes a string parameter, so does the `BeginEcho` method. In addition, the `BeginEcho` method requires a delegate for the callback and an object to which the asynchronous request belongs. Rather than list an entire application to invoke this method, the source code snippet in Listing 4.4.7 demonstrates the use of the asynchronous method invocation.

LISTING 4.4.7   Asynchronous `WebService` Invocation

```
1: //Create the proxy and invoke the BeginEcho method
2: EchoServiceSoapProxy sp = new EchoServiceSoapProxy( );
3: sp.BeginEcho("Hello", new System.AsyncCallback(this.CallBack), sp );
4:
5: //The callback for the asynchronous result
6: protected void CallBack( System.IAsyncResult ar )        {
7:     EchoServiceSoapProxy sp = (EchoServiceSoapProxy)ar.AsyncState;
8:     this.button1.Text = sp.EndEcho( ar );
9: }
```

After the `CallBack` method is invoked, the original `EchoServiceSoapProxy` object is obtained from the `IAsyncResult` interface. Next, the `EndEcho` method is called to obtain the results of the asynchronous WebService `method call`.

Hopefully the `EchoService` is a good introduction to the ease of WebService development and client consumption of such WebServices.

Returning User-Defined Types

It is often necessary to return user-defined types from a method, such as employee or department. When doing so, the WebService serialization will create a generic representation of the data element to return to the client. It is important to understand that WebServices should be used to return data and not objects. Essentially, a memento should be returned rather than trying to instantiate an object and attempt distributed reference counts.

A *memento* represents the current state of an object or the data necessary to describe an object. In the case of an employee, the basic information such as ID, name, department, and photo ID would represent the data associated with the employee.

The serialization services will serialize all public fields and public properties with GET assessors. To support de-serialization, the corresponding properties must also implement SET as well as GET within the accessory. Each field or property will be mapped to an XML element. This default behavior might serve well enough for simple services and serves as a starting point for using User Defined Types (UDT) within the context of a WebService.

Creating the Service

Start by creating a WebService named UDTWebService using VS.NET and rename the default Service1.asmx file to UDTService.asmx. As with all the WebServices created so far, the actual implementation will reside in the code-behind page.

The WebService will provide a method that will locate a person based on his or her last name; hence, the name of the method will be LocatePerson. Before implementing the method, it will be necessary to create a Person class that can be used to return the information to a WebService client (see Listing 4.4.8).

LISTING 4.4.8 The UDTPerson Class

```
 1: namespace UDTWebService
 2: {
 3:     using System;
 4:
 5:     /// <summary>
 6:     ///  The Person Class represents a basic UDT( User Defined Type )
 7:     /// </summary>
 8:     public class UDTPerson
 9:     {
10:         ///Private Fields
11:         private string    m_FirstName;
12:         private string    m_LastName;
13:
14:         //Public Properties
15:         public string FirstName
16:         {
17:             get { return m_FirstName; }
18:             set { m_FirstName = value; }
19:         }
20:
21:         public string LastName
```

Listing 4.4.8   Continued

```
22:          {
23:              get { return m_LastName; }
24:              set { m_LastName = value; }
25:          }
26:
27:
28:          //Constructor(s)
29:          public UDTPerson( )
30:          {
31:              //Default Constructor
32:          }
33:
34:          public UDTPerson( string FName, string LName )
35:          {
36:              m_FirstName = FName;
37:              m_LastName = LName;
38:          }
39:      }
40: }
41:
```

The UDTPerson class represents a basic C# class with no attributes applied to it. So how can it be serialized? Remember the Reflection API? This is the mechanism used to serialize this class. The WebService underpinning will use Reflection to scrape out information from the class and serialize that information. Again, only public fields or properties will be serialized.

With the implementation of UDTPerson completed, the next step is to add the LocatePerson method to the UDTService class. Update the UDTService class using the code appearing in Listing 4.4.9.

Listing 4.4.9   UDTService Source

```
1: using System;
2: using System.Collections;
3: using System.ComponentModel;
4: using System.Data;
5: using System.Diagnostics;
6: using System.Web;
7: using System.Web.Services;
8:
9: namespace UDTWebService
10: {
11:     /// <summary>
```

LISTING 4.4.9   Continued

```
12:      /// Summary description for UDTService.
13:      /// </summary>
14:      public class UDTService : System.Web.Services.WebService
15:      {
16:          private Hashtable    htPeople;
17:
18:          public UDTService()
19:          {
20:              //CODEGEN: This call is required by the ASP.NET Web
➡Services Designer
21:              InitializeComponent();
22:
23:              //Load the hashtable
24:              //Add some people to the hashtable
25:              htPeople = new Hashtable( );
26:              htPeople.Add( "Weeks", new UDTPerson( "Richard", "Weeks" ) );
27:              htPeople.Add( "Powell", new UDTPerson( "Bob", "Powell" ) );
28:              htPeople.Add( "Martschenko",
➡new UDTPerson( "Bill", "Martschenko" ) );
29:              htPeople.Add( "Schumacher",
➡ new UDTPerson( "Greg", "Schumacher" ) );
30:              htPeople.Add( "Pitzer", new UDTPerson( "Jay", "Pitzer" ) );
31:
32:          }
33:
34:      #region Component Designer generated code
35:      /// <summary>
36:      /// Required method for Designer support - do not modify
37:      /// the contents of this method with the code editor.
38:      /// </summary>
39:      private void InitializeComponent()
40:      {
41:      }
42:      #endregion
43:
44:      /// <summary>
45:      /// Clean up any resources being used.
46:      /// </summary>
47:      protected override void Dispose( bool disposing )
48:      {
49:      }
50:
51:      [WebMethod]
52:       public UDTPerson LocatePerson( string LastName ) {
```

LISTING 4.4.9 Continued

```
53:
54:            try {
55:                return (UDTPerson)htPeople[ LastName ];
56:            } catch( Exception ) {
57:            }
58:            return null;
59:        }
60:    }
61: }
```

Rather than retrieving from a database, this example creates a hash table to hold a few different people for whom to search. The LocatePerson method on line 52 takes the LastName as a string parameter. It is important to notice that the method looks no different than the WebMethod found in the EchoService. Because the default serialization mechanism handles the common case, you do not need to provide custom serialization code for the UDTPerson class.

Generating a Client Binding

Again, the WSDL.exe tool can be used to create the necessary client proxy class for invoking the LocatePerson method. Along with the proxy class, WSDL.exe will generate a simple class that represents the UDTPerson return type. The reason for this is that most users of your WebService will not have access to the code behind the service. Instead, they will have to rely on the WSDL description of the site to create the necessary client code to invoke any given service. Listing 4.4.10 shows the generated code produced by the WSDL.exe tool for the UDTService.

LISTING 4.4.10 UDTService Proxy Code

```
 1: //------------------------------------------------------------------
 2: // <autogenerated>
 3: //      This code was generated by a tool.
 4: //      Runtime Version: 1.0.2914.11
 5: //
 6: //      Changes to this file may cause incorrect behavior and
➡will be lost if
 7: //      the code is regenerated.
 8: // </autogenerated>
 9: //------------------------------------------------------------------
10:
11: //
12: // This source code was auto-generated by wsdl, Version=1.0.2914.11.
13: //
```

LISTING 4.4.10   Continued

```
14: using System.Diagnostics;
15: using System.Xml.Serialization;
16: using System;
17: using System.Web.Services.Protocols;
18: using System.Web.Services;
19:
20:
21: [System.Web.Services.WebServiceBindingAttribute(Name="UDTServiceSoap",
➥ Namespace="http://tempuri.org/")]
22: public class UDTService :
➥System.Web.Services.Protocols.SoapHttpClientProtocol {
23:
24:     [System.Diagnostics.DebuggerStepThroughAttribute()]
25:     public UDTService() {
26:         this.Url = "http://localhost/UDTWebService/UDTService.asmx";
27:     }
28:
29:     [System.Diagnostics.DebuggerStepThroughAttribute()]
30:     [System.Web.Services.Protocols.SoapDocumentMethodAttribute(
➥"http://tempuri.org/LocatePerson",
➥Use=System.Web.Services.Description.SoapBindingUse.Literal,
➥ ParameterStyle=System.Web.Services.Protocols.
➥SoapParameterStyle.Wrapped)]
31:     public UDTPerson LocatePerson(string LastName) {
32:         object[] results = this.Invoke("LocatePerson", new object[] {
33:                     LastName});
34:         return ((UDTPerson)(results[0]));
35:     }
36:
37:     [System.Diagnostics.DebuggerStepThroughAttribute()]
38:     public System.IAsyncResult BeginLocatePerson(string LastName,
➥System.AsyncCallback callback, object asyncState) {
39:         return this.BeginInvoke("LocatePerson", new object[] {
40:                     LastName}, callback, asyncState);
41:     }
42:
43:     [System.Diagnostics.DebuggerStepThroughAttribute()]
44:     public UDTPerson EndLocatePerson(System.IAsyncResult asyncResult) {
45:         object[] results = this.EndInvoke(asyncResult);
46:         return ((UDTPerson)(results[0]));
47:     }
48: }
49:
```

LISTING 4.4.10   Continued

```
50: public class UDTPerson {
51:
52:      public string FirstName;
53:
54:      public string LastName;
55: }
```

The WSDL.exe-generated code is basically the same as seen before; the new addition to notice is the UDTPerson class that was generated. Notice that the FirstName and LastName attributes are created as public fields rather than private fields. WSDL.exe has no way of knowing the actual implementation of UDTPerson as it exists on the server; instead, WSDL.exe must utilize the information found in the wsdl document to construct the proxy and referenced types.

Invoking UDTService.LocatePerson from Internet Explorer will produce an XML return and display it in the browser, as shown in Figure 4.4.8. This XML represents the return message from the WebService. Take a minute to study how the XML maps to the UDTPerson class created by the WSDL.exe tool.

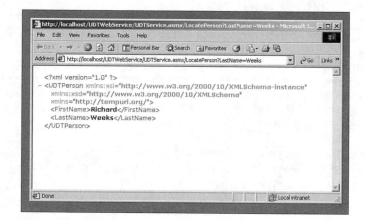

FIGURE 4.4.8
The XML result from LocatePerson.

XML Attributes

So far, we've seen how to return intrinsic types and UDTs from a WebService. The basic serialization provided by WebServices will generally suffice, but there are times when it is necessary to control the representation of elements being returned.

An XML document can have at most one root. An XML root can be defined by making use of the `XMLRootAttribute`. The `XMLRootAttribute` is used to specify the following properties in Table 4.4.1.

TABLE 4.4.1 `XMLRootAttribute` Instance Properties

Property	Meaning
DataType	XML data type of the root element
ElementName	The name of the root element
Form	Qualified or unqualified root element name
IsNullable	Determines if the `XmlSerializer` should serialize if set to `null`
Namespace	Namespace for the root element

A XML root element can contain *N* number of child elements, and each child is capable of containing *N* number of child elements. This recursive definition allows for arbitrary nesting depth with the XML document.

Along with a root element, an XML document consists of child elements and attributes. An element can be considered a contained type of entity of the document. The `XmlElementAttribute` is used to describe these elements. Elements can be a class or members of a class. In addition to specifying `XmlElementsAttributes`, elements can have attributes applied to them by using the `XmlAttributeAttribute` class.

So far, only single-level objects have been returned by the WebServices created. The `XmlSerializer` is quite capable of returning complex XML structures with nested classes. It is also possible to use the various XML attributes in conjunction with structs and to mix in entities with no explicit XML attributes.

To see the power of the `XmlSerializer` in action, a simple WebService will be created to return an `Employee` containing two contained objects—one `Address` class and one `Department` struct. Listing 4.4.11 shows the implementation of the `Employee`, `Address`, and `Department` entities.

LISTING 4.4.11 `Entities.cs`

```
1: namespace XML
2: {
3:     using System;
4:     using System.Xml;
5:     using System.Xml.Serialization;
6:
```

LISTING 4.4.11   Continued

```
7:
8:        [XmlRoot("employee")]
9:        public class Employee
10:       {
11:               private string        m_FirstName;
12:               private string        m_LastName;
13:               private Address        m_Address;
14:               private Department    m_Dept;
15:
16:           //Properties
17:           [XmlAttribute("first_name")]
18:           public string FirstName
19:           {
20:               get{ return m_FirstName; }
21:               set { m_FirstName = value; }
22:           }
23:
24:           [XmlAttribute("last_name")]
25:           public string LastName
26:           {
27:               get { return m_LastName; }
28:               set { m_LastName = value; }
29:           }
30:
31:
32:           [XmlElement("address")]
33:           public Address Address
34:           {
35:               get { return m_Address; }
36:               set { m_Address = value; }
37:           }
38:
39:           [XmlElement("department")]
40:           public Department Department
41:           {
42:               get { return m_Dept; }
43:               set { m_Dept = value; }
44:           }
45:       }
```

LISTING 4.4.11   Continued

```
46:
47:
48:      public class Address
49:      {
50:
51:          //Use Public Fields with XmlAttributes
52:          [XmlAttribute("line1")]
53:          public string Line1;
54:
55:          [XmlAttribute("city")]
56:          public string City;
57:
58:          [XmlAttribute("state")]
59:          public string State;
60:
61:          [XmlAttribute("zip")]
62:          public string Zip;
63:      }
64:
65:      //Use a simple struct
66:      public struct Department
67:      {
68:          //Fields with no XML attributes
69:          public string name;
70:          public int      building_number;
71:      }
72: }
73:
```

The entities in Listing 4.4.11 mix and match the various XML attributes and composite class creation. Both Employee and Address make use of the XML attributes, whereas the Department struct utilizes only public fields. By default, all public fields of a class or struct will be serialized by the WebService XML serialization code. This ability to mix and match provides an impressive power that enables you, the developer, to take complete control over the serialization process.

The result of the composite Employee class after serialization can be seen in Figure 4.4.9.

4.4

WEBSERVICES

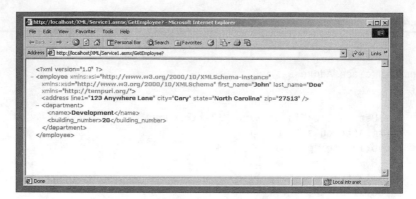

FIGURE 4.4.9
The XML representation of the Employee *class.*

Notice the various XML attributes and how they affect the XML output produced during the serialization of an Employee entity. It is also important to note there is more than one way to decorate a class with XML attributes that achieve the same serialization format. Consider the proxy code generated by the WSDL.exe tool in Listing 4.4.12.

LISTING 4.4.12   Client Proxy-Generated Code

```
 1: // <autogenerated>
 2: //      This code was generated by a tool.
 3: //      Runtime Version: 1.0.2615.1
 4: //
 5: //      Changes to this file may cause incorrect behavior
➥ and will be lost if
 6: //      the code is regenerated.
 7: // </autogenerated>
 8:
 9: //
10: // This source code was auto-generated by wsdl, Version=1.0.2615.1.
11: //
12: using System.Xml.Serialization;
13: using System;
14: using System.Web.Services.Protocols;
15: using System.Web.Services;
16:
17:
18: [
19: System.Web.Services.WebServiceBindingAttribute(
20:                     Name="Service1Soap",
21:                     Namespace="http://tempuri.org/")
```

LISTING 4.4.12 Continued

```
22: ]
23: public class Service1 :
➥System.Web.Services.Protocols.SoapHttpClientProtocol {
24:     public Service1() {
25:         this.Url = "http://localhost/XML/Service1.asmx";
26:     }
27:
28:     [
29: System.Web.Services.Protocols.SoapMethodAttribute(
30: "http://tempuri.org/GetEmployee",
➥MessageStyle=System.Web.Services.Protocols.
➥SoapMessageStyle.ParametersInDocument)
31: ]
32: [return: System.Xml.Serialization.XmlElementAttribute(
➥"employee", IsNullable=false)]
33:     public Employee GetEmployee() {
34:         object[] results = this.Invoke("GetEmployee", new object[0]);
35:         return ((Employee)(results[0]));
36:     }
37:
38:     public System.IAsyncResult BeginGetEmployee(
➥System.AsyncCallback callback, object asyncState) {
39:         return this.BeginInvoke("GetEmployee", new object[0], callback,
➥asyncState);
40:     }
41:
42:     public Employee EndGetEmployee(System.IAsyncResult asyncResult) {
43:         object[] results = this.EndInvoke(asyncResult);
44:         return ((Employee)(results[0]));
45:     }
46: }
47:
48: public class Employee {
49:
50:     [System.Xml.Serialization.XmlElementAttribute(IsNullable=false)]
51:     public Address address;
52:
53:     [System.Xml.Serialization.XmlElementAttribute(IsNullable=false)]
54:     public Department department;
55:
56:     [System.Xml.Serialization.XmlAttributeAttribute()]
57:     public string first_name;
58:
59:     [System.Xml.Serialization.XmlAttributeAttribute()]
```

4.4

WEBSERVICES

LISTING 4.4.12   Continued

```
60:      public string last_name;
61: }
62:
63: public class Address {
64:
65:      [System.Xml.Serialization.XmlAttributeAttribute()]
66:      public string line1;
67:
68:      [System.Xml.Serialization.XmlAttributeAttribute()]
69:      public string city;
70:
71:      [System.Xml.Serialization.XmlAttributeAttribute()]
72:      public string state;
73:
74:      [System.Xml.Serialization.XmlAttributeAttribute()]
75:      public string zip;
76: }
77:
78: [
79: System.Xml.Serialization.XmlTypeAttribute(
80:             Namespace="http://tempuri.org/")
81: ]
82: public class Department {
83:
84:      public string name;
85:
86:      public int building_number;
87: }
88:
```

As usual, the WSDL.exe tool produces the necessary proxy code to invoke the requested WebService method. Along with the proxy code, WSDL.exe also produces the Employee, Address, and Department entities as described by the WebServices wsdl document. Notice the differences between the Employee, Address, and Department developed previously and the source generated by the WSDL.exe tool.

Although each class/struct uses a different approach to produce the proper serialization format, both implementations are orthogonal to each other. Basically, only the names have changed on the decorated fields and properties. In effect, the WSDL.exe tool relies on both the various XML attributes and the use of Reflection to produce the proper serialized format.

Summary

I encourage you to continue to experiment with WebServices because they represent a new development paradigm in the separation of data and presentation logic. Along the way, be sure to inspect the generated proxy code created by WSDL.exe. This will help broaden your understanding of not only WebServices, but also XML and XML mapping between a particular entity and the serialized version.

Component Usage

IN THIS PART

Assemblies

IN THIS CHAPTER

What Is an Assembly?

The term `Assembly` refers to one or more files that make up a logical grouping in .NET. An assembly can be a single DLL or EXE as well as a collection of DLLs and/or EXEs. The notion of an assembly is more of a packaging for .NET components than anything else.

Before the days of .NET, code could reside within an EXE, DLL and, for those of you who remember, an overlay. By breaking compiled code up into smaller blocks, it was possible to reuse existing compiled code for other applications, and to share that code among various applications. This, of course, led to the dreaded DLL hell often referred to in various conversations and articles. *DLL hell* is basically the problem that arises when a new version of a DLL replaces an older version and, as a result, a client application suddenly quits working. The reason for the client's sudden sickness is not always apparent but, due to lack of versioning enforcement of DLLs, a client application was at the mercy of the DLL author.

With .NET assemblies, it is now possible to retain multiple versions of a particular assembly. A client application can choose to use the assembly it was compiled against or to use the latest and greatest version of the assembly. This dynamic binding is controlled by the applications configuration file, located in the same directory as the application. A brief discussion of this dynamic binding will be covered in the "Application Configuration File" in Chapter 5.2, "Signing and Versioning."

Assembly Contents

Each assembly contains a `Manifest` and the compiled code. A `Manifest` is a roster of additional files for a multifile assembly, as well as storing information about the assembly's version, strong name, and other information about the particular assembly. Using `ILDASM`, you can view the `Manifest` of any .NET assembly to see what the `Manifest` actually contains. Figure 5.1.1 shows the `Manifest` for the `mscorlib.dll` assembly.

.NET assemblies are fully self-describing; that is, all information about the assembly's contents is accessible to the runtime and to other .NET clients. In the same way that a COM client could interrogate a COM server about the interfaces it supported, it is possible to query for all entities within an assembly. The last section of this chapter creates a lightweight assembly viewer.

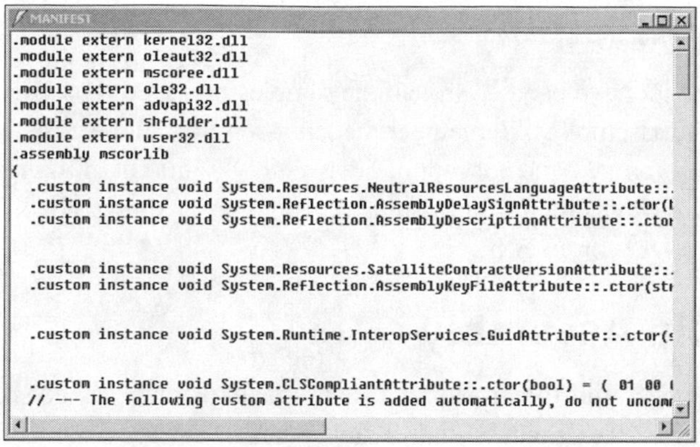

FIGURE 5.1.1
Manifest for mscorlib.dll.

Locating Assembly

The goal of .NET assemblies was to allow for easy client installation of components. It is possible to install an application by merely doing an XCOPY of the application to a directory on the client computer. No registering of components is required, no registry entries for COM. So how does the runtime locate an assembly? The .NET runtime will locate required assemblies using the following options:

- Application path
- Bin directory under the Application path
- Assembly named directory under application path (for example C:\program files\ myapp\myassembly\myassembly.dll)
- Global Assembly Cache (covered in Chapter 5.2)

A more detailed explanation of locating assemblies can be found in MSDN, including topics such as probing heuristics and so on.

For most applications, the use of private assemblies will suffice. A *private assembly* is an assembly that is only used by that particular application. Because no other application is even aware of the existence of the assembly, the assembly should reside within the application directory or a subdirectory of the application. Only if your company is developing a suite of applications that share common assemblies should you consider making use of the Global Assembly Cache.

5.1

ASSEMBLIES

Single File Assembly

Although you might not have been aware, all the samples provided thus far in this book are considered single file assemblies. Remember that an assembly can be either a DLL or an EXE. This, of course, tends to make the concept of an assembly a little hard to grasp. But none the less, a *single file assembly* is the result of some compilation of source code, and/or resources that result in either a DLL or an EXE.

Multiple File Assembly

The process of creating a multifile assembly takes some explaining, as does the use of some command line utilities. A key point to understand is that a *multifile assembly* can contain only one entry point. That is to say that only one class within the assembly can contain a `Main` method. Of course, if the multifile assembly is a DLL, this is not an issue. However, if the multifile assembly is an EXE, it is not possible for the assembly to contain more than one entry point.

To create the multifile assembly, it will be necessary to create two source files and compile them into code modules, which have the extension `.netmodule` by default. Listings 5.1.1 and 5.1.2 contain the source for very simple classes that will comprise the multifile assembly.

LISTING 5.1.1   ClassOne of the Multi-File Assembly

```
 1: using System;
 2: using FileTwo;
 3:
 4: namespace FileOne {
 5:
 6:     public class ClassOne {
 7:
 8:         public static void Main( ) {
 9:
10:             ClassTwo ct = new ClassTwo( );
11:             ct.SayHello( );
12:
13:         }
14:     }
15: }
```

LISTING 5.1.2   ClassTwo of the Multi-File Assembly

```
 1: using System;
 2:
 3:
 4: namespace FileTwo {
 5:
 6:
 7:     public class ClassTwo {
 8:
 9:         public void SayHello( ) {
10:
11:             Console.WriteLine( "Hello From FileTwo.ClassTwo" );
12:         }
13:     }
14: }
```

To create the new assembly, it is necessary to first compile each source file into a module. Note the order and steps of the compilation process:

1. `csc /t:module two.cs`

2. `csc /addmodule:two.netmodule /t:module one.cs`

3. `al one.netmodule two.netmodule /main:FileOne.ClassOne.Main`
   `/out:MultiAsm.exe /target:exe`

The first step is the creation of a code module from the second source file. This is due to the fact that the first source module references `FileTwo.ClassTwo`. Next is the creation of the code module for the first source file, which references the code module created from the second source file. The final step involves using the Assembly Generation Tool (`al.exe`) to create the multifile assembly. Note that if you delete the `.netmodule` files and attempt to execute `MultiAsm.exe`, the runtime will generate an exception due to missing dependencies. Figure 5.1.2 shows the manifest for `MultiAsm.exe`; note the references to `one.netmodule` and `two.netmodule`.

By packaging multiple files together into an assembly, it is possible to ensure proper references and versions of the code being executed.

5.1

ASSEMBLIES

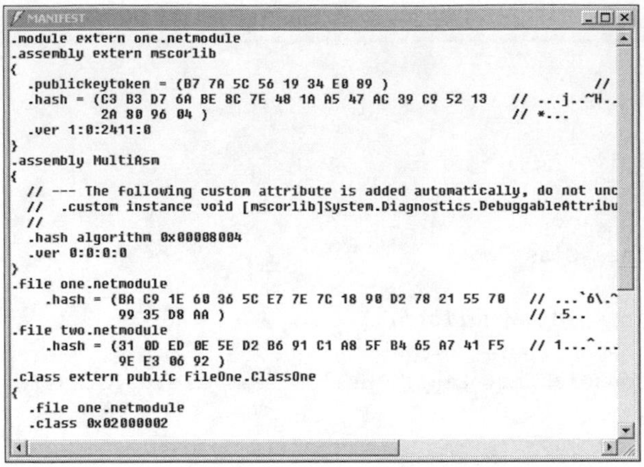

FIGURE 5.1.2
Manifest for MultiAsm.exe.

Assembly Attributes

Every assembly contains various attributes, including the assembly name, company, version, culture, copyright, and description among others. Listing 5.1.3 shows the default AssemblyInfo.cs file included in every C# .NET project.

LISTING 5.1.3 AssemblyInfo.cs

```
 1: using System.Reflection;
 2: using System.Runtime.CompilerServices;
 3:
 4: //
 5: // General Information about an assembly is controlled through the
➥following
 6: // set of attributes. Change these attribute values to modify the
➥ information
 7: // associated with an assembly.
 8: //
 9: [assembly: AssemblyTitle("")]
10: [assembly: AssemblyDescription("")]
11: [assembly: AssemblyConfiguration("")]
12: [assembly: AssemblyCompany("")]
13: [assembly: AssemblyProduct("")]
14: [assembly: AssemblyCopyright("")]
15: [assembly: AssemblyTrademark("")]
16: [assembly: AssemblyCulture("")]
17:
```

LISTING 5.1.3   Continued

```
18: //
19: // Version information for an assembly consists of the following
➥ four values:
20: //
21: //        Major Version
22: //        Minor Version
23: //        Build Number
24: //        Revision
25: //
26: // You can specify all the values or you can default the Revision
➥ and Build Numbers
27: // by using the '*' as shown below:
28:
29: [assembly: AssemblyVersion("1.0.*")]
30:
31: //
32: // In order to sign your assembly you must specify a key to use.
➥ Refer to the
33: // Microsoft .NET Framework documentation for more information
➥ on assembly signing.
34: //
35: // Use the attributes below to control which key is used for signing.
36: //
37: // Notes:
38: //   (*) If no key is specified - the assembly cannot be signed.
39: //   (*) KeyName refers to a key that has been installed in the
➥ Crypto Service
40: //        Provider (CSP) on your machine.
41: //   (*) If the key file and a key name attributes are both specified, the
42: //        following processing occurs:
43: //        (1) If the KeyName can be found in the CSP - that key is used.
44: //        (2) If the KeyName does not exist and the KeyFile does exist,
➥ the key
45: //            in the file is installed into the CSP and used.
46: //   (*) Delay Signing is an advanced option -
➥see the Microsoft .NET Framework
47: //        documentation for more information on this.
48: //
49: [assembly: AssemblyDelaySign(false)]
50: [assembly: AssemblyKeyFile("")]
51: [assembly: AssemblyKeyName("")]
```

5.1

ASSEMBLIES

The attributes for signing an assembly (AssemblyDelySign, AssemblyKeyFile and AssemblyKeyName) are covered in Chapter 5.2. The rest of the attributes should be somewhat familiar to Win32 developers. Every assembly can have information about the company that produced the assembly, including copyright information and current version.

Loading Assemblies at Runtime

The .NET runtime will load all assemblies referenced by the current assembly as detailed within the manifest of the dependant assembly. In plain English, a Windows Forms application will have the System.Windows.Forms.dll assembly loaded by the runtime on its behalf because the application has an explicit reference to the required assembly. However, sometimes it might be necessary to dynamically load .NET assemblies at runtime. Such uses include application extensions and various tools, such as the VS.NET IDE, which is capable of loading new .NET components for use by developers.

Loading an assembly at runtime is a powerful mechanism to extend an application. Consider an application that allows forms to be added to the application at sometime in the future. As an example, the Microsoft Management Console (MMC) allows for the development of snap-ins, which are basically COM components that are hosted within the shell provided by MMC.

FormHost Project

To illustrate the basic plumbing of loading assemblies at runtime for the purpose of extending an application, a small demo application will be created. The demo application will search in a specific subdirectory for DLL assembly files. Each assembly will be loaded, and the types from that assembly will be inspected. If a type within the assembly is derived from the System.Windows.Forms.Form class and the type supports an extension interface, in this case IFormHostClient, the form will be loaded and a menu item added to the host container.

To create the demo, do the following:

1. Create a new blank solution within VS.NET with the name of **DynamicAsmLoad**.

2. After the blank solution is in place, start by adding a new C# Class library project to the solution. Name this library **FormHostSDK**. (The FormHostSDK project will do nothing more than provide for a single interface to be used throughout the entire demo.)

3. Add a new class to the FormHostSDK project named **IformHostClient**.

Listing 5.1.4 shows the interface definition that will be used by both the FormHost project and a FormOne project.

LISTING 5.1.4 IFormHostClient Interface

```
1: ///Simple Interface for forms
2: ///
3: using System;
4:
5: namespace FormHostSDK
6: {
7:     public interface IFormHostClient {
8:
9:         string MenuText {
10:             get;
11:         }
12:     }
13: }
```

The IFormHostClient interface requires only a single property to be implemented. The MenuText property will be used to add a menu entry to the FormHost shell which will be created next.

With a simple interface defined for client forms to be hosted within a shell application, it's now time to develop the actual container application. Add a new C# Windows Application to the project with the name FormHost. This Windows Application will serve as the container application for hosting MDI child forms, which will be located within assemblies and loaded dynamically by the FormHost application. Listing 5.1.5 shows the code for the FormHost application.

LISTING 5.1.5 FormHost

```
1: using System;
2: using System.Drawing;
3: using System.Collections;
4: using System.ComponentModel;
5: using System.Windows.Forms;
6: using System.Data;
7: using System.Reflection;
8: using System.IO;
9: using FormHostSDK;
10:
11: namespace FormHost
12: {
13:     /// <summary>
14:     /// Summary description for MainForm.
15:     /// </summary>
16:     public class MainForm : System.Windows.Forms.Form
17:     {
```

5.1

ASSEMBLIES

LISTING 5.1.5 Continued

```
18:          /// <summary>
19:          /// Required designer variable.
20:          /// </summary>
21:          private System.ComponentModel.Container components = null;
22:          private System.Windows.Forms.MdiClient mdiClient1;
23:          private System.Windows.Forms.MainMenu mainMenu1;
24:          private System.Windows.Forms.MenuItem FileMenuItem;
25:          private System.Windows.Forms.MenuItem FormsMenuItem;
26:          private System.Windows.Forms.MenuItem ExitMenuItem;
27:          private Hashtable             forms = new Hashtable( );
28:
29:          public MainForm()
30:          {
31:              //
32:              // Required for Windows Form Designer support
33:              //
34:              InitializeComponent();
35:
36:              //
37:              // TODO: Add any constructor code after
➥InitializeComponent call
38:              //
39:
40:              LoadForms( );
41:          }
42:
43:          /// <summary>
44:          /// Clean up any resources being used.
45:          /// </summary>
46:          protected override void Dispose( bool disposing )
47:          {
48:              if( disposing )
49:              {
50:                  if (components != null)
51:                  {
52:                      components.Dispose();
53:                  }
54:              }
55:              base.Dispose( disposing );
56:          }
57:
58:          #region Windows Form Designer generated code
59:          /// <summary>
60:          /// Required method for Designer support - do not modify
61:          /// the contents of this method with the code editor.
```

LISTING 5.1.5 Continued

```
62:            /// </summary>
63:            private void InitializeComponent()
64:            {
65:                this.mdiClient1 = new System.Windows.Forms.MdiClient();
66:                this.mainMenu1 = new System.Windows.Forms.MainMenu();
67:                this.FileMenuItem = new System.Windows.Forms.MenuItem();
68:                this.FormsMenuItem = new System.Windows.Forms.MenuItem( );
69:                this.ExitMenuItem = new System.Windows.Forms.MenuItem();
70:                this.SuspendLayout();
71:                //
72:                // mdiClient1
73:                //
74:                this.mdiClient1.Dock =
➥System.Windows.Forms.DockStyle.Fill;
75:                this.mdiClient1.Name = "mdiClient1";
76:                this.mdiClient1.TabIndex = 0;
77:                //
78:                // mainMenu1
79:                //
80:                this.mainMenu1.MenuItems.AddRange(
81:                        new System.Windows.Forms.MenuItem[] {
82:                                this.FileMenuItem,
83:                                this.FormsMenuItem
84:                                                                }
85:                                                    );
86:                //
87:                // FormsMenuItem
88:                //
89:                this.FormsMenuItem.Index = 1;
90:                this.FormsMenuItem.Text = "F&orms";
91:
92:                 //
93:                 // FileMenuItem
94:                 //
95:                 this.FileMenuItem.Index = 0;
96:                 this.FileMenuItem.Text   = "&File";
97:                 this.FileMenuItem.MenuItems.Add( this.ExitMenuItem );
98:
99:                 //
100:                // menuItemExit
101:                //
102:                  this.ExitMenuItem.Index = 0;
103:                  this.ExitMenuItem.Text = "E&xit";
104:                  //
105:                  // MainForm
```

LISTING 5.1.5   Continued

```
106:                        //
107:                        this.AutoScaleBaseSize = new
108: ➥System.Drawing.Size(5, 13);
109:                        this.ClientSize = new
110: ➥System.Drawing.Size(576, 429);
111:                        this.Controls.AddRange(
112:                                new System.Windows.Forms.Control[] {
113:                                        this.mdiClient1
114:                                                                }
115:                                        );
116:                        this.IsMdiContainer = true;
117:                        this.Menu = this.mainMenu1;
118:                        this.Name = "MainForm";
119:                        this.Text = "MainForm";
120:                        this.ResumeLayout(false);
121:
122:                }
123:            #endregion
124:
125:
126:            /// <summary>
127:            /// load any dynamic forms
128:            /// </summary>
129:            protected void LoadForms( ) {
130:                string FormsDir = string.Format(
131:                                "{0}\\DynamicForms",
132: ➥Application.StartupPath
133:                                                        );
134:
135:                //Locate all Assemblies (DLL's only)
136:                string[] Files = Directory.GetFiles( FormsDir, "*.dll" );
137:
138:                foreach( string strFile in Files ) {
139:                 Assembly curAsm = Assembly.LoadFrom( strFile );
140:
141:                    //Look at the exposed types
142:                    Type[] types = curAsm.GetTypes( );
143:                    foreach( Type T in types ) {
144:                        if( T.IsSubclassOf( typeof( Form ) ) ) {
145:                            //Create an instance and add to main menu
146:                            Form frm =
147: ➥(Form)curAsm.CreateInstance( T.FullName );
148:                            forms.Add(
149: ➥((IFormHostClient)frm).MenuText, T );
150:
```

LISTING 5.1.5 Continued

```
151:                               MenuItem newItem = new MenuItem(
152:                                   ((IFormHostClient)frm)
153: ➥.MenuText,
154:                                   new EventHandler(
155: ➥ this.OnFormSelectMenu ) );
156:                       FormsMenuItem.MenuItems.Add( newItem );
157:                   }
158:               }
159:           }
160:       }
161:
162:       /// <summary>
163:       /// Create an instance of the requested form
164:       /// </summary>
165:       /// <param name="sender"></param>
166:       /// <param name="e"></param>
167:       protected void OnFormSelectMenu( object sender, EventArgs e ){
168:           MenuItem mi = (MenuItem)sender;
169:           if( this.forms.ContainsKey( mi.Text ) ) {
170:               Type T = (Type)this.forms[ mi.Text ];
171:               Form frmChild = (Form)Activator.CreateInstance( T );
172:               frmChild.MdiParent = this;
173:               frmChild.Show( );
174:           }
175:       }
176:
177:       /// <summary>
178:       /// The main entry point for the application.
179:       /// </summary>
180:       [STAThread]
181:       static void Main()
182:       {
183:           Application.Run(new MainForm());
184:       }
185:   }
186: }
```

Within the FormHost code, there are really only two methods of interest. The first method, LoadForms, which begins on line 127, is responsible for locating assemblies that contain forms that can be hosted within the shell. The LoadForms method begins by retrieving a list of possible assemblies and then iterating through that list. Each assembly then is loaded using the Assembly.LoadFrom static method. The Assembly class is located within the System.Reflection namespace.

5.1

After an assembly is loaded, the next step is to extract the various types and then compare those types against two simple tests. The first test is to determine if the loaded type is derived from the base type of System.Windows.Forms.Form. If so, chances are that the type also supports the IFormHostClient interface required by the shell application. If the loaded type is correct, the name is added to the Forms menu and the type information is stored in a hash table.

When the loaded form is selected from the menu, the type is retrieved from the hash table and, using the Activator class, a new instance of the form is created and shown within the MDI container.

To finish the demo, add a new C# class library project to the current DynamicAsmLoad project and name the library **FormOne**. The FormOne library will contain a single class derived from System.Windows.Forms and also will implement the required IFormHostClient interface. Remember to add a reference to the FormHostSDK project or DLL. In addition, the current FormHost application searches for assemblies located in a subdirectory named DynamicForms, so be sure that the FormOne project will build into this directory. The easiest way to accomplish this is to set the project build properties to point to this directory. Figure 5.1.3 shows the Project Properties dialog and the settings for the Build information.

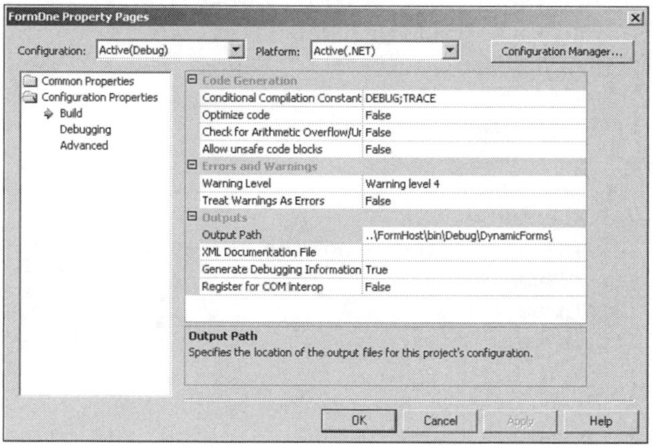

FIGURE 5.1.3

FormOne *Project Properties.*

The source Listing in 5.1.6 shows the implementation of the FormOne class.

LISTING 5.1.6   FormOne

```
1: using System;
2: using System.Drawing;
3: using System.Collections;
```

LISTING 5.1.6 Continued

```
 4: using System.ComponentModel;
 5: using System.Windows.Forms;
 6:
 7: using FormHostSDK;
 8:
 9: namespace FormOne
10: {
11:     /// <summary>
12:     /// Summary description for FormOne.
13:     /// </summary>
14:     public class FormOne : System.Windows.Forms.Form,
➥ FormHostSDK.IFormHostClient
15:     {
16:
17:         /// <summary>
18:         /// Required designer variable.
19:         /// </summary>
20:         private System.ComponentModel.Container components = null;
21:
22:
23:         //Implement the IFormHostClient interface
24:         public string MenuText {
25:             get {
26:                 return "Form One";
27:             }
28:         }
29:
30:
31:         public FormOne()
32:         {
33:             //
34:             // Required for Windows Form Designer support
35:             //
36:             InitializeComponent();
37:
38:             //
39:             // TODO: Add any constructor code after InitializeComponent call
40:             //
41:         }
42:
43:         /// <summary>
44:         /// Clean up any resources being used.
45:         /// </summary>
46:         protected override void Dispose( bool disposing )
```

5.1

LISTING **5.1.6**   Continued

```
47:          {
48:              if( disposing )
49:              {
50:                  if(components != null)
51:                  {
52:                      components.Dispose();
53:                  }
54:              }
55:              base.Dispose( disposing );
56:          }
57:
58:          #region Windows Form Designer generated code
59:          /// <summary>
60:          /// Required method for Designer support - do not modify
61:          /// the contents of this method with the code editor.
62:          /// </summary>
63:          private void InitializeComponent()
64:          {
65:              this.components = new System.ComponentModel.Container();
66:              this.Size = new System.Drawing.Size(300,300);
67:              this.Text = "FormOne";
68:          }
69:          #endregion
70:      }
71: }
```

With the completion of the FormOne class, just build the entire solution and launch the FormHost application. If all goes well, a menu item under the Forms menu should appear and, when selected, the FormOne window will appear as shown in Figure 5.1.4.

FIGURE **5.1.4**

FormHost *with* FormOne *showing.*

Although the demo was not very impressive, it should give you enough to enable larger projects with more advanced features. I would suggest developing a container application similar in nature to that of the Microsoft Management Console. Such a project will give you a good understanding of building shell type applications.

Assembly Viewer Light

Throughout this text, the `Reflection` API has been used to glean information about types and to peer into assemblies. .NET assemblies are so self describing that it is possible to reverse engineer a .NET assembly from IL to C#. The processes of generating C# from IL involves some work, however, generating the basic structure of a .NET class from the description found within an assembly is rather simple.

The Assembly Viewer, shown in Figure 5.1.5, was built in approximately 30 minutes and required no great magic. Although the Assembly Viewer does not import the IL and reverse-engineer it, adding such functionality can be accomplished.

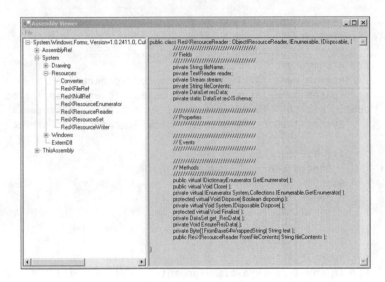

FIGURE 5.1.5
Assembly Viewer.

Rather than presenting the entire source here, only the code responsible for generating the C# code from a given `System.Type` is shown here in Listing 5.1.7.

LISTING 5.1.7   Source for `TypeSourceEngine`

```csharp
 1: using System;
 2: using System.Collections;
 3: using System.Reflection;
 4:
 5: namespace AssemblyViewer.ASMContent
 6: {
 7:     /// <summary>
 8:     /// Summary description for TypeSourceEngine.
 9:     /// </summary>
10:     public class TypeSourceEngine
11:     {
12:         public static BindingFlags BF = BindingFlags.Public |
13:                                         BindingFlags.NonPublic |
14:                                         BindingFlags.Instance |
15:                                         BindingFlags.Static |
16:                                         BindingFlags.DeclaredOnly;
17:
18:
19:         /// <summary>
20:         /// Generate C# code from a given Type
21:         /// </summary>
22:         /// <param name="T">Type used for code generation</param>
23:         /// <param name="stream">Stream object to write to</param>
24:         public static void GenerateCode( Type T, Stream stream ) {
25:             System.IO.StreamWriter sw = new StreamWriter( stream );
26:
27:             if( T.IsEnum )
28:                 GenerateEnum( T, sw );
29:             else
30:                 GenerateClassOrInterface( T, sw );
31:
32:         }
33:
34:         /// <summary>
35:         /// If the Type is a class or interface, generate the proper code
36:         /// </summary>
37:         /// <param name="T"></param>
38:         /// <param name="sw"></param>
39:         private static void GenerateClassOrInterface( Type T,
➥ StreamWriter sw )
40:         {
41:             ArrayList Fields;
42:             ArrayList Properties;
43:             ArrayList Methods;
44:             ArrayList Events;
```

LISTING 5.1.7 Continued

```
45:
46:                    GenerateFields( T, out Fields );
47:                    GenerateProperties( T, out Properties );
48:                    GenerateEvents( T, out Events );
49:                    GenerateMethods(T, out Methods );
50:
51:                    sw.Write( GenerateTypeStmt( T ) );
52:                    sw.Write( "\r\n" );
53:                    Inject( sw, Fields, "Fields" );
54:                    Inject( sw, Properties, "Properties" );
55:                      Inject( sw, Events, "Events" );
56:                      Inject( sw, Methods, "Methods" );
57:                      sw.Write("}");
58:                      sw.Flush( );
59:            }
60:
61:            /// <summary>
62:            /// Generate code for an Enum type
63:            /// </summary>
64:            /// <param name="T"></param>
65:            /// <param name="sw"></param>
66:            private static void GenerateEnum( Type T, StreamWriter sw )
67:            {
68:                ArrayList Fields;
69:                GenerateFields( T, out Fields );
70:                sw.Write( GenerateTypeStmt( T ) );
71:                sw.Write( "\r\n" );
72:                Inject( sw, Fields, "Fields" );
73:                sw.Write("}");
74:                sw.Flush( );
75:            }
76:
77:            /// <summary>
78:            /// Creates a type declaration statement:
79:            /// (public | private) [abstract|sealed]
➥[interface|class|struct] TypeName [: [Base Class], [Interfaces] ]
80:            /// </summary>
81:            /// <param name="T"></param>
82:            /// <returns></returns>
83:            private static string GenerateTypeStmt( Type T ) {
84:                string stmt = "";
85:
86:                if( T.IsPublic )
87:                    stmt = "public ";
88:                else if( T.IsNotPublic )
```

LISTING 5.1.7   Continued

```
89:                    stmt = "private ";
90:
91:            if( T.IsAbstract )
92:                stmt += "abstract ";
93:            else if( T.IsEnum )
94:                stmt += "enum ";
95:            else if( T.IsInterface )
96:                stmt += "interface ";
97:            else if( T.IsSealed )
98:                stmt += "sealed ";
99:
100:            if( T.IsClass )
101:                stmt += "class ";
102:            else if (T.IsInterface )
103:                stmt += "interface ";
104:            else
105:                stmt += "struct ";
106:
107:            bool bHasBase = false;
108:            stmt += string.Format( "{0} ", T.Name );
109:            if( T.BaseType != null ) {
110:                stmt += string.Format(": {0}", T.BaseType.Name);
111:                bHasBase = true;
112:            }
113:
114:            System.Type[] Interfaces  = T.GetInterfaces( );
115:            if( Interfaces.Length != 0 ) {
116:                if( !bHasBase )
117:                    stmt += ": ";
118:                foreach( Type tt in Interfaces ) {
119:                    stmt += tt.Name;
120:                    stmt += ", ";
121:                }
122:                stmt = stmt.Substring(0, stmt.Length - 1);
123:            }
124:            stmt += " {";
125:            return stmt;
126:        }
127:
128:        /// <summary>
129:        /// Inject source into StreamWriter
130:        /// </summary>
131:        /// <param name="al"></param>
132:        /// <param name="EntryType"></param>
133:        private static void Inject( System.IO.StreamWriter sw,
```

LISTING 5.1.7   Continued

```
134:                              ArrayList al,
135:                              string EntryType ) {
136:        sw.Write("\t////////////////////////////////////\r\n");
137:        sw.Write(string.Format("\t// {0}\r\n", EntryType));
138:        sw.Write("\t////////////////////////////////////\r\n");
139:        foreach( string s in al ) {
140:            sw.Write("\t");
141:            sw.Write( s );
142:            sw.Write( "\r\n" );
143:        }
144:        sw.Write("\r\n");
145:    }
146:
147:
148:        /// <summary>
149:        /// Generate Field declarations
150:        /// </summary>
151:        /// <param name="T"></param>
152:        /// <param name="fieldList"></param>
153:        private static void GenerateFields( Type T,
➥out ArrayList fieldList )
154:        {
155:            fieldList = new ArrayList( );
156:            FieldInfo[] fields = T.GetFields( BF );
157:            foreach( FieldInfo fi in fields ) {
158:                fieldList.Add( GenerateFieldStmt( fi ) );
159:            }
160:        }
161:
162:        /// <summary>
163:        /// Generate the actual field stmt
164:        /// ie: private int someFieldMember;
165:        /// </summary>
166:        /// <param name="fi"></param>
167:        /// <returns></returns>
168:        private static string GenerateFieldStmt( FieldInfo fi ) {
169:
170:            string stmt;
171:
172:            if( fi.IsPublic )
173:                stmt = "public ";
174:            else if( fi.IsPrivate )
175:                stmt = "private ";
176:            else
177:                stmt = "protected ";
```

LISTING 5.1.7 Continued

```
178:
179:            if( fi.IsStatic )
180:                stmt += "static ";
181:
182:                stmt += fi.FieldType.Name;
183:                stmt += " ";
184:                stmt += fi.Name;
185:                stmt += ";";
186:                return stmt;
187:        }
188:
189:        private static void GenerateProperties( Type T,
190:                                        out ArrayList propertyList ) {
191:
192:            PropertyInfo[] props = T.GetProperties(  );
193:            propertyList = new ArrayList( );
194:            foreach( PropertyInfo pi in props )
195:                propertyList.Add( GeneratePropStmt( pi ) );
196:
197:        }
198:
199:        private static string GeneratePropStmt( PropertyInfo pi ) {
200:            string stmt = "public ";
201:            stmt += pi.PropertyType.Name;
202:            stmt += " ";
203:            stmt += pi.Name;
204:            stmt += " { ";
205:            if( pi.CanRead )
206:                stmt += "get; ";
207:            if( pi.CanWrite )
208:                stmt += "set; ";
209:            stmt += " }; ";
210:            return stmt;
211:        }
212:
213:
214:        private static void GenerateMethods( Type T,
215:                                        out ArrayList methodList ) {
216:            MethodInfo[] Methods = T.GetMethods( BF );
217:            methodList = new ArrayList( );
218:            foreach( MethodInfo mi in Methods )
219:                methodList.Add( GenerateMethodStmt( mi ) );
220:
221:        }
222:
```

LISTING 5.1.7 Continued

```
223:          private static string GenerateMethodStmt( MethodInfo mi ) {
224:            string stmt;
225:
226:            if( mi.IsPublic )
227:                stmt = "public ";
228:            else if( mi.IsPrivate )
229:                stmt = "private ";
230:            else if( mi.IsFamily )
231:                stmt = "protected ";
232:            else
233:                stmt = "protected internal ";
234:
235:            if( mi.IsVirtual )
236:                stmt += "virtual ";
237:            else if( mi.IsAbstract )
238:                stmt += "abstract ";
239:
240:            stmt += string.Format("{0} {1}( ", mi.ReturnType.Name,
➥ mi.Name );
241:            ParameterInfo[] Params = mi.GetParameters( );
242:            if( Params.Length > 0 ) {
243:                int i;
244:                for( i = 0; i < Params.Length - 1; i++ )
245:                    stmt += string.Format("{0}, ",GenerateParamStmt(
➥Params[i] ) );
246:                    stmt += string.Format("{0} ", GenerateParamStmt(
➥Params[ i ] ) );
247:                }
248:                stmt += ");";
249:                return stmt;
250:        }
251:
252:          private static string GenerateParamStmt( ParameterInfo pi ) {
253:                string stmt = "";
254:                if( pi.IsIn )
255:                    stmt = "[in] ";
256:                else if( pi.IsOut )
257:                    stmt = "[out] ";
258:                else if ( pi.IsRetval )
259:                    stmt = "[ref] ";
260:                stmt += string.Format( "{0} {1}",
➥pi.ParameterType.Name, pi.Name );
261:                return stmt;
262:        }
263:
```

5.1

ASSEMBLIES

LISTING 5.1.7   Continued

```
264:          private static void GenerateEvents( Type T,
265:                                             out ArrayList eventList ) {
266:             EventInfo[] Events = T.GetEvents( BF );
267:             eventList= new ArrayList( );
268:             foreach( EventInfo ei in Events )
269:                 eventList.Add( GenerateEventStmt( ei ) );
270:          }
271:
272:          private static string GenerateEventStmt( EventInfo ei ) {
273:             return string.Format("public {0} {1};",
274:                                  ei.EventHandlerType.Name, ei.Name );
275:          }
276:       }
277: }
```

The code generating C# is fairly simple, although Listing 5.1.7 could certainly use some improvements, it does serve as a basis from which to expand. The first improvement to make is the removal of all hand coding of the C# constructs and using the CodeDom class, located in the System.CodeDom namespace, instead. Next, of course, is retrieving the IL from a .NET assembly and generating appropriate statements for the target language.

Summary

.NET assemblies are a powerful mechanism for packaging not only IL code but also complete type information so that each assembly is completely self describing. In time, I'm sure you will find many uses for the metadata within the assemblies and the ease of working with new assemblies. In the next chapter, the topics of signing and versioning of assemblies is covered. .NET assemblies and the reflection API will prove to be an invaluable resource for extending the life of applications and provide the ability to create assemblies on-the-fly using the Reflection.Emit API. I encourage you to learn every aspect of assemblies and the supporting classes that allow you to work with them.

Signing and Versioning

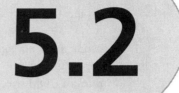

CHAPTER

5.2

IN THIS CHAPTER

DLL Hell

As most of us are aware of by now, one of the goals of creating Win32 DLLs was for code reuse. We are also painfully aware that the version of the DLL could make or break the application. New applications would ship and often contain a newer version of a DLL that another application would depend on and, of course, the new DLL would break existing software. The rules of COM tried to combat this problem through strict rules, but these rules were to be followed by developers and not enforced by any runtime system. As such, even applications that used COM components found that not all COM developers followed the rules, and software would crash when using different versions of supposedly the same component.

With .NET, Microsoft has chosen a new approach to solve the dreaded issue of DLL hell. The .NET runtime enforces versioning of components and even allows for side-by-side installation of components with different versions. Client applications then can choose which version of the DLL to use; by default, an application will load the version of the DLL to which is was originally linked during the initial release build. If a new version of a shared component becomes available, the application then can be configured to use the new version of the DLL or continue to make use of the current DLL.

Global Assembly Cache

The Global Assembly Cache (GAC) is meant to be a replacement for shared components. In the world of COM, each COM `coclass`, `interface`, `progid`, and so on was registered in the system Registry. The COM subsystem used this information to locate the COM component and load the object. In .NET, the global assembly cache serves as the home for all shared components. Any .NET component can be installed into the GAC using the `gacutil.exe` utility shipped with the .NET runtime or by using Windows Explorer and dropping the component into the GAC directory. The GAC is located in a directory under the base system directory; in the case of Windows 2000, all shared components are located in `C:\WINNT\assembly`, assuming that installation defaults were used. Figure 5.2.1 shows the contents of the GAC.

Every .NET component has a manifest as part of the assembly file; this manifest includes versioning information that is used by the CLR loader to enforce .NET component versioning. The version number consists of the following parts:

- Major
- Minor
- Revision
- Build Number

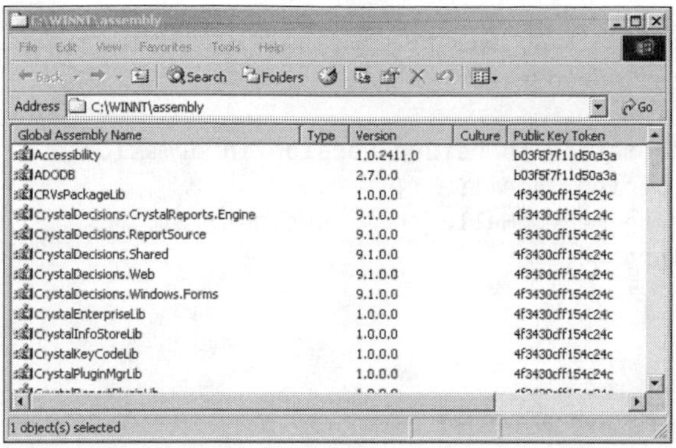

FIGURE 5.2.1
Contents of GAC directory.

These four pieces of version information are used to ensure that the proper .NET component is loaded for a given client application. If a client application requests a version that does not exist, the CLR loader will fail and report the failure information.

Versioning

There are a few steps that need to be followed to create versioned components. At the time of this writing, VS.NET does not support the ability to automatically create signed components. The first step is the generation of a signing key using the SN.exe utility shipped with the .NET SDK. Generally, a company will create such a key and all .NET components built will use this key to sign the component. To generate a public/private key pair, issue the following command:

```
sn.exe -k sams.snk
```

This will create a key file that can be used to sign the assembly. With the key file created, create a new VS.NET project for a C# class library and name the project **SharedComponent**. Next, add a new class, **SharedServer**, to the project and enter the code in Listing 5.2.1.

LISTING 5.2.1   SharedServer Source

```
1: using System;
2:
3: namespace SharedComponent
4: {
5:     /// <summary>
6:     /// Summary description for Class1.
7:     /// </summary>
```

5.2

LISTING 5.2.1   Continued

```
 8:     public class SharedServer
 9:     {
10:         //Single method to return version information
11:         public string WhoAmI( ) {
12:             string me = "Hello from version 1.0";
13:             return me;
14:         }
15:
16:     }
17: }
```

This small class then will be used to test the versioning support provided by the CLR loader. To build the project with signing support, modify the `AssemblyInfo.cs` file and add the key file information, as show in Listing 5.2.2.

LISTING 5.2.2   `AssemblyInfo.cs`

```
1: [assembly: AssemblyDelaySign(false)]
2: [assembly: AssemblyKeyFile("D:\\SAMS\\SAMS.SNK")]
3: [assembly: AssemblyKeyName("")]
```

Notice that the `[assembly: AssemblyKeyFile(...)]` attribute is used to specify the key file used to sign the assembly. This is all there is to it. Now, build the assembly and drag the compiled DLL into the GAC directory located in `C:\WINNT\assembly` using the Windows Explorer. Figure 5.2.2 shows the Windows Explorer of the GAC directory and the newly installed `SharedComponent.dll`.

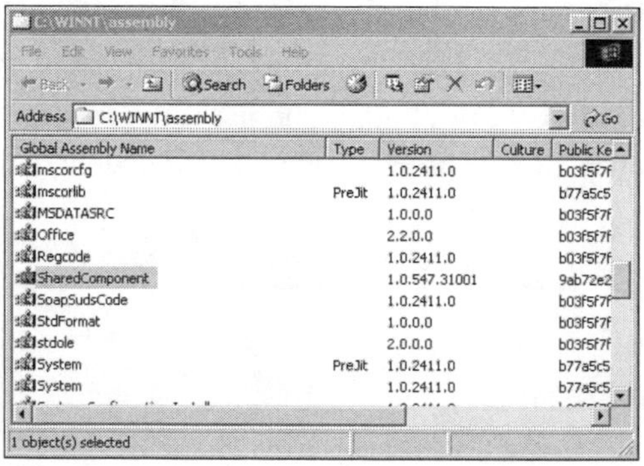

FIGURE 5.2.2
`SharedComponent.dll` in the GAC directory.

With the shared assembly in place, it's time to create a client to use the newly created `SharedComponent.dll`. Create a new Windows Forms project and add a reference to the `SharedComponent` assembly using the Add Reference explorer. (Again, at the time of this writing, VS.NET does not support adding a reference to a component installed within the GAC. Therefore, you can add a reference to the compiled DLL by browsing for it in the `bin\Release` directory of the shared component. Be sure to set the properties of the shared component `CopyLocal` to `false` so that the CLR will search the GAC for the component during execution of the client.)

To test the `SharedComponent`, merely drag a label onto the client form and add the code shown in Listing 5.2.3 to the constructor of the form.

LISTING 5.2.3   Test Harness for `SharedComponent`

```
 1: public Form1()
 2: {
 3:     //
 4:     // Required for Windows Form Designer support
 5:     //
 6:     InitializeComponent();
 7:
 8:     //
 9:     // TODO: Add any constructor code after InitializeComponent call
10:     //
11:     SharedComponent.SharedServer ss = new SharedComponent.SharedServer( );
12:     this.label1.Text = ss.WhoAmI( );
13: }
```

Lines 11 and 12 create a new `SharedServer` object and assign the `Text` property of the label to the returned string of the `WhoAmI` method. Now, compile and run the client application to test the assembly binding. The client should look similar to the window in Figure 5.2.3.

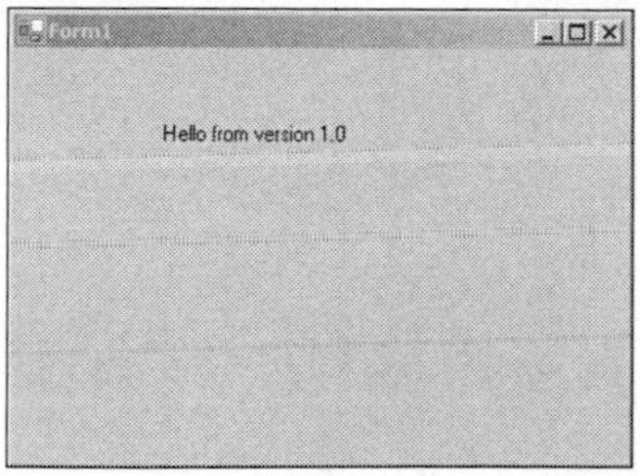

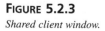

Hello from version 1.0

FIGURE 5.2.3
Shared client window.

The client application is bound to the current version of the shared assembly based on the version information available at the time the client is compiled. In the next segment, a newer version of the component will be created and installed into the GAC. After doing so, the client application will still use the first version of the DLL until it is configured to use a newer version.

Side-By-Side Assemblies

To demonstrate side-by-side versioning support of .NET assemblies, reopen the SharedComponent project and make the following changes:

1. Update the version attribute in AssemblyInfo.cs to 1.1.
2. Change the returned string from the WhoAmI method to reflect the new version information.
3. Build the new assembly.
4. Install the new version of the assembly into the GAC directory.

After these steps are complete, two versions of the SharedComponent.dll should be visible in the GAC, as shown in Figure 5.2.4.

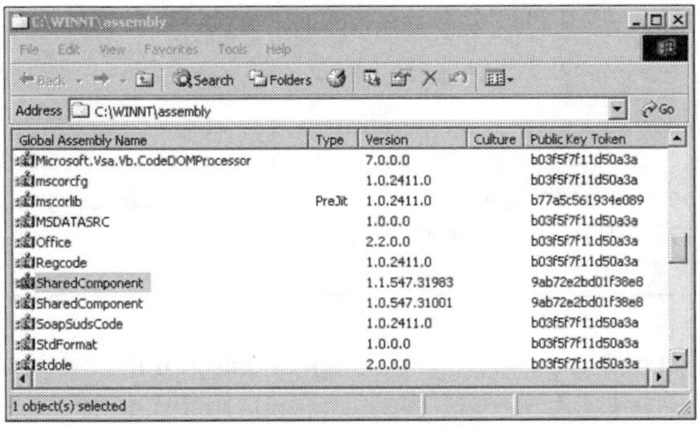

FIGURE 5.2.4
Side-by-side versioning of SharedComponent.dll.

Rerun the client application and notice that the returned message is still "Hello from version 1.0.". It is important **NOT** to recompile the client application because the reference will now be to the newer version of the DLL.

Custom Binding: Application Configuration

To allow the client application to make use of the newly built assembly, an application configuration file must exist in the same directory as the .exe. The configuration file will have the same name as the application name, including the extension. In the case of the Shared

Client.exe program, the configuration file will have the name SharedClient.exe.config. The configuration file listed in Listing 5.2.4 shows the necessary entries to redirect the binding from the 1.0 version to the 1.1 version of the SharedComponent.dll.

LISTING 5.2.4 SharedClient.exe.config

```
 1: <?xml version="1.0"?>
 2: <configuration>
 3:   <runtime>
 4:     <assemblyBinding xmlns="urn:schemas-microsoft-com:asm.v1">
 5:       <dependentAssembly>
 6:         <assemblyIdentity name="SharedComponent"
 7:                           publicKeyToken="9ab72e2bd01f38e8" />
 8:         <bindingRedirect oldVersion="1.0.547.38856"
 9:                          newVersion="1.1.547.38908" />
10:       </dependentAssembly>
11:     </assemblyBinding>
12:   </runtime>
13: </configuration>
```

In the assemblyBinding section, all dependent assemblies are listed for rebinding. Each assembly to be redirected will have an entry. The entries consist of the dependentAssembly section that details the identity of the assembly and the binding information. The config file is a simple XML file used by the runtime to alter the environment for any application. Create a text file named **SharedClient.exe.config** and copy Listing 5.2.4; be sure to verify the version numbers because they will most likely differ from those listed. The version information can be obtained from browsing the GAC directory with Windows Explorer, as shown in Figure 5.2.4.

With the configuration file in place, launch the SharedClient.exe application and notice that the text displayed in the label now says "Hello from version 1.1" (see Figure 5.2.5). This is due to the runtime rebinding the assemblies.

FIGURE 5.2.5
SharedClient.exe *with binding redirect.*

5.2

Rather than creating the configuration file by hand, the .NET framework ships with a MMC snap-in that allows you to configure applications, including the assembly rebinding. In fact, I used the MMC snap-in .NET Admin Tool (`mscorcfg.msc`) to generate the configuration file for the `SharedClient.exe` program. Figure 5.2.6 shows the .NET Admin Tool loaded in MMC.

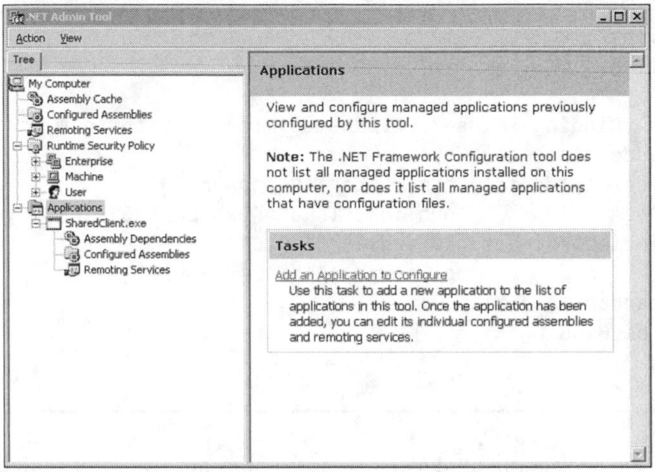

FIGURE 5.2.6
.NET Admin tool.

Microsoft's .NET Admin tool allows for editing of the GAC, configured assemblies, remote services, runtime security policies, and assembly binding. The tool itself is fairly straightforward to use. The first step is to add an application to configure, in this case, `SharedClient.exe`. After the application is added, a new node will appear under the Applications branch (see Figure 5.2.7).

To reconfigure assembly binding, select the Configured Assemblies node and then select Configure an Assembly in the right pane. This will bring up a Wizard Style dialog to walk you through the process. Figure 5.2.8 shows the assembly selection dialog with the `SharedComponent` assembly chosen. For a client application to make use of a newer assembly, the client must either be re-linked to the assembly or a binding configuration must be available to the client. In classic COM, clients generally would use the newest COM object because COM requires all interfaces to be immutable. In .NET, a client application will attempt to load the assembly it was originally linked against unless an application configuration file specifies a different assembly binding.

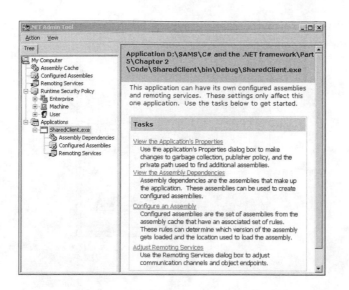

FIGURE 5.2.7
SharedClient.exe *in the Applications group.*

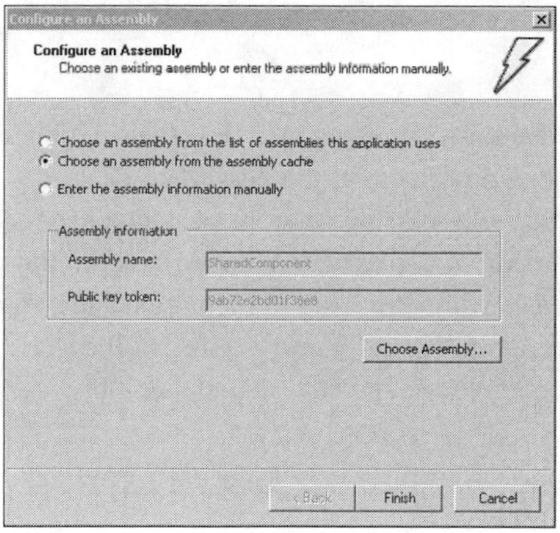

FIGURE 5.2.8
Assembly selection dialog.

When the Finish button is clicked, a Properties dialog is displayed. This dialog can be used to specify the binding policy for the given application. Figure 5.2.9 shows the Properties dialog with the Binding Policy tab selected and the binding information for the SharedComponent.

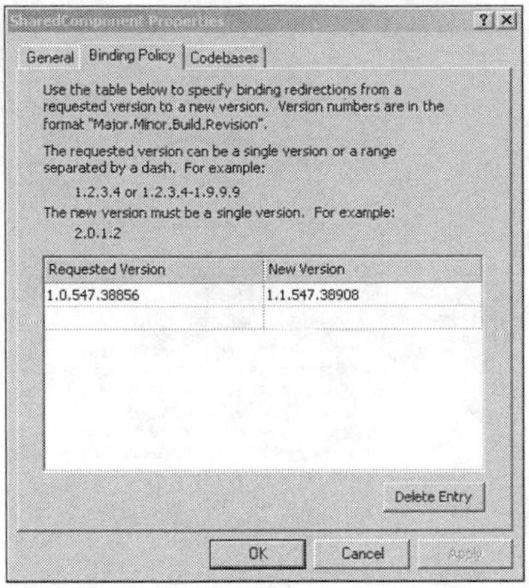

FIGURE 5.2.9
Binding Policy tab.

The output from the .NET Admin tool is an application configuration file located in the same directory as the application. This configuration file then can be used as part of an update to send to clients along with a new version of any shared components.

Summary

Chapters 5.1 and 5.2 have demonstrated the way .NET deals with assemblies and shared assemblies. DLL hell becomes a problem of the past when dealing with shared assemblies as the GAC is capable of hosting side-by-side versions of components, thus allowing client applications to use the proper version of a given component. In addition, application configuration files allow for binding changes without having to recompile and redistribute an application. All that is needed is the configuration file and a new version of the shared component, and clients then can use binding redirection to use the new shared assembly.

COM Interoperability

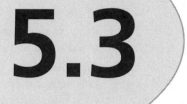
IN THIS CHAPTER

The World of COM

There has always been a long-standing vision of multiple languages sharing common components. In the Windows world, this vision was realized by COM, the Component Object Model. COM's sole purpose was to allow any language that understood the COM binary standard to make use of that component. With the advent of .NET, these issues disappear because all .NET languages can freely interoperate with one another with ease. The combination of the CLS and CLR make such interoperability seamless; gone are the days of Type Libraries and IDL.

Before venturing further, this chapter assumes a certain familiarity with COM. Such topics as Interfaces(such as `IUnknown`, `IDispatch`, and `IEnumVARIANT`), `coclass`, Connection Points, and COM threading should already be understood. .NET provides a rich facility for Managed Clients to interact with Unmanaged COM components and for Managed components to be consumed as though they themselves were classic COM components.

.NET COM Support

For Managed code to consume the services provided by a COM component, a bit of translation must take place. After all, you won't find `CoInitialize` or `CoCreateInstance` within the .NET framework. Such arcane practices, which most of us spent considerable time learning, are no more. Instead, the .NET environment introduces the notion of a Runtime Callable Wrapper or RCW. From the viewpoint of the Managed client there is no real difference between using the RCW and a managed component. Figure 5.3.1 depicts a very generic view of a Managed client using a RCW to interact with a classic COM component.

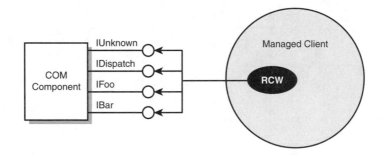

FIGURE 5.3.1
Generalized view of RCW.

An RCW has several responsibilities that shield the developer from tasks such as reference counting, QI, and memory allocation/de-allocation.

RCW's responsibilities include the following:

- Preserving Object Identity
- Maintaining Object Lifetime
- Proxying Unmanaged Interfaces
- Marshaling Method Calls
- Consuming Selected Interfaces

Preserving Object Identity

There is only one RCW for an underlying COM component. This allows the RCW to ensure the identity of the COM object by comparing objects against the `IUnknown` interface. A RCW will appear to implement several interfaces, as provided by the underlying COM object, but the RCW actually only hides the `QueryInterface` calls from the developer. When casting for an interface, the RCW checks for a cached interface of the requested type and, if found, returns it; otherwise, a QI is invoked. When the RCW invokes a QI on the underlying COM object, the returned interface is added to the cache maintained by the RCW. If a requested interface is not found, the standard `InvalidCastException` is thrown by the RCW.

Maintaining Object Lifetime

A single instance of the RCW is necessary for the proper lifetime management of the underlying COM object. The RCW handles the necessary calls to `AddRef()` and `Release()`, thus ensuring proper reference counting and finalization of the COM object. As with any other Managed Object, the RCW is also garbage collected. When the RCWs finalize method is invoked by the GC, the RCW will call `Release()` on all cached interfaces for the underlying COM object. This frees the developer from having to worry about proper `AddRef()` to `Release()` ratios because the RCW is now responsible for reference counting.

Even though the RCW manages the lifetime of the underlying COM object, there are times when it is necessary to force the release of a COM object. Consider a COM object that requires precious resources such as socket connections, database connections, or shared memory. Because there is no deterministic finalization within .NET due to the GC, it might be necessary to pragmatically release the underlying COM object. When a COM object is imported for use in a Managed environment (a topic that will be covered later), the Marshal class includes a static method called `ReleaseComObject( object o)`. In effect, this causes the RCW to call `Release()` on each cached interface within the RCW.

Proxying Unmanaged Interfaces

A typical COM object consists of a coclass that implements one or more custom interfaces. By custom interface, I'm referring to any interface not defined by COM. Standard COM interfaces include `IUnknown`, `IDispatch`, `ISupportErrorInfo`, `IConnectionPoint`, and others. Custom interfaces refer to developer-defined interfaces such as ILoan, IBank, and ISpy. The RCW must provide some mechanism that allows Managed clients to access these Unmanaged interfaces. As such, the RCW appears to implement all interfaces provided by the COM object. In effect, this allows for interface method invocation without explicitly casting to the necessary interface. Consider the following example:

Given the COM object described in Listing 5.3.1, a Managed client can invoke any interface method without an explicit cast for that interface. Listing 5.3.2 demonstrates how to interact with the class COM object detailed in Listing 5.3.1.

LISTING 5.3.1   COM Component Definition

```
 1: [uuid(...)]
 2: interface IFoo : IDispatch {
 3:     [id(...)] HRESULT FooMethod( ... );
 4: }
 5:
 6: [uuid(...)]
 7: interface IBar : IDispatch {
 8:     [id(...)] HRESULT BarMethod( ... );
 9: }
10:
11: [uuid(...)]
12: coclass FooBar {
13:     [default] interface IFoo;
14:     interface IBar;
15: }
```

LISTING 5.3.2   Managed Wrapper Code

```
1: FooBar fb = new FooBar( );
2: //Invoke IFoo.FooMethod
3: //No need for explicit IFoo cast
4: fb.FooMethod( );
5:
6: //Invoke IBar.BarMethod
7: //No need for explicit IBar cast
8: fb.BarMethod( );
```

In the classic COM world, it would be necessary to QI for a particular interface to invoke the methods associated with that particular interface.

Marshaling Method Calls

To invoke a COM Interface method, there are several tasks that need attention. Specifically, these tasks include the following:

- Transition to Unmanaged Code
- Error handling such as HRESULTs to exceptions
- Parameter marshaling such as [in], [out], [in,out], and [out,retval]
- Converting between CLR data types and COM data types

Once again, .NET comes to the rescue because this functionality is provided by the generated RCW.

Consuming Selected Interfaces

Because a Managed client has no need for IUnknown or IDispatch, neither of these interfaces are exposed by the RCW. A complete listing of consumed interfaces can be found on MSDN; therefore, this chapter will not go into great detail about them.

Some of the most common interfaces, such as ISupportErrorInfo, IConnectionPoint, and IEnumVARIANT, are mapped to Managed concepts. In the case of ISupportErrorInfo, the extend error information will be propagated into the exception being thrown.

The IConnectionPoint interface maps to the concept of events and delegates within .NET. When importing a COM object that supports IConnectionPoint, all event methods will be converted to the proper event construct in C# along with the delegate definition.

TlbImp.exe

Up to this point, the concept of RCW has merely been in the abstract without a true physical entity. When it is necessary for a Managed Client to consume a class COM object, there needs to exist a Managed Wrapper—the RCW. This task is generally accomplished with the TlbImp.exe utility that ships with the .NET SDK. TlbImp.exe can be used to create a Managed Wrapper from a COM Type Library or any COM .dll or .exe.

The following is the basic syntax for TlbImp.exe:

```
TlbImp.exe TypeLibName [/out:<FileName>]
```

Simple Object

To gain a better understanding of the relationship between classic COM and .NET RCW, consider the following example COM object (see Listing 5.3.3).

5.3

LISTING 5.3.3 SimpleObject.h

```
 1: // SimpleObject.h : Declaration of the CSimpleObject
 2:
 3: #pragma once
 4: #include "resource.h"        // main symbols
 5:
 6:
 7: // ISimpleObject
 8: [
 9:     object,
10:     uuid("6D854C55-4549-44FB-9CDF-6079F56B232E"),
11:     dual,   helpstring("ISimpleObject Interface"),
12:     pointer_default(unique)
13: ]
14: __interface ISimpleObject : IDispatch
15: {
16:
17:
18:     [id(1), helpstring("method SayHello")]
➥HRESULT SayHello([in] BSTR Name, [out,retval] BSTR* Message);
19: };
20:
21:
22:
23: // CSimpleObject
24:
25: [
26:     coclass,
27:     threading("apartment"),
28:     aggregatable("never"),
29:     vi_progid("SimpleATL.SimpleObject"),
30:     progid("SimpleATL.SimpleObject.1"),
31:     version(1.0),
32:     uuid("D82A38B8-5392-4D3D-ADEC-516C18E6A092"),
33:     helpstring("SimpleObject Class")
34: ]
35: class ATL_NO_VTABLE CSimpleObject :
36:     public ISimpleObject
37: {
38: public:
39:     CSimpleObject()
40:     {
41:     }
42:
43:
44:     DECLARE_PROTECT_FINAL_CONSTRUCT()
```

Listing 5.3.3 Continued

```
45:
46:     HRESULT FinalConstruct()
47:     {
48:         return S_OK;
49:     }
50:
51:     void FinalRelease()
52:     {
53:     }
54:
55: public:
56:
57:
58:     STDMETHOD(SayHello)(BSTR Name, BSTR* Message);
59: };
60:
```

SimpleObject.h defines a single interface ISimpleObject and a coclass CSimpleObject that implements the ISimpleObject interface. ISimpleObject defines a single method SayHello that takes a BSTR input and returns a BSTR. The RCW will marshal the BSTR type as a CLR string. Listing 5.3.4 provides the implementation for the SayHello method.

Listing 5.3.4 SimpleObject.cpp

```
1: // SimpleObject.cpp : Implementation of CSimpleObject
2: #include "stdafx.h"
3: #include "SimpleObject.h"
4:
5: // CSimpleObject
6:
7: STDMETHODIMP CSimpleObject::SayHello(BSTR Name, BSTR* Message)
8: {
9:     // TODO: Add your implementation code here
10:    CComBSTR Msg( "Hello " ); Msg += Name;
11:    *Message = ::SysAllocString( Msg.m_str );
12:
13:    return S_OK;
14: }
15:
```

The SayHello method implementation merely creates a concatenated string. The ATL source was created using VS.NET and attributed ATL, in case you're interested.

To create a RCW for `SimpleATL.dll`, issue the following command:

```
TlbImp SimpleATL.dll /out:SimpleATLImp.dll
```

This will produce the necessary RCW for use by a .NET Managed Client. The Managed Wrapper can then be inspected with ILDASM; as depicted in Figure 5.3.2.

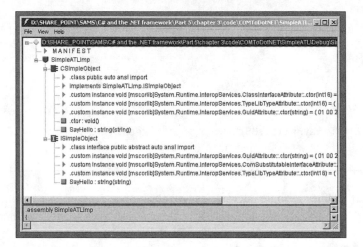

FIGURE 5.3.2
Managed Wrapper in ILDASM.

Early Binding

With the RCW created, using the COM object is a simple matter of adding the appropriate reference to the project. When a reference is added to the project, the object is available for Early Binding. *Early Binding* allows for compile time type checking and method verification (see Listing 5.3.5). For a COM object to be available for Early Binding, it must support dual interfaces. For details on dual/dispatch interfaces, refer to a COM text. If a COM object only supports `IDispatch`, first—the creator of the COM object should be flogged, and then the object can only be accessed with late binding and reflection.

LISTING 5.3.5   Early Binding

```
1: namespace EarlyBinding
2: {
3:     using System;
4:
5:     class Early
6:     {
7:         static void Main(string[] args)
```

LISTING 5.3.5   Continued

```
 8:          {
 9:              SimpleATLImp.CSimpleObject o =
➥new SimpleATLImp.CSimpleObject( );
10:              Console.WriteLine(o.SayHello( "Richard" ));
11:          }
12:      }
13: }
14:
```

With the generated RCW, using a COM object requires no additional code as far as the Managed client is concerned. As far as the client is aware, it is merely making use of another object.

Late Binding

Late binding refers to the use of a COM objects IDispatch interface for runtime discovery of services. The purpose of an IDispatch interface is to provide an interface for use with scripting clients. Scripting clients, such as VBScript or JScript, are unable to make use of raw interfaces and require late bound IDispatch.

.NET also provides the ability to make use of late binding through the IDispatch interface of a COM object (see Listing 5.3.6). Doing so, however, does not allow for compile time type checking. The developer must make use of the Reflection API to access instance methods and properties.

LISTING 5.3.6   Late Binding

```
 1: namespace LateBinding
 2: {
 3:     using System;
 4:     using System.Reflection;
 5:     using System.Runtime.InteropServices;
 6:
 7:     class Late
 8:     {
 9:         static void Main(string[] args)
10:         {
11:             try
12:             {
13:                 Type SimpleObjectType =
➥Type.GetTypeFromProgID("SimpleATL.SimpleObject");
14:                 object SimpleObjectInstance =
➥Activator.CreateInstance( SimpleObjectType );
```

LISTING 5.3.6   Continued

```
15:
16:               Console.WriteLine("SimpleObjectType = {0}",
          ⮬SimpleObjectType.ToString( ) );
17:               Console.WriteLine("SimpleObjectInstance Type = {0}",
18:                 SimpleObjectInstance.GetType( ).ToString( ) );
19:
20:             //Invoke the SayHello Instance Method
21:               string Message =
          ⮬ (string)SimpleObjectType.InvokeMember("SayHello",
22:                     BindingFlags.Default | BindingFlags.InvokeMethod,
23:                     null,
24:                     SimpleObjectInstance,
25:                     new object[] { "Richard" } );
26:             //Did it work?
27:             Console.WriteLine(Message);
28:           }
29:         catch( COMException e )
30:           {
31:             Console.WriteLine("What up? {0} : {1}",
          ⮬e.ErrorCode, e.Message );
32:           }
33:       }
34:     }
35: }
36:
```

Obviously, using a COM object with late binding requires just a bit of code. The advantage of learning how to use late binding is the ability to dynamically load COM objects and use reflection to discover the services it provides. Also, you may end up having a COM object that only supports the IDispatch interface, in which case late binding is the only way.

COM Inheritance? Blasphemy!

You can't inherit from a COM coclass; that's against the rules of COM. COM states that only interface implementation is possible and not implementation inheritance. Not anymore! Because there exists a Managed RCW for the COM object, it, like any other object, can serve as a base class in .NET.

Listing 5.3.7 highlights the extensibility of .NET and the advanced language interoperability. The details of COM have been abstracted away, thus freeing the developer to concentrate on other issues.

LISTING 5.3.7 Extending `CSimpleObject`

```
1: namespace Inherit
2: {
3:     using System;
4:
5:     /// <summary>
6:     /// Use the CSimpleObject coclass as the base class
7:     /// </summary>
8:     public class SimpleInherit : SimpleATLImp.CSimpleObject
9:     {
10:
11:         /// <summary>
12:         /// Extend the functionality of CSimpleObject
13:         /// </summary>
14:         public void NewMethod( )
15:         {
16:             Console.WriteLine("Cool, derived from COM coclass");
17:         }
18:     }
19:
20:
21:     class COMdotNETStyle
22:     {
23:         static void Main(string[] args)
24:         {
25:             //Create new derived class.
26:             SimpleInherit simpleInherit = new SimpleInherit( );
27:
28:             //Invoke COM SayHelloMethod
29:             string s = simpleInherit.SayHello("Me");
30:             Console.WriteLine(s);
31:
32:             //Invoke derived class method
33:             simpleInherit.NewMethod( );
34:         }
35:     }
36: }
37:
```

IConnectionPoint

.NET introduces the notion of events and delegates that handle those events. In COM, there exists a source and a sink. These entities are attached through the `IConnectionPoint` interface in which the sink requests to be advised of events from the source. When an RCW is created

5.3

for a COM object that implements the IConnectionPoint interface, each event method is translated into a corresponding delegate. The notion of events and delegates with .NET is a vast improvement over the work required for classic COM events.

Each event exposed by the COM object will have a delegate with the following naming convention:

```
_I<EventInterface>_<EventName>EventHandler
```

Although it may not be pretty to look at, it does the job and saves you a considerable amount of work. To illustrate the process, consider a simple COM object which implements the following event interface (see Listing 5.3.8).

LISTING 5.3.8   _ISourceObjectEvents Interface

```
 1: // _ISourceObjectEvents
 2: [
 3:     dispinterface,
 4:     uuid("F0507830-BD45-479D-849F-35E422A5C7FA"),
 5:     hidden,
 6:     helpstring("_ISourceObjectEvents Interface")
 7: ]
 8: __interface _ISourceObjectEvents
 9: {
10:
11:     [id(1), helpstring("method OnSomeEvent")]
➥void OnSomeEvent([in] BSTR Message);
12: };
13:
```

The event method OnSomeEvent, line 11, will translate into an event/delegate pair when the RCW is created. The delegate will have the following, somewhat hideous, name:

```
_ISourceObjectEvent_OnSomeEventEventHandler
```

This delegate can then be created and attached to the event OnSomeEvent (see Listing 5.3.9).

LISTING 5.3.9   SimpleSink Source

```
1: namespace CSharpSink
2: {
3:     using System;
4:     using ATLSourceImp;
5:
6:     /// <summary>
7:     ///         Summary description for Class1.
8:     /// </summary>
```

LISTING 5.3.9 Continued

```
 9:     class SimpleSink
10:         {
11:             static void Main(string[] args)
12:             {
13:
14:                 CSourceObject source = new CSourceObject( );
15:                 source.OnSomeEvent +=
16:                     new _
➥ISourceObjectEvents_OnSomeEventEventHandler(OnSomeEvent);
17:
18:                 source.MakeEventFire( "Hello" );
19:             }
20:
21:             public static void OnSomeEvent( string Message )
22:             {
23:                 Console.WriteLine("Have Event: {0}", Message );
24:             }
25:         }
26: }
27:
```

The event hookup is no different than with other .NET event/delegate pairs. The
CSimpleObject class invokes the OnSomeEvent whenever the method is invoked. The COM
Interop layer handles the marshaling of the COM event and directing the event to the proper
delegate on your behalf. For any of you who have had the pleasure of sinking a COM event in
raw C++, this is definitely a better way.

Threading Issues

COM introduced a plethora of threading models from which to choose. COM components
could be Apartment, Both, Free, MTA, Single, or STA—so many choices, so many possible
penalties. If you've never bothered to truly dive into the available COM threading models and
understand COM apartments, consider yourself fortunate. However, when you need to work
with classic COM objects, it is important to understand the implications of the various threading models.

A managed client creates threads within an STA. When using a COM object that also is STA,
there is no penalty incurred when invoking methods on the various interfaces. However, if the
COM object is MTA, it's time to pay the piper. The performance hit comes when marshaling
calls from STA to MTA. Fortunately, a Managed client can change the current threading
model, create the COM object, and save some cycles in the process.

To change the threading model, access the CurrentThread and set the ApartmentState as
needed. Note that the ApartmentState can only be set once. Depending on the application, it

might be beneficial to create a worker thread to access the classic COM object with the thread's `ApartmentState` set to the necessary `Apartment` type. Listing 5.3.10 changes the `ApartmentState` of the current thread to `MTA` to match that of the `MTAObject` being accessed.

LISTING 5.3.10   Changing Apartments

```
1: Thread.CurrentThread.ApartmentState = ApartmentState.MTA;
2: //Create MTA Object
MTAObject o = new MTAObject( );
3: o.Foo( );
```

Making use of threading model changes, the overhead of marshalling COM calls across various apartments will be reduced. In server-side code where speed is critical, saving overhead is paramount, and knowing the threading model used by the COM object allows for maximum call efficiency.

COM Types to .NET Types

The mapping of supported COM types to .NET types is fairly easy to guess. Table 5.3.1 maps out some of the most common COM types and their .NET equivalents.

TABLE 5.3.1   COM to .NET Type Mappings

COM Type	.NET Type
BSTR	string
VARIANT	object
SAFEARRAY	array[]
I1	sbyte
I2	short
I4	int
I8	long
UI1	byte
UI2	ushort
CHAR	char
UI4	uint
R4	float
R8	double
IUnknown**	object
IDispatch**	object
I<SomeInterface>	I<SomeInterface>

Although Table 5.3.1 is by no means complete, it does convey the basic types and their conversions. For a complete listing of the various type conversions, reference MSDN.

Exposing .NET Components as COM Objects

Just as Managed clients can consume class COM objects, the ability to create a COM Callable Wrapper (CCW) also exists. Chances are that the need to create .NET components and expose them as COM objects probably shouldn't come up in general development. As such, I will merely present how to register a .NET component as a COM object and the caveats associated with doing so.

RegAsm.exe

The .NET SDK provides a RegAsm.exe tool that is used to create the necessary entries with the system registry. RegAsm can also generate a type library, .tlb file, to describe the types within the assembly. The Registry entries look like those of a COM object and allow for the loading of the Managed assembly. In addition to using RegAsm.exe to register the Managed assembly, it is also necessary to add the assembly to the GAC, or Global Assembly Cache. The gacutil.exe can be used to accomplish this task.

COM Callable Wrapper

The counter part to an RCW is the COM Callable Wrapper (CCW). Like the RCW, the CCW handles many of the same issues, such as preserving object identity, lifetime management, and so on. The CCW is also responsible for providing interfaces, such as IDispatch and IUnknown, because these interfaces are not part of the managed component. The IDispatch interface allows for scripting clients to make use of Managed components, just as they would use any other IDispatch COM object. Figure 5.3.3 depicts a basic view of the CCW.

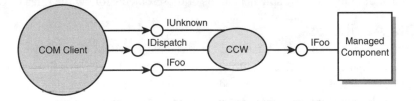

FIGURE 5.3.3

Conceptual view of CCW.

A CCW acts as a proxy between the COM client and the Managed component.

.NET to COM Issues

COM has very strict rules that govern its implementation. To make effective use of exposing a
.NET component to COM, the rules of COM must be followed. Consider the following .NET
class:

```
1: class Foo {
2:     public Foo( string s ) {...}
3:     public static void Bar( ) {...}
4: }
```

An attempt to export class Foo to COM would not be successful for two reasons:

- COM does not support constructors with parameters
- COM does not have a notion of non-instance methods, such as static methods

Class Foo is considered non-COM friendly. Parameterized constructors should be removed and
some initialization method should then be supplied. It is this type of detail that must be
adhered to effectively expose Managed objects to COM.

COM supports the notion of value types, just as .NET does. In COM, however, value types
cannot have instance methods as they can in .NET and even C++.

```
1: public struct Point {
2:     int x;
3:     int y;
4:     void SetXY( int x, int y ) {...}
5: }
```

When the value type Point is exported to COM, the instance method SetXY will be removed
and, because members x and y are private, the Point value type will be of no value.

Before embarking on a project to create .NET components with the intention of exposing them
to COM clients, be sure that the implementations of those objects follow the rules of COM.

.NET COM Attributes

Along with the basics of exposing a Managed class as a classic COM object, several
Attributes exist that allow for finer control of exactly what and how elements are exposed. In
addition, it is also possible to declare user code that should be executed during object registration and un-registration using ComRegisterFunctionAttribute and
ComUnregisterFunctionAttribute respectively (see Listing 5.3.11).

LISTING 5.3.11   .NET COM Attributes Object Registration

```
1: using system;
2: public class MyClass {
```

LISTING 5.3.11 Continued

```
3:      [ComRegisterFunctionAttribute]
4:      public static void RegisterMethod( Type T ) {...}
5:
6:      [ComUnregisterFunctionAttribute]
7:      public static void UnregisterMethod( Type T ) {...}
8: }
9:
```

The methods RegisterMethod and UnregisterMethod must be public and static. Also, the Type T parameter is the object type that is currently being registered/unregistered. Remember that attributes can be restricted to classes, interfaces, methods, parameters, return types, and even fields. In the case of ComRegisterFunctionAttributes and ComUnregisterFunctionAttributes, these attributes can only be applied to methods.

Supporting scripting clients requires an IDispatch interface. Using the ClassInterfaceAttribute controls the interface type generated for the Managed class. This can be designated as Dual, IUnknown-derived, or IDispatch only, depending on the requirements of the consuming client. The InterfaceTypeAttribute controls a similar concept only applied to Managed interfaces.

In addition, the ability to specify the ProgID, ProgIdAttribute, and the Guid (GuidAttribute), allows for even more control over how the exposed object is perceived. Using the GuidAttribute allows for a Managed class to implement a COM-based interface that can be consumed by a COM client.

Summary

Many COM issues that you are likely to encounter were touched on in this chapter. Issues such as consuming COM within a Managed Client, exposing Managed code as classic COM, COM threading models, and the notion that COM supports only a subset of what can be accomplished with C# and the CLR. It is likely that classic COM will exist for years to come, thus requiring most developers to learn the basics of COM Interop with Managed code. For future projects, I would suggest moving away from the restrictions of classic COM. Focus instead on maximizing your return with the facilities provided by C# and language interop for component-based applications.

C# affords a very powerful language for component construction, and .NET facilitates language interoperability that is unparalleled. To effectively interoperate outside of .NET still requires knowledge of the target client and its support for interop. With the large amount of classic COM in existence, chances are that most of your projects will require the consumption of those COM object by a Managed client. Luckily, you've got .NET on your side.

5.3

COM
INTEROPERABILITY

Threads

IN THIS CHAPTER

Multithreading 101

Each application has a main thread of execution. This main thread executes the application code in some specific order; whether based on user interaction or in response to a Windows message. What happens when more than one task or section of code needs to be executed? The order of execution will depend on how the single-threaded application is developed, but only one task at a time will be executed.

Under the Windows environment, it is possible for an application to spawn several threads and to control the interaction of those threads. This allows an application to handle multiple tasks concurrently. Consider your favorite Web browser. When downloading a file, the Web browser will spawn a thread to handle that task and allow you to navigate to another Web page while the download continues. Without the ability to create and control multiple threads within an application, the task of downloading the file from the Web would consume the main application thread. Under such a circumstance, the Web browser would be unable to perform any other task until the file download was complete.

The creation of multithreaded applications can improve performance of an application, but the addition of new execution threads adds a new level of complexity to the design, development, and debugging of such applications. In addition, it is not always a performance gain to start creating new threads without first evaluating the use of the application architecture.

Application Thread

The .NET architecture creates a single thread under an application domain to execute an application. The Main method of a class represents the entry point of the program and also the entry point of the application thread. Each thread created within the application thread is considered a child of the parent thread. This same notion applies to the application thread because the application thread is a child thread of the Application Domain. When the parent thread terminates, all child threads also will terminate. It is important to ensure that all child threads have been properly terminated and resources have been released before terminating the parent thread.

Worker Threads

The most common type of thread is a worker thread. A *worker thread* is used to perform some type of background processing that would otherwise occupy the application thread. Examples of such background processing include file downloading, background printing, and auto save features. When used properly, worker threads allow the main application thread to respond to application messages and give the appearance of a more responsive application.

Creating a Worker Thread

Like the application thread, a worker thread executes a section of code within the program. A basic worker thread example can be used to illustrate this. Listing 5.4.1 shows the basic construction of a worker thread.

LISTING 5.4.1 Basic worker thread

```
1: using System;
2: using System.Threading;
3:
4: namespace BasicWorkerThread
5: {
6:
7:     class Class1
8:     {
9:
10:         static void WorkerThread( )
11:         {
12:             Console.WriteLine("Hello from WorkerThread");
13:         }
14:
15:         static void Main(string[] args)
16:         {
17:
18:             //Create the Worker Thread
19:             Thread WT = new Thread( new ThreadStart( WorkerThread ) );
20:
21:             //Start the Thread
22:             WT.Start( );
23:
24:             //end the application
25:             Console.WriteLine("Press enter to exit");
26:             Console.ReadLine( );
27:         }
28:     }
29: }
30:
```

The first thing to notice about Listing 5.4.1 is the using directive to import the System.Threading namespace. All thread-related classes are found within this namespace. To create a thread, there needs to be a method to act as the thread delegate. That's right: .NET threading uses a delegate to define the method a new thread will use. In the case of the example in Listing 5.4.1, the static method WorkerThread matches the delegate definition required for threads. On line 19, a new Thread object is created. Notice that the constructor for a

5.4

THREADS

Thread takes as a parameter a ThreadStart delegate. As mentioned earlier, the ThreadStart delegate defines which method the newly created thread will execute. Thread delegates have only a single possible signature, which consists of a void return and an empty argument list.

Those of you familiar with traditional Win32 threads, or POSIX threads, might be wondering why there are no arguments to a thread. In Win32 threading, a thread function takes a LPVOID (long pointer to a void) as a parameter. This allows any possible parameter to be passed to the thread function. Unlike Win32 threads, .NET threads can be instance based. That is, a non-static method of an object can be used for the thread. When a non-static method is used, that method and thread have access to all fields, properties, and methods of that object instance. This represents a significant difference from static Win32-type threads. Listing 5.4.2 shows a thread accessing instance data within a class.

LISTING 5.4.2   Instance Thread

```
 1: using System;
 2: using System.Threading;
 3:
 4: namespace InstanceThread
 5: {
 6:     class Bank
 7:     {
 8:
 9:         private string bankName = "First Bank";
10:
11:         public void WorkerThread( )
12:         {
13:             //Access instance member bankName
14:             Console.WriteLine("Bank Name = {0}", this.bankName );
15:         }
16:
17:         public void Run( )
18:         {
19:            Thread WT = new Thread( new ThreadStart( this.WorkerThread ) );
20:             WT.Start( );
21:         }
22:
23:
24:         static void Main(string[] args)
25:         {
26:             Bank b = new Bank( );
27:             b.Run( );
28:         }
29:     }
30: }
```

The code in Listing 5.4.2 is not much different than that found in Listing 5.4.1. In this example, the thread delegate WorkerThread has instance-based access to the private field bankName. Such object-aware threads are a major departure from traditional Win32 based threads. .NET provides a closer notion of object-aware threads than ever before, but it's not quite perfect. There does not exist a base class from which to derive classes that will act as threads. In the .NET framework, the System.Threading.Thread base class is sealed and, as such, is not meant to serve as a base class.

ThreadStatic Attribute

The ThreadStatic attribute provides a mechanism for creating static fields that are thread specific. Each thread created will have its own copy of any field that is attributed with the ThreadStatic attribute. It's also important to note that any field marked with the Thread Static attribute will be zeroed out for threads, regardless of the initial assigned value. The static field will retain the initial value only for the main application thread. Listing 5.4.3 illustrates the use of the ThreadStatic attribute and the effect it has on static fields.

LISTING 5.4.3 ThreadStatic Attribute

```
 1: using System;
 2: using System.Threading;
 3:
 4:
 5:
 6: public class Task {
 7:
 8:     [ThreadStatic] static int m_nId = 10;
 9:
10:     public string            m_strThreadName;
11:
12:     public void Run( string ThreadName ) {
13:         this.m_strThreadName = ThreadName;
14:         Thread T = new Thread( new ThreadStart( threadProc ) );
15:         T.Start( );
16:     }
17:
18:     public void threadProc( ) {
19:
20:         Console.WriteLine( "Thread {0} is running", m_strThreadName );
21:
22:         //loop and increment the m_nId static field
23:         for(int i = 0; i < 10; i++ )
24:         Console.WriteLine("Thread {0} : m_nId = {1}",
25:                           this.m_strThreadName, m_nId++ );
26:     }
```

5.4

LISTING 5.4.3   Continued

```
27: }
28:
29:
30: public class ThreadApp {
31:
32:     public static void Main( ) {
33:
34:         //Create 2 worker Tasks
35:         Task t1 = new Task( );
36:         Task t2 = new Task( );
37:
38:         t1.Run( "Worker 1" );
39:         t2.Run( "Worker 2" );
40:
41:         //Execute on the Main thread
42:         Task t3 = new Task( );
43:         t3.m_strThreadName = "Main Thread";
44:         t3.threadProc( );
45:     }
46: }
```

The output from Listing 5.4.3 will, of course, depend on the order in which each thread is scheduled to run and any thread switching that takes place. However, you can see that each thread, when executed, has a static member m_nId with an initial value of zero. When the threadProc member is executed from the context of the main application thread (line 44), the static field retains its initial value of 10. The ThreadStatic attribute allows each thread to retain its own static member data. If this is not the desired effect, the ThreadStatic attribute should not be used, in which case, any static member will be available to all threads and its value shared among them.

Join—Bringing Threads Together

It often is necessary to spawn one or more threads and have the parent thread wait for those threads to complete before continuing execution. This can be accomplished easily by making use of the Join instance method of a thread. When the Join method is called, the calling thread will suspend until the worker thread completes. After the worker thread has exited, execution will continue within the calling thread (see Listing 5.4.4).

LISTING 5.4.4   Using Join

```
1: using System;
2: using System.Threading;
3:
```

LISTING 5.4.4   Continued

```
 4:
 5:
 6: public class JoinTest {
 7:
 8:
 9:     public static void ThreadProc( ) {
10:
11:         Console.WriteLine("Thread Active");
12:
13:         Thread.Sleep( 30 * 1000 );
14:
15:         Console.WriteLine("Thread Exiting");
16:     }
17:
18:
19:     public static void Main() {
20:         Thread T = new Thread( new ThreadStart( ThreadProc ) );
21:         T.Start( );
22:         T.Join( );
23:         Console.WriteLine("After Join");
24:     }
25: }
```

Thread Synchronization

As stated before, threads can be scheduled to run at any time and in any order. It often is necessary to coordinate various threads and to share resources among threads. One word of initial caution: All multithread applications work in debug mode; it's only in release mode when things start to go haywire. Debugging multithreaded applications takes time and experience; nothing else seems to help make life any easier when dealing with these multi-headed monsters. For some unknown and unexplainable reason, thread scheduling in Debug mode in no way represents the types of scheduling found in Release mode. Mainly, this is a side effect introduced by the debugging environment.

`lock` Keyword

C# has the `lock` keyword. `lock` can be used to synchronize access to both instance and static fields of an object. To synchronize access to instance based fields, an application would use `lock( this )` where `this` is a reference to the current object. To synchronize access to static fields, the `lock` keyword would be used in conjunction with the `typeof` keyword as follows:

```
lock( typeof( class ) )
```

5.4

THREADS

To illustrate the use of the lock keyword and the possible effects of not using it, Listing 5.4.5 shows a simple example of accessing an instance-based array. Two threads are created and each thread attempts to place its hash code into individual cells within the array. When the lock statement is active, the test program runs without any errors. However, to see the effect of not using the lock keyword, merely comment out the lock statement and run the same example.

LISTING 5.4.5 The lock Keyword

```
 1: using System;
 2: using System.Threading;
 3:
 4:
 5: public class ThreadLockTest {
 6:
 7:     private int[]    m_Array = new int[10];
 8:     private int      m_CurrentIndex = 0;
 9:
10:
11:     public  void ThreadProc( ) {
12:
13:         int ThreadId = Thread.CurrentThread.GetHashCode( );
14:
15:         for( int i = 0; i < 10; i++ )
16:            //comment out the lock statement
17:            //and watch the exceptions fly
18:            lock( this ) {
19:                if( m_CurrentIndex < 10 ) {
20:                    Thread.Sleep( (new Random()).Next( 2 ) * 1000 );
21:                    m_Array[m_CurrentIndex++] = ThreadId;
22:                }
23:            }//lock block
24:     }
25:
26:     public void PrintArray( ) {
27:        for( int i = 0; i < 10; i++ )
28:            Console.WriteLine( "m_Array[{0}] = {1}", i, m_Array[i] );
29:     }
30:
31:
32:
33:     public static void Main( ) {
34:
```

LISTING 5.4.5 Continued

```
35:          ThreadLockTest tlt = new ThreadLockTest( );
36:          Thread t1 = new Thread( new ThreadStart( tlt.ThreadProc ) );
37:          Thread t2 = new Thread( new ThreadStart( tlt.ThreadProc ) );
38:
39:          t1.Start( );
40:          t2.Start( );
41:          t1.Join( );
42:          t2.Join( );
43:
44:          tlt.PrintArray( );
45:      }
46: }
```

Again, with the lock statement in place, the test program runs fine and each index of the array will contain the hash code of the given thread. However, if the lock statement is commented out, chances are that an IndexOutOfRangeException exception will be raised. This is due to the test on line 19. After the m_CurrentIndex is checked, the current thread is put to sleep for a random period of time. In that time period, it is possible for the other thread to run and possibly to invalidate the m_CurrentIndex by incrementing the value past 10.

Mutex

Similar to the lock keyword, a Mutex represents mutually exclusive access to one or more resources. Unlike a critical section, a Mutex is a kernel level object and, as such, can be shared across processes. As a side effect, the time required to acquire the Mutex is much longer than that of a critical section using the lock keyword.

Rather than build a small console program to demonstrate the use of a Mutex, a small Windows Forms application will be created. The idea is to show how two different processes can access the same Mutex. For multiple processes to gain access to a shared Mutex, there needs to be some mechanism to acquire the same Mutex. In fact, this is very simple to accomplish and is done by creating a Mutex with a shared name in the form of a formal string parameter. The string parameter then can be used by multiple processes to acquire the kernel level Mutex.

Figure 5.4.1 shows two instances of the WinMutex application. When one process acquires the shared Mutex, a green circle will be drawn in the client area. When the Mutex is released or when waiting to acquire the Mutex, the circle will turn red in color.

5.4

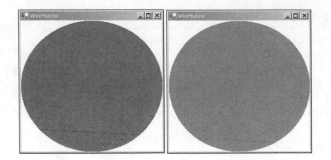

FIGURE 5.4.1
WinMutex *application.*

Listing 5.4.6 shows the implementation for WinMutex. Of particular note is the construction of the Mutex object that will be accessed by multiple instances of this application.

LISTING 5.4.6 WinMutex Application

```
 1: using System;
 2: using System.Drawing;
 3: using System.Collections;
 4: using System.ComponentModel;
 5: using System.Windows.Forms;
 6: using System.Data;
 7: using System.Threading;
 8:
 9: namespace WinMutex
10: {
11:
12:     public class MainForm : System.Windows.Forms.Form
13:     {
14:
15:         private System.ComponentModel.IContainer components;
16:
17:         private Mutex m = new Mutex( false, "WinMutex" );
18:         private bool bHaveMutex = false;
19:
20:         public MainForm() {
21:
22:             InitializeComponent();
23:
24:             //
25:             // TODO: Add any constructor code after
➥InitializeComponent call
```

Listing 5.4.6   Continued

```
26:              //
27:              Thread T = new Thread( new ThreadStart( ThreadProc ) );
28:              T.Start( );
29:
30:          }
31:
32:          /// <summary>
33:          /// Clean up any resources being used.
34:          /// </summary>
35:          public override void Dispose()
36:          {
37:            if (components != null)
38:            {
39:                components.Dispose();
40:            }
41:              base.Dispose();
42:          }
43:
44:          #region Windows Form Designer generated code
45:          /// <summary>
46:          /// Required method for Designer support - do not modify
47:          /// the contents of this method with the code editor.
48:          /// </summary>
49:          private void InitializeComponent()
50:          {
51:              this.components = new System.ComponentModel.Container();
52:              //
53:              // MainForm
54:              //
55:              this.AutoScaleBaseSize = new System.Drawing.Size(5, 13);
56:              this.BackColor = System.Drawing.SystemColors.Window;
57:              this.ClientSize = new System.Drawing.Size(292, 273);
58:              this.Name = "MainForm";
59:              this.Text = "WinMutex";
60:
61:          }
62:        #endregion
63:
64:        protected override void OnPaint( PaintEventArgs e ) {
65:
66:            if( this.bHaveMutex )
67:              DrawCircle( System.Drawing.Color.Green );
68:            else
69:              DrawCircle( System.Drawing.Color.Red );
```

5.4

THREADS

LISTING 5.4.6 Continued

```
70:             }
71:
72:         protected void DrawCircle( System.Drawing.Color color ) {
73:
74:             Brush b = new SolidBrush( color );
75:             System.Drawing.Graphics g = this.CreateGraphics( );
76:             int x = this.Size.Width / 2;
77:             int y = this.Size.Height / 2;
78:
79:             g.FillEllipse( b, 0, 0, this.ClientSize.Width,
    ➥this.ClientSize.Height );
80:
81:             b.Dispose( );
82:             g.Dispose( );
83:
84:         }
85:
86:
87:         protected void ThreadProc( ) {
88:
89:             while( true ) {
90:                 m.WaitOne( );
91:                 bHaveMutex = true;
92:                 Invalidate( );
93:                 Update( );
94:                 Thread.Sleep( 1000 );
95:                 m.ReleaseMutex( );
96:                 bHaveMutex = false;
97:                 Invalidate( );
98:                 Update( );
99:             }
100:         }
101:
102:         /// <summary>
103:         /// The main entry point for the application.
104:         /// </summary>
105:         [STAThread]
106:         static void Main()
107:         {
108:             Application.Run(new MainForm());
109:         }
110:     }
111: }
```

There are a few things to point out about the WinMutex program besides just the use of the shared Mutex. On line 87 of Listing 5.4.6 is the thread procedure ThreadProc. This method is used to acquire the Mutex and to invalidate the parent form so the proper colored circle can be rendered. Why not just call the DrawCircle method from within the ThreadProc method? The answer lies in a little known handle map used by Windows Forms. When attempting to create a graphics context by another thread, an exception will be generated due to a handle map violation. In essence, a duplicate window handle cannot be created, and this is exactly what happens when a child thread attempts to create a graphics context. To avoid this exception, the worker thread merely invalidates the form, which, in turn, generates a WM_PAINT message to be placed in the applications message queue. The main application thread will then process this WM_PAINT message.

Run two instances of WinMutex side by side and you'll notice that the circles are never green at the same time. This is due to the use of the shared Mutex and cross process synchronization achieved by its use.

AutoResetEvent

Another form of cross thread synchronization is that of events. The .NET framework provides both AutoResetEvents and ManualResetEvents. An event is similar to an event in Windows Forms where the application is awaiting some action by the user to generate an event and then responds to that event. In a similar manner, events can be used to synchronize the processing of various threads. The name AutoResetEvent is derived from the fact that the event is reset automatically when a pending thread has been notified of the event.

Consider the following example: One thread is responsible for producing some widget and yet another thread consumes these widgets. This type of problem is known as producer/consumer and is a classic thread synchronization example. In this example, the producer thread will raise an event each time a widget is produced. In response to the raised event, the consumer thread will do something with the newly created widget. Listing 5.4.7 shows the basic use of the AutoResetEvent.

LISTING 5.4.7 The AutoResetEvent

```
1: using System;
2: using System.Threading;
3:
4: namespace ProducerConsumer {
5:
6:     public class Factory {
7:
8:         private int[]  Widgets = new int[100];
```

5.4

THREADS

LISTING 5.4.7   Continued

```
 9:         private int      WidgetIndex = 0;
10:         private AutoResetEvent NewWidgetEvent =
➡ new AutoResetEvent( false );
11:
12:
13:         protected void Producer( ) {
14:
15:             while( true ) {   //run forever
16:
17:                 lock( this ) {
18:                     if( WidgetIndex < 100 ) {
19:                         Widgets[ WidgetIndex ] = 1;
20:                         Console.WriteLine("Widget {0} Produced",
➡ WidgetIndex++ );
21:                         NewWidgetEvent.Set( );
22:                     }
23:                 }
24:
25:                 Thread.Sleep( (new Random()).Next( 5 ) * 1000 );
26:             }
27:         }
28:
29:
30:         protected void Consumer( ) {
31:
32:             while( true ) {
33:                 NewWidgetEvent.WaitOne( );
34:                 int iWidgetIndex = 0;
35:
36:                 lock( this ) {
37:                     iWidgetIndex = --this.WidgetIndex;
38:                     Console.WriteLine("Consuming widget {0}",
➡iWidgetIndex );
39:                     Widgets[ iWidgetIndex-- ] = 0;
40:                 }
41:             }
42:         }
43:
44:         public void Run( ) {
45:             //Create 3 producers
46:             for( int i = 0; i < 3; i++ ) {
47:                 Thread producer = new Thread( new ThreadStart( Producer ) );
48:                 producer.Start( );
49:             }
```

LISTING 5.4.7 Continued

```
50:                    //Create 3 consumers
51:                for( int i = 0; i < 3; i++ ) {
52:                    Thread consumer = new Thread( new ThreadStart( Consumer ) );
53:                    consumer.Start( );
54:                }
55:
56:        }
57:
58:        public static void Main( ) {
59:            Factory factory = new Factory( );
60:            factory.Run( );
61:        }
62:    }
63: }
```

ManualResetEvent

Similar to the AutoResetEvent, the ManualResetEvent also can be used to signal a pending thread regarding some event. The difference is that a ManualResetEvent has to be reset through a method invocation rather than automatically being reset. This is the only difference as far as the mechanics are concerned. The usage difference between an AutoResetEvent and a ManualResetEvent is really dependent on the types of synchronization that are necessary. With a ManualResetEvent, it is possible to monitor the state of the event to determine when the event becomes reset.

Thread Pools

There are many applications that use threads to handle various client requests. Such applications include Web servers, database servers, and application servers. Rather than spawning a new thread each time to fulfill a client request, thread pools allow threads to be reused. By allocating and reusing threads, the overhead involved in constantly creating and destroying threads can be saved. Although the cost of creating a worker thread is generally small, the additive cost of creating and destroying hundreds of threads begins to be a performance issue.

A thread pool will be created under three different circumstances: The first circumstance is the call to QueueUserWorkItem. The timer queue or a registered wait operation queues a callback function. The second circumstance is the number of threads that will be created and managed by the thread pool, which depends on the amount of memory available to the system and the third circumstance is the implementation of the thread pool manager.

5.4

THREADS

QueueUserWorkItem

To demonstrate the use of `QueueUserWorkItem`, consider an insurance company's need to process insurance claims. Using a thread pool, each claim can be considered a work item for a thread to complete. When a new claim arrives, the application can queue the claim as a work item for the thread pool. The `QueueUserWorkItem` method is a static method of the `ThreadPool` class and has the following signature:

```
ThreadPool.QueueUserWorkItem( WaitCallback callback, object state )
```

The first argument is the callback delegate for the thread to execute. Unlike the thread delegates used in the past examples, a `WaitCallback` delegate allows a formal parameter of type `object`. The `object` parameter allows information to be sent to the worker thread. This, of course, differs in the respect that, up until now, there has been no information passing to worker threads. Listing 5.4.8 shows the insurance example using a thread pool to process insurance claims.

LISTING 5.4.8   Thread Pools and `QueueUserWorkItem`

```
 1: using System;
 2: using System.Threading;
 3:
 4:
 5: //The InsClaim represents
 6: //a work item for a particular
 7: //thread
 8: public struct InsClaim {
 9:     public string ClaimId;
10:     public double Amount;
11: }
12:
13:
14: public class App {
15:
16:     public void ProcessInsuranceClaim( object state ) {
17:         //unbox the InsClaim passed in
18:         InsClaim theClaim = (InsClaim)state;
19:
20:         //Process the claim and sleep to simulate work
21:         Console.WriteLine("Processing Claim {0} for ${1} amount",
➥theClaim.ClaimId, theClaim.Amount );
22:         Thread.Sleep( 5000 );
23:         Console.WriteLine("Claim {0} processed", theClaim.ClaimId);
24:     }
25:
```

LISTING 5.4.8 Continued

```
26:
27:     public static void Main( ) {
28:
29:         App app = new App( );
30:
31:         //Create 100 insurance claims
32:         Random r = new Random( );
33:         for( int i = 0; i < 100; i++ ) {
34:             InsClaim claim;
35:             claim.ClaimId = string.Format("INS{0}", i);
36:             claim.Amount = r.NextDouble( ) * 5000;
37:             ThreadPool.QueueUserWorkItem(
➥new WaitCallback( app.ProcessInsuranceClaim ), claim );
38:         }
39:
40:         //allow threads in pool to run
41:         Console.ReadLine( );
42:     }
43: }
```

The insurance claim example in Listing 5.4.8 is fairly straightforward. The `for` loop, used to create 100 insurance claims to be processed, begins on line 33. Each claim then is queued as a work item for a waiting thread within the thread pool. Be sure to notice the interleaving output produced by the sample. As claims are starting to be processed, other claims being processed by other threads are finishing the processing. Thread pools are an effective tool for such background tasks, especially when threads might be spending time waiting for work.

Extending .NET Threads

Although .NET offers a unified approach to threads for all languages that target the .NET platform, there still lacks a true cohesiveness and encapsulation with regards to a thread object. By creating a small abstract base class to represent a worker thread, the ability to extend the basic thread support will prove useful when developing larger applications.

WorkerThread Class

Creating a simple abstract class to represent a worker thread is not that difficult. There are a couple of key concepts that the worker thread base class needs to provide, the first of which is the ability to associate data with a particular thread. This will allow a worker thread to be created and data for the worker thread to be specified. The next item of business is the ability to stop the worker thread in some predictable manner. The simplest way to accomplish this is to provide a Stop method that causes a ThreadAbortException to be generated within the Run method of the worker thread. Listing 5.4.9 shows the implementation for a basic worker thread class.

LISTING 5.4.8   Abstract WorkerThread Class

```
 1: using System;
 2: using System.Threading;
 3:
 4: namespace SAMS.Threading
 5: {
 6:
 7:
 8:     /// <summary>
 9:     /// Encapsulate a worker thread and data
10:     /// </summary>
11:     public abstract class WorkerThread {
12:
13:         private object    ThreadData;
14:         private Thread    thisThread;
15:
16:
17:         //Properties
18:         public object Data {
19:            get { return ThreadData; }
20:            set { ThreadData = value; }
21:         }
22:
23:         public object IsAlive {
24:             get { return thisThread == null ? false : thisThread.IsAlive; }
25:         }
26:
27:         /// <summary>
28:         /// Constructors
29:         /// </summary>
30:
31:         public WorkerThread( object data ) {
32:             this.ThreadData = data;
33:         }
34:
35:         public WorkerThread( ) {
36:             ThreadData = null;
37:         }
38:
39:         /// <summary>
40:         /// Public Methods
```

LISTING 5.4.8 Continued

```
41:         /// </summary>
42:
43:         /// <summary>
44:         /// Start the worker thread
45:         /// </summary>
46:         public void Start( ) {
47:             thisThread = new Thread( new ThreadStart( this.Run ) );
48:             thisThread.Start();
49:         }
50:
51:         /// <summary>
52:         /// Stop the current thread.  Abort causes
53:         /// a ThreadAbortException to be raised within
54:         /// the thread
55:         /// </summary>
56:         public void Stop( ) {
57:             thisThread.Abort( );
58:             while( thisThread.IsAlive ) ;
59:             thisThread = null;
60:         }
61:
62:         /// <summary>
63:         /// To be implemented by derived threads
64:         /// </summary>
65:         protected abstract void Run( );
66:     }
67: }
```

The implementation of the WorkerThread class shows the ease in which creating a wrapper class for existing thread support can be accomplished. A wrapper class is jargon for a class that wraps up some basic functionality to extend a common type or class. The most important method within the WorkerThread class is the abstract Run method. The Run method is meant to be implemented in a derived class and is where the actual work to be performed by the thread will take place.

Dining Philosophers

To put the WorkerThread class to use, a classical threading synchronization problem, known as the Dining Philosophers, will be implemented. In the Dining Philosophers problem, a group of philosophers are seated at a circular table. They each eat and think, eat and think. To eat, however, it is necessary for a philosopher to obtain the chopstick on his or her right and left. Figure 5.4.2 shows the arrangement of the philosophers and the chopsticks.

5.4

THREADS

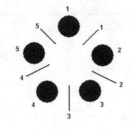

FIGURE 5.4.2
The Dining Philosophers.

Of course, the synchronization issue arises when each philosopher has one chopstick and sits waiting for the other chopstick. This situation is known as a deadlock. In a deadlock situation, various threads are waiting on resources that cannot be obtained due to some circular lock pattern. Thus, the goal is to ensure that a philosopher will only retain both chopsticks and not hold on to a single chopstick. Listing 5.4.9 shows the implementation of the Dinning Philosophers using the WorkerThread base class.

LISTING 5.4.9   The Dining Philosophers

```
 1: using System;
 2: using System.Threading;
 3: using SAMS.Threading;
 4:
 5: namespace DiningPhilosophers
 6: {
 7:
 8:     public struct PhilosopherData {
 9:         public int         PhilosopherId;
10:         public Mutex       RightChopStick;
11:         public Mutex       LeftChopStick;
12:         public int         AmountToEat;
13:         public int         TotalFood;
14:     }
15:
16:
17:
18:     public class Philosopher : WorkerThread
19:     {
20:         public Philosopher( object data ) : base( data ) { }
21:
22:         //Implement the abstract Run Method
23:         protected override void Run( ) {
24:
```

LISTING 5.4.9 Continued

```
25:                PhilosopherData pd = (PhilosopherData)Data;
26:                Random r = new Random( pd.PhilosopherId );
27:                Console.WriteLine("Philosopher {0} ready", pd.PhilosopherId );
28:                WaitHandle[] chopSticks =  new WaitHandle[] {
➥ pd.LeftChopStick, pd.RightChopStick };
29:
30:                while( pd.TotalFood > 0 ) {
31:                    //Get both chop sticks
32:                    WaitHandle.WaitAll( chopSticks );
33:                    Console.WriteLine("Philosopher {0} eating {1} of {2} food",
➥ pd.PhilosopherId, pd.AmountToEat, pd.TotalFood );
34:                    pd.TotalFood -= pd.AmountToEat;
35:                    Thread.Sleep( r.Next(1000,5000) );
36:
37:                    //Release the chopsticks
38:                    Console.WriteLine("Philosopher {0} thinking",
➥pd.PhilosopherId);
39:                    pd.RightChopStick.ReleaseMutex( );
40:                    pd.LeftChopStick.ReleaseMutex( );
41:
42:                    //Think for a random time length
43:                    Thread.Sleep( r.Next(1000,5000) );
44:                }
45:                Console.WriteLine("Philosopher {0} finished",
➥ pd.PhilosopherId );
46:            }
47:        }
48:
49:
50:    public class Restaurant {
51:
52:        public static void Main( ) {
53:            Mutex[] chopSticks = new Mutex[5];
54:
55:            //init the chopSticks
56:            for( int i = 0; i < 5; i++ )
57:                chopSticks[i] = new Mutex( false );
58:
59:            //Create the Five Philosophers
60:            for( int i = 0; i < 5; i++ ) {
61:                PhilosopherData pd;
62:                pd.PhilosopherId = i + 1;
63:                pd.RightChopStick =
➥chopSticks[ i - 1 >= 0 ? ( i - 1 ) : 4 ];
64:                pd.LeftChopStick = chopSticks[i];
```

5.4

THREADS

LISTING 5.4.9   Continued

```
65:              pd.AmountToEat = 5;
66:              pd.TotalFood = 35;
67:              Philosopher p = new Philosopher( pd );
68:              p.Start( );
69:          }
70:
71:          Console.ReadLine( );
72:      }
73:   }
74: }
```

The Dining Philosophers example introduces the use of the static method WaitHandle.WaitAll
to acquire both chopsticks. Effectively, the WaitAll method will not return until it is able to
acquire both of the WaitHandle-derived objects, in this case a pair of Mutex classes for each
chopstick. The WaitAll method also provides two overrides that allow for specifying the time-
out value to wait for the operation and a Boolean flag to determine the exit context. WaitAll
proves useful when it is necessary to acquire several resources before performing an operation
and prevent a deadlock situation that can arise due to circular waiting.

Summary

This wraps up the discussion on thread support provided by the .NET framework. Again,
although the thread classes and mechanism provided are not always adequate for the task at
hand, you have to keep in mind that the .NET framework is meant to target multiple languages.
As such, a completely feature-rich implementation is not always possible and, as such, requires
the developer of a particular language to extend the base offerings as needed. Using the basic
WorkerThread abstract class, you should be able to extend it for your own particular needs and
continue to improve and refine it over time.

INDEX